The Debate Since *Roe*

Making the Case Against Abortion (1975-2010)

Edited by Anne Conlon

© 2010 The Human Life Foundation, Inc.
353 Lexington Avenue, Suite 802
New York, NY 10016

Cover design by Christina Angelopoulos

I am moved by fancies that are curled
Around these images, and cling:
The notion of some infinitely gentle
Infinitely suffering thing.

T.S. ELIOT, "PRELUDES"

Good writing can win battles;
great writing, whole wars.

J.P. MCFADDEN

For Anne Higgins and J.P. McFadden

TABLE OF CONTENTS

PREFACE 6

THE ROAD TO ABORTION (1998/99)
   Mary Meehan 11

A HUMAN LIFE AMENDMENT (1975)
   James L. Buckley 39

THE THEORY OF THE DANFORTH CASE (1976)
   Francis Canavan 52

ABORTION AND THE MORAL REVOLUTION (1979)
   James Hitchcock 61

LOOKING-GLASS LOGIC (1980)
   Ellen Wilson Fielding 71

THE HUMANE HOLOCAUST (1980)
   Malcolm Muggeridge 81

IN RE NEW HUMANS (1981)
   Jérôme Lejeune 90

THE HUMAN LIFE BILL: SOME ISSUES AND ANSWERS (1982)
   Henry J. Hyde 94

LIFE: DEFINING THE BEGINNING BY THE END (2003)
   Maureen L. Condic 108

ABORTION AND THE CONSCIENCE OF THE NATION (1983)
   Ronald Reagan 116

GHOSTS ON THE GREAT LAWN (1986)
   Faith Abbott McFadden 124

DANCING WITH THE SAINTS (2009)
   Patrick Mullaney 131

WHY NOBODY IS REALLY PRO-CHOICE (1992)
   Ann Coulter 142

ON ABORTION: A LINCOLNIAN POSITION (1995)
George McKenna 154

WHAT WE CAN'T *NOT* KNOW (1996)
J. Budziszewski 174

OF LIFE, THE LAW, AND ROSES (2000)
Sandi Merle 184

THE BORN-ALIVE INFANTS PROTECTION ACT OF 2000 (2000)
Hadley Arkes 194

TOGETHER—FOR LIFE (2002)
Richard John Neuhaus 206

SINGER AND THE SONG (2003)
Jo McGowan 218

SCHEIDLER'S SUPREME VICTORY (2003)
Stephen Vincent 222

PARTIAL-BIRTH ABORTION ON TRIAL (2005)
Cathy Cleaver Ruse 229

ROE HOVERS LIKE A MALIGN SHADOW (2007)
Michael M. Uhlmann 247

THE VICTORY OF THE ABSTRACT OVER THE REAL (2006)
Harold O.J. Brown 254

MY CONTROVERSIAL CHOICE TO BECOME PRO-LIFE (2009)
Nat Hentoff 260

THE CHILD CAME TO US (2006)
Mary Kenny 265

IDENTITY, ABORTION AND WALKER PERCY (2008)
Edward Short 271

A NOTRE DAME WITNESS FOR LIFE (2009)
William McGurn 285

ONE MAN'S EVIL (2010)
William Murchison 292

THE FACELESSNESS OF THE UNBORN (2010)
Donald DeMarco 298

PREFACE

"There has to be a record," J.P. McFadden insisted when he started the *Human Life Review* in 1975. "We won't be like Nazi Germany. No one should be able to say, whatever happens, that they didn't know what's actually going on here."

After 35 years of continuous publishing, the quarterly journal McFadden founded has compiled perhaps the most comprehensive record there is of the national debate that began on January 22, 1973—the day seven justices of the Supreme Court declared that women not only had a legal right to kill their unborn children (*Roe* v. *Wade*), but that they could exercise this right at any time throughout nine months of pregnancy (*Doe* v. *Bolton*). "The upshot," wrote Justice Byron White in a dissent joined by William Rehnquist, "is that the people and the legislatures of the 50 States are constitutionally disentitled to weigh the relative importance of the continued existence and development of the fetus, on the one hand, against a spectrum of possible impacts on the mother, on the other hand." It was, White famously protested, "an exercise of raw judicial power . . . an improvident and extravagant exercise of the power of judicial review that the Constitution extends to this Court."

In his introduction to the first issue of the *Review* (Winter 1975), McFadden recalled how the Court's decisions had "shocked and surprised" most people, who up until then simply hadn't been paying much attention. "The majority of Americans," he went on, "although now obviously very interested in the abortion issue, both wants to know more about it, and *needs* to know more if we, as a nation, are to achieve a workable solution to a dilemma that so closely (and often bitterly) divides us." Three-and-a-half decades—and over 50 million abortions—later, the bitterness, if anything, has intensified; and polling on the subject suggests public opinion, while lately tilting in a pro-life direction—especially among young people—is more confused than committed: Most people say they are against most abortions; but most also want abortion to remain legal. In some polls, even many of those who called abortion *murder* didn't want to outlaw it. The search for a workable solution goes on.

Meanwhile other life-and-death issues clamor for public (and judicial) attention: euthanasia and physician-assisted suicide, embryonic-stem-cell research and cloning, fetal genetic screening and designer babies—all emanations of a resurgent eugenic *Zeitgeist*. Consistency of thinking regarding these, however, can't be presumed: Some, who call themselves pro-life because they object to abortion, don't object to physician-assisted suicide. Others, who may be apprehensive about euthanasia, aren't especially concerned about the fate of unwanted unborn babies. And then there are those who declare they are anti-abortion *and* anti-euthanasia while supporting embryonic-stem-cell research and so-called therapeutic cloning.

This much is certain: The Court's 1973 abortion rulings threw over the age-old sanctity-of-life ethic that undergirt centuries of medical, legal, political, philosophical, and theological thinking about the meaning of life and death. Golden Rule-based common sense and decency were rejected in favor of a utilitarian calculus that favors the strong (the mother) over the weak (the baby). In the decades since, we have seen this calculus also applied to end-of-life dilemmas—notoriously by Dr. Jack Kevorkian, who went to prison for committing euthanasia on TV; infamously by a Florida court that ordered the extermination of Terri Schiavo. Recently we have seen it applied when the question concerns the very beginning of life: One of Barack Obama's early acts as president was to make government funds available to researchers who seek "life-saving" cures by killing "leftover" embryos from fertility clinics.

Surely, the need to know more is even greater today than it was when McFadden set out, in his words, to "narrow the information and education gap." But thanks to his *Human Life Review* there is now a record—a rich archive that has made it possible to produce this unique anthology. Culled from tens of hundreds of articles published under McFadden's, and, since his death in 1998, his daughter Maria McFadden Maffucci's editorship, *The Debate Since Roe* presents medical, legal, political, philosophical, and theological arguments for restoring the sanctity-of-life ethic to the nation's jurisprudence, and foremost, as Ronald Reagan urged in the essay of his included here, to its conscience. Most of these essays were written, as was Reagan's, especially for the *Review*. But a few, like George McKenna's "On Abortion: A Lincolnian Position," and Maureen Condic's "Life: Defining the Beginning by the End," were reprinted after being spotted elsewhere, because one or the other McFadden thought it should be part of the *Review*'s record. That record also contains the texts of important political speeches, as well as the testimony of witnesses called before congressional committees convened over the years to consider how legislation might reclaim the ground so rudely arrogated by the Court. Some of that material, such as Senator James Buckley's "A Human Life Amendment" and Hadley Arkes's "The Born-Alive Infants Protection Act of 2000," is featured here.

A pro-life reader of sorts, *The Debate Since Roe* is intended not so much for scholars as for all those who have sat around the kitchen table (or the dorm room) defending the sanctity of human life while wishing they had greater command of the facts and arguments. The essays gathered here were written by doctors and lawyers, politicians and political scientists, philosophers and clerics, journalists, and, to quote McFadden again, those who bring "a layman's view of the meaning of it all." They were chosen not to be a "Best of the *Human Life Review*"—though many would certainly make that cut—but rather to present the reader with as much information, and as little overlap, as possible. The order in which they appear is largely, though not always literally, chronological.

One thing that struck me as I read through these and many other essays in the *Review*'s archive was how little, really, the facts and arguments in defense of life have changed since the Court's abortion rulings. Most of what we know today about fetal development, for example, or certainly what's important to know about it, was available to the justices deliberating the *Roe* and *Doe* cases nearly forty years ago. Yes, we now have the benefit of sonography, which allows parents to see their developing infant—and to proudly pass around his or her first baby picture among family and friends. But from the earliest ages of medicine, doctors have encountered the developing infant in spontaneous abortions; and in recent centuries, artists have created exact models of the infant in all its embryological stages—this is how obstetrics progressed. My point here is that we didn't need sonography to show us what doctors routinely saw—they could have told us.

But they didn't. For decades, pro-abortion propagandists assured the public that what was being destroyed in over a million wombs every year was merely a disembodied "blob of tissue." There was no media stampede of medical professionals to repudiate this and other abortion disinformation— like the claim that we cannot know when life begins. Enshrined by Harry Blackmun in his *Roe* opinion, this ludicrous assertion still hits the airwaves and op-ed pages every election season, confusing the public as it provides cover for pro-abortion Catholic politicians like Nancy Pelosi and Joe Biden, whose Church teaches that life begins at conception. Meanwhile, most members of the scientific community, whose own embryology textbooks also teach that life begins at conception, remain silent. Shame on them.

In 1985, introducing the 10th anniversary issue of the *Review*, McFadden addressed another kind of silence: "In the Abortion War," he asked, "who would command the best 'vendors of words'?" Here's his answer:

> Our bet was: *our* side. What writer proud of his gift would befoul his reputation by supporting the killing of unborn babies, much less use his art to advocate it? And just so, we'd say, it has proved: no renowned writer has yet come forward as the champion of abortion (surely some privately favor the "choice"?), whereas we have had no difficulty whatever in publishing, over the past ten years, perhaps three million words, an impressive number of them authored by fine writers, virtually *all* of them contributed by talented people proud to affirm their open and public support for our "lost cause."

Nor in the twenty-five years since McFadden made that observation has a renowned writer come forward as a champion of abortion. And, with only a few exceptions (e.g., a highly controversial episode of the 1970s TV series *Maude*), television, film, and drama have also avoided abortion advocacy. Indeed, an Oscar for best original screenplay was awarded in 2007 to Diablo Cody, the woman who wrote the popular movie *Juno*, whose heroine—a feisty 16-year-old who becomes pregnant the first time she has intercourse with her high-school boyfriend—decides not to kill her baby but to give him up for adoption. While no one would call *Juno* overtly anti-abortion, the message it communicates, that adoption is indisputably the better "choice," can be applauded by even the most ardent pro-lifer.

Not long before this book went to press, word came that a dear friend and benefactress, Anne Higgins, had died in Washington, D.C. Anne, who handled correspondence for three presidents, and was director of the White House Office of Presidential Correspondence under Ronald Reagan, was an early enlistee in the Abortion War and a longtime supporter of the *Human Life Review*. In his eulogy, Patrick J. Buchanan (her boss in the Reagan years) recounted how each week the president would have Anne select 30 letters—from the thousands the White House received—for Reagan to take to Camp David and read over the weekend; a tape of his replies was delivered to her office every Monday morning. Monday was also the day the president had lunch with senior staff. And, according to Buchanan, Reagan always began by reading them one of these letters. "I recall one," Buchanan said. It was written by a woman in her 80s, who told the president that when her husband had left her, pregnant at the age of 40, she had considered having an abortion. But in the end she decided to have the child, a boy as it turned out, who, now in *his* 40s, was taking care of his mother in her old age. Reagan had been greatly moved by the story. Not so one of his senior advisors, who later asked Buchanan in an exasperated tone: "Where does he get these letters?"

He got them from Anne Higgins, who, Buchanan chuckled, always managed to salt a couple of life-affirming missives into the weekend mix. I think that were J.P. McFadden still with us, he would have insisted that this book be dedicated to his cherished friend and fellow traveler, Anne, who, like him, well knew the power of words.

ANNE CONLON, MANAGING EDITOR
HUMAN LIFE REVIEW

The Road to Abortion

Mary Meehan

Part I: How Eugenics Birthed Population Control

The typical account of the battle for legal abortion in the United States goes something like this: Brave civil libertarians and women's rights advocates, encouraged by liberating currents of the 1960s, dared to raise the abortion issue in public and to prompt serious debate about it. Some of them started amending state anti-abortion laws to allow exceptions beyond life-of-the-mother cases, while others challenged abortion restrictions in the courts. The U.S. Supreme Court gave them a huge victory with its 1973 *Roe* v. *Wade* decision. Yet that decision resulted in a backlash which has kept the issue in politics, and the country badly divided over it. So the brave civil libertarians and feminists soldier on in their lonely battle.

This version, while including a few truths, leaves out so many others that it is deeply misleading. A wealth of inside information, now available in private and government archives, suggests that the eugenics movement (devoted to breeding a "better" human race) led to population control, which in turn had enormous influence on the legalization of abortion. Civil libertarians and feminists were certainly in the picture, but in many cases they were handy instruments of the eugenicists and population controllers. Moreover, far from fighting a lonely battle, abortion supporters received enormous aid from the American establishment or "power elite."

It is important to note the difference between birth control and population control. Birth control, although often used as another label for "contraception," actually includes any method to limit births for any reason. It can be used by individuals or couples with no involvement by government or private agencies.

Population control, however, involves a public or private program to reduce births within a specific area or group (for example, within China or among African-Americans) and/or to increase births elsewhere (for example, within France or among the highly educated). In other words, those running the program have a specific demographic outcome in mind. While equal-opportunity population programs are theoretically possible, in practice one race or nationality generally uses population control against another.

Population control may involve any or all of the following: propaganda in favor of smaller families; pressure for legal change such as raising the legal

Mary Meehan, a Maryland writer and veteran *Human Life Review* contributor, is writing a book about eugenics.

age for marriage or repealing restrictions on contraception and abortion; widespread availability (often including public subsidy) of contraception, sterilization and abortion; the use of specific target numbers for birth control "acceptors" and for reduction of birth rates; economic penalties for having more than one or two children; and physical coercion to use birth control.

Occasional internal disputes among U.S. population controllers have obscured broad areas of agreement. Key figures such as Garrett Hardin and Alan Guttmacher, for example, disagreed over whether it was best to use a radical or a gradualist approach to advance the cause of abortion.

In 1963 Prof. Hardin, an environmentalist who was also an ardent population controller and a member of the American Eugenics Society, made a radical argument for repealing anti-abortion laws. In an approach that would be copied by many others, he put his population and eugenics concerns in the background and based his argument mainly on the welfare and rights of women. To religious objections citing the commandment "Thou shalt not kill," Hardin responded that the Bible "does not forbid killing, only murder." And murder, he said, means "unlawful killing. . . . Murder is a matter of definition. We can define murder any way we want to." Later he said that "it would be unwise to define the fetus as human (hence tactically unwise to refer to the fetus as an 'unborn child')."[1] Hardin had learned well the Humpty Dumpty technique:

"When *I* use a word," Humpty Dumpty said in rather a scornful tone, "it means just what I choose it to mean—neither more nor less." "The question is," said Alice, "whether you *can* make words mean so many different things." "The question is," said Humpty Dumpty, "which is to be master—that's all."[2]

Dr. Alan Guttmacher, President of the Planned Parenthood Federation of America, wrote Hardin that anti-abortion laws could be changed "inch by inch and foot by foot, but not a mile at a time." Later Guttmacher told another correspondent that "I am in favor of abortion on demand, but feel from the practical point of view that such a social revolution should evolve by stages." Publicly he, like Hardin, presented access to abortion as a benefit for women. Guttmacher undoubtedly believed that it helped women; in fact, he had referred patients to an illegal abortionist as early as 1941. Yet he also had other motives, ones indicated by his service as vice president and board member of the American Eugenics Society.[3]

He had a fair amount of medical prestige, which he used to advance the abortion cause. But prestige alone was not enough. Substantial amounts of money were needed to promote the kind of change he wanted.

John D. Rockefeller 3rd, his family, and their foundations provided much of the money. JDR 3rd's grandfather and father (that is, oil baron John D. Rockefeller and his son, John D., Jr.) were members of the American Eugenics Society, and JDR 3rd helped keep the eugenics group afloat financially during the Depression.

While he focused especially on population growth overseas, JDR 3rd was happy to squelch it within the United States as well. In 1967 he told his sister that "the matter of abortion is the principal remaining area in the population field which has not been given the attention it should." He suggested that she join him in giving money to the Association for the Study of Abortion. This sophisticated propaganda group, which pressed for legalization, included major eugenicists such as Guttmacher, ethicist Joseph Fletcher, and statistician Christopher Tietze. JDR 3rd and other Rockefeller sources contributed substantial amounts to the Association. They also gave money to support the winning side in *Roe* v. *Wade*.[4]

Another key figure in the abortion wars was Frederick Osborn, an immensely talented establishment figure who at various times was a businessman, scholar, army general, diplomat, and foundation executive. Osborn was also the strategist of the American Eugenics Society and the first administrator of a Rockefeller enterprise called the Population Council. Well before surgical abortion became a major issue, Osborn promoted Council research on chemical abortion and Council distribution of abortifacient intrauterine devices (IUDs). In 1974 he suggested that birth control and abortion were a great step forward for eugenics, but added: "If they had been advanced for eugenic reasons it would have retarded or stopped their acceptance."[5]

Who are the eugenicists, and why are they so obsessively interested in other people's fertility? When and why did they become involved in abortion?

English scientist Francis Galton, a cousin of Charles Darwin, invented the term "eugenics" in 1883. Taken from the Greek words for "well born," the term is used to describe the movement to "improve" the human race by encouraging the healthy and well-off to have many children and persuading, pressuring or coercing others to have few or none at all. The eugenics movement took root in many Western nations and also in China and Japan, with results that are very much with us today.

Galton, writing in the heyday of the British Empire, shared the profound bias against non-whites typical of his country and time. In one book, for example, he suggested that the "yellow races of China" might eventually push "the coarse and lazy Negro from at least the metaliferous regions of tropical Africa."[6] Racial bias deeply infected Western eugenics from the start; and in the United States, it reinforced bad attitudes of the slavery and segregation eras. Eugenics encouraged superiority attitudes of the upper class and all too many members of the middle class. They flocked to an ideology that seemed to give a scientific seal of approval to bigotry against the poor, non-whites, the immigrants pouring through the Golden Door, and people with physical and mental disabilities.

Several upper-class people devoted portions of their huge fortunes to promote eugenics. Mary Harriman, widow of railroad baron E. H. Harriman, gave large sums to support the Eugenics Record Office. The Rockefellers and George Eastman (of Eastman Kodak) also backed the cause. They supported not only the efforts of academic eugenicists, but also practical efforts to limit births among the poor.

Some eugenics supporters, viewing their own heredity as splendid, had the large families that eugenics doctrine said they should have. John D. Rockefeller, Jr., had six children, as did Frederick Osborn. Some later supporters of population control have continued the tradition: Former President George H. W. Bush, television entrepreneur Ted Turner, and financier George Soros each has five children.

U.S. eugenics in the 1920s and 1930s sometimes looked like a strange assortment of academics, socialites, crackpots and racists who were going off in all directions at once—a circus in need of a ringmaster. Harry Laughlin and Rep. Albert Johnson were fighting to reduce immigration from Southern and Eastern Europe. Margaret Sanger and Clarence Gamble were spreading contraception everywhere they could, but especially among the poor. Paul Popenoe, E. S. Gosney and Harry Laughlin were persuading states to pass laws for compulsory sterilization of "feeble-minded" Americans. Many eugenicists were churning out propaganda, and some were even running "Fitter Families" contests at state fairs.[7]

Late in life, Frederick Osborn would look back upon this era as one that was almost useless in advancing eugenics. Yet there is much to suggest that he was too harsh in his judgment. Eugenics groups recruited many people who remained interested and active in eugenics throughout their careers, often passing on the ideology to children who also became active. Eugenics was firmly established in many prestige institutions, especially Ivy League universities and elite women's colleges. Its influence on the American establishment, through the education of its professionals and politicians and foundation executives, was profound.

Laughlin and his friends, moreover, had great influence on immigration and sterilization policies. Others turned the new birth-control movement in the direction of population control for eugenic purposes.

Margaret Sanger—the charming, articulate and ruthless champion of birth control—was a eugenicist through most of her long career. She was a member of the American Eugenics Society and also a fellow of England's eugenics group.

Her marriage to the wealthy Noah Slee and her enjoyment of the upper-class lifestyle toned down the radicalism of her youth—so much so that she suggested birth control as a solution for unemployment and labor militance during the Depression. After a 1931 demonstration by unemployed marchers in Washington, D.C., she wrote to industrialist George Eastman: "The army of the unemployed—massed before the Capitol yesterday morning—reminded one very forcibly that birth control in practice is the only thing that is going to help solve this economic and current problem."

In one of her early books, Sanger said that eugenicists were showing "that the feeble-minded, the syphilitic, the irresponsible and the defective breed unhindered" and that "society at large is breeding an ever-increasing army of undersized, stunted and dehumanized slaves." In 1932 she called for a Population Congress that would "give certain dysgenic groups in our population their choice of segregation or sterilization." She had in mind "morons, mental defectives, epileptics," suggesting that "five million mental and moral degenerates" would be segregated. She also estimated that a second group of "illiterates, paupers, unemployables, criminals, prostitutes, dope-fiends" could be segregated "on farms and open spaces as long as necessary for the strengthening and development of moral conduct." She mentioned numbers casually and in a confusing way, but apparently was speaking of between fifteen and twenty million Americans to be segregated or sterilized.[9]

Justice Oliver Wendell Holmes, writing for a 1927 Supreme Court majority that upheld a Virginia sterilization law, shared Sanger's cold view of the mentally retarded when he said: "Three generations of imbeciles are enough." The compulsory sterilization laws, aimed at people in public institutions, victimized many poor whites in the South and elsewhere—and not just the retarded, either. A woman who was sterilized as a teenager in 1928, but told she was having her appendix removed, was shocked to learn about the sterilization fifty-one years later. "I wanted babies bad," she said. "Me and him [her husband] tried and tried to have 'em. I just don't know why they done it to me. I tried to live a good life." Her husband, a retired plumber, said that they were "always crazy about kids."

One writer suggests that black people were increasingly targeted for sterilization by the early 1940s, as state institutions in the South were opened to black residents. Targeting poor women—black and white, Native American and Hispanic—continued long after that period. Sometimes it involved mainly the enticement of public subsidy (still offered today), and sometimes pressure or outright coercion.[10]

Abortion was not much discussed in the 1920s, even among eugenicists, for it was a criminal venture widely condemned in the medical profession and the major churches. But there were rumblings of interest in the next decade. In 1933, for example, the Eugenics Publishing Company published a book advocating substantial loosening of anti-abortion laws. At a 1935 high-level meeting of eugenicists and population controllers, Dr. Eric Matsner suggested making abortion law more permissive, but the meeting notes did not mention any discussion of his proposal. Other participants were primarily interested in encouraging births among "good stock" or in spreading contraception. Mrs. Robert Huse of the National Committee on Maternal Health "suggested getting rid of the undesirables before trying to stimulate the birth rates of the top strata of society."[11]

Her committee sponsored a conference on abortion problems in 1942, one that indicated ambivalence on the topic but included suggestions for fighting illegal abortion.[12] This was a serious problem in large cities at the time. Had there been more interest in positive solutions among the conference participants, they might have set up a network of crisis-pregnancy centers to aid women in need. That, however, would have resulted in the births of many children eugenicists would have viewed as inferior.

German eugenicists, including Adolf Hitler, were interested in the American experience with immigration and sterilization. In *Mein Kampf,* published soon after Harry Laughlin and others had persuaded the U.S. Congress to pass immigration restrictions, Hitler suggested that American immigration policy was superior to German policy, although he called American restrictions "weak beginnings" and "slow beginnings." According to Leon Whitney, who had served as executive secretary of the American Eugenics Society and had become a sterilization enthusiast, a Hitler aide "wrote me for a copy of my book, *The Case for Sterilization,* which I sent and which Hitler personally acknowledged." Whitney showed Hitler's letter to Madison Grant, who chaired the eugenics group's immigration committee. Grant's response? "He smiled, reached to a folder on his desk and gave me a letter from Hitler to read. It was in German. It thanked our chairman for writing *The Passing of the Great Race* and said that the book was his Bible." Clarence Campbell, president of another American group called the Eugenics Research Association, attended a 1935 population congress in Berlin, where he offered a banquet toast to "that great leader, Adolf Hitler!"[13]

Frederick Osborn, who was in the process of taking over the American Eugenics Society, realized that hobnobbing with the Nazis had a down side in public relations. In 1938 he remarked that American public opinion was "opposed to the apparently excellent sterilization program in Germany because of its Nazi origin" and warned fellow eugenicists: "We must keep ourselves as Caesar's wife, beyond reproach. And that means the things we do, the people we keep company with, the things we say, and the things other people say about us."[14]

Osborn certainly changed eugenics rhetoric for the better, but he did not really reject class and racial bias. He probably contributed some thoughts to a remarkable chapter on population in Gunnar Myrdal's *An American Dilemma,* the classic 1944 study of race relations in the United States. Osborn was a trustee of the Carnegie Corporation of New York, which funded the massive Myrdal study. Myrdal included Osborn in his acknowledgments and cited Osborn and many other American eugenicists in his footnotes to the population chapter. Myrdal and his wife Alva, although mainly known in the U.S. as Swedish socialists, were also eugenics sympathizers.

As a whole, the Myrdal study was a strong indictment of white cruelties against the black community in America. But his population chapter might be described as intellectually chaotic, deeply cynical, or both. Perhaps his comment about the confusion, ambiguity and inconsistency that lurk "in the basement of man's soul" should be applied first to himself.

Myrdal wrote that "*the overwhelming majority of white Americans desire that there be as few Negroes as possible in America.*" He claimed, though, that the desire for "a decrease of the Negro population is not necessarily hostile to the Negro people." He said that it "is shared even by enlightened white Americans who do not hold the common belief that Negroes are inferior as a race. Usually it is pointed out that Negroes fare better and meet less prejudice when they are few in number."

Myrdal remarked that "all white Americans agree that, if the Negro is to be eliminated, he must be eliminated slowly so as not to hurt any living individual Negroes. Therefore, the dominant American valuation is that the Negro should be eliminated from the American scene, but *slowly.*"

Myrdal genuinely wanted to improve the living standards of the black community, but believed that until reforms could be made, "and as long as the burden of caste is laid upon American Negroes, even an extreme birth control program is warranted by reasons of individual and social welfare." He said that many Negroes "are so destitute that from a general social point of view it would be highly desirable that they did not procreate." Many, he said "are so ignorant and so poor that they are not desirable parents and cannot offer their children a reasonably good home." He suggested that expanding birth control and lowering the black birth rate could relieve "the poverty of the Negro masses" and improve black women's health.[15]

This mishmash of eugenic and humanitarian motivations became standard fare among population controllers in the decades after Myrdal wrote. By no means were all population controllers liberals. But some who were apparently made a bargain with their own consciences: They supported civil-rights laws and programs to fight poverty in the black community, while also supporting birth-control programs to contain or reduce the black population. Many of them probably believed the humanitarian rationale yet also had, deep down, a fear of growing numbers among non-whites.[16]

Myrdal also stressed the problem of sexually transmitted disease in the black community, suggesting contraception to prevent its transmission to children and adding: "A case could also be made for extending the scope of the circumstances under which physicians may legally perform therapeutic abortions." His native Sweden had already done this.[17]

Myrdal was familiar with Margaret Sanger's "Negro Project," although he did not use that term in describing it. Sanger was trying to spread birth control to Southern Negroes in pilot projects that featured black doctors and nurses as well as endorsements by black ministers and other leaders. According to her defenders, Sanger was genuinely concerned about the health and welfare of black women and felt that too-frequent childbearing harmed them. Dorothy Roberts, a black law professor who has studied the Negro Project, says that black women wanted birth control and that many were already using it at the time. Black leaders, she notes, thought it was needed for the advancement of their community. Yet Roberts also remarks that W. E. B. Du Bois "and other prominent Blacks were not immune from the elitist thinking of their time" and "sometimes advocated birth control for poorer segments of their own race in terms painfully similar to eugenic rhetoric."[18]

Possibly some black leaders had a bias against poor members of their own community that started in the house servant/field servant division of the slavery era. But Sanger, who was white, had both class bias and racial prejudice of the paternalistic variety. By dealing with doctors of their own race, she suggested, Negroes could more easily "lay their cards on the table, which means their ignorance, superstitions and doubts." She told another white eugenicist, Dr. Clarence Gamble: "We do not want word to go out that we want to exterminate the Negro population," adding that "the minister is the man who can straighten out that idea if it ever occurs to any of their more *rebellious* members."

Earlier, Dr. Gamble had suggested *buying* black support for the project. He told a Sanger colleague that "relatively minor contributions to local churches might be made which would result in continuous backing of the project by the local ministers." He added: "If colored newspapers are found to be influential it might be found effective to exchange cash for editorial and news support."[19]

Sanger's friend and birth-control colleague, Mary Lasker, won large contributions from her wealthy husband for the Negro Project and other

Sanger ventures. Lasker was a talented strategist in her own right. She and Sanger lobbied relentlessly to get federal and state governments involved in birth control. With help from their mutual friend in the White House, Eleanor Roosevelt, they had some success. The initial federal efforts were relatively small, and quietly arranged, but they provided a precedent when Presidents Lyndon Johnson and Richard Nixon decided to expand federal involvement in a dramatic way.[20]

In the early 1940s, while Sanger worked on her many projects, U.S. troops were fighting in World War II and U.S. policymakers were making careful plans for the postwar era. Much of the planning was done through a secret project called "Studies of American Interests in the War and the Peace," which was financed by the Rockefeller Foundation and conducted by the private Council on Foreign Relations for the U.S. State Department. Major concerns included postwar access to the rich natural resources of colonial areas and the possibility of finding markets everywhere for American products.

Frank Notestein—a eugenicist, an economist/demographer, and a friend and colleague of Frederick Osborn—wrote a paper on population for the project. Rapid population growth in colonial areas, he suggested, would result in great hardships for some of them, including hunger, disease, and war. Such areas, he said, "will be increasingly expensive and troublesome to administer, and unsatisfactory to do business with." He proposed a program of modernization for the colonies, including the development of industries that would "draw a surplus and ineffective agricultural population into effective production," the use of popular education "to create new wants for physical and material well-being," and "propaganda in favor of controlled fertility as an integral part of a public health program."[21] Notestein's proposals for manipulating entire societies had profound effects on other population experts and eventually on government policy.

Jacob Viner, a noted economist, also wrote a paper for the war/peace studies in which he remarked that "higher-standard-of-living populations" made better trading partners for the West than did "low-standard populations even if greater in size." Lower birth rates in the "backward areas," Viner suggested, were "very much to the interest of the United States."[22] This point was extremely important to the businessmen who participated in the Council on Foreign Relations and had great influence on U.S. foreign policy.

As American private and public agencies developed programs of population control over the next several decades, they stressed humanitarian objectives such as fighting poverty and famine and improving the status of women. Some of the population controllers, such as Notestein, actually believed the humanitarian rationale, at least in an abstract or paternalistic way. They did not, however, sit down with poor people as equals to discuss the matter; instead, *they* decided what poor people should have and then manipulated the poor to accept it.

For many population controllers, the humanitarian rationale was a cover for other motivations: (1) the eugenicists' desire to breed a "better" human race by suppressing the birth rate of poor people and non-whites; (2) the goal of retaining access to the natural resources of the old colonial areas and of developing markets there; and (3) as the Cold War intensified, a decision by U.S. leaders to use population control as a way of keeping the lid on poor nations so they would not fall victim to Communist take-overs. These three motivations reinforced one another; all of them were oriented toward keeping the industrialized West, and especially the U.S., dominant in the world.

After World War II, eugenicists started two organizations to promote population control in ex-colonial nations. (Populations there were increasing even more rapidly than predicted because of improved disease control.) Margaret Sanger, C. P. Blacker of England's Eugenics Society, and others formed the International Planned Parenthood Federation (IPPF), which now has worldwide national affiliates. John D. Rockefeller 3rd and Frederick Osborn launched the Population Council, a private foundation that first convinced government leaders in poor nations that they had a serious population problem and then showed them how to solve it through population control.

Osborn, who was the key administrator of the Population Council in its early years, wanted it to keep a low profile in order to avoid charges of U.S. imperialism. At the Council's 1952 founding conference, he had asked, "Supposing a perfect contraceptive should be developed. Should it be announced by the University of Chicago, or Bellevue Hospital . . . or should it get its final development in Japan or India, so it would appear to spring from there?" Using grants and fellowships, he started building in the poor nations a network of population experts with career interests in population control. "We were trying to help foreign countries with large grants," he said years later, "and it was far better to do it quietly, without the public in the foreign countries knowing that this was an American effort."[23]

Osborn, Rockefeller and their colleagues were eager to develop birth-control drugs and devices that could be distributed on a massive basis both at home and abroad. They were interested in chemical abortifacients; for example, they funded research by Dr. J. B. Thiersch on "anti-metabolites" to induce early abortion. Documents on this project show a remarkable lack of concern about its ethical problems—not only abortion, but also the occasional disguise of the project as one involving only "the rat litter and fetus *in utero*" and the use of "institutionalized patients" for toxicity studies. Osborn was concerned about *legal* problems, though, at a time when abortion was illegal in all states with limited exceptions. Noting that an early Thiersch grant application did not "say explicitly that the people he is going to experiment on will be exclusively women certified for therapeutic abortion," Osborn asked, "Shouldn't we be so protected in making the grant?"[24]

The Population Council also put great effort into developing and distributing intrauterine devices, or IUDs. (An IUD can either prevent conception—that is, fertilization—or prevent implantation of the embryo in the womb, thus causing an early abortion.) In 1966 Osborn told a correspondent that the Council was spending major sums on IUDs, adding: "We have felt this could be done far more effectively in the name of the Population Council than in the name of eugenics . . . Personally, I think it the most important practical eugenic measure ever taken."[25]

Possible medical complications of IUDs include cramps, heavy bleeding, anemia, uterine perforation, pelvic infection, infertility, ectopic pregnancy, and even septic abortion and death. Feminist Betsy Hartmann says that the "mortality rate from IUDs in the Third World is roughly *double* that in the West" and the infertility sometimes caused by IUDs can lead to "social ostracism, abandonment, and ultimately destitution" for women.[26]

Long ago, population controllers worked out a way to deflect criticism of abortifacient drugs and devices. At a 1959 conference, one expert suggested "a prudent habit of speech," hinting that it would be wise to consider implantation—rather than fertilization—the beginning of pregnancy. In 1962, in its "model penal code" project, the American Law Institute recommended legalizing the use of "drugs or other substances for avoiding pregnancy, whether by preventing implantation of a fertilized ovum or by any other method that operates before, at or immediately after fertilization."

In a 1964 Population Council conference, eugenicist Dr. Christopher Tietze pointedly reminded his colleagues that theologians and jurists do listen to doctors and biologists. "If a medical consensus develops and is maintained that pregnancy, and therefore life, begins at implantation, eventually our brethren from the other faculties will listen," he said. A committee of the American College of Obstetricians and Gynecologists soon obliged Tietze by defining conception as "the implantation of a fertilized ovum."[27] With that kind of support, the population controllers were off to the races, developing more and more abortifacients, which they usually referred to as "contraceptives" or simply "birth control." The IUDs and the later Norplant devices have proved useful in coercive population control, such as that in China, since it can be difficult and dangerous for non-physicians to remove them.[28]

Part II: How Government Got Hooked

While eugenicists encouraged research on abortifacient drugs and devices, they also turned their attention to surgical abortion as a tool that could be combined with prenatal testing to eliminate the handicapped unborn.

The Nazi era had given compulsory sterilization a bad name, but eugenicists never lost their interest in preventing births of the handicapped. Frederick Osborn and others in the American Eugenics Society had long promoted "hereditary counseling," which they once described as "the opening wedge in the public acceptance of eugenic principles." Scientists were developing prenatal testing for fetal handicaps in the 1950s,[1] but that would not have meant much had abortion continued to be illegal. A Rockefeller-funded project came to the rescue. The foundation was supporting the American Law Institute's production of a "model penal code," which states could use as a guide when amending their criminal laws.

Dr. Alan Guttmacher's twin brother Manfred, a psychiatrist, was a special consultant to the model code project, and Alan himself took part in one or two meetings about it when he was vice president of the American Eugenics Society. (Later he would lead the Planned Parenthood Federation of America.) Another special consultant was a British legal scholar and eugenicist, Glanville Williams. The model code, as adopted by the Institute in 1962, allowed abortions for "substantial risk" of serious handicap in the unborn child, as well as in other hard cases. In the final debate, attorney Eugene Quay declared, to no avail, that "the state cannot give the authority to perform an abortion because it does not have the authority itself. Those lives are human lives, and are not the property of the state."[2]

A number of states changed their abortion laws along the lines suggested in the model penal code. The new laws did not make as much difference as their supporters had hoped—and their opponents had feared—probably because many "respectable" doctors were already doing abortions for hard cases. While abortion supporters were disappointed and soon pressed for abortion-on-demand, the exceptions approach actually had helped their cause in several ways. It had prompted public debate on a "taboo" subject, had softened up the public to the idea of abortion as a "humanitarian" action, and probably had led much of the public to believe that the debate was about hard cases only.

Meanwhile, population experts were increasingly viewing abortion as another tool to control population numbers. They knew that legalized abortion had sharply reduced population growth in Japan after the Second World War. They were particularly interested in suction machines used for abortion in

China, and they worked to spread knowledge of this method. C. Lalor Burdick, a foundation executive and eugenicist, pressed the suction-machine approach with great energy because it could be done on an outpatient basis and was cheaper than other methods. His Lalor Foundation helped finance a training film on suction abortion that was produced by British doctor Dorothea Kerslake and shown widely to doctors in the U.S. and elsewhere.

In 1970 Burdick told a correspondent that some day it might be accepted "that bum pregnancies of whatever character should ipso facto be terminated. And so would come the next step, namely, that the lowest grade people (as determined by performance factors) are not to have children either." He asked, "Isn't an intelligent black or mulatto a lot better than the dippings from the bottom of the white barrel?" Earlier, though, he had told population-controller Hugh Moore, "All channels with which I come in contact speak of the fecklessness of the Indians and of the hopeless inabilities of the Africans." Burdick had also complained that Americans "seem to be deifying our scruffy and unfit by putting them in temples (welfare housing)" and "re-creating some ancient fertility cult where we provide breeding pads and free sustenance for the proliferation of a kind of people that hate us and would destroy us, if they could." This lover of humanity also remarked: "The 'maternal impulse' is partly bunk. De-bunking of this might get some females off their fat duffs and into useful endeavor."[3]

Burdick was not unique. Retired army general William H. Draper, Jr., a leading figure in Planned Parenthood and the Population Crisis Committee, suggested population control as a solution to urban riots. Referring to 1967 riots in Detroit and elsewhere, he told a business executive that "it is pretty obvious that a great many unwanted children have added fuel to the fire." He said that "to cure the present ghetto problems and deal with the population question among the poorer parts of our own population . . . will require valiant and much greater efforts than any exerted in the past." If the executive decided to support Planned Parenthood, Draper added, "you could do no better." In 1966 Dr. Alan Guttmacher, apparently trying to be witty, wrote from Africa to a U.S. colleague: "My trip has been great. I believe I converted the Jews in Israel and now I am working on the pigmented savages." This private comment from Guttmacher (who was Jewish, but not observant) came soon after his Planned Parenthood had given an award to the Rev. Martin Luther King, Jr.[4]

The population controllers started winning major and publicly trumpeted government funding of contraception in the 1960s. Hugh Moore, a Pennsylvania businessman, had done much of the groundwork with a series of "The Population Bomb" booklets mailed to prominent Americans in the previous decade. "We are not primarily interested in the sociological or humanitarian aspects of birth control," Moore and two colleagues said in a 1954 cover letter for the booklet. "We are interested in the use which the Communists make of hungry people in their drive to conquer the earth." A top New York *Times* executive who received the mailing passed it on to his Princeton classmate, Allen Dulles, who happened to be Director of the Central Intelligence Agency. The *Times*man suggested that population control "is a project which officials of our government may not want in any way to promote, but to me it seems to have merit if followed up by some private sources." The archives file containing this letter does not have a reply from Dulles.[5]

Several months earlier, though, Dulles had been informed that CIA economic analyst Edgar M. Hoover was "leaving to go with the Office of Population Studies which is an operation of Princeton University." But Hoover would be "located in Washington," Dulles was told, and would be "an intermittent consultant to the Agency" (the CIA). Hoover and demographer Ansley Coale then produced for the Princeton office (actually called the Office of Population Research, Frank Notestein's fiefdom) a major study partly financed by the Population Council (the Osborn-Rockefeller empire) and the World Bank. They reached this conclusion about low-income nations: ". . . to postpone the reduction of fertility is to forego the opportunity for a more rapid rise in immediate wellbeing, and to shrink the potential growth in incomes per capita for the indefinite future." The Coale-Hoover study, widely distributed by the Population Council, had enormous impact. As one expert later remarked, it "held the field for most of 20 years. It was explained in every population textbook and was the rationale for large population programs by the United States and other countries." Although later challenged effectively by economist Julian Simon and others, the Coale-Hoover theory won the public policy debate early and firmly—as one suspects it was designed to do.[6]

President Dwight Eisenhower, whom Allen Dulles served as CIA Director, was interested in population and asked a foreign-aid study panel to look into it. The panel, headed by retired General Draper and prodded by Hugh Moore, recommended that the U.S. assist other nations with population programs. After U.S. Catholic bishops blasted that notion, though, Eisenhower quickly retreated. "I cannot imagine anything more emphatically a subject that is not a proper political or governmental activity or function or responsibility . . . We do not intend to interfere with the internal affairs of any other government . . . ," the President said in 1959.[7]

Before John F. Kennedy's 1960 election to the presidency, a Senate colleague had asked Kennedy how he, as a Catholic, viewed the issue of making "family planning information" available at home and abroad. Kennedy

24

responded, "It's bound to come; it's just a question of time. The Church will come around. I intend to be as brave as I dare." As President, Kennedy cautiously gave encouragement to those who wanted to involve both the U.S. government and the United Nations in population control. He did not, however, share with the public his views on abortion. According to journalist Benjamin Bradlee, a friend of Kennedy's, in 1963 JFK privately "said he was all for people solving their problems by abortion (and specifically told me I could not use that for publication in *Newsweek*) . . ."[8]

Lyndon Johnson and his immediate successor, Richard Nixon, were the first U.S. presidents who publicly advocated population control abroad and made it a major part of U.S. policy. They also intensified population-control efforts in the United States, partly to demonstrate to leaders of poor countries that the U.S. was willing to restrain its own population growth. But the domestic efforts, like those abroad, primarily targeted poor people and non-whites.

Population control was so carefully wrapped in humanitarian language that most Americans probably thought it simply involved opening birth-control clinics and serving everyone who showed up at the door. But internal government documents from the Johnson administration show: 1) a carefully orchestrated campaign to pressure governments of poor nations to adopt population control, and 2) enormous interest in manipulating cultural attitudes and motivating women to use birth control.

This required a careful approach, since it involved much meddling in the internal affairs of other nations. Thus in 1968 the Agency for International Development (AID) asked U.S. missions abroad "to discreetly investigate" the possibility of having "indigenous social scientists" do research on motivation for fertility reduction. The agency also arranged for the Pathfinder Fund (established years earlier by eugenicist Clarence Gamble) to help "in the establishment of national voluntary associations which would later become members of the International Planned Parenthood Federation." But this, too, had to be done discreetly, and the agency gave its troops information to "deflect any charges" that the Planned Parenthood group was "a creature of AID and the U.S. Government."[9]

Soon after his 1969 inauguration, President Nixon asked White House urban affairs aide Daniel Patrick Moynihan to "develop a specific program" in population and family planning. Moynihan was a brilliant choice for the job—a Catholic, a Democrat, a Harvard professor, and a charming fellow who could handle difficult personalities.

The State Department's top population officer, Philander P. Claxton, Jr., already had such a strong program in place that Moynihan did not have to add much in the international area. Claxton, in fact, helped draft Nixon's 1969

25

population message to Congress, which stressed rapid population growth in the Third World and suggested that it aggravated problems of malnutrition, poor housing, and unemployment.[10]

Of course, there were—and are today—areas of great poverty abroad; but population controllers often ignore the productive and energizing force of a young and growing population. As one Pakistani legislator remarked, a new-born child "comes with one mouth and two hands to earn his livelihood and is gifted with a fertile mind." Population controllers, during the Nixon administration and since, think only of the mouth to be fed; they forget the two hands to raise the food and the mind to devise better ways to raise it. Population controllers also tend to believe that they bear major responsibility for everyone else's lives. They rarely, if ever, ask themselves, "Who appointed me to be General Manager of the Universe?"

In its robust pioneer era, America had very rapid population growth; and many of its pioneer families (the parents of Abraham Lincoln, for example) were just as poor as many Third World families are today. Thomas Malthus himself, in an 1830 essay, said that population increase in the United States apparently "has been more rapid than in any known country . . ." With its huge territory and its current population of 76 persons per square mile, the United States is relatively sparsely populated; yet many countries—including most in South America and many in Africa—have even fewer persons per square mile. Gabon has only 12; Bolivia has 19; Algeria has 33; Brazil has 50; Peru has 53. It is true that China has 345—but so does the Czech Republic; and the United Kingdom, at 634 persons per square mile, is far more densely populated than either. All of this should give pause to Westerners who casually talk about "overpopulation" in low-income nations.

Some nations do, indeed, have too few (developed) resources to meet all the needs of their people. But some records suggest that U.S. leaders have been mainly concerned about our access to their resources. One document in the Nixon White House files, for example, had the usual boilerplate language about humanitarian concerns, but also noted that the U.S. "is in danger of losing markets, investments and sources of raw materials" as less-developed nations "seek ways to increase their resources." A high-level population study, commissioned by President Nixon and Secretary of State/National Security Adviser Henry Kissinger, said that the United States, "with 6 percent of the world's population, consumes about a third of its resources" and that "the U.S. economy will require large and increasing amounts of minerals from abroad, especially from less developed countries." Population pressures in such countries, it suggested, could lead to expropriation, labor troubles, sabotage or civil unrest, so that "the smooth flow of needed materials will be jeopardized."

In addition, Nixon's Special Representative for Trade Negotiations suggested that restraining population growth in poor nations could help U.S. trade there. He remarked that "a people living on a bare subsistence level cannot be a prosperous market for the wide range of goods available in the modern world . . . Even a modest improvement in incomes in Latin America would no doubt be reflected in a greater demand for U.S. products not available at home, notably the products of our advanced industrial technology."[12]

Philander Claxton, with support from Moynihan, pressed ahead with his ambitious effort to harness every possible agency of the U.S. government and the United Nations for the cause of population control. By fiscal year 1969, the Agency for International Development was already spending over $45 million per year on population and giving direct aid to 31 countries. The Peace Corps was also involved; more than 200 of its volunteers had done population work in 1966-69. But criticism of such work in South America had signaled a need for discretion; "we have learned the need for caution in approaching this very explosive topic," the Peace Corps told President Nixon. Yet it soldiered on. In Tonga, a tiny island-nation in the Pacific that "has no acute population problem at this time" but reportedly could have one in two generations, Peace Corps volunteers taught contraception and organized village meetings on the subject. "They also introduced sex education into the schools," according to the Peace Corps report, "and it is now an accepted part of the Ministry of Education curriculum."[13]

The U.S. Information Agency was churning out propaganda to encourage "changes of attitude which will lead to effective family planning programs abroad"; but it added more emphasis on issues such as health, education, and human rights. This broader approach, the agency said, "attempted to offset allegations that the U.S. was practicing a kind of 'demographic imperialism' in seeking only to impose population controls on less-developed countries."[14]

Using the United Nations to spread population control was another way to avoid resentment against the United States. In 1967, for example, the State Department had cabled the American embassy in Indonesia: "We feel it is important to involve UN agencies in support of family planning programs in Indonesia and elsewhere to avoid appearance of sole support by USG [U.S. Government]." But it suggested that the right calibration of funding sources was a tricky matter: "UNICEF role should be possible in manner which would dilute USG visibility without raising total visibility of foreign contribution to unacceptable degree."

The State Department and its allies understood the need to have non-Americans and people of color in up-front population jobs at the UN. In 1969 an American highly placed there recommended Rafael Salas of the Philippines for the top UN population job. According to an American diplomat, the UN official thought Salas "has advantage of color, religion (Catholic), and conviction." Salas was chosen.

As Planned Parenthood's Alan Guttmacher told an interviewer, "If you're going to curb population, it's extremely important not to have it done by the damned Yankee, but by the UN. Because the thing is, then it's not considered genocide." He added: "If the United States goes to the black man or the yellow man and says slow down your reproductive rate, we're immediately suspected of having ulterior motives to keep the white man dominant in the world. If you can send in a colorful UN force, you've got much better leverage."[15]

At the White House, Moynihan tried to boost State Department efforts partly by finding more money for birth-control research at the National Institutes of Health. He told another White House aide that "if the Indians and Pakistanis are going to have workable, inexpensive contraceptives ten years from now, it will only be if we pay for the research now." Moynihan also encouraged legal scholar Luke Lee, who was promoting the notion that "legal reforms in such areas as abortion, taxation, sex education, etc., could not fail to produce significant impact on population growth." That sounded like a great idea to Moynihan and Claxton, and Lee soon received AID money to develop a Law and Population Program at Tufts University. It was a major boost to "policy development," the process by which U.S. officials pressure Third-World governments to change their laws and administrative policies to discourage childbirth.[16]

While documents intended for public consumption rarely, if ever, mentioned abortion in connection with population control, Luke Lee was not alone in talking about it privately. In fact, Dr. Reimert Ravenholt, who headed the AID population program, was promoting abortion aggressively. He, like Lalor Burdick, was an enthusiastic proponent of abortion suction machines. In 1970 Ravenholt and an AID colleague outlined five tiers of birth-control technology. Their fifth tier included all of the usual methods—plus surgical abortion and a self-administered abortifacient that "would ensure the non-pregnant state at completion of a monthly cycle." They reported that AID had earmarked over $10 million to develop such a method, and they suggested that prostaglandins could be the magic-bullet abortifacient. Ravenholt sent a batch of material on prostaglandins over to Moynihan at the White House, commenting that the prospect "for fairly rapid resolution of world excess fertility problems is now far better than it was one year ago."[17]

By 1973 AID contractors were training Third World doctors in abortion techniques. "We want to elevate the reproductive well-being of the human race," said an AID official. So aggressive was Ravenholt in his promotional

28

activity that Senator Jesse Helms, the North Carolina Republican, tried to put AID out of the abortion business in 1973. The original Helms Amendment would have forbidden any use of foreign-aid funds to pay for abortifacient drugs and devices, as well as surgical abortion. But a House-Senate conference committee watered down the amendment, so that it simply barred paying for abortions "as a method of family planning or to motivate or coerce any person to practice abortions."

Ravenholt and his colleagues viewed the Helms Amendment as a major nuisance, and population controllers have complained about it ever since. But AID continued to fund research on abortifacients and massive distribution of drugs and devices that were partly abortifacient, and private groups promoted abortion suction machines. Some distributed abortion equipment even in nations where abortion was illegal.[18] Later they used the problem of illegal abortion in poor nations—a problem they had made far worse—as a reason to legalize abortion.

Population controllers had also worked to legalize abortion within the United States. Here they had much assistance from feminists and civil libertarians (although some within each group strongly opposed abortion) and from lawyers such as Roy Lucas and Sarah Weddington, who had been personally involved in abortion.[19] The lawyers and feminists focused on the up-front, public battles.

The population controllers did some of that; but they excelled in quiet, behind-the-scenes efforts where they could count on friends in high places. They arranged government promotion and funding of abortion through a series of administrative decisions, rather than through the constitutional route of authorization by Congress. This was done so quietly and effectively that when some members of Congress realized what was happening and decided to fight it, they found themselves in a very difficult, uphill battle.

Nixon's domestic population-control programs, like Johnson's, targeted low-income women. In his 1969 population message to Congress, President Nixon suggested that five million poor women had insufficient access to birth control and said that "no American woman should be denied access to family planning assistance because of her economic condition." Whatever Nixon's own motivation, the targeting of poor women continued the old eugenics tradition.

When Congress passed a major domestic "family planning" bill in 1970, it provided that money appropriated for it could not "be used in programs where abortion is a method of family planning."[20] But the Medicaid law, providing medical aid to poor people, had been passed several years earlier, before abortion was even a national issue, and it did not have a similar provision. Apparently operating under the notion that whatever is not specifically forbidden is permitted, one or more officials responsible for Medicaid started paying for abortion on a state-option basis. (Abortion was still illegal in most states then.)

Because some key records are missing from the National Archives, it is extremely difficult to find just when this practice started and whether the President (Johnson and/or Nixon) knew about it. A 1970 paper by two interns at the Department of Health, Education and Welfare (HEW) indicates that the government was funding some abortions then. "The primary fear of the family planning services," the interns wrote, "has been that Congress might cut their appropriations if it were to become known that taxpayer's money was being used to give abortions." They suggested that "for the next two or three years, the primary thrust of the Administration and of HEW officials must remain relatively covert."[21]

The abortion subsidy did remain "relatively covert," partly because HEW officials sometimes gave misleading answers when asked about abortion funding and partly because news media were, to be charitable, less than alert about the issue. But in April, 1971, HEW official John Veneman said that under the Medicaid law, "in those states where abortions are legal and approved as one of the services provided by the states, there are federal funds going in."

This was similar to a states' rights policy that President Nixon had recently ordered military hospitals to follow. "If the laws in a particular state restrict abortion," the President announced, "the rules at the military base hospitals are to correspond to that law." But on the other side of the coin, if the laws of a particular state were permissive toward abortion, then those laws were to be followed by military hospitals in the state. But because Nixon's order changed an earlier Defense Department policy that was more permissive toward abortion, abortion foes viewed his action as helpful. They apparently were distracted, too, by his rhetoric about abortion as "an unacceptable form of population control" and about "my personal belief in the sanctity of human life."[22]

President Nixon may have been inclined to oppose abortion in a general way, at least rhetorically, but he was unwilling to let that inclination overcome his states' rights position. Possibly he, or at least many of his subordinates, wanted to have it both ways. He received political credit among abortion foes for speaking against abortion, at the same time that he (or they) advanced population control by allowing abortion funding.

While funding battles went on behind the scenes, abortion supporters were waging a vigorous fight to legalize abortion nationwide. A population commission, appointed by President Nixon and congressional leaders, did its best to advance that cause by calling for abortion "on request."

Nixon selected John D. Rockefeller 3rd to chair the 24-member commission. An ardent advocate of population control and a Depression-era donor to the American Eugenics Society, Rockefeller was using family money and prestige to depress birth rates through his Population Council. He and other Rockefellers were also helping to fund the Association for the Study of Abortion, which promoted the legalization of abortion. And they were helping to finance the federal court case, *Roe* v. *Wade,* which would soon strike down state laws against abortion.

JDR 3rd had lobbied for establishment of the population commission and had conferred with Moynihan on its membership and assignments. Moynihan described a conversation in which Rockefeller "assured me that, while until recently most persons concerned with population growth had directed their attention to the problem of 'unwanted children,' there is now wide agreement that in the United States, at all events, it is the wanted children who are going to cause the problem."

Another member of the population commission, sociologist Otis Dudley Duncan, was vice president of the American Eugenics Society. Other members included population-control hawks such as Sen. Robert Packwood (a Republican from Oregon) and Sen. Alan Cranston (a Democrat from California), and Population Council president Bernard Berelson. The commission's executive director, Charles Westoff, was a eugenicist; so were many professors who wrote papers for him. Anyone aware of these connections might have predicted that the commission would do what, in fact, it did: endorse legalized abortion and call for public funding of it; ask for more research on fertility control and more subsidy of contraception and sterilization; support sex education and "population education" in the schools; and recommend a national average of two children per couple.[23]

Reynolds Farley of the University of Michigan, in a paper for the commission, showed how the black birthrate could be restrained. Noting the high abortion rate of Negro women in New York after a permissive law was passed there, Farley commented: "Liberalized abortion laws may speed a decline in Negro childbearing, although we cannot be certain that the experience of New York City will be duplicated elsewhere." He estimated that if then-current fertility and mortality rates continued, then the black community, which in 1970 made up 11 percent of the U.S. population, would grow to a 17 percent share by 2020—and that it could go as high as 29 percent if black fertility increased. But with low fertility for both races, the black share of the population would rise to only 12 percent of the population by 1980—and stay there through 2020. The black share has risen somewhat higher than that, but the Census Bureau predicts that it will reach only

14 percent by 2020.[24] The industrial-strength birth control aimed at the black community in recent decades certainly has done much to suppress the birth rate—and the political power—of that community.

Some eugenicists were so concerned about over-all numbers of people that, while they may have wanted black fertility to fall, they did not want white fertility to rise. Frederick Osborn, the key strategist of the American Eugenics Society, had long advocated that people of good heredity have large families, and he himself had six children. But in 1970 he was surprised to find that Otis Dudley Duncan, the Eugenics Society vice president who served on the Rockefeller commission, agreed with "the two-child slogan." Rockefeller, too, seemed to be on the other side of the issue from his old friend Osborn. And Chester Finn, Jr., an aide to Moynihan at the White House, referred to "the extraordinary fecundity of the American middle class—in light of its 'allotted' 2.1 children per couple." (The middle class, was, of course, overwhelmingly white.) Finn also remarked that if "the government can subtly influence social mores such that families *want* to have fewer children, so much the better. But it isn't something we want to talk about."[25]

At first sight, this may suggest that population control was a revolution that turned on its own children. Yet it has always been a hobby of upper-class people. They are happy to use middle-class experts when needed, but do not necessarily have a high opinion of the middle class as a whole. Members of the middle class who support population control might ponder a remark attributed to Winston Churchill: "An appeaser is one who feeds a crocodile—hoping it will eat him last."[26]

Population control marched on triumphantly during and beyond the Nixon administration. After the Supreme Court legalized abortion nationwide in 1973, population controllers pressed hard, and often successfully, for public subsidy of abortions for poor women. Because this was presented as a humanitarian good, eugenicists were able to get credit for doing what they had always done: suppressing the birth rate of poor people and non-whites.

Although the Ronald Reagan and George Bush administrations tried to hold the line against surgical abortion, both supported widespread contraception and sterilization and the distribution of birth-control methods that are partly abortifacient. Then the William Clinton administration campaigned to import into the United States the French abortion pill called RU-486, defended even the horrific "partial-birth abortions," and worked unceasingly for more population control abroad.

Private groups continued to press population control, often as government contractors and often on their own as well. They received massive funding from the Rockefeller, Ford, Mellon, Packard, and many other foundations.[27]

Population programs often looked like war against women and children, and sometimes men as well. Thus in 1978 the Population Crisis Committee speculated on such possible future methods of fertility control as:

- ethanol (ethyl alcohol) abortions that involved injecting ethanol through the cervix;
- prostaglandin suppositories for early abortion;
- chemical sterilization of women by "permanent scarring" with the quinacrine drug;
- investigation of "the possible use of industrial chemicals such as the pesticide DMCP" as male contraceptives;
- experiments with male sterilization using "a mixture of ethanol and formalin," that is, ethyl alcohol plus a solution of water and formaldehyde.[28]

If this calls to mind the Nazi sterilization experiments, the resemblance may not be entirely coincidental. Those who try to breed "better" people—whatever their definition of "better"—eventually find themselves in a war against humanity.

The writer is deeply grateful to archives staff for their assistance and, where needed, for permission to quote from their documents.

Statements about an individual's membership in the American Eugenics Society (later called the Society for the Study of Social Biology or SSSB), unless otherwise indicated, are based on the 1930 Society membership list in the Margaret Sanger Papers, Library of Congress, microfilm reel 41; the Eugenics Quarterly *(especially the membership list in the Dec., 1956 issue); or issues of* Social Biology.

Statements about membership or fellowship in England's Eugenics Society are based on 1928 and 1944 lists in the Norman E. Himes Archive, box 7, folder 78; an Aug., 1957, list bound with 1957 issues of Eugenics Review, *National Library of Medicine, Bethesda, Md.; and Eugenics Watch, "The British Eugenics Society, 1907 to 1994," posted on the Internet (www.africa2000.com).*

Here are the locations of manuscript collections cited in the notes below:

American Eugenics Society Archives, American Philosophical Society Library, Philadelphia, Pa.

Carnegie Institution of Washington Archive, Washington, D.C.

Allen W. Dulles Papers, Seeley G. Mudd Manuscript Library, Princeton University, Princeton, N.J.

Clarence James Gamble Papers (H MS c23), Harvard Medical Library in the Francis A. Countway Library of Medicine, Boston, Mass.

Alan Frank Guttmacher Papers (H MS c155), Harvard Medical Library in the Francis A. Countway Library of Medicine, Boston, Mass.

Norman E. Himes Archive, Francis A. Countway Library of Medicine, Boston, Mass.

Ellsworth Huntington Papers, Manuscripts and Archives, Yale University Library, New Haven, Conn.

Hugh Moore Papers, Seeley G.. Mudd Manuscript Library, Princeton University, Princeton, N.J.

National Committee on Maternal Health Archive, Francis A. Countway Libary of Medicine, Boston, Mass.

Richard M. Nixon Presidential Materials, National Archives, College Park, Md.

Frederick Henry Osborn Papers, American Philosophical Society Library, Philadelphia, Pa.

Planned Parenthood Federation of America Records, Sophia Smith Collection, Smith College, Northampton, Mass.

Population Council Archives, Rockefeller Archive Center (RAC), Sleepy Hollow, N.Y.

Rockefeller Family Archives, Rockefeller Archive Center (RAC), Sleepy Hollow, N.Y.

Rockefeller Foundation Archives, Rockefeller Archive Center (RAC), Sleepy Hollow, N.Y.

Margaret Sanger Papers, Library of Congress, Washington, D.C.

U.S. Commission on Population Growth and the American Future (Record Group 220), National Archives, College Park, Md.

U.S. Department of State (Record Group 59), Central Foreign Policy Files (CFPF), 1967-69, National Archives, College Park, Md.

U.S. National Security Council (Record Group 273), National Archives, College Park, Md.

NOTES (Part I)

1. Garrett Hardin. *Stalking the Wild Taboo* (Los Altos, Calif., 1973), pp. 24-25 & 66. Hardin was a member of the American Eugenics Society as early as 1956. He served on its board in 1972 and remained on it in 1973-74 after the group changed its name to Society for the Study of Social Biology.
2. Lewis Carroll, *Through the Looking-Glass and What Alice Found There* (New York, 1993), p. 124.
3. Alan F. Guttmacher to Garrett Hardin, Dec. 30, 1963, Guttmacher Papers, box 1, folder 12; Alan F. Guttmacher to Emily C. Moore, Dec. 20, 1968, *ibid.,* box 2, folder 31; and Dr. Regine K. Stix to Dr. Boudreau, Feb. 11, 1941, National Committee on Maternal Health Archive, box 9. Guttmacher was vice president of the American Eugenics

Society in 1956-1963 and was on its board in 1955 and 1964-1966.

4. Typed copy of John D. Rockefeller 3rd [hereafter JDR 3rd] to Frederick Osborn, June 30,1936, Huntington Papers, Group 1, Series III, box 77; Rudolph Bertheau to Robert C. Cook, March *12,1942, ibid.,* box 88; JDR 3rd to Mrs. Jean Mauze, Jan. 12, 1967, John D. Rockefeller 3rd Papers, Rockefeller Archive Center [hereafter RAC]; "John D. Rockefeller 3rd Contributions in the Area of Abortion, 1966-1978," *ibid.;* "John D. Rockefeller 3rd Contributions in the Area of Abortion, 1966-1978," April 24, 1978, Record Group (A 79) (Rockefeller Foundation), Series 200A, folders on "Madison Const. Law Institute," RAC.

5. Frederick Osborn, "Notes on Markle and Fox ...," Jan. 25, 1974, Osborn Papers, folder on "Osborn-Paper-Notes on 'Paradigms or Public Relations ...'"

6. Francis Galton, *Inquiries into Human Faculty and Its Development* (London, 1883), pp. 24-25 & 316-317.

7. Daniel J. Kevles, *In the Name of Eugenics* (New York, 1985), pp. 54-56 & 60; Rockefeller Foundation, 1913-14 annual report; folder on "Genetics-Eugenics Record Office/Finance 1918-1940," Carnegie Institution of Washington Archive; Ellen Chesler, *Woman of Valor: Margaret Sanger and the Birth Control Movement in America* (New York, 1992), *passim;* and Elizabeth Brayer, George Eastman (Baltimore, 1996), pp. 474-476. See *Who's Who in America* and *Who Was Who in America* for information on family size of noted population controllers.

8. Frederick Osborn, *"Notes on Markle and Fox . . . ,"* op. cit. (n.5).

9. Margaret Sanger to George Eastman, Dec. 8, 1931, Sanger Papers, microfilm reel 51; Margaret Sanger, *The Pivot of Civilization* (New York, 1922), p. 175; and Margaret Sanger in *Birth Control Review,* vol. 16, no. 4 (April, 1932), pp. 107-108. Sanger appeared on the 1930 and 1956 membership lists of the American Eugenics Society. She was listed as a fellow of England's Eugenics Society in 1928, 1944 and 1957.

10. *Buck* v. *Bell,* 274 U.S. 200, 207 (1927); Richmond *Times-Dispatch,* Feb. 23, 1980; and Dorothy Roberts, *Killing the Black Body* (New York, 1997), pp. 89-98.

11. David Garrow, *Liberty & Sexuality: The Right to Privacy and the Making of Roe v. Wade* (New York, 1994), p. 273; and "Notes on Meeting of Council on Population Policy," Nov. 7, 1935, pp. II & I, Osborn Papers, folder on "Council on Population Policy."

12. National Committee on Maternal Health, *The Abortion Problem* (Baltimore, 1944).

13. Adolf Hitler, *Mein Kampf,* trans. by Ralph Manheim (Boston, 1971, original German version published in 1925-1926), pp. 439-440; Leon Fradley Whitney, (unpublished) autobiography manuscript, pp. 204-205, American Philosophical Society Library, Phila-delphia; *Time* magazine, Sept. 9, 1935, pp. 20-21; New York *Times,* Aug. 29-31, 1935; and Stefan Kühl, *The Nazi Connection* (New York, 1994), pp. 26, 27, 32-35 & 85.

14. "American Eugenics Society, Annual Meeting-May 5,1938," pp. 2 & 1, American Eugenics Society Archives, "Osborn, Frederick Papers I," folder 9. At various times, Osborn served as president, secretary, treasurer and/or board member of the Society; he was its key strategist for about 40 years.

15. Gunnar Myrdal, *An American Dilemma* (New York, 1962, anniv. ed.), pp. lxix & 167-178, emphasis in original. See Nils Roll-Hansen in *British Journal for the History of Science,* vol. 22, part 3, no. 74 (Sept., 1989), p. 342 on Gunnar Myrdal's role in proposing sterilization for handicapped people in Sweden. Alva Myrdal, Gunnar's wife, apparently was a member of the American Eugenics Society; see Norman E. Himes Archive, box 5, folder 56.

16. Myrdal, *op. cit.* (n. 15), pp. 1017-1018; and Hodding Carter III, *The South Strikes Back* (Garden City, N.Y., 1959), pp. 209-210.

17. Myrdal, *op. cit.* (n. 15), p. 177; and Alva Myrdal, *Nation and Family* (London, 1945), pp. 205-212.

18. Roberts, *op. cit.* (n. 10), pp. 82-85.

19. Margaret Sanger to C.J. Gamble, Dec. 10, 1939, Gamble Papers, box 195; and "CJG" to Miss Rose, Nov. 26, 1939, *ibid.,* box 136.
20. David M. Kennedy, *Birth Control in America: The Career of Margaret Sanger* (New Haven, Conn., 1970), pp. 259-267; and Chesler, *op. cit.* (n. 7), pp. 387-391.
21. Frank W. Notestein, "Problems of Policy Toward Areas of Heavy Population Pressure," No. TB 72, April 21, 1944, pp. 6 & 11, in Council on Foreign Relations, *Studies of American Interests in the War and the Peace* (New York, 1944).
22. Jacob Viner, "The United States and the 'Colonial Problem,'" No. E-B 71, June 24, 1944, pp. 10-11, in *ibid.*
23. Beryl Suitters, *Be Brave and Angry: Chronicles of the International Planned Parenthood Federation* (London, 1973); National Academy of Sciences, transcript of "Conference on Population Problems," Williamsburg, Va., June 21, 1952, afternoon session, p. 16, John D. Rockefeller 3rd Papers, RAC; and Frederick Osborn, *Voyage to a New World,* 1889-1979 (Garrison, N.Y., 1979), p. 133.
24. Population Council, 1956, 1957 & 1958 annual reports; Frederick Osborn to Laurance S. Rockefeller, March 31, 1955, Record Group IV3B4.2 (Population Council), box 16, RAC; Frederick Osborn to Warren Nelson, Dec. 6, 1954, *ibid.*
25. Frederick Osborn to P.R.U. Stratton, Jan. 12, 1966, American Eugenics Society Archives, folder on "Osborn, Frederick, Letters on Eugenics."
26. "Patient Package Insert" for ParaGuard T 380A, n.d. (received from Food and Drug Administration in May, 1998); Betsy Hartmann, *Reproductive Rights and Wrongs* (Boston, 1995, rev. ed.), p. 218.
27. Carl G. Hartman, ed., *Mechanisms Concerned with Conception* (Oxford, 1963), p. 386; American Law Institute, *Model Penal Code: Official Draft and Explanatory Notes* (Philadelphia, 1985), pp. 165-166; S.J. Segal et al., ed., *Intra-Uterine Contraception* (Amsterdam, 1965), p. 213; ACOG Terminology Bulletin, no. 1 (Sept., 1965); and Germain Grisez, *Abortion: the Myths, the Realities, and the Arguments* (New York, 1970), pp. 111-116. Dr. Tietze was listed as a member of England's Eugenics Society in 1948, 1957 & 1977.
28. Hartmann, *op. cit.* (n. 26), pp. 77, 164, 180, 211 & 218; and British Broadcasting Corporation, transcript of "The Human Laboratory," Nov. 6, 1995. See, also, Barbara Mintzes *et al.,* ed., *Norplant: Under Her Skin* (Delft, The Netherlands, 1993).

NOTES (Part II)

1. American Eugenics Society, "Five Year Report of the Officers: 1953-1957 (New York, n.d.), p. 10; and *Eugenics Quarterly,* vol. 3, no. 4 (Dec. 1956), p. 200.
2. American Law Institute (ALI), *The American Law Institute 50th Anniversary* (Philadelphia, 1973), pp. 170-174; ALI, *Model Penal Code: Official Draft and Explanatory Notes* (Philadelphia, 1985), pp. xi-xii & 165-166; ALI, *36th Annual Meeting Proceedings,* 1959 (Philadelphia, 1960), pp. 262-263; *Eugenics Quarterly,* vol. 3, no. 2 (June, 1956), pp. 67-68; and *Family Planning Perspectives,* vol. 4, no. 4 (Oct., 1972), p. 5-7.
3. Lalor Foundation, "Program of Research Awards To Be Granted for 1969 and Summary of Activities for 1968," Planned Parenthood Federation of American Records, PPFA (II), box 114; C. Lalor Burdick to Dr. W. Shockley, Jan. 16, 1970, Guttmacher Papers, box 5, folder 18; C. Lalor Burdick to Hugh Moore, Aug. 20, 1968, Moore Papers, box 1 (quotation published with permission of Princeton University Library); *Who's Who in America, 1988-1989.*

4. William H. Draper, Jr., to P. A. Gorman, Sept. [8 or 11], 1967, Guttmacher Papers, box 1, folder 43; Alan F. Guttmacher to Frank Notestein, June 13, 1966, PPFA (II), box 125; and *Congressional Record,* May 10, 1966, pp. 10164-10165.

5. Ellsworth Bunker, Will L. Clayton and Hugh Moore to Julius Ochs Adler, Nov. 26, 1954, & Julius Ochs Adler to Allen W. Dulles, Dec. 15, 1954, Dulles Papers, box 63.

6. Unsigned note to "Mr. Dulles," Aug. 5, 1954, *ibid.,* box 64; Ansley J. Coale and Edgar M. Hoover, *Population Growth and Economic Development in Low-Income Countries* (Princeton, 1958), pp. v, vii & 335; Nathan Keyfitz in *Population Index,* vol. 57, no. 1 (Spring, 1991), p. 8; and Julian L. Simon, *The Ultimate Resource* (Princeton, 1981). (Edgar M. Hoover should not be confused with J. Edgar Hoover, the late FBI Director.)

7. Phyllis Tilson Piotrow, *World Population Crisis: The United States Response* (New York, 1973), pp. 36-47; New York *Times,* Nov. 26, 1959; and *Public Papers of the Presidents: Dwight D. Eisenhower,* 1959 (Washington, 1960), p. 787.

8. John F. Kennedy, quoted in interview of Sen. Joseph S. Clark, Dec. 16, 1965, p. 8, John F. Kennedy Library Oral History Program, Boston, Mass.; Piotrow, *op. cit.* (n. 7), pp. 47-82; and Benjamin C. Bradlee, *Conversations with Kennedy* (New York, 1975), p. 166.

9. U.S. Department of State, Airgram PA 207, July 17, 1968, p. 1, Record Group 59 (State Dept.), Central Foreign Policy Files [hereafter CFPF], 1967-69, box 2963; Airgram XA 72, Oct. 15, 1968, p. 2, *ibid.,* box 2959; and Airgram XA 4280, Sept. 11, 1968, p. 1, *ibid.*

10. "RN" to Daniel P. Moynihan, Feb. 9, 1969, *ibid.,* box 2955; writer's interview of Philander P. Claxton, Jr., July 25, 1997; and *Public Papers of the Presidents: Richard M. Nixon,* 1969 (Washington, 1971), pp. 522-523.

11. Senator Qazi Hussain Ahmad, press release, Sept. 5, 1991, Lahore, Pakistan; Thomas Malthus et al., *On Population: Three Essays* (New York, 1960), p. 16; and Population Reference Bureau, "1998 World Population Data Sheet" (Washington, 1998).

12. "The Population Explosion: A *Present* Danger," filed July 24, 1969, Nixon Presidential Materials, White House Central Files [hereafter WHCF], Subject Files: Welfare, box 29; "NSSM 200: Implications of Worldwide Population Growth for U.S. Security and Overseas Interests," Dec. 10, 1974, chapter III, pp. 36, 43 & 37-38, Record Group 273 (National Security Council), unboxed material; and Carl J. Gilbert to Richard M. Nixon, Nov. 4, 1969, Nixon Materials, WHCF, Subject Files: Welfare, box 29.

13. John A. Hannah and William P. Rogers to the President, Nov. 14, 1969, with attached "Joint Report to the President ..." Part II, pp. 1-2, Record Group 59 (State Dept.), CFPF, 1967-69, box 2955; "Report to the President on Peace Corps Activities in Family Planning," Oct. 24, 1969, pp. 1 & 5, *ibid.*

14. Frank Shakespeare to William P. Rogers, Oct. 31, 1969, p. 1, and attached paper on "USIA and the President's Program on Population Matters," p. 5, *ibid.*

15. U.S. Department of State, telegram to American Embassy in Djakarta, Aug. [28?], 1967, pp. 1-2, *ibid.,* box 2958; U.S. Department of State, telegram to U.S. Mission at United Nations, May 29, 1969, p. 1, *ibid.,* box 2956; and *Baltimore Magazine,* vol. 63, no. 2 (Feb., 1970), pp. 51-52.

16. Daniel P. Moynihan to George Shultz, Oct. 14, 1970, Nixon Materials, WHCF, Subject Files: Welfare, box 30; Luke T. Lee to Daniel Patrick Moynihan, July 26, 1969, *ibid.,* box 31; Daniel P. Moynihan to Luke T. Lee, Aug. 13,1969, *ibid.;* "Checker" Finn to Philander Claxton, Jr., Aug. 13, 1969, *ibid.;* and U.S. Agency for International Development, *Population Program Assistance: Annual Report,* 1975 (Washington, April 1976), pp. 9-17 & 161. See, also, Luke T. Lee and Arthur Larson, ed., *Population and Law* (Leiden, The Netherlands, 1971); and Luke T. Lee in *Journal of International Law and Economics,* vol. 9, no. 3 (December 1, 1974), pp. 375-417.

17. R.T. Ravenholt to Daniel P. Moynihan, Oct. 7, 1970, with attached paper by R.T. Ravenholt and J. Joseph Speidel on prostaglandins, Nixon Materials, WHCF, Subject Files: Welfare, box 30.

18. Dr. Gerald Winfield, quoted in *St. Louis Globe-Democrat,* Oct. 25, 1973; *Congressional Record,* Oct. 1,1973, pp. 32292-32303, Oct. 2, 1973, p. 32529, & Dec. 4,1973, p. 39315. See, also, Donald P. Warwick in James Tunstead Burtchaell, ed., *Abortion Parley* (Kansas City, 1980), pp. 301-322.

19. David J. Garrow, *Liberty and Sexuality: The Right to Privacy and the Making of* Roe v. Wade (New York, 1994), pp. 335-336 & 393-394.

20. *Public Papers of the Presidents, op. cit.* (n. 10), p. 528; and Piotrow, *op. cit.* (n. 7), p. 195.

21. Andrew M. and Janis B. Clearfield, "Socio-Legal Aspects of Abortion: A Policy Proposal,"Aug. 19, 1970, p. 8, Nixon Materials, WHCF, Subject Files: Welfare, box 30. Forty-four boxes of 1968-1975 records from HEW (Accession No. 514-77-0006) could not be found at the National Archives or at its Suitland, Md., records center, despite extensive checking in July, 1997. Staff said the records may have been destroyed by mistake or may be lost somewhere in the system.

22. U.S. Commission on Population Growth and the American Future, "Transcript of Proceedings," April 14, 1971, p. 35, Record Group 220 (temporary agencies), Entry 37110, box 16; and *Public Papers of the Presidents: Richard M. Nixon,* 1971 (Washington, 1972), p. 500.

23. See Part I of this series, n. 4; Daniel P. Moynihan to Arthur F. Burns, June 18, 1969, Nixon Materials, WHCF, Subject Files: EXFG 275, box 1; and U.S. Commission on Population Growth and the American Future, *Population and the American Future* (Washington, 1972), pp. 110-113 & 141-143.

24. Reynolds Farley in Charles F. Westoff and Robert Parke, Jr., ed., *Demographic and Social Aspects of Population Growth* (Washington, 1972), pp. 111-138; and U.S. Bureau of the Census, *Current Population Reports,* Feb., 1996, p. 13.

25. Frederick Osborn to Lee Dice, June 2, 1970, American Eugenics Society Archives, folder on "AES: Correspondence, June 1970"; "Checker" Finn to Dr. Moynihan, Aug. 7, 1969, Nixon Materials, WHCF, Subject Files: Welfare, box 29; and "Checker" Finn to Steve Hess, Sept. 8, 1969, *ibid.*

26. Winston Churchill, as quoted by Walter Winchell, *Reader's Digest,* Dec., 1954, p. 34.

27. Mary Meehan in *Human Life Review,* vol. 10, no. 4 (Fall, 1984), pp. 42-60. See Foundation Center Library, Washington, D.C., for current information on foundation funding of population control.

28. *Draper Fund Report,* no. 6 (Summer, 1978), p. 14 ff. The Population Crisis Committee is now called Population Action International. Most of the methods noted in the 1978 report apparently did not prove successful, although there are recent reports of quinacrine sterilization of women.

A Human Life Amendment

James L. Buckley

The Supreme Court, in a pair of highly controversial, precedent-shattering decisions, *Roe against Wade* and *Doe against Bolton,* ruled that a pregnant woman has a constitutional right to destroy the life of her unborn child. In so doing, the Court not only contravened the express will of every State legislature in the country; it not only removed every vestige or legal protection hitherto enjoyed by the child in the mother's womb; but it reached its result through a curious and confusing chain of reasoning that, logically extended, could apply with equal force to the genetically deficient infant, the retarded child, or the insane or senile adult.

After reviewing these decisions, I concluded that, given the gravity of the issues at stake and the way in which the Court had carefully closed off alternative means of redress, a constitutional amendment was the only way to remedy the damage wrought by the Court. My decision was not lightly taken for I believe that only matters of permanent and fundamental interest are properly the subject for constitutional amendment. I regret the necessity for having to take this serious step, but the Court's decisions, unfortunately, leave those who respect human life in all its stages from inception to death with no other recourse.

To those who argue that an amendment to the Constitution affecting abortion and related matters would encumber the document with details more appropriately regulated by statute, I can only reply that the ultimate responsibility must be borne by the High Court itself. With Mr. Justice White, who dissented so vigorously in the abortion cases:

> I find nothing in the language or history of the Constitution to support the Court's judgment.

The Court simply carved out of thin air a previously undisclosed right of "privacy" that is nowhere mentioned in the Constitution, a right of privacy which, oddly, can be exercised in this instance only by destroying the life and, therefore, the privacy of an unborn child. As Mr. Justice White remarked last January:

> As an exercise of raw judicial power, the Court perhaps has authority to do what it does today; but in my view its judgment is an improvident and extravagant exercise of the power of judicial review which the Constitution extends to this Court.

James L. Buckley, a United States Senator (NY) from 1971 to 1977, introduced his Human Life Amendment on May 31, 1973. This is a slightly abridged version of his Senate address.

In the intervening weeks since the Court's decisions, I have sought the advice of men and women trained in medicine, ethics, and the law. They have given me the most discriminating and exacting counsel on virtually every aspect of the issues involved and have provided invaluable assistance in drawing up an amendment that reflects the latest and best scientific fact, and that comports with our most cherished legal traditions.

What Did the Court Really Do?

Before discussing the specific language of my proposed amendment, I believe it necessary first to analyze the effect and implications of *Wade* and *Bolton,* and then to place them in the context of current attacks on our traditional attitudes toward human life. At the outset, it is necessary to discuss with some care what the Court in fact held in its abortion decisions. This is, I must confess, not an easy task. For parsing the Court's opinions in these cases requires that one attempt to follow a labyrinthine path of argument that simultaneously ignores or confuses a long line of legal precedent and flies in the face of well-established scientific fact.

The Court's labored reasoning in these cases has been a source of considerable puzzlement to all who have the slightest familiarity with the biological facts of human life before birth or with the legal protections previously provided for the unborn child. The Court's substantial errors of law and fact have been so well documented by others that it would be superfluous for me to attempt to add anything of my own.

The full import of the Court's action is as yet incompletely understood by large segments of the public and by many legislators and commentators. It seems to be rather widely held, for example, that the Court authorized abortion on request in the first 6 months of pregnancy, leaving the States free to proscribe the act thereafter. But such is far from the truth. The truth of the matter is that, under these decisions, a woman may at any time during pregnancy exercise a constitutional right to have an abortion provided only that she can find a physician willing to certify that her "health" requires it; and as the word "health" is defined, that in essence means abortion on demand.

The Court attempts to distinguish three stages of pregnancy, but upon examination this attempt yields, in practical effect, distinctions without a difference. In the first 3 months, in the words of the Court, "the abortion decision and its effectuation must be left to the medical judgment of the pregnant woman's attending physician." This means, for all intents and purposes, abortion on request. During the second trimester of pregnancy, the State may—but it need not—regulate the abortion procedure in ways that are reasonably related to maternal health. The power of the State's regulation here is effectively limited to matters of time, place and perhaps manner.

Thus, through approximately the first 6 months of pregnancy, the woman has a constitutionally protected right to take the life of her unborn child, and the State has no "compelling interest" that would justify prohibiting abortion if a woman insists on one.

After the period of "viability," which the Court marks at 6, or alternatively 7, months of pregnancy, the State "may"—but, again, it need not—proscribe abortion except "where it is necessary for the preservation of the life or health of the mother." This provision, which appears at first glance to be an important restriction, turns out to be none at all, as the Court defines health to include "psychological as well as physical well-being," and states that the necessary "medical judgment may be exercised in the light of all factors—physical, emotional, psychological, familial, and the woman's age—relevant to the well-being" of the mother. The Court, in short, has included under the umbrella of "health" just about every conceivable reason a woman might want to advance for having an abortion.

It is clear, then, that at no time prior to natural delivery is the unborn child considered a legal person entitled to constitutional protections; at no time may the unborn child's life take precedence over the mother's subjectively-based assertion that her well-being is at stake.

In reaching these findings, the Court in effect wrote a statute governing abortion for the entire country, a statute more permissive than that enacted by the hitherto most permissive jurisdiction in the country; namely, my own State of New York. Nor is that all. In the course of its deliberations, the Court found it necessary to concede a series of premises that can lead to conclusions far beyond the immediate question of abortion itself. These premises have to do with the conditions under which human beings, born or unborn, may be said to possess fundamental rights. I would like to touch briefly on one or two basic points:

First, it would now appear that the question of who is or is not a "person" entitled to the full protection of the law is a question of legal definition as opposed to practical determination. Thus, contrary to the meaning of the Declaration of Independence, contrary to the intent of the framers of the 14th amendment, and contrary to previous holdings of the Court, to be created human is no longer a guarantee that one will be possessed of inalienable rights in the sight of the law. The Court has extended to government, it would seem, the power to decide the terms and conditions under which membership in good standing in the human race is determined. This statement of the decisions' effect may strike many as overwrought, but it will not appear as such to those who have followed the abortion debate carefully or to those who have read the Court's decisions in full. When, for example, the Court states that the unborn are not recognized by the law as "persons in the whole sense," and when, further, it uses as a precondition for legal protection the test whether one has a "capability of meaningful life," a thoughtful man is necessarily invited to speculate on what the logical extension of such arguments might be.

If constitutional rights are deemed to hinge on one's being a "person in the whole sense," where does one draw the line between "whole" and something less than "whole"? Is it simply a question of physical or mental development? If so, how does one distinguish between the child in his 23rd week of gestation who is lifted alive from his mother's womb and allowed to die in the process of abortion by hysterotomy, and the one that is prematurely born and rushed to an incubator? It is a well known scientific fact that the greater part of a child's cerebral cortex is not formed, that a child does not become a "cognitive person," until some months after normal delivery. Might we not someday determine that a child does not become a "whole" person until sometime after birth, or never become "whole" if born with serious defects? And what about those who, having been born healthy, later lose their mental or physical capacity? Will it one day be found that a person, by virtue of mental illness, or serious accident, or senility, ceases to be a "person in the whole sense," or ceases to have the "capability for meaningful life," and as such is no longer entitled to the full protection of the law?

The list of such questions is virtually endless. The Court in attempting to solve one problem has ended up by creating 20 others. One can read the Court's opinions in the abortion cases from beginning to end and back again, but he will not find even the glimmer of an answer to these questions; indeed, one will not even find the glimmer of an indication that the Court was aware that such questions might be raised or might be considered important.

A second general consideration I should like to raise has to do with the Court's definition of "health" as involving "all factors—physical, emotional, psychological, familial, and the woman's age—relevant to . . . well-being." It is a little remarked but ultimately momentous part of the abortion decisions that the Court, consciously or unconsciously, has adopted wholesale the controversial definition of "health" popularized by the World Health Organization. According to the WHO, "health" is "a state of complete physical, mental, and social well-being, not simply the absence of illness and disease." In this context, the Court's definition acquires a special importance, not only because it can be used to justify abortion any time a woman feels discomfited by pregnancy, but because the Court made pointed reference to the "compelling interest" of the State in matters of health in general and maternal health in particular. One is bound to wonder whether the State's interest in maternal health would ever be sufficiently "compelling" to warrant an abortion against a pregnant woman's will. This is no mere academic matter. An unwed, pregnant teenage girl was ordered by a lower court in Maryland just last year, against her will, to have an abortion. The girl was able to frustrate the order by running away. The order was later overturned by a Maryland appellate court; but the important point is that an analog to the compelling State interest argument was used by the lower court to justify its holding.

Let us consider, for example, the case of a pregnant mental patient. Would the State's compelling interest in her health ever be sufficient to force an abortion upon her? What of the unmarried mother on welfare who is already unable to cope with her existing children? Again, I am not raising an academic point for the sake of disputation. In the abortion cases, the Supreme Court breathed life into the notorious precedent of *Buck against Bell*. The *Bell* cases, it will be recalled, upheld the right of a State to sterilize a mental incompetent without her consent.

The Court held in that case that—

> The principle that sustains compulsory vaccination is broad enough to cover cutting the Fallopian tubes.

One is necessarily bound to wonder whether, by analogous extension, the principle that sustains compulsory sterilization of mental patients is broad enough to cover compulsory abortion of mental patients; and if of mental patients, then why not, as the lower court in Maryland suggested, of unwed minor girls? And if of unwed minor girls, then why not of any other woman? Just how "compelling" is the State's interest in matters of "health"? Where does the power begin or end? In the abortion cases, *Bell* curiously, is cited for the proposition that a woman does not have an unlimited right to her own body, whence the only inference to be drawn is that the reason she doesn't have an unlimited right is that the State may qualify that right because of its "compelling interest" in "health." I find that a strange doctrine to be celebrated by the proponents of women's liberation.

These larger and deeply troubling considerations, may in the long run be as important to us as the special concern that many of us have with the matter of abortion itself. Every premise conceded by the Court in order to justify the killing of an unborn child can be extended to justify the killing of anyone else if, like the unborn child, he is found to be less than a person in the "whole" sense or incapable of "meaningful" life. The removal of all legal restrictions against abortion must, in short, be seen in the light of a changing attitude regarding the sanctity of individual life, the effects of which will be felt not only by the unborn child who is torn from its mother's womb but as well by all those who may someday fall beyond the arbitrary boundaries of the Court's definition of humanity.

Which Ethic Will Govern?

This wider context of the abortion controversy was brought to my attention most forcefully by an unusually candid editorial entitled "A New Ethic for Medicine and Society" that was published two and a half years ago in *California Medicine,* the official journal of the California Medical Association. It was occasioned, as I understand it, by the debate then taking place in our largest State regarding the liberalization of the abortion law.

The thrust of the editorial is simply this: That the controversy over abortion represents the first phase of a head-on conflict between the traditional, Judeo-Christian medical and legal ethic—in which the intrinsic worth and equal value of every human life is secured by law, regardless of age, health or condition of dependency—and a new ethic, according to which human life can be taken for what are held to be the compelling social, economic or psychological needs of others. Mr. President, I ask unanimous consent that the editorial referred to be printed in the *Record* at the conclusion of my remarks.

Let me for a moment dwell on a crucial point in that editorial. The author writes:

> The process of eroding the old ethic and substituting the new has already begun. It may be seen most clearly in changing attitudes toward human abortion. In defiance of the long held Western ethic of intrinsic and equal value for every human life regardless of its stage, condition, or status, abortion is becoming accepted by society as moral, right, and even necessary. It is worth noting that this shift in public attitude has affected the churches, the laws and public policy rather than the reverse. Since the old ethic has not yet been fully displaced it has been necessary to separate the idea of abortion from the idea of killing, which continues to be socially abhorrent. The result has been a curious avoidance of the scientific fact, which everyone really knows, that human life begins at conception and is continuous whether intra- or extra-uterine until death. The very considerable semantic gymnastics which are required to rationalize abortion as anything but taking a human life would be ludicrous if they were not often put forth under socially impeccable auspices. It is suggested that this schizophrenic sort of subterfuge is necessary because while a new ethic is being accepted the old one has not yet been rejected.

Lest there be any ambiguity as to the ultimate thrust of the "new ethics," the *California Medicine* editorial went on to state the following in discussing the growing role of physicans in deciding who will and will not live:

> One may anticipate further development of these roles as the problems of birth control and birth selection are extended inevitably to death selection and death control whether by the individual or by society . . .

I find the editorial a powerful, eloquent, and compelling statement of the ultimate questions involved in the abortion controversy. The question in issue—the Supreme Court to the contrary notwithstanding—is not to determine when life begins, for that is one of scientific fact requiring neither philosophical nor theological knowledge to answer. The question, rather, is what value we shall place on human life in general and whether unborn human life in particular is entitled to legal protection.

Whether or not our society shall continue its commitment to the old ethic, or transfer its allegiance to the new, is not a question to be decided by a transitory majority of the Supreme Court, but by the people acting through their political processes. I concur in Mr. Justice White's condemnation of the *Wade* decision as "an exercise of raw judicial power" that is "improvident and extravagant." I concur in finding unacceptable the Court's action in "interposing a constitutional barrier to State efforts to protect human life and in investing mothers and doctors with the constitutionally protected right to exterminate it."

The majority of the Court, however, has rendered its decision. We as a people have been committed by seven men to the "new ethic"; and because of the finality of their decisions, because there are now no practical curbs on the killing of the unborn to suit the convenience or whim of the mother, those who continue to believe in the old ethic have no recourse but to resort to the political process. That is why I intend to do what I can to give the American people the opportunity to determine for themselves which ethic will govern this country in what is, after all, quite literally a matter of life or death. That is why I send my proposed Human Life Amendment to the desk and ask that it be printed and appropriately referred.

The Proposed Amendment

In doing so, Mr. President, may I say how deeply gratified I am to be joined in introducing this amendment by my distinguished colleagues from Oregon, Iowa, Utah, Nebraska, Oklahoma, and North Dakota. Senators Hatfield, Hughes, Bennett, Bartlett, Curtis, and Young* are known in this body and elsewhere as exceptionally thoughtful and dedicated men whose

---

* Shortly thereafter, these Senators were joined by Senator James O. Eastland, Democrat, of Mississippi and Senator Jesse Helms, Republican, of North Carolina.

day-to-day political activities are informed by devotion to first principles. When such a geographically, ideologically, and religiously diverse group of Senators can agree on a major issue like this, it suggests that opposition to abortion is truly ecumenical and national in scope. These Senators honor me by their co-sponsorship, and I consider it a privilege to work together with them in this great cause. I would simply like to take this occasion to extend to each of them my personal gratitude for their help and cooperation and to say how much I look forward to working jointly with them in the months ahead.

The text of our amendment reads as follows:

Section 1. *With respect to the right to life, the word "person," as used in this Article and in the Fifth and Fourteenth Articles of Amendment to the Constitution of the United States, applies to all human beings, including their unborn offspring at every stage of their biological development, irrespective of age, health, function or condition or dependency.*
Section 2. *This Article shall not apply in an emergency when a reasonable medical certainty exists that continuation of the pregnancy will cause the death of the mother.*
Section 3. *Congress and the several States shall have power to enforce this Article by appropriate legislation within their respective jurisdictions.*

The amendment's central purpose is to create, or rather, as will be made clear below, to restore a constitutionally compelling identity between the biological category "human being" and the legal category "person." This has been made necessary by two factors: First, the more or less conscious dissemblance on the part of abortion proponents, by virtue of which the universally agreed upon facts of biology are made to appear as questions of value—a false argument that the Supreme Court adopted wholesale; and second, the holding of the Court in *Wade* and *Bolton* that the test of personhood is one of legal rather than of biological definition. The amendment addresses these difficulties by making the biological test constitutionally binding, on the ground that only such a test will restrain the tendency of certain courts and legislatures to arrogate to themselves the power to determine who is or who is not human and, therefore, who is or is not entitled to constitutional protections. The amendment is founded on the belief that the ultimate safeguard of all persons, born or unborn, normal or defective, is to compel courts and legislatures to rest their decisions on scientific fact rather than on political, sociological, or other opinion.

Such a test will return the law to a position compatible with the original understanding of the 14th amendment. As the debates in Congress during consideration of that amendment make clear, it was precisely the intention of Congress to make "legal person" and "human being" synonymous categories.

By so doing, Congress wrote into the Constitution that understanding of the Declaration of Independence best articulated by Abraham Lincoln; namely, that to be human is to possess certain rights by nature, rights that no court and no legislature can legitimately remove. Chief among these, of course, is the right to life.

On the specific subject of abortion, it is notable that the same men who passed the 14th amendment also enacted an expanded Assimilative Crimes Statute, April, 1866, which adopted recently passed State anti-abortion statutes. These statutes, in turn, had been enacted as a result of a concerted effort by medical societies to bring to legislators' attention the recently discovered facts of human conception. The Court's opinion in *Wade* totally misreads—if the Court was aware of it at all—the fascinating medico-legal history of the enactment of 19th-century anti-abortion statutes, and ignores altogether the fundamental intention which animated the framers of the 14th amendment.

Section 1 of the proposed amendment would restore and make explicit the biological test for legal protection of human life. The generic category is "human being," which includes, but is not limited to, "unborn offspring—at every stage of their biological development." It is a question of biological fact as to what constitutes "human being" and as to when "offspring" may be said to come into existence. While the basic facts concerning these matters are not in dispute among informed members of the scientific community, the ways in which these facts are to be ascertained in any particular case will depend on the specifications contained in implementing legislation passed consistent with the standard established by the amendment. Such legislation would have to consider, in the light of the best available scientific information, the establishment of reasonable standards for determining when a woman is in fact pregnant, and if so, what limitations are to be placed on the performance of certain medical procedures or the administering of certain drugs.

Section 1, it will also be noted, reaches the more general case of euthanasia. This is made necessary because of the widespread and growing talk of legalizing "death with dignity," and because of the alarming dicta in the *Wade* opinion by which legal protection seems to be conditioned on whether one has the "capability of meaningful life" or whether one is a "person in the whole sense." Such language in the Court's opinion, when combined with the Court's frequent references to the State's "compelling interest" in matters of "health," is pointedly brought to our attention by the revival in *Wade* of the notorious 1927 case of *Buck against Bell*—which upheld the right of the State to sterilize a mentally defective woman without her consent. The *Wade* and *Bolton* opinions taken as a whole seem to suggest that unborn children are not the only ones whose right to life is now legally unprotected. Thus, the proposed amendment explicitly extends its protections to all those whose physical or mental condition might make them especially vulnerable victims of the "new ethic."

Regarding the specific subject of abortion, section 2 makes an explicit exception for the life of the pregnant woman. There seems to be a widespread misimpression that pregnancy is a medically dangerous condition, when the truth of the matter is that under most circumstances a pregnant woman can deliver her child with minimal risk to her own life and health. There is, however, an exceedingly small class of pregnancies where continuation of pregnancy will cause the death of the woman. The most common example is the ectopic or tubal pregnancy. It is our intention to exempt this unique class of pregnancies, without opening the door to spurious claims of risk of death.

Under the amendment, there must be an emergency in which reasonable medical certainty exists that continuation of pregnancy will cause the death of the woman. This is designed to cover the legitimate emergency cases, such as the ectopic pregnancy, while closing the door to unethical physicians who in the past have been willing to sign statements attesting to risk of death when in fact none exists or when the prospect is so remote in time or circumstance as to be unrelated to the pregnancy. Contrary to the opinion of the Supreme Court, which assumes that pregnancy is a pathological state, modern obstetrical advances have succeeded in removing virtually every major medical risk once associated with pregnancy. As Dr. Alan Guttmacher himself remarked nearly a decade ago, modern obstetrical practice has eliminated almost all medical indications for abortion. In certain limited instances, however, a genuine threat to the woman's life remains, and it is felt that excepting such situations is compatible with long-standing moral custom and legal tradition.

What Kind of Society?

I profoundly believe that such popularity, as the idea of abortion has acquired, derives from the ability of the proponents of abortion to dissemble the true facts concerning the nature of unborn life and the true facts concerning what is actually involved in abortion. I further believe that when these facts are fully made known to the public, they will reject abortion save under the most exigent circumstances; that is, those in which the physical life of the mother is itself at stake. In recent weeks, in discussing this matter with friends and colleagues, I have found that, like many of the rest of us, they labor under certain misimpressions created by the proponents of permissive abortion. I, therefore, believe that it would be useful for me to call our colleagues' attention to clinical evidence upon these points.

First, I will quote a particularly felicitous description of the biological and physical character of the unborn child by Dr. A. W. Liley, research professor in fetal physiology at National Women's Hospital, Auckland, New Zealand, a man renowned throughout the world as one of the principal founders and masters of the relatively new field of fetology. Dr. Liley writes:

In a world in which adults control power and purse, the foetus is at a disadvantage being small, naked, nameless and voiceless. He has no one except sympathetic adults to speak up for him and defend him—and equally no one except callous adults to condemn and attack him. Mr. Peter Stanley of Langham Street Clinic, Britain's largest and busiest private abortorium with nearly 7,000 abortions per year, can assure us that "under 28 weeks the foetus is so much garbage—there is no such thing as a living foetus." Dr. Bernard Nathanson, a prominent New York abortionist, can complain that it is difficult to get nurses to aid in abortions beyond the twelfth week because the nurses and often the doctors emotionally assume that a large foetus is more human than a small one. But when Stanley and Nathanson profit handsomely from abortion we can question their detachment because what is good for a doctor's pocket may not be best for mother or baby.

Biologically, at no stage can we subscribe to the view that the foetus is a mere appendage of the mother. Genetically, mother and baby are separate individuals from conception. Physiologically, we must accept that the conceptus is, in very large measure, in charge of the pregnancy, in command of his own environment and destiny with a tenacious purpose.

It is the early embryo who stops mother's periods and proceeds to induce all manner of changes in maternal physiology to make his mother a suitable host for him. Although women speak of their waters breaking or their membranes rupturing, these structures belong to the foetus and he regulates his own amniotic fluid volume. It is the foetus who is responsible for the immunological success of pregnancy—the dazzling achievement by which foetus and mother, although immunological foreigners, tolerate each other in parabiosis for nine months. And finally it is the foetus, not the mother, who decides when labour should be initiated.

One hour after the sperm has penetrated the ovum, the nuclei of the two cells have fused and the genetic instructions from one parent have met the complementary instructions from the other parent to establish the whole design, the inheritance of a new person. The one cell divides into two, the two into four and so on while over a span of 7 or 8 days this ball of cells traverses the Fallopian tube to reach the uterus. On reaching the uterus, this young individual implants in the spongy lining and with a display of physiological power suppresses his mother's menstrual period. This is his home for the next 270 days and to make it habitable the embryo develops a placenta and a protective capsule of fluid for himself. By 25 days the developing heart starts beating, the first strokes of a pump that will make 3,000 million beats in a lifetime. By 30 days and just 2 weeks past mother's first missed period, the baby, 1/4 inch long, has a brain of unmistakable human proportions, eyes, ears, mouth, kidneys, liver and umbilical cord and a heart pumping blood he has made himself. By 45 days, about the time of mother's second missed period, the baby's skeleton is complete, in cartilage not bone, the buds of the milk teeth appear and he makes his first movements of his limbs and body—although it will be another 12 weeks before mother notices movements. By 63 days he will grasp an object placed in his palm and can make a fist.

Most of our studies of foetal behavior have been made later in pregnancy, partly because we lack techniques for investigation earlier and partly because it is only the exigencies of late pregnancy which provide us with opportunities to invade the privacy of the foetus. We know that he moves with a delightful easy grace in his buoyant world, that foetal comfort determines foetal position. He is responsive to pain and touch and cold and sound and light. He drinks his amniotic fluid, more if it is artificially sweetened and less if it is given an unpleasant taste. He gets hiccups and sucks his thumb. He wakes and sleeps. He gets bored with repetitive signals but can be taught to be alerted by a first signal for a second different one. Despite all that has been written by poets and song writers, we believe babies cry at birth because they have been hurt. In all the discussions that have taken place on pain relief in labour, only the pain of mothers have been considered—no one has bothered to think of the baby.

This then is the foetus we know and indeed each once were. This is the foetus we look after in modern obstetrics, the same baby we are caring for before and after birth, who before birth can be ill and need diagnosis and treatment just like any other patient. This is also the foetus whose existence and identity must be so callously ignored or energetically denied by advocates of abortion.

I consider this issue to be of paramount importance. As we stand here on this day, quite literally thousands of unborn children will be sacrificed before the sun sets in the name of the new ethic. Such a situation cannot continue indefinitely without doing irreparable damage to the most cherished principles of humanity and to the moral sensibilities of our people. The issue at stake is not only what we do to unborn children, but what we do to ourselves by permitting them to be killed. With every day that passes, we run the risk of stumbling, willy-nilly, down the path that leads inexorably to the devaluation of all stages of human life, born or unborn. But a few short years ago, a moderate liberalization of abortion was being urged upon us. The most grievous hypothetical circumstances were cast before us to justify giving in a little bit here, a little bit there; and step by step, with the inevitability of gradualness, we were led to the point where, now, we no longer have any valid legal constraints on abortion.

What kind of society is it that will abide this sort of senseless destruction? What kind of people are we that can tolerate this mass extermination? What kind of Constitution is it that can elevate this sort of conduct to the level of a sacrosanct right, presumptively endowed with the blessings of the Founding Fathers, who looked to the laws of nature and of nature's God as the foundation of this Nation?

Abortion, which was once universally condemned in the Western World as a heinous moral and legal offense, is now presented to us as not only a necessary, sometime evil, but as a morally and socially beneficial act. The Christian counsel of perfection which teaches that the greatest love consists in laying down one's life for one's friend, has now become, it seems, an injunction to take another's life for the security and comfort of one's own. Men who one day argue against the killing of innocent human life in war will be found the next arguing in praise of killing innocent human life in the womb. Doctors foresworn to apply the healing arts to save life now dedicate themselves and their skills to the destruction of life.

To enter the world of abortion on request, Mr. President, is to enter a world that is upside down: It is a world in which black becomes white, and right wrong, a world in which the powerful are authorized to destroy the weak and defenseless, a world in which the child's natural protector, his own mother, becomes the very agent of his destruction.

I urge my colleagues to join me in protecting the lives of all human beings, born and unborn, for their sake, for our own sake, for the sake of our children, and for the sake of all those who may someday become the victims of the new ethic.

The Theory of the Danforth Case

Francis Canavan

The late Justice Felix Frankfurter of the U.S. Supreme Court once remarked that "constitutional law . . . is not at all a science but applied politics." There is much truth in what he said. Students of constitutional law understand the extent to which it is a part of the process of practical politics. But, after reading the Supreme Court's latest abortion decision, I am inclined to modify Justice Frankfurter's dictum slightly and to see the Court's opinions on abortion as essays in applied political theory. Let me attempt to explain my reasons for so thinking.

On July 1, 1976, the Court decided the case of *Planned Parenthood of Central Missouri et al.* v. *Danforth, Attorney General of Missouri et al.* Popularly known as the *Danforth* case, it concerned the constitutionality of a law enacted by the State of Missouri to regulate abortions in the aftermath of the Court's 1973 decision in *Roe* v. *Wade* (410 U.S. 113). In that case the Court had held that the States could not constitutionally prohibit abortion. In the *Danforth* case, the majority of the Court found five provisions of the Missouri law incompatible with *Roe* v. *Wade* and therefore unconstitutional. But, for our purposes here, we shall ignore a large part of the Court's opinion and concentrate on the two most important of the Missouri provisions found unconstitutional.

Section 3 (3) and (4) of the Missouri law provided that no abortion could be performed prior to the end of the first twelve weeks of the pregnancy except with the written consent of the woman's husband, if she were married, or with the written consent of one parent or person *in loco parentis,* if she were unmarried and under eighteen years of age. In each instance the qualifying phrase was added, "unless the abortion is certified by a licensed physician to be necessary to save the life of the mother." In *Roe* v. *Wade* the Court had held that a woman's freedom to decide to have an abortion was a "fundamental right" protected by the Constitution against State interference; here it held that this freedom cannot be limited by a State requirement that the woman's husband or parent must consent to the abortion.

Mr. Justice Blackmun wrote the opinion of the Court, as he had in *Roe* v. *Wade.* He therefore spoke for the majority of the Court. It remains nonetheless that he wrote the opinion, that he chose its phraseology and its arguments, and that the political theory which it embodies is in the first instance

Francis Canavan, S.J. (1917-2009), a longtime professor of political science at Fordham University, was an authority on Edmund Burke and the author of many books.

his. I stress this point because Justice Blackmun would surely deny that any theory at all was in his mind when he wrote the opinion of the Court. Unfortunately it would be all too easy to agree with him. He is not a profoundly reflective man and is quite capable of believing that he was only expounding the meaning of the Constitution when he was in fact unconsciously bringing a particular theory to bear on it. The theory is *there* just the same.

But first let us look at Justice Blackmun's reasons for finding the husband's and the parent's consent clauses of the Missouri law unconstitutional. *Roe* v. *Wade* had determined that during the first trimester of pregnancy the mother and her physician were free to decide upon and carry out an abortion without interference by the State. But it was precisely during this first trimester (or twelve weeks) that the Missouri law required the consent of husband or parent. "Clearly," said Justice Blackmun, "since the State cannot regulate or proscribe abortion during the first stage, when the physician and his patient make that decision, the State cannot delegate authority to any particular person, even the spouse, to prevent abortion during the same period."

A woman's husband is thus presented as an individual whose right to prevent the abortion of his own child can only be a derived right, delegated to him by the State. Justice White commented in his dissenting opinion that Blackmun's argument rested on a misapprehension. White pointed out that under the Missouri law "the State is not . . . delegating to the husband the power to vindicate the *State's* interest in the future life of the fetus. It is instead recognizing that the husband has an interest of his own in the life of the fetus which should not be extinguished by the unilateral decision of the wife." Even if, he continued, we accept the principle that, in regard to an abortion, the mother's interest outweighs the State's interest, it does not follow "that the husband's interest is also outweighed and may not be protected by the State. A father's interest in having a child—perhaps his only child— may be unmatched by any other interest in his life." The husband's right therefore stands on an independent base and is not one delegated to him by the State.

In a footnote to his own opinion, Blackmun answered White, saying that the latter did not understand the implication of the Missouri law: that the State had granted the husband "the right to prevent unilaterally, and for whatever reason, the effectuation of his wife's and her physician's decision to terminate her pregnancy." But the State had no power to do this. As Blackmun put it in the section of the opinion dealing with the parental consent clause, "the State does not have the constitutional authority to give a third party an absolute and possibly arbitrary veto over the decision of the physician and his patient to terminate the patient's pregnancy, regardless of the reason for withholding the consent." This is the essential premise of the Court's decision in regard to the consent clauses. To require the consent to an abortion of anyone other than the woman and her doctor is to grant a unilateral veto power on the exercise of a constitutional right.

There is, however, an obvious problem with this insistence on the unilateral character of the "veto power." Justice Blackmun dealt with it in these words:

> We recognize, of course, that when a woman, with the approval of her physician but without the approval of her husband, decides to terminate her pregnancy, it could be said that she is acting unilaterally. The obvious fact is that when the wife and the husband disagree on this decision, the view of only one of the two marriage partners can prevail. Since it is the woman who physically bears the child and who is the more directly and immediately affected by the pregnancy, as between the two, the balance weighs in her favor.

But to say this is to admit that the essential flaw of the Missouri law was not that it granted someone a unilateral right, but that it gave such a right to someone other than the mother. Justice Blackmun, and the majority of the Court with him, apparently cannot conceive of the issue posed by laws regulating abortion in any way but as a conflict of rights. In this conflict, one side always wins and, for all practical purposes, wins totally. So far, the winner has always been the woman who wants an abortion.

Thus, in *Roe* v. *Wade,* the Court considered the conflict between a woman's right to abort her unborn child and the child's right to keep his life. Speaking through Justice Blackmun, the Court remarked: "We need not resolve the difficult question of when life begins. When those trained in the respective disciplines of medicine, philosophy, and theology are unable to arrive at any consensus, the judiciary, at this point in the development of man's knowledge, is not in a position to speculate as to the answer." With that remark, the mother's right to abort became absolute and the unborn child became merely a "potential life," and in no way the subject of a constitutional right to life. From that point on in the Court's opinion, having lost the battle in the conflict of rights, the child simply faded out of the picture.

This was true to the point where, later in the same opinion, when the Court granted that the State might prohibit the abortion of a viable child—one capable of living outside the womb—the most it would concede was the following: "If the State is interested in protecting fetal life after viability, it may go so far as to proscribe abortion during that period except when it is necessary to preserve the life or health of the mother." But this was not to recognize any inherent right of the child as against the mother, since the child would be protected only if the State were interested in protecting it.

Next, still in *Roe* v. *Wade,* the Court considered the conflict between the woman's right to abort and the State's right to proscribe or to regulate abortion. This conflict was resolved in accordance with a doctrine that the Court had worked out since *Griswold* v. *Connecticut* (381 U.S. 479) in 1965. The doctrine teaches that the Constitution implicitly guarantees to every individual a "right of privacy." *Roe* v. *Wade* determined that privacy includes the right to decide upon an abortion. But the doctrine also holds that the right of privacy can be overridden by a "compelling State interest," and therefore is not an absolute right. But in *Roe* v. *Wade* the Court found no "compelling" State interest in protecting "the potentiality of human life" prior to the point of viability. Up to that point, therefore, the woman's right to abort was in effect absolute, not only as against her child but as against the State. The *Danforth* decision merely carried this line of reasoning farther by absolutizing the woman's right to abort as against the conflicting claims of her husband or her parents. As we said, in *every instance* the issue has been reduced to a conflict of rights, in which the mother's right is always found superior.

The opinion of the Court in the *Danforth* case therefore deserves the comment that Justice White made on it in his dissent: "It is truly surprising that the majority finds in the United States Constitution, as it must in order to justify the result it reaches, a rule that the State must assign a greater value to a mother's decision to cut off a potential human life by abortion than to a father's decision to let it mature into a live child." Presumably, however, the Court would uphold a mother's right to bear a live child as against her husband's alleged right to make her submit to an abortion. In that sense the Court could claim to be neutral about abortion, and could say that all it requires is that the State assign a greater value to a mother's decision about abortion, whether for it or against it, than to a father's. Justice White's comment is nevertheless justified.

Justice White clearly assigns a greater value to human life than to its extinction. He would favor the father, not because he is the father, but because he wants to preserve his child's life, while the mother wants to destroy it. For Justice White, the content of the decision is important. For the majority of the Court, all that matters is that the mother should make the decision because, as they say in England, she has to carry the baby.

By making the mother's wishes the controlling consideration, the Court is forcing the State into an attitude of utter indifference toward what, in the Court's own terminology, is at least a potential human life. The only admissible object of public policy, in the Court's jurisprudence, is protection of the mother's untrammeled right to decide on the life or death of her child. The law may show no bias in favor of life, even if the male parent wants to preserve it, but must zealously safeguard the female parent's right to kill it.

But this legal indifference is a specious neutrality: a legal system that refuses to have, or is not allowed to have, a bias in favor of life winds up with a bias against it.

The majority of the Court, in subscribing to the words that Justice Blackmun wrote for them, reveal just such a bias against life. The constitutional flaw they found in the Missouri law, as we saw above, is that it gave "a third party"—husband or parent—the right to exercise an absolute and possibly arbitrary veto over the mother's decision to have an abortion. But the Court thereby only confirmed the mother's absolute right to make a possibly arbitrary decision in favor of abortion. The Court thus subordinated the value of life to the allegedly higher value of an individual's autonomy—her freedom to do her own will. The Court also came very close to regarding the termination of pregnancy as a positive good, since nothing must be allowed to stand in its way, once the mother, with the advice and consent of her physician, has decided on it.

In the mind of the Court, of course, what I have called a bias against life is only a bias in favor of a woman's freedom to make the abortion decision. This freedom was upheld against the State in *Roe* v. *Wade* and, in the *Danforth* case, against the family. The Court, however, would not accept my way of describing its decision in the *Danforth* case. Its position, rather, was that the family as an institution was simply not involved in the case. Nothing was involved but a conflict between individuals: wife v. husband, unmarried minor v. parent. Given that definition of the issue, the only question before the Court was which individual's right should prevail. But to frame the question in those terms is to deny that any rights in the matter arise out of the marriage or the family relationship. There are only individuals with conflicting claims of rights.

The attorneys for the State of Missouri had tried to make the family a factor in the case. They argued that the clause requiring the husband's consent to an abortion had been enacted in the light of the legislature's "perception of marriage as an institution," and that "any major change in family status is a decision to be made jointly by the marriage partners." Similarly, a Federal district court had upheld the clause requiring the consent of the parent of a minor and unmarried mother because of the State's interest "in safeguarding the authority of the family relationship." Justice Blackmun dismissed both arguments and made light of the notion that giving husband or parent a "veto power" over the abortion decision would do anything to strengthen the marriage bond or the family relationship. More significantly, he rejected the premise that the relationship of husband and wife, or of parent and child, furnished any ground for requiring a joint or institutional consent to an abortion. All that he could see was the conflicting wills of distinct individuals, one of whose wills must prevail.

Justice Blackmun was indeed anxious to avoid giving the impression that he had anything but the highest regard for marriage and the family. To demonstrate his true feelings, he inserted a footnote quoting the opinion of the Court in *Griswold* v. *Connecticut*:

> Marriage is a coming together for better or for worse, hopefully enduring, and intimate to the degree of being sacred. It is an association that promotes a way of life, not causes; a harmony in living, not political faiths; a bilateral loyalty, not commercial or social projects. Yet it is an association for as noble a purpose as any involved in our prior decisions.

It is worth remembering, however, why the opinion of the Court in the *Griswold* case included this little *paean* in praise of marriage. The issue in that case was a Connecticut law that prohibited the *use* of contraceptives. In order to find the law unconstitutional, the Court stressed the argument that its enforcement would involve an unwarranted intrusion into the "privacy surrounding the marriage relationship." It was precisely the relationship that was to be defended against the State.

That was in 1965. By 1972, in *Eisenstadt* v. *Baird* (405 U.S. 438), it turned out that the marriage relationship had little to do with the constitutionality of laws regulating contraception. They were now found unconstitutional whether the persons wishing contraceptive information and devices were married or not. Justice Brennan, speaking for the Court, explained:

> It is true that in Griswold the right of privacy in question inhered in the marital relationship. Yet the marital couple is not an independent entity with a mind and heart of its own, but an association of individuals each with a separate intellectual and emotional makeup. If the right of privacy means anything, it is the right of the *individual,* married or single, to be free from unwarranted governmental intrusion into matters so fundamentally affecting a person as the decision whether to bear or beget a child.

In his opinion in the *Danforth* case, Justice Blackmun quoted the above words (from "the marital couple" on) in the footnote immediately following the one in which he quoted the *Griswold* opinion in praise of marriage. It apparently did not occur to him that what was said in the *Eisenstadt* case effectively negated what had been said in the *Griswold* case. The right to contraception, it now appeared, in no way arose out of or was conditioned by the marital relationship. The right of privacy belongs to individuals simply as individuals, prior to and independently of such relationships as marriage and the family. This was the doctrine that Justice Blackmun applied to the right to abortion in the *Danforth* case. It is a doctrine whose roots reach much farther back in intellectual history than perhaps he realizes.

The doctrine is ultimately rooted in what is known as the social contract theory of the state. This in turn had its remote origins in the philosophical school of late medieval nominalism, according to which only individual substances are real, while essences or common natures, and the relations that spring from them, are mere constructs of the human mind. As a political philosophy, the social contract theory flowered in the seventeenth century, where it found its classic expression in the writings of Thomas Hobbes and John Locke. In the eighteenth century it became the dominant mode of political thought and strongly influenced the ideologies of the American and French Revolutions.

The main lines of the theory are as follows. The starting point is a "state of nature," i.e., the state that men are in by their very nature. Men are conceived of as being by nature independent individuals, without inherent or natural political relations to one another; in the more radical versions of the theory, men are thought of as not being by nature even social beings. The state of nature, therefore, is a pre-political state, in which there is no political community, no government and no man-made law.

Every individual in the state of nature is sovereign over himself and subject to no authority but his own. In most versions of the theory the sovereign individual is indeed subject to the "law of nature," which is the law of God as Author of nature. But the primary function of the law of nature is to confer on the individual his natural rights, which Locke summarized as life, liberty and estate (i.e., property). The only obligation imposed by the law of nature is the derivative one of respecting the rights of other individuals. In this theory, then, the individual is first and foremost a subject of rights, free to do what he will with his person and property (and here we may see foreshadowed a woman's now-famous "right to control her own body").

If men would live up to the law of nature and would respect each other's rights, there would be no need of government and human law. Bad men, however, encroach on the rights of others, and so conflicts arise. Since there is no common authority in society, every individual is the interpreter of the law of nature and the judge of his own natural rights. Consequently, there is in the state of nature no peaceable way of settling disputes over rights. Men therefore decide to form a civil society with a government empowered to settle disputes among individuals under general and standing laws. Civil society is formed by a social contract by which every individual surrenders to the community and its government his original right to be the judge in his own cause.

In this theory, civil society is not natural in the sense of being needed for the full development of human nature. It is a purely artificial construct, made necessary by men's wickedness and not by the innate needs of human beings. It is brought into existence by the contractual act of individual wills, each of which was originally sovereign, and which surrender their sovereignty only in order to set up a government that can protect their rights more effectively than they can themselves.

Such a theory rests on an atomistic conception of human nature. Man is no longer seen as a social and political animal (as Aristotle and Aquinas had seen him) whose very nature determines his basic relations to other persons in community. Man, as man, is an individual and nothing more. His relations to other individuals, consequently, are external, factitious and contractual, i.e., established by acts of free choice. The relations that are thus established will be consented to by each individual with a view to his own interests alone. There are no truly common interests, only a pooling of individual interests, because there is no natural community and hence no genuine common good of men.

The result is a political theory that divides society between individuals and the state. Individuals have their reserved and guaranteed rights; the state has its necessary and legitimate power as the protector of their rights. The task of political theory is to draw the proper line between these two spheres, much as the Supreme Court draws it between the "right of privacy" and "compelling state interest." In such a theory, all other associations in society are private and voluntary, the product of individuals pooling their interests and rights. There are no natural associations with their own naturally given structures, powers and rights. All the rights and powers of associations are delegations by individuals and/or by the state.

The social contract theory, in its classical form, was a political theory, concerned only with explaining the nature of the political community and the relations between individuals and the state. It generally took marriage and the family for granted. But if one were to carry the logic of the theory through and apply it to marriage, one would come out with a conception of the marriage contract similar to the one now being advocated in certain quarters. That is, the marriage contract not only unites man and woman in matrimony, it determines the entire content and substance of marriage. Marriage implies no rights and obligations except those specified in the contract. That is to say, the marriage relationship has no given nature; it is whatever the two contracting parties choose to make it (including, for example, sanctioned extramarital larks, if they so specify in the contract).

The U.S. Supreme Court certainly has never gone so far as to put its blessing on that conception of the marriage contract. But one begins to understand the kind of thinking that explains its opinion in the *Danforth* case, and why the social contract theory is relevant to it. As a formal political philosophy, the theory is now out of date, and one no longer expects to find references to the state of nature and the social contract in public documents. But the suppositions of the theory—its atomism, its radical individualism, its obsession with individual autonomy, its tendency to reduce social issues to conflicts of rights— are all powerfully operative in contemporary liberal societies and exercise a profound influence on our thinking today, not least on the thinking of the Supreme Court.

That is why the majority of the Court reduced the issue in the *Danforth* case to a conflict of purely individual rights and to the question: Which individual's right prevails? That is why they could see a woman's husband or parents as having no rights in regard to the abortion decision except as delegates of the State, since no rights in the matter arise out of the marital or family relationship. The majority's basic fault is not that they decided in favor of the mother. If the content of the decision is irrelevant and the only question is which individual has the right to make the decision, it might as well be the mother. Justice Blackmun and the majority erred because they asked the wrong question and thereby ignored the family as a natural community and the basic unit of society. And this they did, not because the Constitution made them do it, but because their minds are still dominated by the suppositions of an outmoded political theory.

Abortion and the Moral Revolution

James Hitchcock

The act of abortion is sometimes characterized as a tragic necessity, in the classical sense of a situation in which two undeniable goods conflict with one another, one or both fated to give way in the face of the requirements of the other.

Yet in practice those who advocate the morality of abortion rarely treat it as though it were tragic in any sense at all. A utilitarian calculus in which the needs of the mother are weighed against the needs of the unborn child and the former given precedence is, however unacceptable, at least comprehensible. But such a calculus, if truly employed, could not help but induce in its users a profound sense of ambivalence. Recognizing the legitimate claims of the child, the mother could never feel altogether justified in her choice, however necessary she might believe it to be. For a truly moral person, no matter how much persuaded that abortion is sometimes permissible, the act could never leave behind a wholly peaceful conscience.

In fact, however, the present cultural attitude towards abortion in no way includes this ambivalence. Although the word "tragic" is bandied about by those who seek merely a convenient verbal formula for disposing of scruples, the possibility that the child has rights is never seriously considered and is routinely and implicitly denied. The regular employment of the utilitarian calculus would actually mark a moral improvement, since it would bring the question at least to the point of admitting that the child's rights must be consciously weighed.

The ploys by which these rights have been denied are too well known to require discussion—the use of terms like "product of pregnancy" and "evacuation of the womb" to obscure what is really happening, the assertion that the fetus is merely a parasite on the mother, and the absolutist claim (made by ostensible moral relativists) that the mother's rights alone matter.

In any moral social atmosphere those who support the permissibility of abortion would treat anti-abortionists with at least a certain deference, admitting that hard moral choices are involved and that those who insist on asking pointed questions are right to do so. They would recognize that the general moral sense of society is protected from atrophy by those who demand that acts like abortion not slip into the realm of unexamined routine. In the end they would be prepared to say at least that anti-abortionists are right in the

James Hitchcock, a professor of history at St. Louis University, is the author of many books, including *The Supreme Court and Religion in American Life* (Princeton, 2004).

abstract, even if their ethic is too demanding and must be compromised in practice. It would then follow that those who support abortion would feel a strong obligation to minimize its use. Having identified certain cases where they believe abortion is the lesser of two evils, they would be at great pains to insure that it was resorted to only in such cases, and they would exercise rigorous vigilance to prevent its becoming a routine practice. (If there is truly a parallel between abortion and capital punishment, the equivalent would be for the defenders of the latter to be determined that no innocent people should be executed.)

Instead a quite different situation prevails. Although legal abortion was advocated on the basis of the familiar "hard cases"—in this instance rape, incest, and danger to the mother's life—virtually all knowledgeable people now admit that such cases are rare. Abortion has indeed become routine and, as many even of its defenders now admit, is simply used as the ultimate method of contraception.

Women who seek abortions need not demonstrate any motive greater than an aversion to inconvenience. In no way does this situation seem to embarrass pro-abortionists; most seem to welcome it as a sign of progress.

Despite what is often asserted, the debate over abortion is not a conflict between two opposed moralities, not even between an absolutist valuing of human life and a relativist one. In a quite literal sense those who support abortion have no moral position. Their position is based precisely on the denial of morality, at least in this instance. Their greatest crime is, in one sense, not their willingness to countenance and even encourage abortion but their determination not to permit the morality of the question even to be discussed. In the interest of securing the practice against attack, they are prepared to suppress all considerations of morality whatever.

Anti-abortionists see parallels between themselves and the anti-slavery abolitionists before the Civil War, and the parallel is nowhere more pronounced than at this point. Although some defenders of slavery may have regarded it as a tragic necessity, and although some slave-owners (like Thomas Jefferson) had bad consciences over the practice, the burden of pro-slavery opinion came to be a flat denial that any moral question was even involved. With slavery as with abortion, those who insisted on raising the moral questions were themselves attacked as immoral. In both cases an act which, morally speaking, could be characterized as at best dubious was elevated to the status of a virtue.

In the case of slave-owners, vested property interests, plus the legitimacy which any long-standing social practice automatically enjoys, largely explains the determination to defend the indefensible. Here the parallel with abortion diverges. Except for those who actually perform abortions, no one has an economic stake in the practice and, far from enjoying the sanction of custom, legalized abortion is a shockingly new and radical idea. What then accounts for the ferocity with which its defenders insist that evil is good?

Mere convenience seems inadequate to explain the passion involved, even though convenience may be the single most common motive for women's seeking abortions. Many morally dubious things are done for the sake of convenience, but such actions are usually justified, if at all, without much apparent conviction, indeed almost furtively. Why do many people passionately support a woman's "right" to kill her unborn offspring even when they themselves will probably never be in a position to seek an abortion?

Much of the passion, the ferocity which shades into hate, can perhaps be taken as a hopeful sign. Surely in many cases it indicates that there is indeed a conscience at work, a conscience which does not permit the easy acceptance of a horrendous deed, and which gives the individual a semblance of peace only to the degree that the moral tables are turned. The defender of human life must be cast as the aggressor, the taker of innocent life, the victim. When the ferocious passions of the pro-abortionists have subsided, when they no longer trouble to vilify their opponents, the cause for worry will be much greater, because it will signify the final disappearance of even the residue of moral sense on the question.

The practical questions surrounding abortion, especially of course the huge number of human lives lost, are enormous. However, it is crucial to the anti-abortion cause to recognize also how the practical questions are increasingly overshadowed by the symbolic. Defenders of abortion are not interested in the question whether fetuses are human and whether, therefore, it is moral to kill them. They dismiss such questions as unanswerable, which means that they do not wish to examine them in any serious way. But the very word "abortion" carries resonances of a kind which accompany few other terms in the language. Stating one's position on this single issue has the effect of calling into play a whole range of moral and social attitudes, and people are now often for or against abortion apart from any consideration of its concrete effects.

A preliminary distinction can be made between right-wing and left-wing pro-abortion sentiment. The former, which is found among many people of conservative beliefs, rests on the perception that legal (and governmentally funded) abortions help solve certain social problems—there will be fewer "unwanted" children, hence less social pathology and less need for expensive welfare programs. People who accept this largely utilitarian principle are usually not militant on the subject of abortion, however, and are not actively part of the group which presses constantly to push back the established limits of protection for human life (euthanasia and infanticide being obviously related issues).

Left-wing pro-abortionists are by definition part of the moral avant-garde of society, and it is their beliefs which are most influential and effective in establishing public policy. Their opinions, in fact, dominate the media, academic life, and the majority of public and private social agencies. Utilitarian considerations certainly enter their thoughts, and utilitarian arguments are especially used to attract popular support. But for most such people the symbolic issues are finally more important than the practical. (Thus liberals remain unmoved by the charge that governmentally funded abortion programs serve to restrict the black population. They are not primarily interested in the practical results of such programs.)

The symbolic issues exist in a series of concentric circles which support and complement one another. The outermost of these circles is that of class conflict—the perception that anti-abortionists are uneducated, crude, and irrational, while their opponents are enlightened, and civilized.[1] Although this stereotype is deliberately concocted for propaganda purposes (it is a stereotype which the media are only too glad to propagate), those who employ it probably also believe it.

It is a generally unrecognized fact about contemporary social life that virtually all change, no matter what populist banner it marches behind, achieves success or failure largely on the basis of what response it evokes from the educated and articulate segments of the middle class. (The black civil rights movement is a classic example.) In fact, very few movements in contemporary life do have populist roots. Most often, movements which appear populist are really the creation of an educated elite.

Abortion is a major instance of this phenomenon. Public support for abortion was initially solicited in the form of sympathy for the "victim" of restrictive laws—allegedly young, poor women either butchered in back alleys or forced to bear unwanted children, while rich mothers flew to safe clinics in foreign countries. Yet the number of women who actually could and did go to foreign countries for abortions was always very small, and the drive for legalized abortion aimed to provide a convenient service for well-off middle-class women. The middle-class couple who have decided that they want no more children, and who, should their daughter become pregnant outside wedlock, would not want her life to be "ruined," are the backbone of pro-abortion opinion in America. All the "needs" of the poor are asserted largely as a rationale for middle-class benefits.

In recent years, holding the correct political and social opinions, and associating oneself with the right kind of causes, has become an important badge of middle-class fashion in America, a phenomenon with which attitudes on abortion are intimately involved. Growing out of the civil-rights and anti-war movements, a conflict has been postulated between an allegedly narrow, bigoted, violent, and irrational white lower and lower-middle class and an educated, enlightened, and progressive upper-middle class. Although in fact social and political attitudes cannot be predicted with nearly such neatness, this image is an important part of the self-esteem of many educated people who take their superior economic status for granted but especially pride themselves on their advanced social views. In particular such people have fallen into the habit of assuming that every belief sanctioned by tradition is likely to be false and that the well-being of the human race is carried forward by constant intellectual and moral innovation.

Such people see themselves as the "cutting edge" of social change in America, and to be associated with avant-garde (and slightly daring) movements is for many of them a psychological necessity. Apart from the specifics of the issue, they see anti-abortion sentiment as representing all those backward attitudes which society must seek to erase. (Liberals who complain about the alleged right-wing dominance of the anti-abortion movement miss the most obvious point—if liberals themselves were to espouse the cause with vigor, conservatives would automatically be deprived of an issue.) Because the anti-abortion movement is as close to a genuinely populist cause as can be found in America, it is hated with special ferocity.

The English historian E. R. Norman has remarked that there is talk about "pluralism" only during the period of transition from one orthodoxy to another. Once the new orthodoxy has become established, its defenders no longer show any interest in the values of tolerance and multiple viewpoints which they previously extolled.

Defenders of traditional orthodoxies have frequently used overt censorship to inhibit the spread of heterodox ideas. Defenders of the new orthodoxies recognize that this is often counter-productive. Much more effective is the kind of censorship they practice, which consists in creating a climate of opinion in which people have the bare legal right to express dissenting views but in which such views are made to seem so eccentric as to be literally incredible. On almost all questions pertaining to sexual behavior, for example—contraception, abortion, extra-marital sex, unmarried cohabitation, homosexuality—defenders of traditional values have, within less than a decade's time, been put on the defensive, their beliefs stigmatized in the media and the educational system as symptomatic merely of narrow and insecure personalities.

Although the rhetoric of change emphasizes merely the right of each "alternative life style" to be tolerated, the struggle is never merely for toleration. Of necessity the media, the schools, and public and private social agencies must take positions with regard to all controversial belief and behavior, and it is the aim of the apostles of the avant-garde to insure that these institutions adopt their own beliefs as normative, relegating traditional values to the closet.

Although the rhetoric of relativism is freely used—the assertion that no absolutes exist and that all beliefs are therefore equally valid—in practice a new absolutism is espoused. Those who believe in sexual "liberation," for example, commonly do not recognize sexual abstinence as a valid way of life. At most they concede it a legal right to exist, and they generate massive social pressures against it.

The new orthodoxy fits closely with the reality of class conflict, already discussed, in that this orthodoxy is essentially located in what has often been called the "new class"—those persons who regard themselves as enlightened and emancipated in their opinions and who are maximally receptive of new ideas. In essence these people believe that moral belief, although necessary to society, is also dangerous because of the passions it arouses. Publicly they espouse the idea of relativism and equal toleration of all opinions, in order to dampen possible outbreaks of moral passions of which they disapprove. In practice, however, they concede to themselves the sole right to have moral passions, the sole right to mount moral crusades. Moral passion is treated as a dangerous substance which must in effect be licensed.

Since the late 1960's there has been talk of a "conscience constituency" in American politics, meaning an element among the voters who shun traditional party loyalties and traditional considerations of economic self-interest in favor of political behavior based on the perceived moral importance of particular issues. These are issues—war, racism, poverty, ecology, the "Third World"—which ordinary politics either takes little interest in or seeks to avoid, precisely because they are emotional and divisive. The intense hatred which many "new politics" people have for the anti-abortion movement stems from their feeling that the kind of people who are opposed to abortion (especially if they are demonstrably religious) have no right engaging in moral crusades. Such crusading is permissible only if directed towards subjects which have been certified as genuine issues of conscience. Conceiving themselves as the authentic keepers of the public conscience, such people are rendered angry and frightened at the prospect of others—the wrong kind of people—claiming the authority of conscience for their own concerns.

Those "single-issue" voters who have allowed their political loyalties to be guided solely by considerations involving, say, war or the Equal Rights

Amendment are commonly admired, within the "conscience constituency," for their purity, even if their single-mindedness is sometimes thought a bit short-sighted. Those who cast their ballots solely on the question of abortion, however, are accused of being dangerous fanatics and threats to the democratic system, the remedy for such a threat being a renewed sense of party loyalty, in which anti-abortion voters would not hold politicians accountable for betraying them.

During the anti-war movement those who engaged in acts of civil disobedience were treated as heroes by most of the "enlightened" element in America, and those who went beyond disobedience to acts of destruction were usually "understood" even if not precisely condoned. In the late 1970's it has been anti-abortionists, and especially young anti-abortionists, who have shown a comparable willingness to risk themselves and their futures. Yet their witness has been largely ignored, or else dismissed as mere fanaticism, and acts of destruction directed against abortion clinics, even when there has been no evidence as to who perpetrated them, have been treated as almost sacrilegious, proof of the fundamental immorality of the anti-abortionists.

The moral avant-garde requires, in politics, a constant series of symbolic victories, which both serve to proclaim the triumph of the enlightened class of people over the backward and the continued and progressive triumph of advanced opinions over traditional beliefs. The terms of permissible public discourse, and the permissible style of those who engage in public discourse, are defined to that end, and supporters of the new manage thereby to keep the momentum always with themselves, their opponents constantly on the defensive.[2]

With regard to abortion, as on other questions, what is being tested in part is the media's ability to mold public opinion, and much of the media's hostility to the anti-abortion movement stems from that movement's stubborn refusal to allow the media to instruct it in correct opinions.

Two other concentric circles are perhaps really dimensions of the previous one. They are constituted by two particular orthodoxies which have, within a decade, managed to establish themselves as beyond question. Their fortuitous coming together accounts almost entirely for the sudden triumph of the pro-abortion position in the public realm.

The first of these is the population question, the assertion that the world is threatened by the prospect of too many people and that all means of population control, including abortion, should be unstintingly used. The ramifications of this contention are too vast to be adequately discussed here. However, two relevant points can be noted. One is that, consciously or otherwise, the mentality of Zero Population Growth and the related philosophy of eugenics express the traditional elitist idea that the world would be a better place if there were fewer people, and if those few were also more carefully selected. In short, it envisions a world in which only those who fit into the enlightened consensus have a right to exist. Secondly—a point which is rather obvious, though seldom noted—there could be no more effective road to totalitarian control in the democratic West than by invoking draconian measures to insure the survival of the race. Furthermore, through such measures (especially as they affect the sacred area of sexual behavior), the enlightened elite can compel the backward masses to behave correctly. Many ardent civil-libertarians show an odd ambivalence towards proposals forcibly to regulate human breeding. (So also, few alarmists on the subject of population seem to be alarmed at the prospect of life created in the laboratory. The symbolism of yet another astonishing "break-through" far outweighs the practical demands of their cause. Many of them would probably prefer a society in which all life were created in the laboratory and little was left to human activity.)

The second unimpeachable orthodoxy is feminism, which neatly complements population-control in its tendency to denigrate motherhood as at best a specialized talent suitable for a relative few, and at worst a form of tyranny. Again the complete ramifications of this orthodoxy are too large for discussion. However, feminists who are opposed to abortion (as some sincerely are) are rather in the same position as Catholics who support it—the official doctrine of feminism does not treat abortion as peripheral, negotiable, or even debatable. The unrestricted right to an abortion is rather taken as basic to any authentic feminism.

There is compelling logic in this, in the sense that the shattering of the hitherto sacred bond between mother and child is necessary for creating the kind of "freedom" that orthodox feminism seeks. Arguably, all aspects of women's traditional social role stem ultimately from either the fact of or the potentiality for motherhood, and it is crucial to the orthodox feminist position that women be able to deny any finally binding obligations which they have towards children. Orthodox feminism is an especially militant manifestation of a larger, and increasingly prevalent, social philosophy which holds that the "needs" of the individual are self-validating and that no person or institution may restrict those needs. Abortion is perceived by many feminists as the acid test of real commitment to the cause—if even that deeply rooted scruple can be overcome, then the individual is indeed a true believer. With feminism as with other fashionable political causes, no considerations of mere morality can be allowed to dilute the degree of commitment to the movement.

The innermost circle, the very core of the militant pro-abortion position, is the simple act of moral iconoclasm itself, and it is the fanaticism which this act breeds which fuels the passions motivating the other circles.

The "conscience constituency" engages in moral innovation in two opposite ways. On the one hand it seeks to define as immoral actions which most people do not think of as such—driving automobiles, building dams, smoking tobacco, eating steak—while on the other it declares permissible and even virtuous certain actions which are commonly deemed immoral—using drugs for enjoyment, homosexual relations, abortion, viewing pornography. The assumption beneath both sets of positions is that the moral perceptions of ordinary people are not only distorted but topsy-turvy, and that it is the duty of the avant-garde precisely to effect a "transvaluation of values." Crucial to this revolution is the necessity of keeping the pressure high. One or two radical moral ideas are likely to suffer the fate of social isolation and be rejected. A moral revolution occurring on all fronts simultaneously will, however, so weaken the public sense of self-confidence, so distort the overall moral perspective, as to make virtually any idea seem plausible, so long as it is advanced with sufficient eloquence.

The pragmatic arguments for abortion, including the "hard cases" alluded to above, were never intended to be final. Rather they were necessary tactical preludes to the central symbolic act of iconoclasm, the assault on two of the most deeply rooted of all human moral institutions—the imperative to protect defenseless life and the sacred bond between mother and child. Anti-abortionists wonder how two such profound moral instincts, both supported by powerful and ancient religious, legal, and social taboos, could possibly be discarded so cavalierly, how the act of abortion could be so swiftly transformed from a heinous crime into a work of charity. The answer is that it is precisely because of the sacredness of the prohibition that such a transformation had to occur. The avant-garde mentality is not content simply to transgress moral prohibitions when they are inconvenient, which has been done in all ages of history. Rather the avant-garde recognizes only one wholly binding moral imperative, namely, in the words of the sociologist Philip Rieff, "the systematic hunting down of all settled convictions." Precisely because the act of aborting is widely perceived as immoral, it must be defiantly asserted. It is the crucial test case to demonstrate that traditional moral values, especially those which have roots in religion, shall not prevail.

The sometimes grotesque contortions through which the moral implications of abortion are denied are indication enough that a large residue of guilt still plagues those who insist that this is a surgical procedure merely equivalent to extracting inflamed tonsils. There have been some notable public conversions by people who began with a belief in the rightness of abortion but whose consciences would finally no longer permit this rationalization.

However, there is only limited comfort to be had from the existence of this moral residue, because it is precisely of the nature of the avant-garde mind to treat guilt as an atavism, an admittedly powerful force which must be systematically rooted out. Only when people suffer no guilt for their acts will they feel truly free. Abortion is the most important test case to determine whether, given massive propaganda doses, people can be made to overcome their deepest inhibitions. It is an experiment with immense relevance for the future.

The ultimate aim of this moral iconoclasm is the establishment of a morality which is wholly a human creation, not only in the sense of having no divine referent but also in the sense of being precisely a creation, that is, an emanation from the self, an exercise of the sovereign human will.[3]

The final result of this exercise—a result already achieved by many of the avant-garde—is that morality as such ceases to exist. This fact is generally overlooked because of the intense moralizing in which many of these same avant-garde indulge. But when the same law which withdraws its protection from unborn children subsequently extends it to snail darters, and when these legal decrees are hailed by enlightened opinion as signs of moral progress, it is clear that what is operative is not moral sense but mere fashion. There is no longer any right or wrong except that which has become enshrined in the ebbing and flowing of approved causes.

The struggle over the legal and moral status of abortion in America extends far beyond the lives of the millions of unborn, important though those lives are. It is finally a struggle over whether morality as such will endure, and will be allowed to make its claims on the way human beings live.

NOTES

1. See Peter Skerry, "The Class Conflict over Abortion," *The Public Interest,* Summer 1978; reprinted in *The Human Life Review,* Vol. IV, No.4, Fall 1978, pp. 34-41.
2. See Hitchcock, "The Dynamics of Popular Intellectual Change," *The American Scholar,* XLV, 4 (Winter 1976), pp. 522-35, and "Power to the Eloquent," *The Yale Review,* LXVI, 3 (Spring, 1977), pp. 374-87.
3. See Hitchcock, "The Roots of American Violence," *The Human Life Review,* Vol. III, No.3. Summer, 1977, pp. 17-29.

Looking-Glass Logic

Ellen Wilson Fielding

"Contrariwise," continued Tweedledee, "if it was so, it might be; and if it were so, it would be; but as it isn't, it ain't. That's logic."

"When I use a word," Humpty Dumpty said, in rather a scornful tone, "it means just what I choose it to mean—neither more nor less."

Through the Looking Glass

To the untutored layman trying to make sense of the way courts handle abortion, arguments seem to go by contraries. Like the world through Alice's looking glass, the Supreme Court seems a place where words mean their opposites, where parallel lines of argument may intersect, where elementary logic may be overturned, inverted, and then filed away for future jurisprudential use. In this review lawyers trained to travel the maze-worlds of majority and minority opinions conduct guided tours of recent Supreme Court decisions, and pending decisions. My aim is less ambitious. Returning to the looking-glass image, I am going to bypass the scientific explanations of reflection and refraction, with their diagrams of light waves bouncing off mirrors, and simply describe what anyone may see.

The Abortion Decisions

Abortion, so one is told, is an issue of privacy. NARAL said so, way back before 1973 when it was the National Association for the Repeal of Abortion Laws. Feminist pro-abortionists said so, ACLU (American Civil Liberties Union) people said so, and finally, in 1973, the Supreme Court said so, when it warned governments and citizens alike to honor a woman's reproductive privacy. For the Supreme Court discovered, not only that abortion is about privacy, but that privacy (except during census years) is a constitutional right. Inquirers were directed to the Bill of Rights and the 14th Amendment, where the relevant penumbrae could be viewed.

The first question which comes to mind, then, is what the Court *means* by privacy? Do the justices distinguish their notion of privacy from that of the 13-year-old who keeps a Secret Diary? Do they mean only that American women have a constitutional right to keep secrets? It would appear not, for

Ellen Wilson Fielding, a longtime senior editor of the *Human Life Review*, is the author of *An Even Dozen* (Human Life Press, 1981).

private citizens and government officials have long since recognized large limitations on this kind of privacy.

For example, a citizen's right to keep a secret about criminal guilt is recognized and protected if the guilt is his own (see the Fifth Amendment), but denied if the guilt is another's (subpoenas, perjury laws, etc.). A minor's right to privacy is severely abridged, particularly in his earlier stages of development, and so is the right of one spouse to be "private" from the other. Then there is the yearly abridgement of our right of privacy by the IRS. The elusive constitutional penumbra of privacy has never deterred them.

We may agree, then, that this sort of "privacy" is scarcely inviolate, whether in theory or in practice. We may further decide that "privacy" is not "the most appropriate word for what NARAL and Justice Blackmun are talking about. (The substance of the pregnant woman's complaint can't really be that her unborn is eavesdropping on her.) Let us rename this right, or more scrupulously define it as the right to form and carry out independent decisions ("personal autonomy" is the way one ACLU lawyer describes it) affecting ourselves and our future. Even so, the shackles remain. For even the less imaginative of the disciples of John Stuart Mill recognize that the right to do as one pleases is qualified: Others resent the liberties we take with their liberties. Thus is built up a great cloud of mutually-eclipsing penumbrae for the political scientists to contend with, and the delineation of their limits is neither as easy nor as clear-cut as the "right to privacy" may suggest.

Other people have pointed out the difficulty of first identifying and then expediting everyone's right to privacy, but the courts and their beneficiaries seem almost obstinately to overlook the problem, seem even to think they have solved it. But this right to privacy, this right to do as one pleases when it is allowable to do as one pleases, carries us no further toward a resolution of the abortion question. It merely restates the problem, but in a submerged, incomplete, and ultimately deceptive manner. The question both parties asked the Court was "Does the woman's right to do as she pleases with her pregnancy collide with other rights of greater or equal significance?" But that question presupposed the answering of another: Is the human fetus human? The Supreme Court has stigmatized this as a "moral" or "religious" question outside the purview of the Court; the major newspapers and magazines have labelled it a divisive question which threatens the First Amendment, party politics, and pluralism; Sens. Kennedy and Moynihan and other tender consciences in the Congress have labelled it a "personal" question which resists the formulation of a "public" opinion. What none of them say is that it is the proper question to ask. If two people are arguing about the square root of two, their opposing viewpoints will not be reconciled by learning that the

Normans invaded England in 1066. The Supreme Court has been trying to change the subject—to privacy, minor's rights, etc.—for seven years now, and it has been reaping its just reward in a long series of litigants trying to bring it back to the point. One could understand a muddled majority of nine men deciding that the human fetus is not human. One cannot understand a majority of nine jurists offhandedly ruling that the question is irrelevant. For if the unborn is human, then of course his right to life will collide with the mother's right to jettison him; if he is "just a mass of tissue" (aren't we all, in one sense), then by all means, respect her privacy.

Even some pro-abortionists were embarrassed by the poor argumentation of the Abortion Decisions. Charged with the defense of a judicial decision so mediocre, they scrambled for more sophisticated arguments for their newly-won right. Embroidering on the privacy principle, one school has declared the (unwanted) fetus an aggressor within the womb, and abortion the moral and legal equivalent of self-defense. But the line of this argument retraces that of the original one. Both, after all, are merely sophisticated versions of "I didn't ask to get pregnant," which, as argument, ranks with the eight-year-old's "I didn't ask to be born." Here, as in the Supreme Court's abortion decisions, the key question is slurred over: Is the unborn human? If so, a pregnant woman's physical (and sometimes psychological) distress is being weighed against a human life. If not, then what is all the fuss about?

But there is an additional point to be made about this privacy of the womb, and that is, that except in rare cases of rape and incest, it hasn't been violated. The woman, whether or not she "planned" the pregnancy, *did* grant admission to the sperm which fertilized her ovum. Further, the attempt to call a fetus an "aggressor" in the womb of all places is ridiculous. What else are wombs *for,* to put the question in Aristotelian terms? Where else would a human fetus be? And where else would that particular human fetus be, formed from the fusion of invited sperm and home-bred ovum? This is not, after all, a vagrant fetus seeking shelter wherever it may be found.

All in all, it would seem the fetus has quite as much claim to privacy as the mother: He should be allowed to develop naturally in the womb. But now we are "presupposing" the fetus' humanity, and that is an act of intellectual temerity from which the Supreme Court still shrinks.

The Minor's Right to Privacy

A court incompetent to deal with the central issue of the abortion cases—upon which all our constitutional rights depend, since they are predicated upon our humanity—would hardly seem qualified to intrude upon mother-daughter relations. Yet that has been the second arena in which the abortion right has been contested. I mentioned earlier that the "right to privacy" brought to mind adolescent diaries kept under lock and key. State and Federal courts in cases such as *Bellotti* have, with obvious discomfort but a manful sense of duty, defended the right of a teenage girl to keep certain diary entries, at least, private from their mothers. For they appear to have awarded the minor a bonus right: Not only may she decide for herself whether to have an abortion, but recent decisions have allowed her to decide privately, without parental consultation and without disclosing her decision or even her pregnant condition.

Others have explored the legal precedents upset by such decisions, the inconsistency of requiring parental consent for almost any kind of medical treatment (or legal contract) *except* abortion, the foreboding implications of these decisions for other aspects of family law, etc. What should be evident, however, is that privacy is not the preeminent issue at stake. Or at least, if both parties have concentrated on the issue of privacy, it is because courts have sacrificed the family's privacy for the sake of a peculiarly interpreted right of privacy for the teenager (as though statute books were to record penalties for disregarding the "Do Not Disturb" sign on her bedroom door).

But consider the merely semantic difficulties into which the Supreme Court's looking-glass logic has embroiled it. The Court has seemingly committed itself to the notion that the minor's right of privacy can only be guaranteed by ensuring that she consult with a public servant—a judge. That it is a more private act to consult with a total stranger than with the people who gave you life and nourished it, is not intuitively obvious. That doctor, judge, and pregnant minor should combine in a conspiracy of silence, with the sole intent of deceiving those directly responsible for the minor's welfare, is not self-evidently wise, or just, or even commonsensical. Worst of all, perhaps, is the Court's justification for this conversion of a dubious right into a part of the judicial process: For their argument that "confidentiality" may be in the minor's best interest amounts to little more than a thinly veiled acknowledgement that Mom and Dad would be very sore if they knew what was going on.

The justices would claim that abortion is an extremely serious and difficult matter (agreed); that there are parents who do not make the right decisions for their children (no quarrel there); and therefore, that an impartial authorizing body must be available to provide the minor with a more promising second opinion. To which the layman would reply that judges are as fallible as parents, and in addition, their training peculiarly *ill*-equips them for juggling just those individual circumstances which, presumably, justify judicial intrusion in the first place. Parents know their children better than strangers do; with few exceptions, they love them better, and in addition they are motivated by a heavier, more constant, and more immediate sense of responsibility than the stranger can share. And as C.S. Lewis reminds us, there is this crucial distinction between love and the sympathetic liking a stranger or acquaintance may feel:

> Kindness, merely as such, cares not whether its object becomes good or bad, provided only that it escapes suffering. . . . It is for people whom we care nothing about that we demand happiness on any terms: with our friends, our lovers, our children, we are exacting, and would rather see them suffer much than be happy in contemptible and estranging modes.

To a benevolent judge or a kindly doctor (to take the best case), confronted with a child whose future will be agonizingly complicated by a pregnancy, abortion will often appear the simple and most beneficial course. But the minor's parents, conscious of continuing responsibility and instructed by love, will more likely consider the kind of person their daughter should be, the kinds of truths she must own up to in order to reach maturity. They, who first introduced her to small responsibilities, will not wish her to shirk greater ones, though they will wish that they could spare her the pain and sacrifices these may entail.

But the looking-glass court has decided that ignorance may judge more justly than knowledge, and a child's welfare be better directed by institutionalized benevolence than by love. This is the second kind of ignorance which the Supreme Court is embracing as judicial principle, for the court counsellors of the minor's abortion decision have already bound themselves to ignorance of what it is the pregnant girl bears in her body.

Federal Funding and the Right of Privacy

Surprise (and even disbelief) over the Supreme Court's interpretation of the right to privacy has been dulled by seven years' familiarity. Outrage over the co-opted rights of families has been diluted by a series of decisions involving spouses and children which have stretched across the intervening years. Looking-glass logic, like Euclidean geometry, comes more easily to the mind with practice. But now Judge Dooling's decision that Medicaid funds must be appropriated for abortions marks a further expansion of the judicially defined right of privacy. The argument now runs that the right of privacy casts its own pale penumbra, requiring not only legalization of abortion-on-demand, but conscription of public funds as well. It is perhaps stretching patience to run through the arguments at length. I do so quickly to reacquaint the reader with the other rights, large and small, which the abortion right is toppling.

It would appear self-evident that if abortion is merely a matter of private choice (if it is one of that class of activities that may legally be engaged in or avoided), there is no obvious obligation for the taxpayer to subsidize someone else's fancy for an abortion. We do not ordinarily subsidize fancies or their fulfillment, whether they are trivial (baseball, Rhine wines) or more important (marriages, sex-change operations). We leave private tastes to private purses.

But pro-abortionists open up a "second front" argument for public funding, which supports the first not so much by force of logic (in reality, the two coexist uneasily) as by drawing our attention away from the details of either. They argue that the abortion decision is so important, so grave in its effect, so likely to alter the mother's lifestyle and redirect her future, that *only* the prospective mother can weigh all the arguments, debate the options, and decide upon the correct course. On these terms, whatever decision the pregnant woman makes is the correct one *for her,* and if the woman is too poor to (in the bureaucratic phrase) "implement that decision," then the public must step in.

This second front argument is distracting, but unconvincing, either by itself or in tandem with the first one. To begin with, if the good or evil of an abortion is preponderantly subjective (as it must be if only the pregnant woman is qualified to judge the matter), then we on the outside cannot tell whether she made the "right" decision. Misinformation, distraught emotions, outside pressure, an uninstructed or misinformed conscience—all could have skewed her reasoning or warped her judgment. We have no reason to assume she made the right decision (used her materials properly, so to speak), and cannot, on that basis, bear a responsibility to realize it for her.

Further, we lack precedents for such funding in other areas. Most important personal decisions are not publicly funded. The choice of a career, for instance, is very important, particularly if it will require long and costly preparation. Yet the nation recognizes no duty to fulfill every adolescent's dream of becoming a doctor or lawyer or dancer or electrician. Even if we were sure that every person could correctly estimate his abilities, as well as his long-term appetite for the job, we wouldn't force taxpayers to send a kid to Harvard or Juilliard.

There is another difficulty with the personalist or subjectivist argument. The idea of an abortion decision so personal that it cannot be evaluated or entered into by the outsider, can backfire against the pro-abortionist. The argument from American Pluralism can cut both ways. Judge Dooling claims that the Hyde Amendment violates the First Amendment freedom of religion rights of those indigent women who have a "religious" belief in the innocence of abortion. (Such case histories exist. There is the female Methodist minister who referred to her own abortion as one of the holiest experiences of her life.) Judge Dooling's opponents have replied quite reasonably on behalf of those taxpayers who feel at least as strongly that abortion is wrong. What are the qualifications of pro-abortionists for judging the circumstances of their opponents' decision *not* to finance abortions? They are, though they won't admit it, hoist on their own subjectivist petard. Anti-abortionists contend that abortion is wrong in and of itself; pro-abortionists claim that it is a matter for individual consciences to decide, implying if not openly stating that it may at least sometimes be a *good.* On what grounds can they object when another's Inner Light directs him to withhold funding for abortions? What has happened to the right of privacy of the anti-abortionist, or is he presumed to have forfeited it by forfeiting his right to have an abortion? The abortionist's right of privacy has been let loose to devour whatever other rights impede it.

Finally, for those who wish to take the pragmatic view, there is the chilling argument that poor people's abortions may be in the national interest—may, to seek out constitutional fiat, "promote the general welfare." Aborting Welfare babies would reduce the crop of Welfare children and teenagers, and eventually Welfare adults and old people. On this theory one could justify the putting to sleep of all adults approaching eligibility for Social Security payments. And this is where it goes wrong: It is *not* a theory; its adherents do not consider the assumptions which underlie it. For the utilitarian position leads us back to our old unanswered question. After all, it is not the *fetus* who will consume thousands of dollars worth of government food, clothing, and education: It is the "post-fetus." When pro-abortionists calculate costs of live births versus abortions in order to demonstrate the expediency of abortion, they are really calculating relative expenses of life versus death. It is not the first nine months, but the succeeding four score and ten years, that make the difference. Death, it turns out, is a great economy move. But have we considered whether it is proper—whether it is *safe*—to encourage a nation to be so grudging of life?

Which leads us back to our opening question. We know the expensive fourscore and ten years is human life. Is the relatively economical first nine months also human life? If so, it can't be sacrificed to balance budgets, public or private. The slavery analogy which John Noonan has employed so well in the *Human Life Review* and elsewhere again provides an appropriate parallel. During the Lincoln-Douglas debates, Stephen Douglas explained his "personally opposed, *but...*" position on the expansion of slavery into the territories. He wanted the issue to be resolved by popular sovereignty, and claimed not to care "whether it is voted up or down." Lincoln's reply exposed Douglas' underlying assumption:

> Any man can say that who does not see anything wrong in slavery, but no man can logically say it who does see a wrong in it; because no man can logically

say he don't care whether a wrong is voted up or down . . .. He contends that whatever community wants slaves has a right to have them. So they have if it is not a wrong. But if it is a wrong, he cannot say people have a right to do a wrong.

And so the abortion issue stands today. If abortion *doesn't* determine the fate of a tiny human life, then let it be voted up or down. If it does, then it belongs to that class of questions which does not take kindly to compromise. If it is relatively unimportant whether abortion is legal or illegal, publicly or privately funded, then the government can have no strong national interest in it, individuals may freely differ without dire repercussions, and the courts are not justified in searching the Constitution for a bill of attainder against Henry Hyde. If abortion is a matter of life and death, then it must be decided correctly. And that can't be done by a court which has declared its incompetency to deal with the question.

Logic along a Single Track

I have been talking about judicial looking-glass logic, confusions of public and private, preoccupations with side-issues while central questions are neglected, and the inability of the Supreme Court to see that political philosophy and epistemology are the underpinnings of the Constitution they interpret. The thing to hold in mind is that looking-glass logic is not the suspension of logic: It is logic developed along one line at the expense of all the rest (this was Chesterton's definition of madness). It is logic lost to proportion, divorced from first principles, or tied too closely to just one. More frightening than present contradictions or inconsistencies in Supreme Court thinking is the Supreme Court's devotion to drawing out one or two pet principles at the expense of the rest, and neglecting the substance of cases for the more ornamental and politically consequential accidents of cases. Minds so constituted may easily go from bad to worse: They may go from anything to anything, as long as they are allowed to follow the same logical track. They are like trolley-car conductors who imagine that the city limits mold themselves to the line of the track, so that nothing important escapes their view. So far, I have been describing the bad thinking that has been and is being done; now I turn to the worse that may be, or might be, or would be, if the courts and their advocates had the courage of their logical convictions. But like science-fiction societies which remain unrealized because they are *too* logical, the full force of the Court's logic may not be inflicted on us.

The argument for privacy, when used to advocate the abortion right, presupposes that only wanted children should be born. An unwanted child is a double offense: marring the happiness of his mother, and bringing upon himself, unwittingly, his own unhappiness. But is any child fully wanted in his final form—or most of his intermediate stages of development? Is any child ever "expected," in the non-gynecological sense? And aren't we kept in suspense about the degrees of unacceptability, not only in the months before a child is born, but for a number of years thereafter? Of course, the most common case is one in which the parent "wants" the child more at one age than at another. A placid one-year-old may become a day-dreaming, inattentive eight-year-old; a loving youngster may become a stand-offish adolescent; the child's tastes may grow either towards or away from those of his parents. In the fullest sense of the word, parents can't know what they're in for.

Consider the plight of Dr. William Shockley, Nobel laureate and recent contributor to a eugenicist's sperm bank, who has confessed in an interview that his middle child possesses mediocre talents and intelligence. How greatly may that child have been wanted while his shortcomings were concealed within the womb, and how progressively unwanted (in one sense) he may have become thereafter. G. K. Chesterton once exposed the delusions of the eugenicist in this way:

> Mr. Blatchford, with colossal simplicity, explained to millions of clerks and workingmen that the mother is like a bottle of blue beads and the father like a bottle of yellow beads; and so the child is like a bottle of mixed blue beads and yellow . . . It is not like blue beads mixed with yellow beads; it is like blue mixed with yellow; the result of which is *green,* a totally novel and unique experience, a new emotion . . . . Every birth is as lonely as a miracle. Every child is as uninvited as a monstrosity.

But if the Supreme Court is right, and abortion a question of taste or preference, with no unpleasant ethical considerations to complicate the issue, then why shouldn't parents have the option of delayed abortion? Why not extend the privilege and allow mothers to do away with four-year-olds who fuss or 10-year-olds who flunk math?

One obvious answer to this is that such children, if not always "wanted," are almost always loved. They are loved even when they are not always liked, or understood. But this is not a complete or fully satisfying answer. It begins at the middle rather than at the beginning. It is situational, concerned with effects rather than principles. It is logical, and as far as it goes, it is "true"—it deals with real, possible situations. The problem is, it does not cover all situations. In fact, it bears the hallmark of Supreme Court thinking in its preference for incidentals at the expense of fundamentals. We do not refrain from killing people simply because we love them, just as we do not (if we are sane and law-abiding) kill people simply because we dislike them. We refrain from killing people because they are people.

Some truths are so fundamental that it requires conscious effort to bring them to mind. And most of the time there is no need to. But because an object is large is no excuse for ignoring its existence, and even fundamental truths may be endangered at times. If we do not ask whether the unborn are human, we will never know whether they share with us a common humanity. If we do not, upon occasion, question the foundation of our rights, we will have no answer for those who wish to chip away at them in the name of social goals or subsidiary rights. If we do not know why we have the right to privacy, we will not know how to draw the limits of that right. "We refrain from killing people because they are people": Would the current Supreme Court know what to make of that explanation?

The Humane Holocaust

Malcolm Muggeridge

One of the most curious encounters I ever had in a television studio was participating in a BBC program set up when the South African surgeon, Dr. Christiaan Barnard, had just carried out his first heart-transplant operation in the Groote Schuur Hospital in Pretoria. The program was billed as "Dr. Barnard Faces His Critics," which, as I well knew, was BBC-ese for "Dr. Barnard Faces His Adulators," as, indeed, proved to be the case. One of the great contributions of television to preparing the way for the collectivist-authoritarian way of life towards which all western countries are, in their different ways, sleep-walking, is its capacity to present consensus in terms of ostensible controversy.

The studio was packed with medical practitioners of one sort and another, including distinguished figures like Lord Platt, all of whom were in a state of euphoria about Dr. Barnard's achievement. As befitting such an occasion, the Church was represented, in the person of the appropriately named Dr. Slack, who on its behalf gave full approval, not just to the particular transplant operation that was being celebrated, but to transplants in general as and when required, whatever the organ concerned. In the event, I found myself pretty well the lone representative of the critics Dr. Barnard had been billed as meeting.

When the time came for me to put a question, one shaped itself insistently in my mind. Was Dr. Barnard, I asked him, the first surgeon to chance his arm with a heart-transplant operation, whereas elsewhere there were still qualms and hesitations, because in South Africa the doctrine of apartheid had devalued human flesh, reducing it from something God had deigned to put on, to a mere carcass?

The question, when I put it, was extremely ill-received. Some of the doctors present went so far as to manifest their displeasure by hissing, while Lord Platt rose to apologize to Dr. Barnard, pointing out that I represented no one but myself, and that he, and he was sure all the others in the studio, would wish to dissociate themselves from my insulting question. Dr. Barnard himself, I should imagine deliberately, misunderstood what I had asked, assuming that what troubled me was a fear lest he had transplanted a black African's heart in a white African's body. In fact, the donor was a white girl.

Malcolm Muggeridge (1903–1990), the English journalist and satirist, authored many works, including *Something Beautiful for God* (1971; reissued 2009, Lion Hudson plc) the book which introduced Mother Teresa to the world.

As Dr. Barnard made no serious effort to answer my question, I persisted, to the further displeasure of the doctors, pointing out that his and their attitude showed little sense of the sanctity of life, which, in the Hippocratic oath they had all presumably taken, they had sworn to respect. As a Christian, I said, I worshipped a God who, according to the New Testament, could not see a sparrow fall to the ground without concern, and quoted Blake's beautiful couplet in the same sense:

> A Robin Redbreast in a Cage
> Puts all Heaven in a Rage.

This caused a titter of amusement, and I lapsed into silence. It is the usual practice after such programs for all the participants to make for the hospitality room, there to continue the discussion over a drink. For once, I just made off, having no taste for any further contact with Lord Platt, Dr. Slack and the others. It was comforting subsequently to receive a letter from a doctor who had once worked at Groote Schuur Hospital, but had left, he explained, because he found the attitude there to surgery to be more veterinary than medical.

Dr. Barnard's own attitude to his surgery is well conveyed in his autobiography, *One Life*. His account of his first post-mortem is almost lascivious; as are his first essays with animals, whose snug little abattoir, he tells us, "smelt of guinea pigs, rabbits and hundreds of mice. Yet it was like heaven, and even today those odours excite me with memories of our first days, so filled with hope and dreams." One of his dreams was to "take a baboon and cool him down, wash out his blood with water, then fill him up with human blood"; another, to graft a second head on a dog, as has allegedly—though I don't believe it—been done in the USSR.

All this was but a prelude to the great moment when the two hearts—the donor's lively one and the recipient's failing one—were ready, and all was set for the first heart-transplant operation. "This isn't a dog," Dr. Barnard reflected exultantly. "*It's a man!*" And then a doubt seized him; was he, after all, entitled to experiment with a human being? His hesitation lasted only for a few seconds, though; the excitement of the occasion, with, as it seemed, the whole world looking on, restored his confidence, and he got to work with his knife.

As it happened, there was one other moment of, if not doubt, then wonderment. The donor, Denise Darvall, was in a respirator; it would be necessary to stop the respirator, and take her heart, which was still beating. Another doctor, de Klerk, was participating in the operation; he wanted Denise's kidneys, but Dr. Barnard made it quite clear what were the priorities. His instructions were to "cut for the heart and let de Klerk worry about his kidneys afterwards." In the event, having stopped the respirator, they waited for the heart to stop beating before transferring it to the recipient, Washkansky. "What intermingling of mythology and ritual," Dr. Barnard asks himself, "prevented us from touching a heart in a body which had been declared clinically dead?" and, like Pontius Pilate on another dramatic occasion, does not wait for an answer.

Washkansky received Denise's heart, and, presumably, de Klerk her kidneys. The heart worked, and the patient in a manner of speaking, lived. Congratulatory messages came pouring in; the television cameras rolled—exclusive TV rights had been disposed of, resulting in unseemly scenes in the hospital. Washkansky, but not Denise, was brought into the act; the arc lights shone on him, a meeting with his loving relatives was set up, and he succeeded in uttering a few cheerful words into a specially sterilized microphone. At the end of eighteen days, he thankfully expired. "They're killing me," he managed to get out before he died. "I can't sleep, I can't eat, I can't do anything. They're at me all the time with pins and needles . . . All day and all night. It's driving me crazy."

Washkansky's successor, Dr. Philip Bleiberg, a dentist, managed to survive for two years, though his private account of how he fared roughly coincided with his predecessor's. In the published version—these rights, too, had been disposed of—he was obliged to put on a brave face, and only three weeks after he had received his new heart, he was able to tell an expectant world that he had succeeded in having sexual intercourse. It was the twentieth-century certification of being fully alive: *copula ergo sum.* Behind the mania about transplant operations, lies the mad hope that in due course genital transplants may become possible—new ballocks in old crotches—so that sated lechers can begin all over again.

The Barnard experience stayed in my mind, and as I thought about it, I realized that it amounted to a sort of parable illustrating a basic dilemma of our time, as between the sanctity of life as conceived through the Christian centuries and the quality of life as conceived in a materialist society. Those doctors in the BBC studio rejoicing in the new possibilities in surgery that Dr. Barnard seemed to have opened up, saw human beings as bodies merely, and so capable of constant improvement, until at last perfection was achieved.

No more sick or misshapen bodies, no more disturbed or twisted minds, no more hereditary idiots or mongoloid children. Babies not up to scratch would be destroyed, before or after birth, as would also the old beyond repair. With the developing skills of modern medicine, the human race could be pruned and carefully tended until only the perfect blooms—the beauty queens, the Mensa I.Q.'s, the athletes—remained. Then at last, with rigid population control to prevent the good work being ruined by excessive numbers, affliction would be ended, and maybe death itself abolished, and men become, not just like gods, but in their perfect mortality, very God.

Against this vision of life without tears in a fleshly paradise, stands the Christian vision of mankind as a family whose loving father is God. Here, the symbol is not the perfected body, the pruned vine, the weeded garden, but a stricken body nailed to a cross, signifying affliction, not as the enemy of life, but as its greatest enhancement and teacher. In an army preparing for battle the unfit are indeed discarded, but in a Christian family the handicapped are particularly cherished, and give special joy to those who cherish them.

Which vision are we for? On the one hand, as the pattern of our collective existence, the broiler house or factory-farm, in which the concern is solely for the physical well-being of the livestock and the financial well-being of the enterprise; on the other, mankind as a family, all of whose members, whatever physical or mental qualities or deficiencies they may have, are equally deserving of consideration in the eyes of their creator, and whose existence has validity, not just in itself, nor just in relation to history, but in relation to a destiny reaching beyond time and into eternity. Or, in simple terms, on the one hand, the quality of life; on the other, the sanctity of life.[1]

The sanctity of life is, of course, a religious or transcendental concept, and has no meaning otherwise; if there is no God, life cannot have sanctity. By the same token, the quality of life is an earthly or worldly concept, and can only be expressed legalistically,[2] and in materialistic terms; the soul does not come into it. Thus a child conceived in conditions of penury, or with a poor heredity, or against its mother's wishes, or otherwise potentially handicapped, may be considered as lacking the requisite quality of life prospects, and so should not be born. Equally, it follows, at the other end of our life span, that geriatrics unable any longer to appreciate what this world has to offer in the way of aesthetic, carnal and egotistic satisfaction, in other words, by virtue of their years losing out on quality of life, should be subjected to euthanasia or mercy-killing, and discreetly murdered.

On this basis, for instance, Beethoven would scarcely have been allowed to be born; his heredity and family circumstances were atrocious, a case history of syphilis, deafness and insanity. Today, his mother's pregnancy would be considered irresponsible, and as requiring to be terminated. Dr. Johnson, when he was born, was scrofulous, and already showed signs of the nervous disorders which plagued him all his life. He, too, under present conditions would probably not have been allowed to survive. Indeed, a good number of the more notable contributors to the sanctity of life, like Dr. Johnson, would have failed to make the grade on quality of life, the supreme example being the founder of the Christian religion. Imagine a young girl, unmarried and pregnant, who insists that the Holy Ghost is responsible for her pregnancy, and that its outcome, according to a vision she has been vouchsafed, would be the birth of a long-awaited Messiah. Not much quality-of-life potential there, I fancy, and it wouldn't take the pregnancy and family-planning pundits long to decide that our Saviour, while still at the fetus stage, should be thrown away with the hospital waste.

These are hypothetical cases; near at hand, we have been accorded, for those that have eyes to see, an object lesson in what the quest for quality of life without reference to sanctity of life, can involve. Ironically enough, this has been provided by none other than the great Nazi holocaust, whose TV presentation has lately been harrowing viewers throughout the western world. In this televised version, an essential consideration has been left out—namely, that the origins of the holocaust lay, not in Nazi terrorism and anti-Semitism, but in pre-Nazi Weimar Germany's acceptance of euthanasia and mercy-killing as humane and estimable. And by one of those sick jokes which haunt our human story, just when the penitential holocaust was being shown on American, and then on German and other Western European TV screens, a humane holocaust was getting under way, this time in the countries that had defeated Hitler's Third Reich, and, at the Nuremberg War Crimes Tribunal, condemned as a war crime the very propositions and practices with which the Nazi holocaust had originated, and on which the humane one was like-wise based.

No one could have put the matter more cogently and authoritatively than has Dr. Leo Alexander, who worked with the Chief American Counsel at the Nuremberg Tribunal:

> Whatever proportion these crimes finally assumed, it became evident to all who investigated them that they had started from small beginnings. The be-ginnings at first were merely a subtle shift in emphasis in the basic attitudes of the physicians. It started with the acceptance of the attitude, basic in the euthanasia movement, that there is such a thing as life not worthy to be lived. This attitude in its early stages concerned itself merely with the severely and chronically sick. Gradually, the sphere of those to be included in this category was enlarged to encompass the socially unproductive, the ideologically un-wanted, the racially unwanted, and finally all non-Germans. *But it is important to realize that the infinitely small wedged-in lever from which the entire trend of mind received its impetus was the attitude towards the non-rehabilitable sick* [my italics].[3]

Surely some future Gibbon surveying our times will note sardonically that it took no more than three decades to transform a war crime into an act of compassion, thereby enabling the victors in the war against Nazi-ism to adopt the very practices for which the Nazis had been solemnly condemned at Nuremberg. Then they could mount their own humane holocaust, which in its range and in the number of its victims may soon far surpass the Nazi one. Nor need we marvel that, whereas the Nazi holocaust received lavish TV and film coverage, the humane one just goes rolling along, largely unnoticed by the media.

It all began in the early twenties, in the decadent years in the post-1914-18 war Germany which have been so glorified by writers like Christopher Isherwood, but which, as I remember them at first hand, were full of sinister portent for the future. All the most horrible and disgusting aspects of the last decades of the twentieth century—the pornography, the sadism, the violence, the moral and spiritual vacuum—were already in evidence there.

In this sick environment, the notion of mercy-killing was put forward in 1920 in a book entitled *The Release of the Destruction of Life Devoid of Value* by Alfred Hoche, a reputable psychiatrist, and Karl Binding, a jurist. The authors advocated killing off "absolutely worthless human beings," pointing out that the money spent on keeping them alive thus saved could be used to better purpose—for instance, on helping a young married couple to set up house. Frederick Wertham, in his scholarly and deeply disturbing book, *A Sign for Cain,* says that the Hoche-Binding book influenced, or at least crystalized the thinking of a whole generation.

From these beginnings, a program of mercy-killing developed which was initiated, directed and supported by doctors and psychiatrists, some of them of considerable eminence—all this when the Nazi movement was still at an embryonic stage, and Hitler had barely been heard of. Initially, the holocaust was aimed, not against Jews or Slavs, but against handicapped Aryan Germans, and was justified, not by racial theories, but by Hegelian utilitarianism, whereby what is useful is *per se* good, without any consideration being given to Judeo-Christian values, or, indeed to any concept whatsoever of Good and Evil. Subsequently, of course, the numbers of the killed rose to astronomical figures, and the medical basis for their slaughter grew ever flimsier; but it should never be forgotten that it was the euthanasia program first organized under the Weimar Republic by the medical profession, which led to and merged into the genocide program of 1941-45. "Technical experience gained first with killing psychiatric patients," Wertham writes, "was utilized later for the destruction of millions. The psychiatric murders came first."

Can this sort of thing happen in countries like Canada and England and the

United States? In my opinion, yes; in fact, it is already happening. Abortion on demand has come to be part of our way of life; in the world as a whole there are estimated to have been last year something in the neighborhood of fifty million abortions—an appalling figure, which, however, with media help did not loom very large, or throw any kind of shadow over 1979 as the Year of the Child. To quieten any qualms Christians might have about it, an Anglican bishop has devised an appropriate prayer for use on the occasion of an abortion which received the approval of the Archbishop of Canterbury. It runs, "Into Thy hands we commit in trust the developing life we have cut short," though whether with the idea of God's continuing the interrupted development elsewhere, or of extinguishing in Heaven the life that was never born on earth, is not clear. In the case of euthanasia, a hymn may seem more in keeping with the occasion—"The life Thou gavest, Lord, we've ended. . . ."

Euthanasia, it is true, has not yet been legalized except in some American states, but notoriously it is being practiced on an ever-increasing scale. Already among old people there is reluctance to go into government institutions for fear of being done away with. As for governments—hard-pressed financially as they all now are, and unable to economize on defense expenditure for fear of laying themselves open to the charge of jeopardizing national security, or on welfare expenditure for fear of losing votes—will they not look ever more-longingly at the possibility of making substantial savings by the simple expedient of mercy-killing off the inmates of institutions for the incurably sick, the senile old, the mentally deranged and other such? With abortions and family-planning ensuring a zero population growth rate, and euthanasia disposing of useless mouths among the debilitated old, besides mopping up intervening freaks, the pursuit of happiness should be assured of at any rate financial viability.

In Christian terms, of course, all this is quite indefensible. Our Lord healed the sick, raised Lazarus from the dead, gave back sanity to the deranged, but never did he practice or envisage killing as part of the mercy that held possession of his heart. His true followers cannot but follow his guidance here. For instance, Mother Teresa, who, in Calcutta, goes to great trouble to have brought into her Home for Dying Derelicts, castaways left to die in the streets. They may survive for no more than a quarter of an hour, but in that quarter of an hour, instead of feeling themselves rejected and abandoned, they meet with Christian love and care. From a purely humanitarian point of view, the effort involved in this ministry of love could be put to some more useful purpose, and the derelicts left to die in the streets, or even helped to die there by being given the requisite injection. Such calculations do not come into Mother Teresa's way of looking at things; her love and compassion reach out to the afflicted without any other consideration than their immediate need, just as our Lord does when he tells us to feed the hungry, shelter the homeless, clothe the naked. She gives all she has to give at once, and then finds she has more to give. As between Mother Teresa's holocaust of love and the humane holocaust, I am for hers.

There is an episode in my own life which, though it happened long ago, provides, as I consider, a powerful elucidation of the whole issue of euthanasia—a study, as it were, in mercy-living in contradistinction to mercy-killing. Some forty years ago, shortly before the outbreak of the 1939-45 war, the person whom I have most loved in this world, my wife Kitty, was desperately ill, and, as I was informed by the doctor attending her, had only an outside chance of surviving. The medical details are unimportant; probably today, with the great advances that have taken place in curative medicine, her state would not be so serious. But as the situation presented itself then, she was hovering between life and death, though, needless to say, there was no voice, as there might well be nowadays, to suggest that it might be better to let her go.

The doctor explained that an emergency operation was essential, and, in honesty, felt bound to tell me that it would be something of a gamble. Her blood, it appeared, was so thin as a result of a long spell of jaundice that before he operated a blood-transfusion was desperately needed—this was before the days of plasma. As he said this, an incredible happiness amounting to ecstacy surged up inside me. If I could be the donor! My blood-count was taken, and found to be suitable; the necessary gear was brought in, very primitive by contemporary standards—just a glass tube one end of which was inserted in her arm and the other end in mine, with a pump in the middle drawing out my blood and sending it into her. I could watch the flow, shouting out absurdly to the doctor: "Don't stint yourself, take all you want!", and noting delightedly the immediate effect in bringing back life into her face that before had seemed grey and lifeless. It was the turning point; from that moment she began to mend.

At no point in our long relationship has there been a more ecstatic moment than when I thus saw my life-blood pouring into hers to revivify it. We were at one, blood to blood, as no other kind of union could make us. To give life— this was what love was for; to give it in all circumstances and eventualities, whether God creating the universe, or a male and female creating another human being; whereas to destroy life, be it in a fertilized ovum one second after conception, or in some octogenarian or sufferer from a fatal illness, was the denial of life and so the antithesis of love. In life-denying terms, as we have seen, compassion easily becomes a holocaust; garden suburbs and gulags derive from the same quest for quality of life, and the surgeon's knife can equally be used to sustain and extinguish life. Dostoevsky makes the same point: "Love toward men, but love without belief in God, very naturally leads to the greatest coercion over men, and turns their lives completely into hell on earth." We should never forget that if ever there was a killing without mercy, a death without dignity, it was on Golgotha. Yet from that killing, what a pouring out of mercy through the subsequent centuries! From that death, what a stupendous enhancement of human dignity!

NOTES

1. See the interesting Study Paper put out by the Law Reform Commission of Canada in its "Protection of Life" series, *Sanctity of Life or Quality of Life.*
2. *Ibid.*
3. From a paper—"Medical Science Under Dictatorship"—by Dr. Alexander, now a Boston psychiatrist, which appeared in the *New England Journal of Medicine* of July 4, 1949, and quoted in an article in the Spring, 1976 issue of the *Human Life Review* entitled "The Lesson of Euthanasia" by Fr. Virgil C. Blum, S.J. and Charles J. Sykes. Another article in the Spring, 1977 issue of the *Human Life Review* to which I am greatly beholden is "The Slide to Auschwitz" by Dr. C. Everett Koop, a pediatric surgeon of international renown and a devout Christian.

In Re New Humans

Jérôme Lejeune

My name is Jérôme Lejeune. Doctor in Medicine and in Science, I am in charge of the mentally defective outpatients at the Hôpital des Enfants Malades (Sick Children's Hospital of Paris). After spending ten years in full-time research, I am professor of fundamental genetics at the University Rene Descartes. Some twenty-three years ago I described the first chromosomal disease in our species, the extra chromosome 21, typical of mongolism. For this work I had the privilege of receiving the Kennedy award from the late President and the William Allen memorial medal from the American Academy of Arts and Sciences. With my colleagues at the Institut de Progenese of Paris, we are involved in the description of basic facts in human heredity. By a comparative study of many mammalian species, including the great apes, we are studying the chromosomal variations which occurred during evolution. In our species, we analyze more precisely the deleterious effects of some chromosomal aberrations. This very year we have demonstrated for the first time that a chromosomal disease could be amenable to therapy. In this fragile-X syndrome, associating a fragility of the X chromosome and severe mental retardation we have shown that a chemical treatment can cure the chromosomal lesion in tissue culture. Moreover, appropriate supply of these chemicals (monocarbons and their carrier molecules) also improves the behavior and the mental abilities of the affected children. Thus, the most fundamental research on mechanisms of life can lead to direct protection of endangered human lives. When does a man begin is the question to which I'll try to give the most precise answer actually available to Science. Modern biology teaches us that ancestors are united to their progeny by a continuous material link, for it is from the fertilization of the female cell (the ovum) by the male cell (the spermatozoa) that a new member of the species will emerge. Life has a very, very long history but each individual has a very neat beginning, the moment of its conception.

The material link is the molecular thread of DNA. In each reproductive cell this ribbon, roughly one meter long, is cut into pieces (23 in our species). Each segment is carefully coiled and packaged (like a magnetic tape in a mini-cassette) so that under the microscope it appears like a little rod, a chromosome.

Jérôme Lejeune (1926-1994) was a French pediatrician and geneticist. This is the text of his testimony (delivered on April 23, 1981), during Senate subcommittee hearings held in 1981 on then-North Carolina Senator Jesse Helms's version of the Human Life Bill (S 158).

As soon as the 23 paternally derived chromosomes are united, through fertilization, with the 23 maternal ones, the full genetic information, necessary and sufficient to express all the inborn qualities of the new individual, is gathered. Exactly as the introduction of a minicassette inside a tape recorder will allow the restitution of the symphony, the new being begins to express himself as soon as he has been conceived.

Nature sciences and the sciences of law speak the same language. Of an individual enjoying a robust health, a biologist would say he has a good constitution; of a society developing itself harmoniously to the benefit of all its members, a legislator would state, it has an equitable constitution.

A legislator could not conceive what a given law is, before all its terms have been clearly and fully spelled out. But when this full information has been given, and when the law has been voted for, then it can help defining the terms of the constitution.

Nature works the same way. The chromosomes are the tables of the law of life and when they have been gathered in the new being (the voting process is the fertilization) they fully spell out his personal constitution.

What is bewildering is the minuteness of the scripture. It is hard to believe, although beyond any possible doubt, that the whole genetic information necessary and sufficient to build our body and even our brain, the most powerful problem-solving device, even able to analyze the laws of the universe, could be epitomized so that its material substratum could fit neatly on the point of a needle!

Even more impressive, during the maturation of the reproductive cells, the genetic information is reshuffled in so many ways that each conceptus receives an entirely original combination which has never occurred before and will never again. Each conceptus is unique, and thus irreplaceable. Identical twins and true hermaphrodites are exceptions to the rule: one man one genetic make-up; but interestingly enough, these exceptions have to take place at the time of conception. Later accidents could not lead to harmonious development.

All these facts were known long ago and everybody was agreeing that test-tube babies, if produced, would demonstrate the autonomy of the conceptus, over which the bottle has no title of property. Test-tube babies now do exist.

If the ovum of a cow is fertilized by a bull's sperm, the tiny conceptus, floating freely in the liquid, starts immediately its cattle career. Normally it would travel for a week, through the fallopian tube, and reach the uterus. But thanks to modern technology it can travel much farther, even across the ocean! The best shipping equipment for such a two milligram cattle being is to introduce it into the fallopian tube of a female rabbit. (Air freight is much less than for a pregnant cow). At destination, the miniscule animal is carefully removed and delicately settled inside the uterus of a recipient cow. Months after the calf exhibits all the genetic endowment it received from its true parents (the donors of the ovum and of the sperm) and none of the qualities of its temporary container (the rabbit) nor of its uterine foster mother.

How many cells are needed to build an individual? Recent experiments spell out the answer. If very early conceptuses of mice are artificially disassembled (by a peculiar enzymatic treatment) their cells come apart. By mixing such suspensions of cells, coming from different embryos, one sees them reassembling again. If the tiny mass is then implanted in a recipient female, some little mice (very few indeed) manage to develop to term, completely normal. As theoretically expected by B. Mintz and demonstrated by Market and Peter, a chimeric mouse can derive from two or even three embryos, but no more. The maximum number of cells cooperating in the elaboration of an individual is three.

In full accordance with this empirical demonstration, the fertilized egg normally cleaves itself in two cells, one of them dividing again, thus forming the surprising odd number of three, encapsulated inside their protective bag, the *zona pellucida*.

To the best of our actual knowledge, the prerequisite for individuation (a stage containing three fundamental cells) is the next step following conception, minutes after it.

All this explains why Dr. Edwards and Steptoe could witness in vitro the fertilization of a ripe ovum from Mrs. Brown by a spermatozoa from Mr. Brown. The tiny conceptus they were implanting days later in the womb of Mrs. Brown could not be a tumor or an animal. It was in fact the incredibly young Louise Brown, now three years old.

The viability of a conceptus is extraordinary. Experimentally a mouse conceptus can be deep frozen (even to -269C°) and, after careful thawing, implanted successfully. For further growth, only a recipient uterine mucosa can supply the embryonic placenta with appropriate nutriments. In his life-capsule, the amniotic bag, the early being is just as viable as an astronaut on the moon in his space-suit: refueling with vital fluids is required from the mother-ship. This nurture is indispensable for survival but does not "make" the baby; no more than the most sophisticated space shuttle can produce an astronaut. Such a comparison becomes even more cogent when the fetus moves. Thanks to a refined sonar-like imagery, Dr. Ian Donald from England succeeded a year ago in producing a movie featuring the youngest star of the world, an eleven weeks old baby dancing in utero. The baby plays, so to speak, trampoline!

He bends his knees, pushes on the wall, soars up, and falls down again. Because his body has the same buoyancy as the amniotic fluid, he does not feel gravity and performs his dance in a very slow, graceful, and elegant way, impossible in any other place on the earth. Only astronauts in their gravity-free state can achieve such gentleness of motion. By the way, for the first walk in space, technologists had to decide where to adapt the tubes carrying the fluids. They finally chose the belt buckle of the scaphander, reinventing the umbilical cord.

Mr. Chairman and members, when I had the honor of testifying previously before the Senate, I took the liberty of referring to the universal fairy-tale of the man, smaller than the thumb.

At two months of age, the human being is less than one thumb's length from the head to the rump. He would fit at ease in a nut-shell, but everything is there: hands, feet, head, organs, brain, all are in place. His heart has been beating for a month already. Looking closely, you would see the palm creases and a fortune teller would read the good adventure of that tiny person. With a good magnifier the fingerprints could be detected. Every document is available for a national identity card.

With the extreme sophistication of the technics, we have invaded his privacy. Special hydrophones reveal the most primitive music: A deep, profound, reassuring hammering at some 60-70 per minute (the maternal heart), and a rapid, high-pitched cadence at some 150-170 (the heart of the fetus). These mixed tempos mimic those of the counterbass and of the maracas, which are the basic rhythms of any pop music.

We now know what he feels, we have listened to what he hears, smelled what he tastes and we have really seen him dancing full of grace and youth. Science has turned the fairy-tale of Tom Thumb into a true story, the one each of us has lived in the womb of his mother.

And to let you measure how precise the detection can be: If at the very beginning, just after conception, days before implantation, a single cell was removed from the little berry-looking individual, we could cultivate that cell and examine its chromosomes. If a student, looking at it under the microscope, could not recognize the number, the shape, and the banding pattern of these chromosomes, if he was not able to tell safely whether it comes from a chimpanzee being or from a human being, he would fail in his examination.

To accept the fact that, after fertilization has taken place, a new human has come into being is no longer a matter of taste or of opinion. The human nature of the human being from conception to old age is not a metaphysical contention, it is a plain experimental evidence.

The Human Life Bill:
Some Issues and Answers

Henry J. Hyde

Section 1. (a) The Congress finds that the life of each human being begins at conception.

(b) The Congress further finds that the fourteenth amendment to the Constitution of the United States protects all human beings.

Section 2. Upon the basis of these findings, and in the exercise of the powers of Congress, including its power under section 5 of the fourteenth amendment to the Constitution of the United States, the Congress hereby recognizes that for the purpose of enforcing the obligation of the States under the fourteenth amendment not to deprive persons of life without due process of law, each human life exists from conception, without regard to race, sex, age, health, defect, or condition of dependency, and for this purpose "person" includes all human beings.

Section 3. Congress further recognizes that each State has a compelling interest, independent of the status of unborn children under the fourteenth amendment, in protecting the lives of those within the State's jurisdiction whom the State rationally regards as human beings.

Those three sections of the pending Human Life Bill present some of the most fascinating legal and biological questions ever to face the Congress or the Courts.

Of course there are other controversial issues in this legislation, such as a proposed limitation of lower federal court jurisdiction, but the questions of when a human being's life begins, when personhood attaches and the constitutional power of Congress to make such determinations are of more interest to me and are presently engaging some of the finest medical and legal minds in the country.

Before addressing the question of when a human life begins, it is prudent to inquire whether an answer is possible, and if so, whether it makes any difference.

A certain amount of courage (or stubbornness—they are often the same) is required to press this inquiry in the face of the explicit contempt of such as A. Bartlett Giamatti, President of Yale, who advised his freshman class to avoid Moral Majority types as " . . . those who presume to know what God

---

Henry J. Hyde, a Republican member of the U.S. House of Representatives (IL) from 1975 to 2007, was the author of the Hyde Amendment, prohibiting (most) federal funding of abortion.

alone knows, which is when human life begins."

I am convinced that biology can tell us when an individual's human life begins. Wasn't the significance of the birth of Louise Brown that her conception was in a test tube?

It is instructive to study the semantic tactics of some academicians and biologists who support the abortion ethic. They choose to pose the relevant question as "when does human life begin?" and then to answer that there is no answer —we are dealing with an unsolvable mystery. But pose the question "when does an individual's life begin?" and answers are possible.

One need not be an historian to draw interesting parallels between the 17th Century astronomer Galileo and his struggle at the hands of "misguided ecclesiastics" unable to reconcile their theology with his notion of a unified cosmos. Today we see these roles exactly reversed, with many churchmen (among others) insisting that an individual's life begins at conception (and hence ought to be legally protectable) and some scientists and certain university presidents denying that such scientific information is even discoverable.

As for the need for such inquiry, it seems only sensible that Congress— which so often legislates on matters of life and death —seek to inform itself on when an individual's life commences. Legal consequences and constitutional rights come into play once we commence dealing with a human life. The time frame for attaching these consequences and rights cannot be a matter of indifference to responsible legislators.

The whole controversy became national in scope when the Supreme Court, in *Roe* v. *Wade* (410 U.S. 113, 1973), with Justice Blackmun speaking for the majority, asserted:

> We need not resolve the difficult question of when life begins. When those trained in the respective disciplines of medicine, philosophy and theology are unable to arrive at any consensus, the judiciary, at this point in the development of man's knowledge, is not in a position to speculate as to the answer.

As I read this statement, the Court is making at least three important points:

1. There is no consensus as to when life begins;

2. We (the Court) are therefore incompetent to make a declaration on this "difficult" question;

3. In any event, we don't need to do so to decide that the unborn is a non-person. It is not disrespectful to note that Dred Scott stands for the proposition (among others, of course) that the Supreme Court is not infallible. Its self-confessed inability to determine when a human's life begins does not foreclose Congress from exploring the question. Congress is uniquely structured to

hold hearings and evaluate conflicting testimony as a basis for determining public policy. The business of Congress is legislation, and the business of the Courts *ought* to be adjudication. It is crucial that we differentiate between several important inter-related but somewhat different terms—"actual human life," "biological human life" and "personhood." One leading doctor, opposed to this legislation (Dr. Leon Rosenberg of Yale University Medical School), told the Senators during the hearing that he knows of "no scientific evidence which bears on the question of when actual human life exists." This assertion was roundly criticized in a letter to the magazine *Science* (July 31, 1981) from Dr. C. B. Goodhart of Gonville and Caius College, Cambridge, England, who replied in part:

> But, leaving aside the question of what the word *actual* means with its theological overtones, Rosenberg would surely agree that the new *biological* human life begins with the activation of the egg at fertilization. The fertilized egg is certainly human, since it belongs to no other species than *Homo sapiens;* it is certainly alive, since it can die (as good a definition of life as most!); and it certainly constitutes a uniquely separate human organism, no longer forming any part of its mother's body and already genetically as distinct from both of its parents as it will ever be, right from the start. It is no less a separate organism because at this stage it may not represent one single individual, being still capable of developing into monozygotic twins; if there are problems here, they are theological rather than biological ones, however.
>
> Presumably, what Rosenberg means is that there is no scientific evidence bearing on the question of the existence of the human *person,* as distinct from biological life. Since only a human can have the status of a person, this is not a problem which arises with the development of other animal species. The biological life of a chimpanzee, for instance, starts with the fertilization of the egg, as it does with a human, and it then regularly develops to maturity and death. It is only with humans that there is this further problem as to whether and when the developing organism begins to exist as a person.

Clearly, it is the law's task (rather than biology's) to determine what value society will place on this biological human life, once it has begun. If we are to postpone "personhood" until some arbitrary time after biological life has begun, we must accept the anomaly of a class of humans—alive—but not to be recognized as possessing the human rights inherent in every person. There are plenty of historical precedents for this (the institution of slavery, as an obvious example) but no confirmed utilitarian can doubt that involuntary euthanasia of handicapped infants, the aged and unwanted, and the abortion of the innocently inconvenient pre-born are facilitated by simply classifying these defective or unwanted humans as non-persons.

The Fourteenth Amendment provides: "Nor shall any State deprive any person of life, liberty or property without due process of law." Could express words and intention be clearer in setting out a separate constitutional right to life?

Contrast this explicit constitutional guarantee of a right to life with the fuzzy foundation of the right to abortion which the Court said rested in a right to privacy it took them 105 years to discover.

How can this right to life be secured or enforced if life cannot be defined? The Court pronounced itself incapable of providing a definition and thereby signed a death warrant for over one and a half million unborn children annually. In the face of this inaction by the Court, in response to this massive epidemic of destruction, Congress has the responsibility to provide a definition securing the right to life guaranteed by the Fourteenth Amendment to every human, even if it is just a tiny island of humanity known as the fetus.

If it is accepted that human rights have a hierarchy, then the right to life must be primal. It provides the foundation for the structure of all other human rights, including the newly discovered constitutional right of privacy.

Now science not only has an answer, but it has *the* answer to the question of life's beginnings. This answer is based on fact, not opinion, on reason and observation rather than emotion and speculation. Science is not tainted by religious or philosophical bias, nor should it be colored by pro-abortion or anti-abortion prejudice.

So let us advance our inquiry one logical step at a time, remembering we are not asking a generic question about human life but rather about when *an individual's* human life has its beginning.

It is worth noting that of all the 22 expert witnesses who testified before the Senate Subcommittee on the Separation of Powers (chaired by Senator John East, of North Carolina) on the medical and biological questions, none ever claimed that unborn children are not alive nor that they belonged to any other species than human, or even that they were a part of the mother rather than a distinct individual human being.

Some, however, refused to acknowledge that "human being" means any individual which is genetically human. Rather they chose to define "humanness" with reference to various qualities of life that they deemed essential. But these were essentially philosophical or moral preferences having nothing to do with answering the medical-biological question "when does a human life begin?"

A fair summary of the voluminous testimony would conclude that the life of each human being (or any other individual belonging to a species that reproduces sexually) begins at conception. The male sperm cell and female egg cell, prior to conception, are only parts of the parents-to-be. When the sperm cell and egg cell unite in conception (a process also called fertilization) a new distinct individual being is created, of the same species as the parents.

Medical and biological literature universally agree on the origin of each human life. The report of Senator East's subcommittee has set out a representative sampling of this literature.[2]

Other testimony offered before the Subcommittee confirms that the life of each human being begins at conception. Though it was argued that human life is a continuum with no identifiable beginning, the words of Jerome Lejeune, M.D. (Professor of Fundamental Genetics, University of Rene Descartes, Paris, France) show that such arguments are not to the point of the Human Life Bill. "Life has a very, very long history, but each individual has a very neat beginning—the moment of its conception." Dr. Watson Bowes, Professor of Obstetrics and Gynecology at the University of Colorado School of Medicine testified that, "If we are talking, then, about the biological beginning of a human life or lives, as distinct from other human lives, the answer is most assuredly that it is at the time of conception—that is to say, the time at which a human ovum is fertilized by a human sperm." Dr. Bowes ended his prepared remarks by saying, "In conclusion, the beginning of a human life from a biological point of view is at the time of conception. This straightforward biological fact should not be distorted to serve sociological, political, or economic goals."[3]

When Is a Human Being a Person?

Acknowledging that biological life commences at fertilization of the female egg by the male sperm, the crucial question yet remains, "What value shall we assign to this new genetic package, this new entity that is both alive and of the human species?"

Obviously we now go beyond a purely scientific inquiry and are in the realm of philosophy.

When one asks "What is a person?" the answer supplied by Robert E. Joyce, Ph.D., Chairman of the Philosophy Department of St. John's University in Minnesota, is helpful. He has written that:

> A person is essentially a being that is naturally gifted (not self-gifted) with capacities or potentialities to know, love, desire, and relate to self and others in a self-reflective way. The person is—not by self but by nature—*able* to be aware of who he or she is and *able* to direct his or her own self in *accord with* this nature. A tree acts in accord with its nature, but does not direct itself that way—it is not consciously a tree. A dog or a dolphin acts in accord with its nature, but does not and cannot direct itself *as a self* in accord with its nature. A person can. The person's dignity and freedom are, at least partly, based on his or her capacity for *freely* acting in accordance with nature, rather than

merely existing. Our freedom as persons resides not so much in our ability to do as we please, but in our ability to act freely and deliberately as we were gifted.[4]

In his book, *Abortion, Law, Choice, and Morality,* Daniel Callahan has said:

> Abortion is not the destruction of a human person—for at no stage of its development does the conceptus fulfill the definition of a person, which implies a developed capacity for reasoning, willing, desiring, and relating to others—but is the destruction of an important and valuable form of human life.[5]

This view harmonizes with that of the majority in *Roe* v. *Wade*. But in response to this, Professor Joyce asserts:

> I would suggest that a person is not an individual with a *developed* capacity for reasoning, willing, desiring, and relating to others. A person is an individual with a *natural* capacity for these activities and relationships, whether this natural capacity is ever developed or not—i.e., whether he or she ever attains the functional capacity or not. Individuals of a rational, volitional, self-conscious *nature* may never attain or may lose the functional capacity for fulfilling this nature to any appreciable extent. But this inability to fulfill their nature does not negate or destroy the nature itself, even though it may, for us, render that nature more difficult to appreciate and love. That difficulty would seem to be a challenge for us as persons more than it is for them.
>
> Neither a human embryo nor a rabbit embryo has the functional capacity to think, will, desire, read, and write. The radical difference, from the very beginning of development, is that the human embryo actually has the natural capacity to act in these ways, whereas the rabbit embryo does not and never will. For all its concern about potentialities, the developmentalist approach fails to see the actuality upon which these potentialities are based. Every potential is itself an actuality. A person's potential to walk across the street is an actuality that the tree beside him does not have. A woman's potential to give birth to a baby is an actuality that a man does not have. The potential of a human *conceptus* to think and talk is an actuality. Even the potential to actuation (called "passive potency" by traditional philosophers) is itself an actuality that is not had by something lacking it.

These concepts argue that personhood is an endowment, not an achievement, and assert in Joyce's phrase that "Nature does not revolve around function. Function revolves around nature. Functions can come and go, but nature is dynamically stable." Often pre-born children are referred to as possessing "potential human life." But a little reflection reveals this is grossly inaccurate. At any moment of its existence a whole living entity—whether a goldfish or a fetus—is either alive or it is not. If it is alive, it is what its *nature* is, even though it is incomplete in its functional development. This idea is sometimes expressed by stating that a pregnant woman always gives birth to a human being—not a puppy or a rabbit.

Thus there really is no such thing as a potentially living organism. It either is alive or it is not. It possesses great potentiality but is not itself potential life. Therefore the single-celled person at conception is fully possessed of its personhood. It is thus endowed, but will use its inherent potential to achieve. It is no less a person because its functions are as yet undeveloped and thus cannot fully express its personality.

(This fact rejects the rationale for the pro-abortion term "pro-choice." Presumably the choice is whether or not the pregnant woman is to have a baby. But she already *has* a baby implanted in her womb, needing only time and nourishment to be born. The "choice," then, is whether to carry the baby to term—let it live and be born—or to kill it through abortion. Every pregnancy terminates. Abortion seeks to exterminate a pregnancy.)

At its roots we have a conflict of immense proportions between the Quality of Life ethic and the Sanctity of Life ethic. If Darwinism is to govern the human aspects of our society, then indeed the handicapped, retarded, insane, sickly, terminally ill, incorrigibly poor and the unwanted everywhere can be too much of a financial and emotional drain on those favored elite not so disadvantaged and who arrogate to themselves the crucial decisions as to who shall live and which of us fail to measure up—and thus should die. The implications of the Quality of Life ethic can be rather chilling depending on which group you belong to. I've often thought that the Quality of Life must have been pretty poor at Valley Forge where nearly 3000 men froze or starved to death. But to their everlasting glory, there was something more important to suffer and struggle for—and we should be grateful they shared this commitment.

It is not merely convenient—it is necessary—that combat soldiers dehumanize the enemy. This is the same necessary tactic employed by those advocating abortion in their war against the unborn—dehumanizing them.

That humanity (or humanness) is an objective fact rather than a subjective determination has important implications. If the latter were true, any human being that the State found undesirable could be re-defined as a non-person and hence disposable. Defenders of slavery justified their position in this manner.

The Philadelphia *Inquirer* in its magazine section of Sunday, August 2, 1981, published a feature story on "The Dreaded Complication." The complication so dreaded by abortionists is that the "products of conception" they seek to terminate will be born alive. The article describes a live, two-and-a-half-pound baby boy who survived the abortion whereupon " . . . a nurse took the squirming infant to a closet where dirty linens were stored . . . it was nothing new."

Much needs to be written about the struggle between the two competing ethics, the Quality of Life versus the Sanctity of Life. Suffice it for the purposes of this article to say that this country's tradition and history reflect a deeply ingrained respect for the Sanctity of Life. The Declaration of Independence affirms this belief in the majestic words:

> We hold these truths to be self-evident, that all men are created equal, that they are endowed by their Creator with certain unalienable rights, that among these are life, liberty, and the pursuit of happiness.

That some persons are unwanted or unloved does not exclude them from the family of humanity but, on the contrary, society must take special care of those who are least loved—if we maintain we are a caring and humane society.

As George Will has pointed out, we measure a society's ascent from barbarism by how it takes care of people. The unloved and unwanted are still human beings unless the State reserves the right of redefining them as subhuman. One of the clearest and most dispassionate outlines of the struggle is contained in a September 1970 editorial appearing in *California Medicine*—over two years before *Roe* v. *Wade* was decided:

> In defiance of the long-held Western ethic of intrinsic and equal value for every human life regardless of its stage, condition or status, abortion is becoming accepted by society as moral, right, and even necessary. It is worth noting that this shift in public attitude has affected the churches, the laws and public policy rather than the reverse.
>
> Since the old ethic has not yet been fully displaced, it has been necessary to separate the idea of abortion from the idea of killing, which continues to be socially abhorrent. The result has been a curious avoidance of the scientific fact, which everyone really knows, that human life begins at conception and is continuous whether intra- or extra-uterine until death.
>
> The very considerable semantic gymnastics which are required to rationalize abortion as anything but taking a human life would be ludicrous if they were not often put forth under socially impeccable auspices.

A final and troublesome question remains: Does Congress have the power to legislate in contradiction of a Supreme Court interpretation of the Constitution? In other words, is the Supreme Court really Supreme?

Professor Joseph P. Witherspoon, Maxey Professor of Law, University of Texas School of Law, has done the most exhaustive research I have seen on the problem. According to him, prior to adoption of the Thirteenth, Fourteenth and Fifteenth Amendments, various political leaders in America held that the Supreme Court could not bind the co-equal branches of the federal govern-ment so as to divest them of the power to perform their specific functions as delegated to them by the Constitution.

Thomas Jefferson, for example, stated his views as follows:

> To consider the judges as the ultimate arbiters of all constitutional questions— [is] a very dangerous doctrine indeed, and one which would place us under the despotism of an oligarchy. Our judges are as honest as other men, and not more so. They have, with others, the same passions for party, for power, and the privilege of their corps. Their maxim is, "boni judicis est ampliare jurisdictionem," and their power [is] the more dangerous as they are in office for life, and not responsible, as the other functionaries are, to the elective control. The Constitution has erected no such single tribunal, knowing that, to whatever hands confided, with the corruptions of time and party, its members would become despots. It has more wisely made all the departments coequal and cosovereign within themselves.[6]
>
> My construction of the Constitution is . . . that each department is truly independent of the others, and has an equal right to decide for itself what is the meaning of the Constitution in the cases submitted to its action, and especially where it is to act ultimately and without appeal.
>
> [Otherwise] [t]he Constitution . . . is a mere thing of wax, in the hands of the judiciary, which they may twist and shape into any form they please. It should be remembered, as an axiom of eternal truth in politics, that whatever power in any Government is independent, is absolute also; in theory only at first, while the spirit of the people is up, but in practice as fast as that relaxes. Independence can be trusted nowhere but with the people in mass.[7]

Similarly, President Andrew Jackson, in the message setting forth his veto of the Bank Bill on July 10, 1832, observed that

> It is maintained by the advocates of the bank that its constitutionality in all its features ought to be considered as settled by the precedent and by the decision of the Supreme Court. To this conclusion I cannot assent . . .
>
> If the opinion of the Supreme Court covered the whole ground of this act, it ought not to control the coordinate authorities of the Government. The Congress, the Executive, and the Court must each for itself be guided by its own opinion of the Constitution . . . It is as much the duty of the House of Representatives, of the Senate, and of the President to decide upon the constitutionality of any bill or resolution which may be presented to them for passage or approval as it is of the supreme judges when it may be brought before them for judicial decision. The opinion of the judges has no more authority over Congress than the opinion of Congress has over the judges, and on that point the President is independent of both. The authority of the Supreme Court must not, therefore, be permitted to control the Congress or the Executive when acting in their legislative capacities, but to have only such influence as the force of their reasoning may deserve.[8]

The views of Thomas Jefferson and Andrew Jackson, as well as the similar views of James Madison,[9] were very influential with the framers of the Thirteenth, Fourteenth and Fifteenth Amendments and with the States that ratified these amendments. In his debates with Senator Stephen A. Douglas, Abraham Lincoln had stated the nature and basis of the authority of the Congress to legislate in contradiction of a Supreme Court decision which it believed to be erroneous:

> We oppose the Dred Scott decision in a certain way . . . as a political rule which shall be binding on the voter, to vote for nobody who thinks it wrong, which shall be binding on the members of Congress or the President to favor no measure that does not actually concur with the principles of that decision. We do not propose to be bound by it as a political rule in that way, because we think it lays the foundation for spreading the evil (of slavery) into the States themselves. We propose so resisting it as to have it reversed if we can, and a new judicial rule established upon that subject.[10]

In his first inaugural address Lincoln stated one of the underlying reasons for the Republican Party position that Congress could by legislation give effect to an interpretation of the Constitution contrary to that of the Supreme Court:

> Nor do I deny that such decisions [of the Supreme Court on constitutional questions] must be binding in any case upon the parties to a suit as to the object of that suit, while they are also entitled to very high respect and consideration in all parallel cases by all other departments of the Government . . . At the same time, the candid citizen must confess that if the policy of the Government upon vital questions affecting the whole people is to be irrevocably fixed by decisions of the Supreme Court, the instant they are made in ordinary litigation between parties in personal actions the people will have ceased to be their own rulers, having to that extent practically resigned their Government into the hands of that eminent tribunal.[11]

Legal scholars dispute whether the Supreme Court's finding that the preborn is a non-person (*Roe* v. *Wade*) can be challenged by an Act of Congress. It is the position of many that once the Court has adjudicated this issue only the Court itself can reverse its finding.

But the Court, in *Roe* v. *Wade,* asserted its own incompetency to determine when human life begins, pointing out what they termed the absence of consensus on this issue. This factual vacuum would no longer be present should the Human Life Bill be adopted and signed into law. After hearings, the taking and evaluating of testimony, the findings of Congress—based on these hearings—should, according to established legal precedents, receive great deference by the Court. After all, Congress, a coordinate branch of government, will have filled the Court's proclaimed factual vacuum with its own findings and so a further Congressional determination that each pre-born human life is also a person within the meaning of the Fourteenth Amendment presents the Court with a fundamentally different question of Constitutional law than in *Roe* v. *Wade*.

Once the factual issue of whether the pre-born are human beings is determined in their favor, the Congress, based on this finding can properly declare each human life as endowed with personhood and hence protectable under the Constitution.

The legal environment, the legal landscape, will be different for the Court this time around. Instead of a vacuum there will be Congressionally legislated findings upon which to posit personhood and protection for the pre-born.

Of course the Supreme Court has the responsibility for interpreting the Constitution as it applies to specific cases. But where the Court confesses its inability to resolve questions that buttress such important and specific Constitutional rights—questions literally of life and death—is Congress powerless to do what it is uniquely structured to do, hold hearings, make findings and determine public policy?

As the East report states the issue, "The purpose of this legislation is not to impair the Supreme Court's power to review the Constitutionality of legislation, but to exercise the authority of Congress to disagree with the result of an earlier Supreme Court decision based on an investigation of facts and a decision concerning values that the Supreme Court declined to address."

The Human Life Bill will be reviewed by the Supreme Court, and thus the Court *will* have the last word. But in the interim, important dialogue will ensue between Congress and the Court and the void that supports *Roe* v. *Wade* will be supplanted by a legislative foundation that the Court will not and cannot be indifferent to.

The Fourteenth Amendment specifically forbids a State to deprive a person of life, and Section 5 of that Amendment expressly confers authority to Congress for the purpose of enforcing this guarantee through appropriate legislation. The Court is entitled to respect and deference in its adjudications and interpretations, but Congress likewise is entitled to respect and deference in its efforts to deal with questions of immense significance and fraught with profound public policy consequences.

To assert that Congress is necessarily impotent in the face of the Court's confessed impotence on the fundamental issue of when a human life begins is to concede a powerlessness on an issue of paramount importance that the Founding Fathers would be the first to reject, if not denounce.

The status of abortion, the existence and value to be accorded pre-natal life, are questions, in a democracy, that the elected representatives of the people must not be foreclosed from considering.

Anyone who has been involved in this controversy knows only too well that no subject generates emotional reaction more than abortion. Each side views the other as monstrously inhuman and uncaring—and thus demonstrates that each side *does* care, only from a different perspective and with a different set of values.

Ironically, support for protecting endangered species (the famous snail darter, for example) is a constant theme in Congress. "Save the Whale" organizations and legislation seeking to outlaw the trapping of wild animals have their effective spokesmen. Some Congressmen have even shared an ice floe with baby harp seals to dramatize their plight. But, strangely, many of those active in the cause of humane treatment for animals cannot bring themselves to much concern for the plight of the endangered unborn.

The heart of this issue, of course, is the humanity of the unborn. If you view the fetus as a blob of tissue, a sort of tumor, then surely it is disposable. But if you value the fetus as a pre-born child and respect human life as the ultimate value, all other considerations become secondary. Of course one's religious views can have an impact on whether the pre-born ought to be protected or not. Should you accept the notion that we humans are permitted to share with God as co-creators in the perpetuation of the human race, then clearly the act of conception (which is creation) takes on a special value.

This is not to say that many persons whose lives embrace religious convictions do not support abortion, because indeed they do, including some clergy.

On the other hand, Bernard N. Nathanson, M.D., an admitted atheist, in his 1979 book *Aborting America*[12] relates his personal odyssey from being a prominent abortionist to becoming a pro-life advocate. He bases his present conviction that abortion is a moral wrong on the Golden Rule—the very basis for a civilized society. He is unable to answer the question as to why he changed so dramatically except to say, as a medical doctor, he opened his mind to "the data" on human life, and its beginnings.

The humanity of the unborn has been called the "13th floor of human society." Everyone really knows it's there, but it is often more convenient to pretend it's not.

I'm not sure I want to passively accept a society in which parents have been told they have no responsibility toward their unborn children, and in which children are told they have no responsibilities toward their parents. This doesn't fit my definition of the caring humane society we pretend to be.

The views expressed 41 years ago during World War II by Dr. Joseph D.

Lee, a leader in modern obstetrical practice, which were printed in the 1940 edition of the *Yearbook of Obstetrics and Gynecology* are more relevant than ever:

> At the present time, when rivers of blood and tears of innocent men, women and children are flowing in most parts of the world, it seems almost silly to be contending over the right to life of an unknowable atom of human flesh in the uterus of a woman.
>
> No, it is not silly. On the contrary, it is of transcendent importance that there be in this chaotic world one high spot, however small, which is safe against the deluge of immorality and savagery that is sweeping over us. That we, the medical profession, hold to the principle of the sacredness of human life and of the rights of the individual, even though unborn, is proof that humanity is not yet lost . . .

NOTES

1. The three sections are quoted from the text of the current Senate version (S. 1741), re-introduced by Sen. Helms on Oct. 15, 1981; they differ somewhat in language (but little in content) from the original versions introduced by Sen. Jesse Helms in the Senate (S. 158) and by Rep. Henry Hyde in the House (H.R. 900) on Jan. 19, 1981; there is also another House version (H. R. 3225) at this writing. —JPM, Ed.
2. The Committee Print of Sen. East's subcommittee hearings, held April 23-June 19, 1981, was reported to the full Senate Judiciary Committee in December, 1981; the text of the Committee print (*sans* dissenting opinions), including the quotations from medical texts, is reprinted as *Appendix A* in this issue.—JPM, Ed.
3. The Subcommittee heard much testimony in the same vein. Dr. Hymie Gordon, Professor of Medical Genetics and physician at the Mayo Clinic, testified that, "[t]he individuality of the unborn baby is established at the very first second of its conception." Later, Dr. Gordon elaborated:

   > . . . I think we can now also say that the question of the beginning of life—when life begins—is no longer a question for theological or philosophical dispute. It is an established scientific fact. Theologians and philosophers may go on to debate the meaning of life or the purpose of life, but it is an established fact that all life, including human life, begins at the moment of conception.

   Later, Dr. Gordon remarked:

   > I have never ever seen in my own scientific reading, long before I became concerned with issues of life of this nature, that anyone has ever argued that life did not begin at the moment of conception and that it was a human conception if it resulted from the fertilization of the human egg by a human sperm. As far as I know, these have never been argued against.

   Dr. Micheline Matthews-Roth, a principal research associate in the Department of Medicine at the Harvard Medical School, after reviewing the scientific literature on the question of when the life of a human being begins, concluded her statement with these words:

   > So, in summary, it is incorrect to say that biological data cannot be decisive. In biology, as in any other branch of science, experiments repeated and confirmed by many different

workers using many different species of organisms do, indeed, prove that a particular biological finding is true.

And, so it is with the biological finding that an organism reproducing by sexual reproduction starts its life as one cell—the zygote—and throughout its existence belongs to the species of its parents. No experiments have disproved this finding.

So, therefore, it is scientifically correct to say that an individual human life begins at conception, when egg and sperm both join to form the zygote, and that this developing human always is a member of our species in all stages of life.

4. Robert E. Joyce, "When Does a Person Begin?" from *New Perspectives on Abortion* (Aletheia Books, 1981).

5. Daniel Callahan, *Abortion, Law, Choice and Morality* (The Macmillan Co.: New York, 1970), pp. 497-498.

6. Letter to William C. Jarvis, September 20, 1820, *The Writings of Thomas Jefferson* (Ford ed. (899), 160.

7. Letter to Judge Roane, September 6, 1819, as quoted by Rep. Philemon Bliss, *Cong. Globe, 35* Cong., 2nd Sess (Feb. 7, (1859), App. 7.

8. *Messages and Papers of the Presidents II* (Richardson ed. 1896), 576, 581-83.

9. Elliot, *Debates of the Federal Constitution* 4. (1836), 549-50.

10. *The Collected Works of Abraham Lincoln I* (Basler ed. 1953), 494, 516.

11. Richardson, *Messages and Papers of the Presidents* 5 (1897), 9-10.

12. Nathanson, *Aborting America* (Doubleday & Co.: New York, 1979).

Life: Defining the Beginning by the End

Maureen L. Condic

W hat defines the beginning of human life? This question has been the topic of considerable legal and social debate over the years since the Supreme Court's *Roe* v. *Wade* decision—debate that has only been intensified by the recent controversies over human embryonic stem cells and human cloning. Answers to this question run the full gamut from those who argue that life begins at conception (the view of more than one major world religion) to those arguing that babies are not to be considered fully human until a month after birth (the position of Princeton Professor of Bioethics Peter Singer).

The range of dissent and disagreement on the question of when human life begins has led many to believe it cannot be reasonably resolved in a pluralistic society. Courts have ruled that the diversity of opinion on the topic precludes a judicial resolution, requiring instead that the matter be addressed in the political arena, where accommodation of divergent views can be wrought through debate and compromise. Many Americans appear equally unwilling to impose a single interpretation on society, preferring instead to allow decisions regarding the beginning of life to be largely a matter of personal choice.

While reluctance to impose a personal view on others is deeply ingrained in American society, one must question the legitimacy of such reluctance when the topic of our "imposition" is a matter (quite literally) of life and death. Few beyond the irrationally obdurate would maintain that human embryos are anything other than biologically Homo sapiens and alive, even at the earliest developmental stages. Equally few would contest the fact that, at early stages of embryonic development, human embryos bear little resemblance to anything we easily identify as "human." For most people, reconciling these two facts involves the uncomfortably fuzzy process of drawing a line somewhere during the continuously changing process of human prenatal development and asserting: "There. That's when human life begins—at least for me." It is precisely the subjectivity and inaccuracy of this decision that fuels our discomfort at "imposing" it on others.

In contrast to the widespread disagreement over when human life begins, there is a broad social and legal consensus regarding when human life ends. Rarely has the point been made that the definition of human death can be

Maureen L. Condic is an Associate Professor of Neurobiology and Anatomy at the University of Utah. This essay, reprinted in the Spring 2003 *Human Life Review,* originally appeared in *First Things* and is reprinted with permission. Copyright (c) 2003 First Things 133 (May 2003).

applied to the question of when life commences with compelling symmetry. The definition of when life ends is both scientific and objective, and does not depend on personal belief or moral viewpoint. The current medical and legal understanding of death unambiguously defines both when human life ends and when it begins in a manner that is widely accepted and consistent with the legal and moral status of human beings at all stages of life.

Death is something most people readily recognize when they see it. People express very little confusion about the difference between a living person and a corpse. Surprisingly, however, the distinction is not as clear from a medical and scientific perspective. There is very little biologic difference between a living person in the instant before death and the body of that person an instant after death. Yet some property has clearly departed from the body in death, and that property is precisely the element that defines "human life." What, then, is the difference between live persons and dead ones? How is death defined medically and scientifically?

The question of when and under precisely what conditions people are viewed as "dead" has itself been the subject of considerable debate. Traditionally, the medical profession considered a person dead when his heart stopped beating—a condition that rapidly results in the death of the cells of the body due to loss of blood flow. As the life-saving potential of organ transplants became increasingly apparent in the 1960s, the medical community undertook a reexamination of the medical standards for death. Waiting until the heart stops beating results in considerable damage to otherwise transplantable organs. After a long and contentious debate, a new standard of death was proposed in 1968 that defined "brain death" as the critical difference between living persons and corpses, a standard that is now widely (although not universally) accepted throughout the world.

Brain death occurs when there has been irreversible damage to the brain, resulting in a complete and permanent failure of brain function. Following the death of the brain, the person stops thinking, sensing, moving, breathing, or performing any other function, although many of the cells in the brain remain "alive" following loss of brain function. The heart can continue to beat spontaneously for some time following death of the brain (even hearts that have been entirely removed from the body will continue to beat for a surprisingly long period), but eventually the heart ceases to function due to loss of oxygen. The advantage of brain death as a legal and medical definition for the end of life is that the quality of organs for transplant can be maintained by maintaining artificial respiration. So long as oxygen is artificially supplied, the heart will continue to beat and the other organs of the body will be maintained in the same state they were prior to death of the brain.

Defining death as the irreversible loss of brain function remains for some a controversial decision. The fact that the cells and organs of the body can be maintained after the death of the individual is a disturbing concept. The feeling that corpses are being kept artificially "alive" as medical zombies for the convenient culture of transplantable organs can be quite discomforting, especially when the body in question is that of a loved one. Nonetheless, it is important to realize that this state of affairs is essentially no different from what occurs naturally following death by any means. On a cellular and molecular level, nothing changes in the instant of death. Immediately following death, most of the cells in the body are still alive, and for a time at least, they continue to function normally. Maintaining heartbeat and artificial respiration simply extends this period of time. Once the "plug is pulled," and the corpse is left to its own devices, the cells and organs of the body undergo the same slow death by oxygen deprivation they would have experienced had medical science not intervened.

What has been lost at death is not merely the activity of the brain or the heart, but more importantly the ability of the body's parts (organs and cells) to function together as an integrated whole. Failure of a critical organ results in the breakdown of the body's overall coordinated activity, despite the continued normal function (or "life") of other organs. Although cells of the brain are still alive following brain death, they cease to work together in a coordinated manner to function as a brain should. Because the brain is not directing the lungs to contract, the heart is deprived of oxygen and stops beating. Subsequently, all of the organs that are dependent on the heart for blood flow cease to function as well. The order of events can vary considerably (the heart can cease to function, resulting in death of the brain, for example), but the net effect is the same. Death occurs when the body ceases to act in a coordinated manner to support the continued healthy function of all bodily organs. Cellular life may continue for some time following the loss of integrated bodily function, but once the ability to act in a coordinated manner has been lost, "life" cannot be restored to a corpse—no matter how "alive" the cells composing the body may yet be.

It is often asserted that the relevant feature of brain death is not the loss of integrated bodily function, but rather the loss of higher-order brain activities, including consciousness. However, this view does not reflect the current legal understanding of death. The inadequacy of equating death with the loss of cognitive function can be seen by considering the difference between brain death and "persistent vegetative state" or irreversible coma. Individuals who have entered a persistent vegetative state due to injury or disease have lost all higher brain functions and are incapable of consciousness. Nonetheless, integrated bodily function is maintained in these patients due to the continued activity of lower-order brain centers. Although such patients are clearly in a lamentable medical state, they are also clearly alive; converting such patients into corpses requires some form of euthanasia.

Despite considerable pressure from the medical community to define persistent vegetative state as a type of brain death (a definition that would both expand the pool of organ donors and eliminate the high medical costs associated with maintaining people in this condition), the courts have repeatedly refused to support persistent vegetative state as a legal definition of death. People whose bodies continue to function in an integrated manner are legally and medically alive, despite their limited (or absent) mental function. Regardless of how one may view the desirability of maintaining patients in a persistent vegetative state (this being an entirely distinct moral and legal question), there is unanimous agreement that such patients are not yet corpses. Even those who advocate the withdrawal of food and water from patients in persistent vegetative state couch their position in terms of the "right to die," fully acknowledging that such patients are indeed "alive." While the issues surrounding persistent vegetative state are both myriad and complex, the import of this condition for understanding the relationship between mental function and death is clear: the loss of integrated bodily function, *not* the loss of higher mental ability, is the defining legal characteristic of death.

What does the nature of death tell us about the nature of human life? The medical and legal definition of death draws a clear distinction between living cells and living organisms. Organisms are living beings composed of parts that have separate but mutually dependent functions. While organisms are made of living cells, living cells themselves do not necessarily constitute an organism. The critical difference between a collection of cells and a living organism is the ability of an organism to act in a coordinated manner for the continued health and maintenance of the body as a whole. It is precisely this ability that breaks down at the moment of death, however death might occur. Dead bodies may have plenty of live cells, but their cells no longer function together in a coordinated manner. We can take living organs and cells from dead people for transplant to patients without a breach of ethics precisely because corpses are no longer living human beings. Human life is defined by the ability to function as an integrated whole—not by the mere presence of living human cells.

What does the nature of death tell us about the *beginning* of human life?

From the earliest stages of development, human embryos clearly function as organisms. Embryos are not merely collections of human cells, but living creatures with all the properties that define any organism as distinct from a group of cells; embryos are capable of growing, maturing, maintaining a physiologic balance between various organ systems, adapting to changing circumstances, and repairing injury. Mere groups of human cells do nothing like this under any circumstances. The embryo generates and organizes distinct tissues that function in a coordinated manner to maintain the continued growth and health of the developing body. Even within the fertilized egg itself there are distinct "parts" that must work together—specialized regions of cytoplasm that will give rise to unique derivatives once the fertilized egg divides into separate cells. Embryos are in full possession of the very characteristic that distinguishes a living human being from a dead one: the ability of all cells in the body to function together as an organism, with all parts acting in an integrated manner for the continued life and health of the body as a whole.

Linking human status to the nature of developing embryos is neither subjective nor open to personal opinion. Human embryos are living human beings precisely because they possess the single defining feature of human life that is lost in the moment of death—the ability to function as a coordinated organism rather than merely as a group of living human cells.

What are the advantages of defining the beginning of human life in the same manner that we define its end, based on the integrated organismal function of human beings? To address this question, the alternative arguments regarding when life begins must be briefly considered. While at first inspection, there appear to be many divergent opinions regarding when human life commences, the common arguments are only of three general types: arguments from form, arguments from ability, and arguments from preference. The subjective and arbitrary nature of these arguments stands in stark contrast to the objective and unambiguous definition that organismal function provides for both the beginning and end of human life.

Of all the arguments regarding when human life begins, the most basic, and perhaps most intuitive, is that to be human, one must *look* human. Early human embryos are often described as "merely a ball of cells," and for many, it is difficult to imagine that something that looks more like a bag of marbles than a baby could possibly be a human being. Fundamentally, this argument asserts that human life is worthy of respect depending on appearance. When plainly stated, this conclusion is quite disturbing and also quite problematic. What level of malformation are we willing to accept before we revoke the right to continued existence? How are we to view children whose mature form will not be completely manifest until puberty? Form alone is a profoundly trivial and capricious basis for assigning human worth, and one that cannot be applied without considerable and obvious injustice.

The superficiality of equating worth with form is sufficient for most to reject this argument and retreat to a functional definition: form per se is not the issue; rather, it is the ability to function as a human being that defines the beginning of human life. Human beings are capable of a number of distinctive functions (self-awareness, reason, language, and so forth) that are acquired gradually over prenatal life as development proceeds. Therefore, the argument goes, human worth is also gradually acquired, with early embryos being less human than more developed fetuses.

A number of seemingly independent arguments regarding when life begins are in fact variations on this argument from ability. Thus, the proposal that human life begins when the fetus becomes "viable," or capable of surviving outside of the womb, is a subset of the ability argument that gives conclusive weight to the suite of abilities required for survival independent of the mother. Similarly, the common argument that embryos are human when they are in the womb of the mother (where they can develop into babies), while embryos generated in the laboratory are not, is also a variation on the ability argument that equates developmental ability with human life and worth.

While the argument from ability is less superficial than the argument from form alone, it is no less problematic. As noted above, functional definitions have been repeatedly rejected as a legal basis for the definition of death, in part due to their arbitrary nature. One can certainly identify any number of elderly and disabled people who are less functionally adept than newborn infants—and perhaps even late-term fetuses. While Western culture has a strong tradition of meritocracy, providing greater economic and social rewards to those who demonstrate greater achievement, basic human rights are not meted out according to performance. Unless we are willing to assign "personhood" proportionate to ability (young children, for example, might be only 20 percent human, while people with myopia 95 percent), the limited abilities of prenatal humans are irrelevant to their status as human beings.

The final and perhaps the most emotionally compelling argument for assigning human status to a developing embryo is the extent to which parents desire a child. Yet the argument from being wanted, which equates status as a human being with the desire of a second party who has the power to confer or deny that status, essentially reduces the definition of a human being to a matter of preference. You are human because I choose to view you that way. The fact that human status can be positively conferred for "wanted" embryos as well as denied for the "unwanted" illustrates the fundamental arbitrariness of this argument. The preferences of individuals who possess the power to impose them on others are hardly a compelling basis for legislation on human life.

Despite the apparent diversity of views regarding when human life begins, the common arguments thus reduce to three general classes (form, ability, and preference), all of which are highly subjective and impossible to reconcile with our current legal and moral view of postnatal human worth. It is, in fact, the subjectivity and inconsistency of these views, rather than their diversity, that makes them so unsatisfying as a basis for legislation on human life.

Unlike other definitions, understanding human life to be an intrinsic property of human organisms does not require subjective judgments regarding "quality of life" or relative worth. A definition based on the organismal nature of human beings acknowledges that individuals with differing appearance, ability, and "desirability" are, nonetheless, equally human. It is precisely the objective nature of such a definition (compared to vague "quality of life" assessments) that has made organismal function so compelling a basis for the legal definition of death.

Once the nature of human beings as organisms has been abandoned as the basis for assigning legal personhood, it is difficult to propose an alternative definition that could not be used to deny humanity to virtually anyone. Arguments that deny human status to embryos based on form, ability, or choice can be readily turned against adult humans who have imperfect form, limited ability, or who simply constitute an inconvenience to more powerful individuals or groups. Indeed, such arguments can be quite protean in their ability to deny rights to anyone not meeting an arbitrary criterion for humanity. Abraham Lincoln made this very point regarding arguments based on form, ability, and choice that were put forth in his day to justify the institution of slavery:

> It is *color*, then; the lighter having the right to enslave the darker? Take care. By this rule, you are to be slave to the first man you meet with a fairer skin than your own.
>
> You do not mean *color* exactly? You mean the whites are *intellectually* the superiors of the blacks, and, therefore, have the right to enslave them? Take care again. By this rule, you are to be slave to the first man you meet with an intellect superior to your own.
>
> But, say you, it is a question of *interest*; and, if you can make it your *interest*, you have the right to enslave another. Very well. And if he can make it his interest, he has the right to enslave you.

Postnatal humans run very little risk that embryos will someday organize politically to impose restrictions on the rights of "the born." However, once society has accepted a particular justification for denying rights to one class of individuals, the same justification can readily be applied to other classes by appealing to the simple argument: "Society has *already determined* that form, ability, or preference defines human life and thereby restricts human rights. Why should the same standard not be applied in this case?" In American society and jurisprudence, arguments from accepted precedent carry great emotional and legal force. Society must determine whether it is willing to accept the current subjective and arbitrary basis for determining the status of prenatal human beings as a legitimate precedent for future legislation on human rights.

Embryos are genetically unique human organisms, fully possessing the integrated biologic function that defines human life at all stages of development, continuing throughout adulthood until death. The ability to act as an integrated whole is the *only* function that departs from our bodies in the moment of death, and is therefore the defining characteristic of "human life." This definition does not depend on religious belief or subjective judgment. From the landmark case of Karen Ann Quinlan (1976) on, the courts have consistently upheld organismal function as the legal definition of human life. Failure to apply the same standard that so clearly defines the end of human life to its beginning is both inconsistent and unwarranted.

The conclusion that human life is defined by integrated (organismal) function has wide-reaching implications, both political and moral. While the public domain has limited authority to promote morality, it does have both the power and the responsibility to prevent harm to individuals. A consistent definition of what constitutes human life, both at its beginning and at its end, requires that current legislation dealing with prenatal human life be considered in light of both biological fact and accepted legal precedent regarding the definition of human life. If current legislation enables and supports the killing of human beings based on a scientifically flawed understanding of human life, laws can and should be revised. Clearly, such a revision would not be without political cost. Yet allowing life-or-death decisions to be based on arbitrary or capricious definitions is also a course of action that is not without considerable social and moral cost.

Abortion and the Conscience of the Nation

Ronald Reagan

The 10th anniversary of the Supreme Court decision in *Roe* v. *Wade* is a good time for us to pause and reflect. Our nationwide policy of abortion-on-demand through all nine months of pregnancy was neither voted for by our people nor enacted by our legislators—not a single state had such unrestricted abortion before the Supreme Court decreed it to be national policy in 1973. But the consequences of this judicial decision are now obvious: Since 1973, more than 15 million unborn children have had their lives snuffed out by legalized abortions. That is over ten times the number of Americans lost in all our nation's wars.

Make no mistake, abortion-on-demand is not a right granted by the Constitution. No serious scholar, including one disposed to agree with the Court's result, has argued that the framers of the Constitution intended to create such a right. Shortly after the *Roe* v. *Wade* decision, Professor John Hart Ely, now Dean of Stanford Law School, wrote that the opinion "is not constitutional law and gives almost no sense of an obligation to try to be." Nowhere do the plain words of the Constitution even hint at a "right" so sweeping as to permit abortion up to the time the child is ready to be born. Yet that is what the Court ruled.

As an act of "raw judicial power" (to use Justice White's biting phrase), the decision by the seven-man majority in *Roe* v. *Wade* has so far been made to stick. But the Court's decision has by no means settled the debate. Instead, *Roe* v. *Wade* has become a continuing prod to the conscience of the nation.

Abortion concerns not just the unborn child, it concerns every one of us. The English poet, John Donne, wrote: " . . . any man's death diminishes me, because I am involved in mankind; and therefore never send to know for whom the bell tolls; it tolls for thee."

We cannot diminish the value of one category of human life—the unborn—without diminishing the value of all human life. We saw tragic proof of this truism last year when the Indiana courts allowed the starvation death of "Baby Doe" in Bloomington because the child had Down's Syndrome.

Many of our fellow citizens grieve over the loss of life that has followed *Roe* v. *Wade*. Margaret Heckler, soon after being nominated to head the largest department of our government, Health and Human Services, told an audience that she believed abortion to be the greatest moral crisis facing our

Ronald Reagan was the fortieth president of the United States. He wrote this essay, which was first published in 1983, especially for the *Human Life Review*.

country today. And the revered Mother Teresa, who works in the streets of Calcutta ministering to dying people in her world-famous mission of mercy, has said that "the greatest misery of our time is the generalized abortion of children."

Over the first two years of my Administration I have closely followed and assisted efforts in Congress to reverse the tide of abortion—efforts of Congressmen, Senators and citizens responding to an urgent moral crisis. Regrettably, I have also seen the massive efforts of those who, under the banner of "freedom of choice," have so far blocked every effort to reverse nationwide abortion-on-demand.

Despite the formidable obstacles before us, we must not lose heart. This is not the first time our country has been divided by a Supreme Court decision that denied the value of certain human lives. The *Dred Scott* decision of 1857 was not overturned in a day, or a year, or even a decade. At first, only a minority of Americans recognized and deplored the moral crisis brought about by denying the full humanity of our black brothers and sisters; but that minority persisted in their vision and finally prevailed. They did it by appealing to the hearts and minds of their countrymen, to the truth of human dignity under God. From their example, we know that respect for the sacred value of human life is too deeply engrained in the hearts of our people to remain forever suppressed. But the great majority of the American people have not yet made their voices heard, and we cannot expect them to—any more than the public voice arose against slavery—*until* the issue is clearly framed and presented.

What, then, is the real issue? I have often said that when we talk about abortion, we are talking about two lives—the life of the mother and the life of the unborn child. Why else do we call a pregnant woman a mother? I have also said that anyone who doesn't feel sure whether we are talking about a second human life should clearly give life the benefit of the doubt. If you don't know whether a body is alive or dead, you would never bury it. I think this consideration itself should be enough for all of us to insist on protecting the unborn.

The case against abortion does not rest here, however, for medical practice confirms at every step the correctness of these moral sensibilities. Modern medicine treats the unborn child as a patient. Medical pioneers have made great breakthroughs in treating the unborn—for genetic problems, vitamin deficiencies, irregular heart rhythms, and other medical conditions. Who can forget George Will's moving account of the little boy who underwent brain surgery six times during the nine weeks before he was born? Who is the *patient* if not that tiny unborn human being who can feel pain when he or she is approached by doctors who come to kill rather than to cure?

The real question today is not when human life begins, but, *What is the value of human life?* The abortionist who reassembles the arms and legs of a tiny baby to make sure all its parts have been torn from its mother's body can hardly doubt whether it is a human being. The real question for him and for all of us is whether that tiny human life has a God-given right to be protected by the law—the same right we have.

What more dramatic confirmation could we have of the real issue than the Baby Doe case in Bloomington, Indiana? The death of that tiny infant tore at the hearts of all Americans because the child was undeniably a live human being—one lying helpless before the eyes of the doctors and the eyes of the nation. The real issue for the courts was *not* whether Baby Doe was a human being. The real issue was whether to protect the life of a human being who had Down's Syndrome, who would probably be mentally handicapped, but who needed a routine surgical procedure to unblock his esophagus and allow him to eat. A doctor testified to the presiding judge that, even with his physical problem corrected, Baby Doe would have a "non-existent" possibility for "a minimally adequate quality of life"—in other words, that retardation was the equivalent of a crime deserving the death penalty. The judge let Baby Doe starve and die, and the Indiana Supreme Court sanctioned his decision.

Federal law does not allow federally assisted hospitals to decide that Down's Syndrome infants are not worth treating, much less to decide to starve them to death. Accordingly, I have directed the Departments of Justice and HHS to apply civil rights regulations to protect handicapped newborns. All hospitals receiving federal funds must post notices which will clearly state that failure to feed handicapped babies is prohibited by federal law. The basic issue is whether to value and protect the lives of the handicapped, whether to recognize the sanctity of human life. This is the same basic issue that underlies the question of abortion.

The 1981 Senate hearings on the beginning of human life brought out the basic issue more clearly than ever before. The many medical and scientific witnesses who testified disagreed on many things, but not on the *scientific* evidence that the unborn child is alive, is a distinct individual, or is a member of the human species. They did disagree over the *value* question, whether to give value to a human life at its early and most vulnerable stages of existence.

Regrettably, we live at a time when some persons do *not* value all human life. They want to pick and choose which individuals have value. Some have said that only those individuals with "consciousness of self" are human beings. One such writer has followed this deadly logic and concluded that "shocking as it may seem, a newly born infant is not a human being."

A Nobel Prize winning scientist has suggested that if a handicapped child "were not declared fully human until three days after birth, then all parents could be allowed the choice." In other words, "quality control" to see if newly born human beings are up to snuff.

Obviously, some influential people want to deny that every human life has intrinsic, sacred worth. They insist that a member of the human race must have certain qualities before they accord him or her status as a "human being."

Events have borne out the editorial in a California medical journal which explained three years before *Roe* v. *Wade* that the social acceptance of abortion is a "defiance of the long-held Western ethic of intrinsic and equal value for every human life regardless of its stage, condition, or status."

Every legislator, every doctor, and every citizen needs to recognize that the real issue is whether to affirm and protect the sanctity of all human life, or to embrace a social ethic where some human lives are valued and others are not. As a nation, we must choose between the sanctity-of-life ethic and the "quality-of-life" ethic.

I have no trouble identifying the answer our nation has always given to this basic question, and the answer that I hope and pray it will give in the future. America was founded by men and women who shared a vision of the value of each and every individual. They stated this vision clearly from the very start in the Declaration of Independence, using words that every schoolboy and schoolgirl can recite:

> We hold these truths to be self-evident, that all men are created equal, that they are endowed by their Creator with certain unalienable rights, that among these are life, liberty, and the pursuit of happiness.

We fought a terrible war to guarantee that one category of mankind—black people in America—could not be denied the inalienable rights with which their Creator endowed them. The great champion of the sanctity of all human life in that day, Abraham Lincoln, gave us his assessment of the Declaration's purpose. Speaking of the framers of that noble document, he said:

> This was their majestic interpretation of the economy of the Universe. This was their lofty, and wise, and noble understanding of the justice of the Creator to His creatures. Yes, gentlemen, to all His creatures, to the whole great family of man. In their enlightened belief, nothing stamped with the divine image and likeness was sent into the world to be trodden on . . . . They grasped not only the whole race of man then living, but they reached forward and seized upon the farthest posterity. They erected a beacon to guide their children and their children's children, and the countless myriads who should inhabit the earth in other ages.

He warned also of the danger we would face if we closed our eyes to the value of life in any category of human beings:

> I should like to know if taking this old Declaration of Independence, which declares that all men are equal upon principle and making exceptions to it where will it stop. If one man says it does not mean a Negro, why not another say it does not mean some other man?

When Congressman John A. Bingham of Ohio drafted the Fourteenth Amendment to guarantee the rights of life, liberty, and property to all human beings, he explained that *all* are "entitled to the protection of American law, because its divine spirit of equality declares that all men are created equal." He said the rights guaranteed by the amendment would therefore apply to "any human being." Justice William Brennan, writing in another case decided only the year before *Roe* v. *Wade,* referred to our society as one that "strongly affirms the sanctity of life."

Another William Brennan—not the Justice—has reminded us of the terrible consequences that can follow when a nation rejects the sanctity of life ethic:

> The cultural environment for a human holocaust is present whenever any society can be misled into defining individuals as less than human and therefore devoid of value and respect.

As a nation today, we have *not* rejected the sanctity of human life. The American people have not had an opportunity to express their view on the sanctity of human life in the unborn. I am convinced that Americans do not want to play God with the value of human life. It is not for us to decide who is worthy to live and who is not. Even the Supreme Court's opinion in *Roe* v. *Wade* did not explicitly reject the traditional American idea of intrinsic worth and value in all human life; it simply dodged this issue.

The Congress has before it several measures that would enable our people to reaffirm the sanctity of human life, even the smallest and the youngest and the most defenseless. The Human Life Bill expressly recognizes the unborn as human beings and accordingly protects them as persons under our Constitution. This bill, first introduced by Senator Jesse Helms, provided the vehicle for the Senate hearings in 1981 which contributed so much to our understanding of the real issue of abortion.

The Respect Human Life Act, just introduced in the 98th Congress, states in its first section that the policy of the United States is "to protect innocent life, both before and after birth." This bill, sponsored by Congressman Henry Hyde and Senator Roger Jepsen, prohibits the federal government from performing abortions or assisting those who do so, except to save the life of the mother. It also addresses the pressing issue of infanticide which, as we have seen, flows inevitably from permissive abortion as another step in the denial of the inviolability of innocent human life.

I have endorsed each of these measures, as well as the more difficult route of constitutional amendment, and I will give these initiatives my full support. Each of them, in different ways, attempts to reverse the tragic policy of abortion-on-demand imposed by the Supreme Court ten years ago. Each of them is a decisive way to affirm the sanctity of human life.

We must all educate ourselves to the reality of the horrors taking place. Doctors today know that unborn children can feel a touch within the womb and that they respond to pain. But how many Americans are aware that abortion techniques are allowed today, in all 50 states, that burn the skin of a baby with a salt solution, in an agonizing death that can last for hours?

Another example: Two years ago, the *Philadelphia Inquirer* ran a Sunday special supplement on "The Dreaded Complication." The "dreaded complication" referred to in the article—the complication feared by doctors who perform abortions—is the *survival* of the child despite all the painful attacks during the abortion procedure. Some unborn children *do* survive the late-term abortions the Supreme Court has made legal. Is there any question that these victims of abortion deserve our attention and protection? Is there any question that those who *don't* survive were living human beings before they were killed?

Late-term abortions, especially when the baby survives, but is then killed by starvation, neglect, or suffocation, show once again the link between abortion and infanticide. The time to stop both is now. As my Administration acts to stop infanticide, we will be fully aware of the real issue that underlies the death of babies before and soon after birth.

Our society has, fortunately, become sensitive to the rights and special needs of the handicapped, but I am shocked that physical or mental handicaps of newborns are still used to justify their extinction. This Administration has a Surgeon General, Dr. C. Everett Koop, who has done perhaps more than any other American for handicapped children, by pioneering surgical techniques to help them, by speaking out on the value of their lives, and by working with them in the context of loving families. You will not find his former patients advocating the so-called "quality-of-life" ethic.

I know that when the true issue of infanticide is placed before the American people, with all the facts openly aired, we will have no trouble deciding that a mentally or physically handicapped baby has the same intrinsic worth and right to life as the rest of us. As the New Jersey Supreme Court said two decades ago, in a decision upholding the sanctity of human life, "a child need not be perfect to have a worthwhile life."

Whether we are talking about pain suffered by unborn children, or about late-term abortions, or about infanticide, we inevitably focus on the humanity of the unborn child. Each of these issues is a potential rallying point for the sanctity of life ethic. Once we as a nation rally around any one of these issues to affirm the sanctity of life, we will see the importance of affirming this principle across the board.

Malcolm Muggeridge, the English writer, goes right to the heart of the matter: "Either life is always and in all circumstances sacred, or intrinsically of no account; it is inconceivable that it should be in some cases the one, and in some the other." The sanctity of innocent human life is a principle that Congress should proclaim at every opportunity.

It is possible that the Supreme Court itself may overturn its abortion rulings. We need only recall that in *Brown* v. *Board of Education* the Court reversed its own earlier "separate-but-equal" decision. I believe if the Supreme Court took another look at *Roe* v. *Wade,* and considered the real issue between the sanctity-of-life ethic and the quality-of-life ethic, it would change its mind once again.

As we continue to work to overturn *Roe* v. *Wade,* we must also continue to lay the groundwork for a society in which abortion is not the accepted answer to unwanted pregnancy. Pro-life people have already taken heroic steps, often at great personal sacrifice, to provide for unwed mothers. I recently spoke about a young pregnant woman named Victoria, who said, "In this society we save whales, we save timber wolves and bald eagles and Coke bottles. Yet, everyone wanted me to throw away my baby." She has been helped by Sav-a-Life, a group in Dallas, which provides a way for unwed mothers to preserve the human life within them when they might otherwise be tempted to resort to abortion. I think also of House of His Creation in Coatesville, Pennsylvania, where a loving couple has taken in almost 200 young women in the past ten years. They have seen, as a fact of life, that the girls are *not* better off having abortions than saving their babies. I am also reminded of the remarkable Rossow family of Ellington, Connecticut, who have opened their hearts and their home to nine handicapped adopted and foster children.

The Adolescent Family Life Program, adopted by Congress at the request of Senator Jeremiah Denton, has opened new opportunities for unwed mothers to give their children life. We should not rest until our entire society echoes the tone of John Powell in the dedication of his book, *Abortion: The Silent Holocaust,* a dedication to every woman carrying an unwanted child:

"Please believe that you are not alone. There are many of us that truly love you, who want to stand at your side, and help in any way we can." And we can echo the always-practical woman of faith, Mother Teresa, when she says, "If you don't want the little child, that unborn child, give him to me." We have so many families in America seeking to adopt children that the slogan "every child a wanted child" is now the emptiest of all reasons to tolerate abortion.

I have often said we need to join in prayer to bring protection to the unborn. Prayer and action are needed to uphold the sanctity of human life. I believe it will not be possible to accomplish our work, the work of saving lives, "without being a soul of prayer." The famous British Member of Parliament, William Wilberforce, prayed with his small group of influential friends, the "Clapham Sect," for *decades* to see an end to slavery in the British empire. Wilberforce led that struggle in Parliament, unflaggingly, because he believed in the sanctity of human life. He saw the fulfillment of his impossible dream when Parliament outlawed slavery just before his death.

Let his faith and perseverance be our guide. We will never recognize the true value of our own lives until we affirm the value in the life of others, a value of which Malcolm Muggeridge says: ". . . however low it flickers or fiercely burns, it is still a Divine flame which no man dare presume to put out, be his motives ever so humane and enlightened."

Abraham Lincoln recognized that we could not survive as a free land when some men could decide that others were not fit to be free and should therefore be slaves. Likewise, we cannot survive as a free nation when some men decide that others are not fit to live and should be abandoned to abortion or infanticide. My administration is dedicated to the preservation of America as a free land, and there is no cause more important for preserving that freedom than affirming the transcendent right to life of all human beings, the right without which no other rights have any meaning.

Ghosts on the Great Lawn

Faith Abbott McFadden

You know Erma Bombeck, and how funny she can be. Millions read her syndicated newspaper column regularly. But sometimes she's not funny.

One of her own favorite columns is reprinted from time to time, when she's on vacation. Thus, last summer, her fans saw again her sober column titled "The Phantom Senior Classes." It's about teenagers who die in drunk-driving accidents. Erma imagines a Central High ("somewhere in the midwest") which "until this moment" had a senior class of about 200, but this year, she writes, there will be *no* senior class at Central—nor any such classes for the next 45 years, because during that time some 9,000 young drunk-driving victims won't live to get their diplomas.

In a futuristic flashback, she adds that Central High closed its doors in 2029, because of "decreasing enrollment"—indeed, 44 more Centrals would also close down, because in those 40-some years over 400,000 young people would also be victims of such tragic accidents.

It struck me, because I too had been thinking about phantom children, not at Central High but on the Great Lawn in New York's Central Park, during the big Fourth of July Liberty Weekend celebration, when President Reagan joined the millions who came to see the refurbished Statue of Liberty's torch relighted.

The following Monday, the tabloid New York *Daily News'* front-page banner headline roared "IT WAS SOME PARTY"—the historic six-million throng, the story reported, had "one big bash . . . ate 750,000 hot dogs, and drank two million drinks." There were millions in the subways; the longest lines *ever* waited above; the statistics ran on and on. And then this: the "Most Well-Mannered Crowd: the 800,000 at the Central Park Concert."

There have been many concerts in Central Park, including Rock affairs that got out of hand, with drug disasters, muggings, even riots, involving as many as a half-million "youths" of all ages. But this one was to be different. A half-million people were expected, but the police didn't expect big troubles from a crowd coming to hear the New York Philharmonic. (Who goes out of control when Zubin Mehta conducts, Yo Yo Ma plays his cello, Itzhak Perlman fiddles, and the soloists are Marilyn Horne, Placido Domingo, and Sherrill Milnes?) The 1,700 cops mobilized were there mainly to handle pedestrian traffic in and out of the park. A police Captain said: "Zubin Mehta groupies are not generally trouble-makers."

Faith Abbott McFadden is a senior editor of the *Human Life Review* and author of the memoir, *Acts of Faith* (Ignatius Press, 1995).

And it *was* a great night, with the enthusiastic crowd exceeding predictions and reaching the 800,000 the *News* reported. (Have *you* ever seen that many people in one place?)

On the blistering hot afternoon before the concert I had walked across the Great Lawn on the way to higher ground from which I hoped to view the First Ever Annual Great Blimp Race. The Lawn had begun filling up since early morning; from atop the Belvedere Castle (yes, we did see the five blimps, between buildings) I saw whole families with picnic and "survival" apparatus. But I had no idea of what a *capacity* crowd on the Great Lawn would look like, until that night, when I watched the concert live on TV and saw the aerial view from the blimps. And when I read Monday's *News,* I thought: So that's what 800,000 looks like.

Numbers have always left me cold: I have No Head for Figures—zeroes and commas play tricks on me: hundreds turn into thousands and vice-versa. From earliest memory (when I told friends about my great-grandmother who died at age 30l—actually she was run over by a milk cart at 103) through my first job, when my boss began to look for a *new* job because, he said, he needed to make a "five-figure salary" (which someone later explained meant $10,000-up) up to the present, my inability to translate figures into what they represent has been a practical disability and a social embarrassment.

So I have had to make a sort of game about numbers. A kind of Sesame Street for adults, where you see the numbers and then envision abstract images. And since adult heads must deal with many more than ten oranges or witches or whatever, there must be an expanded concept: a spatial concept, if hundreds and thousands up to millions are to make any sense.

Time magazine recently had a clever Sesame Street-type visual aid, for people who can't conceptualize a sea depth of 12,500 feet, at which the remains of the *Titanic* lie: Ten Empire State buildings were stacked up atop each other. So if you can visualize how tall the Empire State is, you get the idea of how deep is the ocean over the *Titanic.*

My first numerical-visual aid was 2,000, which was the size of the student body in my high school. When I would hear that some demonstration or celebration had drawn a crowd of something-thousand, I'd remember my high school auditorium as a standard of comparison.

After the *Roe* v. *Wade* decision in 1973, I began attending the annual March for Life in Washington, and my numbers game expanded: One year there were 35,000 marchers (we stood on a street corner and watched them march by); another year 50,000; one year 70,000. From Capitol Hill one got a conceptual idea of what 70,000 *looked* like. Anything to do with the *million* category was still an abstraction. Until my Great Lawn experience.

A few days after I'd read in the *News* about the 800,000 people at the concert (more than ten times the size of that Washington mob), I received a copy of an ad which had appeared in the New York *Times* on May 26th (we had not seen it earlier because it was in the *Times'* "National Edition," which goes outside New York). The ad, sponsored by Doctors for Life, offered Congratulations to the 8th Grade Graduates of 1986 and Condolences to "Your classmates who didn't make it"—the 745,000 souls who would have been 8th grade graduates in 1986 had they not been aborted.

The ad said: "Many of you (3,137,000) were born in 1973—the year abortion was legalized. Over 745,000 of your Class of '86 were aborted in the same year—the Massacre of 1973." Now that the figure 800,000 was indelible in my mind, I could "see" 745,000. And 750,000 hot dogs dispensed that Liberty Weekend? Just about one for each absent member of that class.

And of course these 8th graders would become, in the fall, the first high school freshman class in American history to have been decimated by abortion. I imagined the Great Lawn filled with silent 8th grade graduates, Class of 1986, standing upright, the ghosts of the Class That Wasn't There.

"Where there is no vision, the people perish." Would a vision—a viewing—of the perished help make sense of their sheer numbers, I wondered? Of course there can't be pictures of my ghosts on the Great Lawn, those victims of "the massacre of 1973." I remembered the pictures of the mere 900 victims of the Jonestown Massacre. Who can forget all those full-color magazine photos of the victims of fanatacism and cyanide-laced Kool-Aid, lying there on the ground in Guyana. Horrible, we shuddered. Still, though, *that* happened somewhere else, not "close to home." Not on Central Park's Great Lawn. But we *had* seen 800,000 people on the Great Lawn, which is almost exactly *half* the number of babies unborn-in-America every year, so I could visualize them covering *two* Great Lawns with a capacity crowd of ghosts. Probably all of Central Park could be populated by ghosts, at the current rate of snuffing-out.

But 1.6 million *is* hard to visualize. Break that figure down, though, into the *daily* rate of snuffing-out, and you get about four thousand ghosts created every day. Twice the size of my high school auditorium. Two full assemblies a day, wiped out: vaporized.

The other day, I caught myself saying (as who doesn't?) "Gee, thanks a million." And suddenly I wondered how long it would take to say "thanks" a million times. It would take a lot longer to count to 1.6 million: It *is* more awesomely horrible to *know* that that many babies are killed each year.

The ad said that only 600,000 had been killed in all our wars. That amazed me, so I looked it up. The total I found was 652,000 deaths in battle, plus another 500,000—plus "other" war deaths. I looked up that famous disaster, the 1918 Flu epidemic. It killed "only" a half million Americans. I'm told that an estimated 18 million unborn babies have died since *Roe* v. *Wade,* which must make abortion the worst epidemic in history.

Dwelling on this tends to make my Numbers Game work *too* well. Before you know it, you're thinking: How many each hour, each minute—how many, from here to the subway? *That* sort of thing.

Especially when there are visual aides, from here to the subway. Each summer day in Manhattan one sees large groups of name-tagged little kids erupting from the subway, being maneuvered along 86th Street toward Central Park: happy, fun-time-anticipating kids, two by two. Their day-camp counselors stop them every so often to take yet another head-count and remind the kids to stick with their partners. My mind wanders and I see one single line of kids. Their buddies aren't there. One out of how many, I wonder, got vaporized in the few years since these day-campers were born? Nobody can do a head-count of those little ghosts.

Not to overdo it, but there's another big story in town this summer that makes the abortion issue "hit home"—babies falling out of windows.

One can't imagine New Yorkers saying: "So what?" when they read that yet another child has fallen to its death from an unbarred window. No: We are compassionate. We agonize over needless deaths. The *News* (August 11) headlined: "9th child falls to death," and the New York *Times,* the same day, told us it was "the 77th time that a child has fallen through a window in the City. Nine of the falls have resulted in deaths, including four within the last three weeks."

We think: how *needless.* Why don't these parents/babysitters learn from the papers about window-bars? We *feel* for the bereaved parents even as we accuse them of negligence (and as we check our *own* window-bars).

Even when we know and can quote the statistics about abortion; even when we see the annual statistics broken down into daily and hourly fatalities, we tend—automatically—to make a distinction between *statistics* and *individual* victims of preventable fatalities, whose names and ages are reported in the papers, with their baby pictures.

What if the media informed us that, this year, 1.6 million babies would fall to their deaths from unguarded windows? At the rate of about 4,000 daily, almost three every minute? We wouldn't feel just "compassion" but horror. We'd raise hysterical cries about committing national suicide, about what it all meant for the *future.*

The reality is that 1.6 million babies were victims of preventable deaths last year. Is there any difference, ultimately? There is no future for the nine small children with names who have died so far this year from window falls: There is the same no-future for the un-named, unbirth-dated babies who are also victims of needless death. But *these* victims of preventable deaths never make it to the stage where *we* have "feelings" about them. The 4,000 per day aborted babies are statistics of a *different* sort; we don't read about how they died; we don't know their names; we can be rhetorical about Unborn Millions, but not about three babies falling out of windows every minute, even though the end result is the same. There are no degrees of death.

Maybe it's because abortion statistics have all those zeroes. We think of the aborted in terms of zeroes if we think about them at all. It's easier to deal with "mass murder" than to think about individual victims. To think of the victims as one-at-a-time individuals offends one's sensibilities. But that is how they died, one at a time, just as the window-victims died. Just as the window-victims had been *born,* one at a time; just as you and I were born, and will die. So the fatalities of legal abortion would have been born one at a time, had they not been "terminated." Each of the 1.6 million victims unborn in America every year has an identity.

It's as if the unborn don't count. They do, however, count up. The next window victim will be the 10th. Somewhere, there has been (or soon will be) abortion victim 18,000,001.

"Where there is no vision, the people perish." One wonders if even the most ardent pro-abortionists, given a vision of several empty Great Lawns and *knowing* what the empty spaces represented, would say: So what? More likely they'd say Yes, but . . . most likely, they'd not say anything, because they are too busy with numbers: *theirs.* (Stand up and be counted, all in favor of women's reproductive rights.) Their numbers represent the *born* who are now free of burdensome unwanted babies.

And what was Ellie Smeal's National Organization for Women doing in our nation's capital on July 7th, the day the *Daily News* raved about New York's Feedom Party? Picketing the U.S. Catholic bishops, that's what. About 25 women (*that's* a crowd I have no trouble visualizing) bearing signs about Civil Rights, and also carrying umbrellas, marched outside the bishops' headquarters, chant-ing: "Let it rain. Let it pour. We know what we're marching for."

Ellie Smeal's supporters had done better last March in Washington: An estimated 80,000 demonstrated for Abortion Rights. On July 7th, they were protesting the bishops' endorsement of an amendment for the so-called Civil Rights Restoration Act now pending in Congress. They want the government to force institutions to support abortion: That's what "civil rights" is all about, of course. Indeed, "We know what we're marching for." *What,* not *who.* So that was how NOW joined in celebrating Liberty Weekend.

NOW cares about *now*. What about the future? Is their Emperor eternally resplendent in new clothes? Don't they know that decimated populations will affect everyone? Even if they (being very cerebral people) don't weep over the unborn, don't they worry about, say, economics? Don't they know that they, and the children they *have* allowed to live, face tremendous financial burdens? That there won't be enough people for jobs, children for schools, soldiers to defend the nation—and who will take care of the NOW Generation in *its* old age?

One might say that they have their backs to the future. Yet it is often these same people, oblivious to the ramifications of a dwindling population, who crusade for "conservation." Who ask: Have you thought about the future? Save our trees! Be good to ozone layers. Save the whales. We must not allow this-or-that animal to become extinct. Conserve, preserve! Save our National Parks. (Save our Great Lawns, so that someday they *can* be empty?)

Erma Bombeck touched on that, too: "The people of this country champion the lives of helpless seals, unborn babies, abandoned dogs and cats, abused children, alcoholics, the elderly and the disease-ridden. When will we weep for the phantom classes at Central High?"

I wish Erma had listed unborn babies next to phantom classes rather than between helpless seals and abandoned animals—I trust Erma would correct this, if she thought about it. After all, what unborn children and her phantom teenagers have in common is that they *all* are "would-have-beens and should-have-beens."

There is no doubt that the concert on the Great Lawn had a strong emotional impact on everyone there, as well as on television viewers (some of whom, like us, could rush to our windows to see the fire-works, live, at the grande finale). It was a shared experience, a sort of group emotion. But such "emotional experiences" can lead to a heightened perception of reality.

When I read the Doctors for Life ad, and had that spatial-visual concept of how many ghosts there must now be from sea to shining sea, I felt "personally" involved. I *felt* the reality of how many aren't, and won't ever be, there to share in our So Proudly Hailing; to join in the final Ode to Joy, which had everyone standing up. Then everyone sang God Bless America (even Kate Smith would have been impressed). In the land of the free and the home of the brave, these twilight ghosts were unfree to ask God to bless America. For them, Freedom's Birthday had come too late.

More from Erma Bombeck's column: "The halls echoed with school songs that were never sung, valedictorians who never spoke and cheers that were never heard."

The *News* had also mentioned, in connection with the well-behaved 800,000, that 1,200 plastic bags had been given to the concert-goers, to clean up after themselves; and that they'd left behind only 250 cubic yards of trash. I do not have a concept of cubic yards, but I figured 250 of them must be a mere drop in the sanitation truck bucket. And then I remembered stories I'd read about the disposal of fetuses, in just such trash bags, and I had no wish to conceptualize. I did not want to play my Numbers Game.

A few years ago President Reagan published an essay, *Abortion and the Conscience of the Nation.* Conscience has to do with knowing and feeling, it seems to me: A conscience is *formed* by the working-together of the heart and the mind. If there is one point of agreement on both sides of the abortion issue, it is that this is "a battle for hearts and minds." It has to be fought in the courts, but nothing will ultimately change until hearts and minds do. Whichever gets most involved *first* doesn't seem to matter all that much, since eventually both must come together. If we are *whole*—and I don't know anyone who would like to be considered fragmented.

There are dedicated anti-abortion people who *feel* so deeply about the unborn that they use sheer emotional bombardment as a weapon. You know, all those graphic pictures, etc. But people will not see what they don't want to see. Shock tactics simply turn them off.

Then there are those whose approach is basically cerebral: They know that seeing is not necessarily believing; nevertheless they are convinced that seeing *statistics* will lead to comprehension. (If people only knew the *facts* about unborn babies, they would rise up and say: "This killing has got to stop!") Which is a bit like saying: If teenagers only *knew* the Facts of Life, they'd stop getting pregnant—education is the answer. But we know that a whole generation of Sex Ed has produced the highest pregnancy/abortion rate in history.

Abortion and the Conscience of the Nation? It may be that until there is a coming-together of seeing and believing and knowing, in individual consciences, there can't be any formation of a national conscience; and 1.5 or 1.6 million—all those innocent zeroes—will continue to be slaughtered, one at a time, every few seconds, every single year. But their little ghosts will continue to not go away.

The nonsensical nursery rhyme becomes less nonsensical:

> The other day
> Upon the stair
> I saw a man
> Who wasn't there.
> He wasn't there again today:
> I wish that man
> Would go away.

Dancing with the Saints

Patrick Mullaney

We live in a society that has exempted the value of life from the democratic process by making life an individual constitutional right.[1] However, despite this and the fact that there is now little serious disagreement that life exists before birth, unborn life has somehow been un-exempted from the Constitution's protection.

One need look no further than *Roe* v. *Wade* for an explanation. There, in support of its primary holding that abortion is a Due Process liberty, the Supreme Court also held that the unborn child is not a "person" within the meaning of the Fourteenth Amendment, thus declaring the entire class outside the Due Process Clause. Moreover, this "non-person" aspect of *Roe* is agreed to by many pro-life commentators and jurists. The standard pro-life argument is that abortion should not be a constitutional right, that it is a political issue to be resolved legislatively by the states. However, many pro-life leaders, for reasons we'll explain later, take no exception to *Roe*'s holding that the unborn child is not entitled to have its life protected under either Fifth or Fourteenth Amendments.[2]

About 20 years ago, I decided to get involved in the abortion battle. I knew very little about the finer constitutional points. In fact, my interest was pretty simple: I thought it was wrong to kill and didn't think it was such a good idea for the Constitution to find virtue in it. I also thought it wasn't much of an idea to decide who lives and who dies by voting on it. I'm as big a fan of democracy as anybody else, but there seemed to me to be something decidedly un-American about subjecting the value of life to a vote. Beyond all that, however, what really bothered me was the acceptance of the idea that an entire class of humanity could be exempted from the protection of an enumerated right to life.

My involvement soon became what I'd have to describe as a remarkable journey. I'd like to share part of my journey here, what happened and why. In particular, I'd like to share my experiences with three extraordinary people I met along the way, Mother Teresa of Calcutta, Dr. Jérôme Lejeune, and John Cardinal O'Connor. (For simplicity, I'll occasionally refer to them as "the Saints").[3] I'd like to explain how they were part of that journey, and, more importantly, why they lent their support to a cause that some very learned people on both sides of the abortion debate could or would not support.

Patrick Mullaney, an attorney practicing in New Jersey, represented Alex Loce from 1990 to 1994.

My story revolves around a then-27-year-old man named Alex Loce. In late 1990, Alex was living in Queens, N.Y. He was engaged to a young lady living near Morristown, N.J. She'd become pregnant and, despite his offers to marry her and care for their child, she'd decided to obtain an abortion at a Morristown clinic. She told Alex about her intentions, including her scheduling of a procedure at the clinic on September 8, 1990.

Alex came to Morristown on a Friday, the day before the abortion. With the help of attorneys—Richard Traynor, Michael Carroll, and me—he applied late in the evening to the New Jersey Superior Court in Morristown for a temporary restraining order halting the procedure. His application was denied. He then appealed on an emergent basis to the Appellate Division in Springfield via conference call. After this failed, the appeal was continued to the New Jersey Supreme Court, on the same Friday night: A sole judge, Justice Robert Clifford, heard the appeal sometime after midnight in his Chester living room. After hearing from all the parties who had gathered over the course of the evening—Alex, his fiancée's attorney, the ACLU, NOW, and a few others—Justice Clifford affirmed the lower courts: Alex's baby would be aborted the next day.

But Alex was a determined young man. The next morning, he, joined by a number of sympathizers, chained himself to the door of the clinic. He managed to close the clinic down for about seven hours until the Morristown police obtained a set of graphite metal cutters from the New York Police Department. Eventually he was removed and his baby aborted. He was charged with trespassing and prosecuted in Morristown's municipal court.

The case received an enormous amount of local publicity. This was a father trying to remain a father, a father trying to care for his child. This was a father who had been to the highest court in the state to save that child's life, a father who for all his efforts was being criminally prosecuted. If ever there was a case to bring forward the missing piece of abortion jurisprudence—the unborn child's life right—this could be it.

Alex would defend himself by invoking that missing piece. The argument was simple: His child was alive prior to the abortion and therefore entitled to have its life protected by the Due Process Clause, just as anyone else's would be. Further, in removing Alex from the clinic under the authority of the trespass statute, Morristown had allowed the abortion to take place and thereby violated the child's right to life. As the state cannot prosecute somebody while simultaneously violating somebody else's constitutional rights, Alex was entitled to raise his unborn child's life right in his own defense.

Of course, in order to establish such a right, we had to prove that there is such a thing as unborn life. So Dick Traynor and I wrote to Cardinal O'Connor in New York, explaining the nature of the effort and asking him to assist. Specifically, we requested his assistance in obtaining the testimony of Dr. Jérôme Lejeune, a world-renowned geneticist and pediatrician based at the Sorbonne. He is often referred to as the "Father of Human Genetics" for his discovery, among other things, of the genetic basis for Down Syndrome, the first human abnormality known to be attributable to a genetic defect. But Dr. Lejeune was more than the sum of his professional credentials: His traits of character were much more impressive even than his prodigious intellect. He did not claim the status of anything more than an observer and describer of what he saw as God's work. From his extraordinary position to observe, he saw in the physical world a material fidelity to the commands of life's author and he could explain even the most complex of life's scientific realities with a childlike simplicity.

It's safe to say that requesting the presence and assistance of such a man at a municipal-court proceeding in New Jersey was something of a stretch. However, immediately upon receipt of our request, Cardinal O'Connor faxed Dr. Lejeune a letter informing him of what the Cardinal saw as the importance of the case and virtually imploring him to lend his service on Alex's behalf.

Dr. Lejeune came to Morristown to testify at Alex's trial on April 13, 1991. Those in attendance were spellbound as he described the wonders of life as it passes from generation to generation, how there is no gap in the human continuum, how one generation is undeniably connected to the last at the moment of conception. He received an ovation when his testimony was completed. (Not an everyday event in criminal prosecutions.) Most important, the trial judge, Michael Noonan, basing his opinion largely on Dr. Lejeune's scientific testimony, held that—as a matter of scientific fact—life begins at conception. I'm told that that was a first in an abortion-related case. Although Judge Noonan was forced to find Alex guilty based on *Roe*'s precedent, he went on to describe the abortion of Alex's child as a "legal execution"—something else no one had ever heard from an American court.

These findings gave the case something of a national status, something to be built upon. At about this time the Cardinal let me know that John Paul II was following the events closely, even considering including the Loce Case (as it became known) in a note of an encyclical he was writing.[4] That was all it took for me to ask Cardinal O'Connor if he'd approach the Pope and see if he, the Pope, wouldn't publicly get behind the effort. Certainly that would be a boost. After some time the Cardinal got back to me and said that after much thought and prayer he didn't think it was a good idea to involve the Holy See in the internal affairs of sovereign governments. Knowing, however, that we needed support going forward (and I'm paraphrasing only a little), he went on to say, "How about Mother Teresa?"

It thus came to pass that Mother Teresa became involved in the Loce Case. Her first contribution was to the New Jersey Supreme Court, as the appeal was taken there in early 1993. She addressed a letter—typed, I'm told, by her, on an old typewriter in her room in Calcutta—to the justices, imploring them to review the case and grant to the unborn child its life right. The letter, simple and to the point, reads:

54-A A.J.C. Bose Road
Calcutta 700016, INDIA

Justices of New Jersey
The Supreme Court of New Jersey
Trenton, New Jersey 08625

Re: State of New Jersey v. Alex Loce

Dear Justices of New Jersey,

To make it easier for us to love and protect one another, Jesus made us this promise . . . "Whatever you do to the least of my brethren, you did to me." "When you receive a little child in my name . . . you receive me." Today, the least and most unprotected of our brethren, is the little unborn child. We have all been created by the same loving hand of God, It is your responsibility to protect the rights of all God's children that come before you, regardless if they can speak for themselves or not. As you are making your decision to hear this case, I beg you to protect the rights of God's poorest of the poor, please do not turn your back and reject the rights of the little unborn child. I beg of you to do what Jesus would do in this situation.

My gratitude to you is my prayer for you, for the work that you are doing and the people whom you serve.

Mother M. Teresa, M.C.
Calcutta

Mother Teresa's letter was delivered to me through care of the Cardinal in February 1993. At the suggestion of a friend, I gave the Supreme Court copies and kept the original. It hangs on the wall of my office to this day.

Unfortunately, none of the seven justices on the New Jersey Supreme Court, including those known to be opposed to *Roe*, voted to grant certification. So we moved on to the Supreme Court of the United States. By now, *Loce* had become a rallying point. Dedicated and competent people undertook to organize groups from around the world to submit amicus briefs to the Supreme Court requesting the Court to take the case and properly resolve the question of the unborn life right. By the time they were done, 170 Friends of the Court from 60 nations had filed briefs.

Dr. Lejeune, who was then dying of cancer in Paris, composed a handwritten note to Cardinal O'Connor, referring to Mother Teresa as the "true Mother of the disinherited," and imploring her to continue to aid in the Loce effort. Through the Cardinal I was soon advised that she'd agreed to submit a formal amicus brief on Alex's behalf. I'm told she'd never directly petitioned a government in her life—for reasons similar to the Holy See's—but considered the unborn life right to be so fundamental that an exception was called for.

Being associated with Mother Teresa was a unique experience. Everybody loved her: the ACLU, NOW, Catholics for a Free Choice—everybody. Even if they disagreed violently with everything she said, few dared to disagree strongly in public, let alone criticize her. She attracted universal good will.

Mother Teresa came to Washington in February 1994 to deliver a speech at the National Prayer Breakfast. The speech has become very well known: She spoke passionately to President and Mrs. Clinton and Vice President and Mrs. Gore of the obligation to protect the unborn. A Washington public-relations firm—donating its services—had arranged for Mother Teresa, following the prayer breakfast, to deliver personally her amicus brief to the Clerk of the Supreme Court. They had also arranged for her to be escorted by Peter Jennings and Cokie Roberts as she climbed the outside stairs, entered the building, and proceeded to the Clerk's office. Her support of the Loce Case was to be featured on the evening news. The same firm had also arranged for her to appear for the same purpose later that night on *Nightline*. I was invited along, I guess for technical support. I'd been told that Mother Teresa had refused to grant media interviews for a ten-year period prior to her coming to us. She was going to make yet another exception, for the unborn child.

As you might imagine, this was all pretty heady stuff for me. Advocating a simple point and being involved for a very short time, I found myself and my colleagues about to visit the seat of power, escorted by Saints. Those in power, the justices of the Supreme Court, were about to be requested by the most beloved person in the world to consider an issue they had never seriously addressed, the crux of the abortion debate, the obligation of law to life. I couldn't help but think that no one wants to be on the other side of a moral issue from Mother Teresa, not even Supreme Court justices. It all seemed too good to be true. Such a thing could not possibly happen.

And it didn't.

A few days before the prayer breakfast, I received a phone call from

Cardinal Hickey's office in Washington informing me that the Cardinal had "requested" that Mother Teresa not deliver her brief to the Court personally. His concern was that she might embarrass the president, who had personally invited her to come to the United States to address the political leaders.

I was also told that Mother Teresa would honor his request. Gone was the national exposure, gone was the momentum that the networks may have provided. Gone was a lot of effort from a lot of very good people.

Picking up the ball, Cardinal O'Connor told me that it was important to see the effort through to its end and that someday I'd understand. He offered to fly Mother Teresa to New York to have the brief signed there. She did and the brief was eventually filed by her attorneys, Robert George and William Porth. Still, a great opportunity had been lost.

Shortly thereafter, the Supreme Court denied Alex's petition for certiorari. Not one justice—not even those who had long opposed *Roe*—voted to take the case. It simply ended there. None of the 16 justices sitting on the Supreme Court of New Jersey and the Supreme Court of the United States saw fit even to hear the case.

I've had many years to consider the events of the Loce Case. At first I kept on asking, simply, how could all this have happened? Why had these remarkable people—the moral leaders of the world—gotten behind an obscure prosecution defended by an obscure attorney in an obscure municipal court? My thoughts over time began to center on the differences between the Saints and the justices who'd refused to hear the Loce Case. What was it? Why had the Saints so fervently advocated the case, and the justices so fervently discarded it? I wasn't expecting much from the justices who favored abortion rights. But I did expect something from those who didn't. So I began to ask myself: What is the difference between the Saints and those justices who represent the mainstream of pro-life thought, who not only oppose abortion's constitutional status but also see it as a moral wrong? How can the obvious solution—to declare an enumerated constitutional protection against a fundamental moral breach—simply be discarded?

I think the central fact is that the Saints *knew* of the proper moral order, and insisted that the political order *conform* to it. It sounds strange today, in an age where all moral points of view are tolerated, even valued, to say that someone *knows* the moral order. To the Saints, though, it's not only known, it's the starting point of a continuum between it and the political order.

About 700 years ago, St. Thomas Aquinas taught that every man is at the outset a blank tablet (*tabula rasa*), knowing nothing. As we go through life, each of us begins to acquire knowledge through the senses, first with awareness of particular tangible things, like this table and that chair. From the particular we proceed actively to abstract general concepts. We come to know what tables and chairs are generally by *intellectualizing*—a capacity of the human reason—upon our sensory perceptions of particular tables and chairs.[5]

The moral order, however, is intangible. So St. Thomas went on to consider whether we can know things beyond the physical. He answers that, yes, we can; that, being human, the intellect must start with sensing physical things, but, being *intellect*, it may proceed farther, to the metaphysical. He goes on to make the distinction between the direct sensory knowledge we can gain of physical things through observation and our knowledge of the metaphysical. The latter is not direct; rather, it is relational—or analogical—to the physical. All material things, he teaches, *manifest* God and their relationship to God, yielding to us an analogical and imperfect knowledge of God's nature—a knowledge of permeating, universal goodness.[6]

It is upon this knowable reality of goodness that St. Thomas establishes the knowledge of a moral order. He states that all creatures are by their particular natures ordered to God as their *purpose*. Men, rational by nature, are ordered to God through their reason and rational intellect. Thus, the free intellect is always properly used toward God through the pursuit of God's nature—the good (*bonum*). And it is through this proper ordering of the free will that we come to know the first moral principle of practical reason—that good is to be done and evil avoided.[7]

St. Thomas considers the political order within the same context. For him, the State is a natural institution in that it also properly reflects the nature of man. The State's *purpose*—the reason it exists—is to serve as a continuum of the moral order. Thus, a democratic state requires a collective use of reason in pursuit of the good.[8] A constitutional order would similarly require elements of its constitutional structure, such as individual rights, to be applied in the pursuit of the good. In general, to St. Thomas any human law or institution must be an application of truth; within its context an application of that revealed first through the Jews and then through Christ culminating in the Great Commandment to love one another.[9] To St. Thomas, human law's reach is no farther than its end in goodness, and to the extent that the law violates goodness it "will not be a law but a perversion of law."[10]

I think this suggests an understanding of the Saints' advocacy in the Loce Case. They simply believed that an unprotected portion of humanity—the unborn—be included within the protection of an enumerated constitutional right to life as part of the Constitution's obligation to pursue the good. As per St. Thomas, that advocacy was of a proper continuum of the moral order to the political as it currently exists in America. More important, to the Saints there is not—and may not be—a moral void in the political order, a void where competing concerns render irrelevant or subordinate the moral, at least as to the law's obligation to life.

Let's now turn to the competing thoughts of the justices who decided not to consider the Loce case. We can focus first on the pro-life justices, those who disagree with the legitimacy of the abortion liberty, but would deny the unborn life right. Judge Robert Bork perhaps outlines their position best in his October 2003 *First Things* article, "Constitutional Persons: An Exchange on Abortion." There he wrote, concerning the Due Process Clause as encompassing unborn life: "That reading seems to me *absurd*. The Constitutional question is not what biological science tells us today about when human life begins. *No doubt conception is the moment. The issue, instead, is what the proponents and ratifiers of the Fifth and Fourteenth Amendments understood themselves to be doing.*" (Emphasis added.) As to whether the proponents and ratifiers may have intended such a result, he goes on to say: "I think that the Constitution has nothing to say about *abortion*, one way or another, leaving the issue as the Constitution leaves most moral questions, to *democratic determination.*" (Emphasis added.)

We can see at first blush that Judge Bork's concerns on abortion's constitutional status are different from those of the Saints. His concerns are political. They're based on the solid premise that if constitutional rights are not limited to the original intent of those who drafted the text of the Constitution, any number of rights found nowhere within it, such as abortion, may be undemocratically imposed upon all of us simply because the Supreme Court at some time may like them. That's a great argument against abortion as a constitutional right. But he goes on to conclude that because abortion is not a valid constitutional right, neither is the unborn life right.

This seems to conflict with the facts. Abortion may not be an enumerated right—but life certainly is. It seems that the drafters intended to protect life, without classification or exclusion of any kind, as they put it in the Constitution, not once, but twice. It's always seemed to me that Judge Bork's democratic concerns—and the similar concerns of all the pro-life justices and many commentators—simply do not apply to the argument for the unborn life right.

Let's examine exactly what Judge Bork's methodology does. It subordinates the value of life to a competing political—democratic—concern. It argues that since an original intent to protect unborn life specifically within the abortion context is not found, the conceded facts that unborn life exists and that abortion takes that life become irrelevant. This political aspect of the argument—a concern about runaway federal judges—thus supersedes the primary moral obligation of the law to protect life, subordinating life to a political concern. Simultaneously, the Constitution is made a moral void on the issue as it denies an entire class of humanity the protection of an enumerated and fundamental human right.

We should also take a minute to note that, in one respect, the pro-life justices have something in common with the pro-abortion justices. They all subordinate life to a competing concern: the pro-abortion justices to personal autonomy, the pro-life justices to the mandates of original intent. They all deny the law's obligation to protect life within that subordination.

Here we can see the difference between the Saints and the justices: To the Saints, there can be no moral void within the Constitution resulting from these competing concerns. To the justices, there can.

Now, to most Americans this difference isn't offensive. We are well conditioned to the reality that our political institutions and our laws function in a moral void. And, as Judge Bork makes clear, we can address moral issues within the democratic process. So, one may ask, what's the big deal about Judge Bork's position? If abortion has a moral component, why not just address it at the ballot box? What's lost in classifying unborn life out of Due Process protection?

It's here that I have to introduce John Paul II into the Loce journey. I'd mentioned above that Cardinal O'Connor told me in 1992 that the Holy Father was following the case closely, even considered using it in an encyclical note. Later, I was told that the Holy Father kept copies of the briefs we'd filed with the Supreme Court on the altar of his private chapel as he said Daily Mass while the case was pending before the Court.

His encyclical *Evangelium Vitae*, released in 1995 and written during the Loce years, took up the issue of the law's obligation to unborn life. It did so in three steps. First, it affirmed the existence of a right to life *prior* to the political process—a right found in the natural law, before the human law, and based on a faithful and reasonable knowledge of the sacred value of human life and the dignity of the person from conception to natural death. Second, much like St. Thomas, John Paul II declared the recognition of the right to life as *the purpose* of the subsequent political community.[11] Finally, he went on to consider the consequences of its being denied by that political community, writing:

> [If] the original and inalienable right to life is *questioned or denied* on the basis of a parliamentary vote or will of the people—even if it is the majority . . . the right ceases to be such, because it is no longer founded in the inviolable dignity of the person, but is made subject to the will of the stronger part. In this way democracy, contradicting its own principles, effectively moves towards a form of totalitarianism . . . *when this happens the process leading to the breakdown of a genuinely human co-existence and a disintegration of the State itself has already begun.* [Emphasis added.][12]

That's pretty strong stuff: movement towards totalitarianism, disintegration of the state. But let's look at what John Paul II is saying. First and foremost, government *exists* to recognize the life right. Thus, government's *denying* the right corrupts its own purpose. It does so by recasting the right's essential nature. No longer original (prior to the political process) and inalienable, it is now contingent upon other, competing concerns. The state has thus contradicted its core principles, making its foundation something other than the recognition of life, the recognition of the dignity of the human person. John Paul II sees this contradiction as so fundamental a breach that a society undertaking it cannot endure.

It can be argued that John Paul II speaks only of the democratic process, not the constitutional adjudication of rights. But I think his point is broader. His condemnation of denying life was not from any particular governmental perspective. Rather, it was from a core mandate applicable wherever the issue is presented: The right to life must prevail over *all* competing concerns, including Judge Bork's.

When I read *Evangelium Vitae*, I began to understand the Loce journey: The Loce Case was presenting precisely the point that was being considered by the Holy Father. As I began to understand the point and its magnitude, I began to understand why the Cardinal had gone to such extraordinary lengths; why he'd engaged Dr. Lejeune and Mother Teresa; why Dr. Lejeune and Mother Teresa had unquestioningly lent themselves to our effort. They say great minds think alike. I guess holy minds do as well. To those minds, the United States must honor, not deny, life in its law. I began to understand how they'd seen that the United States had in fact honored life at our law's summit; exempting it from the dangers of the democratic process by recognizing and protecting it individually. I began to understand how they saw that that honoring was now being lost, not only by the recognition of abortion as an individual right, but also by the denial of the life right to the unborn by all who considered the issue. I began to understand how the Loce Case was an opportunity for them to advocate the proper status of life within the law.

Maybe most important, it began to dawn on me how people like the Saints see both unity and fragility within the world. They see that fidelity to the moral order spoken of by Saint Thomas, not to politics or policy, is what allows a society to exist as an integrated whole. They see that integration as resting upon the proper use of a society's free will, including the collective will in the form of its laws, in pursuit of the moral order, in pursuit of God's nature, in pursuit of the good. They also see that the moral order is as fragile as it is strong; and they see the consequences—laid out in no uncertain terms by John Paul II—of its being fundamentally violated on topics of basic human concern.

I certainly can't claim to know if our treatment of life is leading us down the path that John Paul II suggests. I'm well aware that as far as the topic of constitutional protection for the unborn goes, a lot of good people don't seem concerned at all. We've seen that Judge Bork dismissed the argument as "absurd." Paul Linton, in his Summer 2007 *Human Life Review* article, "Sacred Cows, Whole Hogs and Golden Calves," similarly described its practical advocacy as a "counsel of despair dressed up in the guise of a false hope."

It seems pretty clear that the Saints would disagree. No, they saw nothing absurd or desperate in what Alex Loce tried to do. After these many years, I think what they saw was an attempt to bring Truth to the law, as St. Thomas so long ago suggested. In its temporal struggle with abortion, they saw America as engaged in the eternal struggle between Truth and Freedom, how to conform the power of Freedom with the mandate of Truth. I think that what they were trying to tell us, in the end, was what John Paul II put so well in *Fides et Ratio*: "Truth and freedom either go hand-in-hand or together they perish in misery."[13]

NOTES

1. The Due Process Clauses of both the Fifth and Fourteenth Amendments set forth "life" as an individual right.
2. See Bork, "Constitutional Persons: An Exchange on Abortion," *First Things*, January 2003; *see also* Linton, "Sacred Cows, Whole Hogs, and Golden Calves," *Human Life Review*, Summer 2007.
3. Mother Teresa of Calcutta was beatified by John Paul II on October 19, 2003. Dr. Lejeune was proposed for beatification by Cardinal Fiorenzo Angelini at the Pontifical Academy for Life in Rome on February 20, 2004. In April 2007, Paris Archbishop Andre Vingt-Trois launched the process for his beatification. To those who knew Cardinal O'Connor, his own beatification is just a matter of time.
4. The Loce Case was not mentioned, though the encyclical turned out to be *Evangelium Vitae*. As set forth *infra*, John Paul II advocated a recognition and protection of unborn life precisely as was being advocated in the Loce Case.
5. *Summa Theologica, Ia,* 84, 7, 3; *see also* Copleston, A *History of Philosophy*, Vol. II, Medieval Philosophy, at 393-4, Doubleday. (Further references to *Summa Theologica* shall be designated as *S.T.*; further references to *A History of Philosophy* by Father Copleston shall be referenced as *Copleston* with appropriate Volume and Page indications.)
6. *Copleston*, Vol. II at 390-4.
7. *S.T.*, 1a, IIae, 94, 2; *Copleston*, Vol. II at 406.
8. *De Regimine Principum,* I; *Copleston,* Vol. II at 413.
9. *Copleston*, Vol. II at 418.
10. *S.T.* Ia, IIae, 95, 2; *Copleston*, Vol. II at 419.
11. *Evangelium Vitae*, N. 2, N. 20.
12. *Evangelium Vitae*, N. 20.
13. *Fides et Ratio*, N.90.

Why Nobody Is Really Pro-Choice

Ann Coulter

I don't know how to talk or write without arguing so this will be in the nature of an argument with myself over when life begins. This is an advantage because it means I can dictate who wins. But on the question of whether a fetus merits treatment as a human being, no advantage is necessary.

Although I know little about such facts as when various stimuli are present in a fetus or what medical advances will shorten the period to viability, I do know that at some point before the child is actually born you have something that looks like a human life, and that's all I've ever needed to know to persuade people that abortion is immoral and wrong. No one is pro-choice, it is an impossible position. I suppose my title could also be taken to mean that people who claim to be pro-choice are frequently, in fact, active proponents of abortion, which I happen to think is also true, but that isn't what my talk is on.

The argument is analogous to those I've had with swaggering swains at law school who claim to be atheists. I point out to them that atheists ought to be able to eat human beings. They generally eat chicken and beef—indeed, all but the most incorrigible and sickly vegetarians will at least eat eggs and caviar. But only a Jeffrey Dahmer would eat a human or a human fetus. Obviously it is understood that there is something unique about humans. What is that if not a soul?

Atheists should also be willing to take their clothes off in public: They don't keep their Dalmation's private parts covered in warm weather. Unless there is something special about being human, such personal modesty is inexplicable. Not coincidentally, many of Madalyn Murray O'Hare's followers resided in nudist colonies. Social convention alone cannot explain why atheists wear clothes. Arranged marriages, calling cards, vomitoriums, nose rings, wigs for men and pants for women, and innumerable other social customs that were once common—some even unbreachable—have completely disappeared or vary from culture to culture. Only a few are invariably present in civilized society: marriage, for one, and coverings for certain parts of the body.[1] Moreover, it seems to me, if I lived in a society in which everyone believed some silly little nursery limerick such as "step on a crack, break your mother's back" and I went around dismissing the veracity of the rhyme, I think people would have reason to doubt me if I steadfastly refused to step on

Ann Coulter is an attorney and best-selling author. Her latest book is *Guilty: Liberal "Victims" and Their Assault on America* (Crown Forum, 2009). This article was adapted from a talk she gave to a Catholic women's group in Connecticut in 1992.

a crack. Only the statistically irreverent crank is constitutionally capable of really putting his atheism to practice by being a nudist. And those who cannot manifestly operate on the assumption that there is a human soul. They can claim they don't believe in God all they want, but unless they're willing to act on that belief by walking around buck naked and eating humans, they understand that humans have souls.

This is the way most alleged atheists behave—and ultimately is the way the abortion argument goes. The pro-abortionist is forced to apply principles to the potential life within the fetus that he would accept in no other area of his life, in no other circumstances. Because precepts that are necessary to support abortion are specifically and uniformly rejected in analogous situations, there is reason to doubt the sincerity of the "pro-choice" position.

The abortion advocate must have concluded that the entity being aborted is not a human life, and contrarily, the abortion opponent, that it is a human life. The only point at issue is not whether people will harm themselves attempting to break laws against abortion or whether such laws will disproportionately affect the poor, but whether the fetus is a human life. What sorts of indicia normally operate as evidence of human life would seem to be relevant to this inquiry. Although it ought to be incumbent on the person who says it is okay to kill to establish that what is being killed is more like crabgrass or a virus than it is like a human being, the question is generally phrased: "Who are you to say when life begins?"

Invariably, people who have said this have never seen a fetus, have no idea when a heartbeat begins, don't know when the pain receptors or brain waves are present. People who claim to be pro-choice apparently are not in favor of there being a lot of information out there that would seem to be relevant to make an informed choice. While newspapers and television news programs are splattered with pictures of dead and maimed bodies from famine and wars and natural disasters, I have yet to see any major newspaper or television display a picture of a mangled fetus. You aren't going to learn what you don't want to know. But the media's bias is hardly a novel point.

So starting at the end, could it be that a fetus is not a life until it emerges from the womb? Very few people arguing seriously will take that line, although one occasionally hears the argument made in retreat. About a year ago there was a story in the New York tabloids of a man who fed a newborn baby, one day old, to a dog. I think the city was properly revulsed at this and I don't understand under what definition of life the same act could be conceived of as an acceptable activity had it occurred twenty-four hours earlier. I don't think that can really be explained. But if life begins at birth, twenty-four hours earlier it would have been appropriate to feed the exact same being, the exact same entity, to a dog.

Can it be that life does not begin until birth because the child is still dependent on another? That seems preposterous—for the first several years of its life the child is dependent on someone else. If left to its own devices it would perish in the first days after birth. Is it that the fetus relies on one specific person for whom no one can substitute? What if an infant were lost in the woods with one adult. The child would be entirely at the disposal of this adult, the only person who can save it. Would people say at that point it would be all right for the adult to feed the infant to a dire wolf because the child is totally dependent on that single person for its survival? Would it matter if the child were an "unwanted intruder" or "uninvited guest," as the fetus is frequently termed? I think that would not make a difference.

In fact, on the principle that dependence on one particular person refutes the existence of a human life, it would be a morally acceptable choice to ignore an invalid's cries for help if no one else were around. A person could be in his home, alone with an ailing parent who is crying out for medicine, for food, for a doctor. If that person were the only one in a position to hear the pleas, he could say: "Oh well, Pops is entirely dependent on me now, so I'm on the road again." No one would countenance such an ethic (or would they?). Or at least no one *ought* to countenance such an ethic. And fortunately, with the possible exception of Derek Humphry and the euthanasia devotees, no one does.

And such a principle of behavior would be no more palatable if a person were going to be stuck alone in a cabin with an invalid parent for a full nine months and it were a dreadful burden to keep interrupting his complex souffles and novel-reading to attend to his parent. Nor would it make a difference to anyone if the adult and child lost in the woods were sure to remain lost for nine long months, if it were an enormous hassle for the adult to care for the child all that time, and if, in addition, the adult would become emotionally attached to the child during their sojourn together. I don't think anyone would dispute that it would be a vicious, monstrous act to feed a child to a wolf under those circumstances or even to let it perish on its own by benign neglect—although there, the analogy breaks down. Abortion is not benign neglect but an active and purposeful destruction of the fetus.

So if dependence on another being cannot be the criterion defining life, the next plausible dividing line is viability. Viability generally comes up as a bald assertion that something is not cognizable as a human life until it is viable. There are a lot of problems with this. To begin with, the fetus *is* viable from conception—provided it remains attached to an umbilical cord. For viability to mean something other than dependence for life on one other person, which continues at most until birth in any event, it must refer strictly to the fetus's ability to survive entirely on its own.

But the survival-on-its-own definition of human life would disenfranchise from the definition of life a non-trivial portion of people who rely on artificial respirators or intravenous feeding machines, even people who have to go to kidney dialysis twice a week are not really viable beings. They cannot survive on their own. It cannot be that these people were viable at one point and then lost their viability that anoints them with the privilege of life. Some children are born instantly needing machines, they must go on respirators or into incubators immediately. I was in an incubator for some number of weeks; would it have been morally neutral for my mother's obstetrician to have strangled me to death at her instruction while I lay in the incubator? Do people who depend upon some sort of artificial device for their entire lives never attain humanity?

There is also a disingenuous aspect to the viability argument. If the argument is that a being must be viable, but there is a sort of grandfather clause protecting beings who have already been viable at some point, then a person who was once an able-bodied human who is judged completely brain-dead because of an accident, disease, or old age and is kept alive only by virtue of a battery of machines would have to fit the definition of life. At all costs this person would have to be kept alive. Whether or not that would be a good idea, I am pretty sure there are not a lot of pro-choicers who absolutely insist that life support systems be employed to extend the physical life of humans with no intellectual awareness.

Although society's treatment of the brain-dead should not dictate its treatment of fetuses—fetuses are not brain-dead—there is an inconsistency in employing a grandfathered previous viability as the definition of life, but then not demanding life-support systems for the terminally comatose. Or, rather, the only consistency is the impulse to always err on the side of death. It is inconsistent as a coherent body of ethical principles.

A peculiar thing about the argument that life begins at viability is that it always ends up being self-defining. If it is not dependence on one other person, and if it's not the capacity to survive on one's own, nor to have previously attained independent existence, then the definition of life—whatever one is left with—begins to look suspicious. Human life comes to be defined as whatever the fetus, and the fetus alone, is not.

Suppose a definition of life were proposed that would exclude everything that is defined by a word that begins with "f." Someone points out that Frenchmen would thereby be fair game, so then the definition is modified to exclude anything that begins with "f" but that also contains only five letters; that's not a life. Then the Finns are mentioned and the definition becomes: anything that begins with "f," has five letters, and includes the letter "e." Ignoring the substance of such a definition, which is absurd in and of itself, the farrago of limitations and exceptions is enough to cast some doubt on its usefulness.

Viability as the definition of human life can be made consistent with other principles accepted by normal people only if so many amendments and codicils are attached that the viability in question refers exclusively to that of a fetus. But there ought to be some independent grounds for viability being a rational reason to define something as a life and that rationale must be applied consistently. I don't think there is a principle that would permit the killing of a nonviable fetus that people would be willing to apply across the board. It becomes a mere tautology: "Life begins at viability because life begins at viability and that's just what I believe."

One of the most absurd aspects of viability as the definition of life is that the point of viability is constantly changing. It is preposterous to have a definition of when human life begins that was different a century ago. That means Homer and Shakespeare possessed souls—or whatever it is about humans that makes cannibalism repulsive—at a point in their developments much later than we do today. It means that, even today, souls do not enter the bodies of babies born in Swaziland as soon as they do in babies born in the United States. This is simply an incoherent position.

Alternatively, it could be argued that only beings whose lives depend upon a physical attachment to another human being do not deserve protection. The popular version of this definition of life compares the developing fetus to a parasite that has climbed on to the back of a woman and begins to rely on the woman for its own life. Phrased thus, the argument has an obvious visceral appeal: Parasites are vermin, viruses, and weeds, not human beings. Moreover, stripped down to its essential facts without descriptive coloration, it is not easy to argue against a definition of life that excludes physical attachment to another human being because of the difficulty in hypothesizing scenarios relevant to its application outside the abortion context.

Siamese twins may provide the most analogous real life phenomenon capable of testing the general acceptability of the human parasite argument. Even if it were common practice to surgically remove *one* Siamese twin and allow it to die so that the *other* could lead a more full life, it would seem peculiar to place that decision in the hands of the twin who stood to survive. Indeed, Solomonic justice would militate for killing off whichever twin were to request his sibling's death and to preserve the twin who would not consider demanding that the other die.

But to fairly equate a Siamese twin to a woman with child, only one twin would be dependent on the other for its existence, and the dependency would last no more than nine months. I submit that the decision to destroy the dependent twin would still not be thought to properly reside alone with his sibling, nor would any conscientious decision-maker consider the nine months of physical attachment adequate grounds for compelling the death of the inferior twin.

Furthermore, neither Siamese twin is vaguely responsible for his condition, thus the twin example is a fair comparison to a pregnancy only in the small fraction of cases in which the pregnancy results from rape. Accepting the highest estimates of rape-induced pregnancies, one is still left with approximately 1.6 million abortions per year in which the woman had a hand in creating the life that then depends on her for its survival. In those cases, a more accurate comparison requires that the independent twin had taken some volitional action which in turn placed the other at his mercy. And then the decision to kill off the dependent twin in order to give the superior twin nine unencumbered months would be absurd.

So what do we look at to decide if a human life is present? The definition of life cannot exclude beings attached to an umbilical cord by virtue of their dependence on or physical attachment to another human being, and it cannot exclude beings incapable of independent existence. Moving it all the way back, at the moment of conception, the fetus is, as it is referred to, a clump of cells. This clump of cells has all the genetic material that will determine whether it is a male or female, and what its blood type, hair color, eye color and fingerprints will be. Still, many people have difficulty conceiving of a clump of cells as a human life and I'll give them that. I don't need that concession. It is very, very small at that point.

Incidentally, it is so little at the beginning, that the little clump of cells that people have difficulty recognizing as a life is also too small to abort. In those rare cases in which a woman discovers that she is pregnant within three weeks of conception, which is extremely unusual, she is told to wait until the fetus is six to eight weeks old so that the abortionists can be sure to get it. It's not a pleasant procedure; it's not like laser surgery or an x-ray. The doctor has to make sure he gets all of the baby out, and at three weeks, at four weeks, it's too small for the abortionist to know he's got it. It has to be at least six or eight weeks old.

Remaining agnostic for the moment about the potential life in a recently conceived fetus, we do know that there is a heartbeat at three weeks, brain waves within five to six weeks, and pain receptors at six to seven weeks. I think the most dogmatic pro-choicer cannot deny that these are strong indicia of life and that, by around six or seven weeks at the least, there is a reasonable possibility that the fetus constitutes a human life. Several weeks after that, the fetus will thrash around wildly when the abortionist's tool comes after it. No one can look at that and say that it is not a human life.

Whether life can be conclusively seen by unanimous consent at the moment when there is brain activity, a heart beat, pain receptors, little fingers and toes, or further on down the line is irrelevant. At some point, long before birth, there is a tiny little being that no honest person can deny is a human life. And whichever incarnation of the developing fetus is accepted as indisputably human, the previous stages are at the very least, possibly, though not indisputably, human life. At that point the question has to be: how do people normally react when there is a possibility that they are killing a human?

Suppose a particularly scrupulous crime-avoider were to discharge a gun into all opaque telephone booths he passed in New York City in order to insure that no mugger lurked within. This is obviously extremely convenient for him. He eliminates some muggers who would otherwise have harmed him first. Before he shoots, he cannot see that there is a human life in the booth; he certainly has no idea whether he is taking a human life until the body tumbles out. And if he doesn't look, he may not know until he reads the police roster of dead bodies found in telephone booths that year. If he shoots every telephone booth he passes, the odds of someone being in any one are extremely small. When he takes a shot, he can't say with any degree of certainty, "I know that there's a life in there."

Is that an acceptable moral choice? Do most people think this would be an appropriate way to behave? More likely he would be rather severely counseled against ever shooting into even one opaque telephone booth simply because he *might* be taking a human life. And that is the *least* that can be said about a developing fetus: it might be a human life.

What if some people derived enormous pleasure or merely found it inordinately convenient to whiz their cars through piles of leaves at high speeds with the knowledge that one in every twenty piles of leaves contained hidden children playing in the leaves? Each time a car careened through the leaves there would be only a 5% chance that a child or two would die. Could people accept those odds? Would that be considered an acceptable moral choice? Would it make a difference if it were somewhat difficult to avoid the piles of leaves and, therefore, the state refused to issue drivers' licences to a certain number of drivers?

The most astonishing argument I heard on this point was from a fireman who told me he didn't know when life began, abortion was convenient for women, and that's why he was pro-choice. I pointed out to him that he operates on such a principle in no other area of his life, that, in fact, in his chosen profession he runs into burning buildings risking his own life—not because he knows there is a life inside that burning building but on account of a mere possibility that a human life may be on the verge of being extinguished.

Occasionally society is, and must be, willing to shoulder some risk of death that accompanies a greater good. In those cases, however, not only must the benefits outweigh the costs, but those whose lives are sacrificed should be designated by fate, not preselected. Thus, for example, although the use of automobiles and airplanes raises the possibility of fatal car accidents and airplane crashes, ultimately the benefits of rapid transportation outweigh the costs of accidents, even on its own terms—human lives. While automobile and airplane crashes cause deaths, ambulances, fire engines, and hospital airplanes directly save lives and the rapid transmission of people, goods, and information indirectly saves and extends lives. Moreover, the benefits are spread across the general population, as are the risks.

In the case of abortion, however, the cost-benefit analysis overwhelmingly opposes permitting abortion even if there is only a non-negligible possibility of life in the unborn child. The benefit is not that lives are saved—laws against abortion always make an exception for the life of the mother—but a convenience is provided to women who want the option of refusing to carry a baby to term.[2] On the risk side, however, we play for life: The costs are measured in lives and potential lives. Every time an abortion takes place, *something* is killed. The odds are thus one hundred percent that something will die during an abortion; the only uncertain odds attend the question of whether what has been killed is a human life.

In addition, both the beneficiaries and the risk-bearers of abortion are known in advance; women who wish they had not become pregnant in the former category and the unborn babies of those women in the latter category. And when the doctor begins the abortion procedure, there is one specific entity singled out to bear the full risk that the unborn clump of cells is not yet a human—that particular unborn clump of cells itself.

A societal decision to accept a certain level of risk in order to obtain some concomitant benefit is least justifiable when the detriment is to be borne entirely by one identifiable subgroup. And when the targeted class not only receives none of the benefits, but has no say in the decision to take on those risks, society's acceptance of the risk would seem to be at its lowest possible ebb—especially when the risk being taken is that the subgroup at issue is being murdered.

Even accepting the perspective of the most skeptical observer and granting an extremely restrictive view of when life begins, society's normal calculus of risk militates against deferring to an admittedly enormous convenience for women with unwanted pregnancies and in favor of avoiding the killing of the voiceless unborn who may be human beings.

Moreover, I think there is no way a line can be drawn at any point during the pregnancy without seriously implicating the little clump of cells that form immediately after conception. In other words, it cannot be said that it looks like a life at five weeks, so that the line can be drawn at five or six weeks but not when it's that little clump of cells. Five or six weeks, or even months, is not a long time to wait for something to become human even if it bears few of the indicia of humanity during that time.

Indeed, we typically wait longer periods on smaller possibilities that a comatose person will become cognizably human than the period between conception and the existence of a tiny baby with arms and legs and fingers and toes and a brain and pain receptors. I have a friend who was in a coma for about six weeks and I think he was probably less a potential life during that time than the fetus is during its first trimester. The doctors did not know whether my friend was ever going to come out of his coma. He did and he is a fine fellow and successful journalist, an ABC correspondent in Moscow at the moment, I believe. Should his father have asked that the plug be pulled because the doctors were not sure that his son was going to come out of it? At five weeks should he have said that?

What if it could have been known that instead of six weeks, the coma would last six months, but then would end? In that case, surely, it would have been barbaric *not* to wait out those six months. There was a quite uncertain possibility my comatose friend would ever revive, whereas from the moment of conception the overwhelming majority of fetuses will develop into full-fledged human beings—if they do not end up fighting for their lives against the abortionist's tool, and losing, always losing.

The point of all of this is that the pro-choice position cannot be maintained without assembling a Frankenstein's monster patchwork of principles that people are willing to apply to no other aspects of their lives. Once it is established that the mere possibility of human life is at stake, people err on the side of life; we err on the side of life without question in all kinds of circumstances, and we should err on the side of life here.

And at that point the other arguments for choice just become absurd. Thus—I am personally opposed to abortion but don't want to impose my moral principles on others. Are people who say this similarly indignant about the state imposing its moral views on Joel Steinberg, who beat to death his adopted daughter, Lisa? She had apparently become an enormous inconvenience to Steinberg, indeed, she drove him to the point of viciously beating her. Perhaps, it was an extremely difficult decision for him. Of course, no one is in *favor* of child abuse, but who are we to impose our moral views on such an intimate aspect of the family as child discipline? He made the difficult and personal decision to beat his child to death. He was in his own home at the time and he had acquired proprietary rights to the child by adopting it—albeit under the table. Are we, as a society, willing to accept the prospect of the authorities bursting into people's homes and policing what they do with their children? It seems we are.

The argument that only wealthy women will be able to obtain abortions is no more interesting or effective an argument against abortion than it is in the legions of other contexts in which it is raised. Every time it occurs to a liberal that it's better to be rich than poor, he thinks he's had an epiphany. But if laws had to be repealed because the wealthy can evade or tolerate them more easily than the poor, there couldn't be laws against anything.

Traffic laws, for example, would definitely be verboten. It is obviously much easier for a person who is wealthy to pay a traffic ticket than for a poor person to pay a traffic ticket. Moreover, now that Claus Von Bulow has gotten off, laws against murdering one's wife would be out. It is always better to be rich than poor and that fact does not militate for or against any rules of behavior.

Inadvertently supporting my point that no one is really pro-choice is this fund-raising letter I received last night from Planned Parenthood. Somehow I've gotten on the Planned Parenthood mailing list for New York City. The cover letter does not mention abortion—the word abortion is not used once. Rather, the letter is ostensibly about "right-wing zealots" and the "gag rule" and "formidable [challenges]" to "reproductive health care." This is how abortion fund-raising letters refer to their mission.

Although abortion is not the only service provided by Planned Parenthood, the letter is obviously referring to that particular service by its focus on right-wing zealots and the "gag rule." As far as I can tell, that is, Operation Rescue workers would not be getting arrested over and over again, dragged to jail, beaten, strip-searched and forced to pay huge fines if all Planned Parenthood were doing were passing out birth control pills. It is abortion they are concerned with. But the word abortion is avoided here; instead it is termed "reproductive freedom," "our rights," "birth control," and "reproductive health care." The name "Planned Parenthood" itself is a little absurd. Apparently not a lot of planning went into these pregnancies that are subsequently "unwanted."

One would assume that the two-page insert would have to get around to the actual subject at issue, but the obfuscation continues. Here there is "reproductive freedom," "family planning," "vital medical care," "health care," and, finally, in the sixth paragraph there are a few mentions of abortion, and then back to "reproductive freedom," "medical services," "reproductive life."

Only three of sixteen paragraphs use the word "abortion."

One of them says, "In New York abortion is legal, safe and funded." But abortion is never safe for the fetus. It is as if there were a group of men lobbying for the right to beat their wives. Bumper stickers would declare "Keep wife-beating safe and legal," and newspaper headlines would proclaim "Ten thousand men injured trying to beat their wives last year."

Another paragraph states:

> In Washington, the Supreme Court has denied doctors free speech with their decision in our case, *Rust* v. *Sullivan,* which upholds the "gag rule." Right-wing conservatives want to eliminate Title X funding for family planning programs and the administration is pandering to them. Millions of poor women are at risk of losing vital medical care.

That is an astonishing formulation. Reading that paragraph—even reading it closely, several times over—one would never know it is discussing a case in which the Court declined to find unconstitutional an administrative regulation denying tax monies for abortion procedures and referrals. The point at issue was whether our money, my money, is to be used to pay for abortion, something I, along with many other taxpayers, consider outright murder. But all one reads about is the "gag rule" and "free speech." The peculiar phraseology of the "pro-choice" movement is not only Orwellian but tacitly admits their own understanding of what a repulsive thing an abortion is.

A sociologist undertook a study of ethnic groups and their nicknames once and concluded that disfavored ethnic groups tend to change their names every few years because, as long as they remain part of the underclass, whatever name they assume begins to take on bad associations. It is not until they have achieved some sort of established status in society that they stick with the last name they were called. Analogously, it is wholly irrelevant what the pro-abortionists call themselves or call the procedure. They can call themselves pro-choice, pro-women's rights or pro-reproductive freedom—they can call themselves "the green people" for all I care. Abortion is an ugly thing and whatever name they adopt is going to become ugly within a few years.

Interestingly, one does not even see the euphemism "terminate a pregnancy" anymore. I think that was what abortion was being called for a while. They just keep running from whatever it is called. People don't like it. People who do not particularly identify themselves as pro-life nonetheless intuitively understand that abortion is a dirty little procedure, the same way my friends who claim to be atheists subliminally pay tribute to the human soul by their refusal to eat humans. By so calculatingly abjuring the word "abortion," Planned Parenthood acknowledges the beastliness of its cause.

My final point concerns all the insipid blathering about whether the anti-abortion position will be a vote-getter, and whether the Republican Party should, perhaps, modify its platform stance. In all great moral battles over the centuries—slavery, Nazism, Stalinism—there have been two sides. Now those wars are over. And when the battle is fought and the patriots win, we look back and everyone seems to presume that he would have been on the side of the angels, courageously facing down the bad guys, had he been alive during the abolitionist movement, World War II, or the Salem witch trials. But at the time, someone *had* to be on the wrong side and it wasn't so easy to be on the right side. It is only easy to be on the right side of important moral struggles in retrospect. It is never easy when it counts—otherwise there would be no battles.

Now you have a chance to see which side you will be on irrespective of the short-term consequences, irrespective of social censure, irrespective of the Leviathan media, and irrespective of your political party. We are right on this. I am right on this. If the Republican Party abandons its pro-life position, abandon the Republican Party. The Republican Party freed the slaves; now it's time to rescue the millions of unborn babies continuously sentenced to the abortionist's abattoir. Thank you.

NOTES

1. I have it on the authority of Professor Alvin Bernstein, who taught "Rome of the Caesars" at Cornell University, that in no civilized society have women walked about publicly with their breasts exposed.
2. The claim that women will die in back-alley abortions if abortion is outlawed cannot be included in the cost-benefit analysis of abortion because it essentially amounts to a threat that the law's opponents will commit suicide. It is as if the Amish were to lobby for a maximum national speed limit of five miles per hour on the grounds that the Amish themselves are likely to take their cattle and livestock for strolls on interstate freeways, thus increasing the odds of fatal accidents if the speed limit is any more than five miles per hour. The law should simply forbid the Amish from meandering onto highways, but cannot allow the threat of lawbreaking to be a function in the calculation of the most efficient speed limit—or of the net costs and benefits of abortion.

On Abortion: A Lincolnian Position

George McKenna

Twenty-two years ago abortion was made an individual right by the Supreme Court. Today it is a public institution—one of the most carefully cultivated institutions in America. It is protected by courts, subsidized by legislatures, performed in government-run hospitals and clinics, and promoted as a "fundamental right" by our State Department. As Supreme Court Justice Sandra Day O'Connor observed in the 1992 *Casey* decision, which reaffirmed *Roe* v. *Wade,* a whole generation has grown up since 1973 in the expectation that legal abortion will be available for them if they want it.

Today our nation's most prestigious civic groups, from the League of Women Voters to the American Civil Liberties Union, are committed to its protection and subsidization. The Accreditation Council for Graduate Medical Education now requires that abortion techniques be taught in all obstetrics-and-gynecology residency training programs. Influential voices in politics and the media are now demanding the assignment of U.S. marshals to protect abortion clinics against violence, and a federal law passed last year prescribes harsh criminal penalties for even nonviolent acts of civil disobedience if they are committed by demonstrators at abortion clinics. Some private organizations that administer birth-control programs and provide abortions, notably Planned Parenthood, are closely tied to government bureaucracies: Planned Parenthood receives one third of its income from the federal government. Abortion today is as American as free speech, freedom of religion, or any other practice protected by our courts.

With this difference: Unlike other American rights, abortion cannot be discussed in plain English. Its warmest supporters do not like to call it by its name.

Abortion is a "reproductive health procedure" or a "termination of pregnancy." Abortion clinics are "reproductive health clinics" (more recently, "women's clinics"), and the right to obtain an abortion is "reproductive freedom." Sometimes the word "abortion" is unavoidable, as in media accounts of the abortion controversy, but then it is almost invariably preceded by a line of nicer-sounding words: "the right of a woman to choose" abortion. This is still not enough to satisfy some in the abortion movement. In an op-ed piece that appeared in the the *New York Times* shortly after a gunman killed some employees and wounded others at two Brookline, Massachusetts, abortion

George McKenna is Professor Emeritus of Political Science at City College of New York. His latest book is *The Puritan Origins of American Patriotism* (Yale, 2007). This essay was reprinted from the *Atlantic Monthly* (September 1995) with the author's permission.

clinics, a counselor at one of the clinics complained that the media kept referring to her workplace as an abortion clinic. "I hate that term," she declared. At the end of the piece she suggested that her abortion clinic ought to be called "a place of healing and care."

The Clinton Administration, the first Administration clearly committed to abortion, seems to be trying hard to promote it without mentioning it. President Bill Clinton's 1993 healthcare bill would have nationalized the funding of abortion, forcing everyone to buy a "standard package" that included it. Yet nowhere in the bill's 1,342 pages was the word "abortion" ever used. In various interviews both Clintons acknowledged that it was their intention to include abortion under the category of "services for pregnant women." Another initiative in which the Clinton Administration participated, the draft report for last year's United Nations International Conference on Population and Development, used similar language. Abortion, called "pregnancy termination," was subsumed under the general category of "reproductive health care," a term used frequently in the report.

Why, in a decade when public discourse about sex has become determinedly forthright, is "abortion" so hard to say? No one hesitates to say "abortion" in other contexts—in referring, for example, to aborting a plane's takeoff. Why not say "abortion of a fetus"? Why substitute a spongy expression like "termination of pregnancy"? And why do abortion clinics get called "reproductive health clinics" when their manifest purpose is to *stop* reproduction? Why all this strange language? What is going on here?

The answer, it seems to me, is unavoidable. Even defenders and promoters of abortion sense that there is something not quite right about the procedure. "I abhor abortions," Henry Foster, President Clinton's unconfirmed nominee for Surgeon General, has said. Clinton himself, who made no secret of his support for abortion during his 1992 campaign, still repeats the mantra of "safe, legal, and rare" abortion. Why "rare"? If abortion is a constitutional right, on a par with freedom of speech and freedom of religion, why does it have to be "rare"? The reason Clinton uses this language should be obvious. He knows he is talking to a national electorate that is deeply troubled about abortion. Shortly before last year's congressional elections his wife went even further in appealing to this audience by characterizing abortion as "wrong" (though she added, "I don't think it should be criminalized").

Sometimes even abortion lobbyists show a degree of uneasiness about what it is they are lobbying for. At the end of 1993 Kate Michelman, the head of the National Abortion and Reproductive Rights Action League, was interviewed by the *Philadelphia Inquirer* about NARAL's new emphasis on the prevention of teen pregnancies. The reporter quoted Michelman as saying,

"We think abortion is a bad thing." Michelman complained that she had been misquoted, whereupon she was reminded that the interview had been taped. Nevertheless, NARAL issued a statement a few days later declaring that Michelman "has never said—and would never say—that 'abortion is a bad thing.'" Michelman, who had reason to know better, sought only to "clarify" her remark in a letter to the *Inquirer.* "It is not abortion itself that is a bad thing," she wrote. "Rather, our nation's high rate of abortion represents a failure" of our system of sex education, contraception, and health care. But a month later Michelman herself, testifying before a House subcommittee on energy and commerce, insisted that "the reporter absolutely quoted me incorrectly," and she later told a *Washington Post* reporter, "I would never, never, never, never, never mean to say such a thing." Not until the *Post* reporter showed her the transcript did Michelman finally acknowledge—somewhat evasively—that she had said it: "I'm obviously guilty of saying something that led her to put that comment in there."

Whatever else Michelman's bobbing and weaving reveals, it shows how nervous abortion advocates can get when the discussion approaches the question of what abortion *is.* Even if we accept Michelman's amended version of her remark, which is that it is not abortion but the "high rate" of abortion that is a bad thing, the meaning is hardly changed. If one abortion is not a bad thing, why are many abortions bad? What is it about abortion that is so troubling?

The obvious answer is that abortion is troubling because it is a killing process. Abortion clinics may indeed be places of "healing and care," as the Planned Parenthood counselor maintains, but their primary purpose is to kill human fetuses. Whether those fetuses are truly "persons" will continue to be debated by modern scholastics, but people keep blurting out fragments of what was long a moral consensus in this country. Once in a while even a newscaster, carefully schooled in *Sprachregelungen,* will slip up by reporting the murder of "a woman and her unborn baby," thus implying that something more than a single homicide has taken place. But that "something" must not be probed or examined; the newscaster must not speak its name. Abortion has thus come to occupy an absurd, surrealistic place in the national dialogue: It cannot be ignored and it cannot be openly stated. It is the corpse at the dinner party.

Douglas and the Democrats

Only one other institution in this country has been treated so evasively, and that is the institution that was nurtured and protected by the government during the first eighty-seven years of our nation's existence: the institution of slavery.

The men who drafted the Constitution included representatives from slave states who were determined to protect their states' interests. Yet they were all highly vocal proponents of human liberty. How does one reconcile liberty with slavery? They did it by producing a document that referred to slavery in three different places without once mentioning it. Slaves were "persons"— or, sometimes, "other persons"—in contrast to "free persons." The slave trade (which the Constitution prohibited Congress from banning until 1808) was referred to as "the Migration or Importation of such Persons as any of the States now existing shall think proper to admit." Free states were required to return fugitive slaves to their masters in the slave states, but in that clause a slave was a "person held to Service or Labour" and a master was "the party to whom such Service or Labour may be due."

At least the founders recognized the humanity of slaves by calling them "persons"; but in the next generation the status of slaves, and of blacks in general, steadily declined. By the end of the 1820s slaves were reduced to a species of property to be bought and sold like other property. Thomas Jefferson, who in 1776 had tried to insert into the Declaration of Independence a denunciation of the King for keeping open "a market where MEN should be bought & sold," now agonized only in private. Publicly all he could say on the fiftieth anniversary of the Declaration (the last year of his life) was that the progress of enlightenment had vindicated the "palpable truth, that the mass of mankind has not been born with saddles on their backs, nor a favored few booted and spurred, ready to ride them legitimately, by the grace of God," adding vaguely, "these are grounds of hope for others."

Jefferson often shied away from public controversy, but even the most flamboyant political leaders of the early nineteenth century could become suddenly circumspect when the talk turned to slavery. Andrew Jackson left office in 1837 blaming the South's secession threats on those northerners who insisted on talking about "the most delicate and exciting topics, topics upon which it is impossible that a large portion of the Union can ever speak without strong emotion." Such talk, he said, assaulted "the feelings and rights" of southerners and "their institutions." Jackson, usually a plainspoken man, would not mar the occasion of his last presidential address by saying the words "abolitionist" and "slavery." When slavery was discussed during the antebellum period, it was usually in the language of "rights"—the property rights of slaveholders and the sovereign rights of states. In 1850 the famous Whig senator Daniel Webster defended his support for a tough fugitive-slave law on such grounds. What right, he asked, did his fellow northerners have "to endeavor to get round this Constitution, or to embarrass the free exercise of the rights secured by the Constitution to the persons whose slaves escape from them? None at all, none at all."

Webster supported the Compromise of 1850, which attempted to settle the

question of slavery in the territories acquired from Mexico by admitting California as a free state and Utah and New Mexico "with or without slavery as
their constitution may provide at the time of their admission." This last principle was seized upon by Stephen A. Douglas, the "little giant" of the Democratic Party, and made the basis of the Kansas-Nebraska Act, which Douglas pushed through Congress in 1854. Nullifying the Missouri Compromise
of 1820, it opened the remaining territories to slavery if the people in them
voted for it. Douglas's rationale was "popular sovereignty," a logical extension of
states' rights. The premise of states' rights was that any institution a state
wanted to have, it should have, so long as that didn't conflict with the Constitution. Since slavery not only did not conflict with the Constitution but was
protected by it, Douglas said, it followed that each state had "a right to do as
it pleases on the subject of slavery," and the same principle should apply to
the territories. Douglas's appeal was not to the fiery pro-slavery minorities in
the South, who insisted that slavery was morally right, but to the vast majority
in the North, who simply felt uncomfortable talking about the subject. He
assured them that they didn't have to—that they could avoid the subject
altogether by leaving it to the democratic process. Let the people decide: If
they "want slavery, they shall have it; if they prohibit slavery, it shall be prohibited." But what about the rights of slaves? That, Douglas said, was one of
those issues that should be left to moralists and theologians. It did not belong
in the political or legal realm. In speaking of the right to own slaves, he said,

> I am now speaking of rights under the Constitution, and not of moral or reli-
> gious rights. I do not discuss the morals of the people of Missouri, but let them
> settle that matter for themselves. I hold that the people of the slaveholding
> States are civilized men as well as ourselves, that they bear consciences as well
> as we, and that they are accountable to God and their posterity and not to us.
> It is for them to decide therefore the moral and religious right of the slavery
> question for themselves within their own limits.

Looking back today on Douglas's words, now 137 years old, one is struck
by how sophisticated and "modern" they seem. He ruled out of order any
debate on the morality of slavery. That was a "religious" question. It had no
place in a constitutional debate, and we had no right to judge other people in
such terms. In one of his debates with Lincoln in 1858, Douglas scolded his
opponent for telling the people in the slave states that their institution violated
the law of God. "Better for him," he said, to cheers and applause, "to adopt
the doctrine of 'judge not lest ye be judged.'"

The same notions and even some of the same language have found their
way into the abortion debate. In *Roe* v. *Wade*, in 1973, Justice Harry Blackmun

observed that philosophers and theologians have been arguing about abortion for centuries without reaching any firm conclusions about its morality. All "seemingly absolute convictions" about it are primarily the products of subjective factors such as one's philosophy, religious training and "attitudes toward life and family and their values." As justices, he said, he and his colleagues were required to put aside all such subjective considerations and "resolve the issue by constitutional measurement free of emotion and of predilection." As the abortion debate intensified, particularly after Catholic bishops and Christian evangelicals entered the fray in the 1970s, the word "religious" was increasingly used by abortion defenders to characterize their opponents. They used it in exactly the same sense that Douglas used it in the slavery debate, as a synonym for "subjective," "personal," and thus, finally, "arbitrary." In this view, religion is largely a matter of taste, and to impose one's taste upon another is not only repressive but also irrational. This seems to be the view of the philosopher Ronald Dworkin in his book *Life's Dominion* (1993) and in some of his subsequent writings. What the opposition to abortion boils down to, Dworkin says, is an attempt "to impose a controversial view on an essentially religious issue on people who reject it."

The approach has served as useful cover for Democratic politicians seeking to reconcile their religious convictions with their party's platform and ideology. The most highly publicized use of the "religious" model was the famous speech given by Mario Cuomo, then the governor of New York, at the University of Notre Dame during the 1984 presidential campaign. Characterizing himself as an "old-fashioned" Catholic, Cuomo said that he accepted his Church's position on abortion, just as he accepted its position on birth control and divorce. But, he asked rhetorically, "must I insist you do?" By linking abortion with divorce and birth control, Cuomo put it in the category of Church doctrines that are meant to apply only to Catholics. Everyone agrees that it would be highly presumptuous for a Catholic politician to seek to prevent non-Catholics from practicing birth control or getting a divorce. But the pro-life argument has always been that abortion is different from birth control and divorce, because it involves a nonconsenting party— the unborn child. At one point in his speech Cuomo seemed to acknowledge that distinction. "As Catholics," he said, "my wife and I were enjoined never to use abortion to destroy the life we created, and we never have," and he added that "a fetus is different from an appendix or a set of tonsils." But then, as if suddenly recognizing where this line of reasoning might lead, he said, "But not everyone in our society agrees with me and Matilda." In other words, it was just a thought—don't bother with it if you don't agree. *De gustibus non est disputandum.*

Lincoln and the Republicans

Cuomo's speech received considerable press coverage, because it was perceived as a kind of thumb in the eye of New York's Cardinal John O'Connor, who had been stressing the Church's unequivocal moral condemnation of abortion. The argument, then, was newsworthy but not at all original. New York Senator Daniel Patrick Moynihan, another pro-choice Catholic, had been saying much the same thing since the mid-1970s, and by the 1980s it had become the standard argument. One hears today from the Clintons, from spokespeople for the American Civil Liberties Union, and from the philosopher Ronald Dworkin, the journalist Roger Rosenblatt, and the celebrity lawyer Alan Dershowitz, and from legions of others that opposition to abortion is essentially religious, or private, and as such has no place in the political realm. There is a patient philosophical response to this argument, which others have spelled out at some length, but it finds no purchase in a mass media that thrives on sound bites. There is also a primal scream— "Murder!"—that is always welcomed by the media as evidence of pro-life fanaticism. But is there a proper *rhetorical* response, a response suited to civil dialogue that combines reason with anger and urgency? I believe there is, and the model for it is Abraham Lincoln's response to Stephen Douglas.

Lincoln had virtually retired from politics by 1854, having failed to obtain a much-coveted position in the Administration of Zachary Taylor. Then came the passage of the Kansas-Nebraska Act, Stephen Douglas's masterwork, which permitted the extension of slavery into the territories. Lincoln was horrified. In his view, slavery was like a cancer—or a "wen," as he called it. It could be eliminated only if it was first contained. If it ever metastasized, spreading into the new territories, it could never be stopped. He viewed the Kansas-Nebraska Act as a stimulant to the growth of the cancer because it invited slave-owning "squatters" to settle in the new territories, create electoral majorities, and establish new slave states. One of the longest and most passionate of Lincoln's speeches was his 1854 address on the act, which rehearsed many of the themes that would reappear in his debates with Douglas.

Douglas had boasted that the Kansas-Nebraska Act furthered democracy by leaving the question of whether or not to adopt slavery up to the people in the territories. Lincoln quickly homed in on the critical weakness in this "self-government" argument: "When the white man governs himself, that is self-government; but when he governs himself and also governs *another* man, that is *more* than self-government—that is despotism." It would not be despotism, of course, if slaves were not human: "That is to say, inasmuch as you do not object to my taking my hog to Nebraska, therefore I must not object to you taking your slave." This, Lincoln said, "is perfectly logical, if there is no difference between hogs and negroes." Lincoln kept returning to the question of the humanity of slaves, the question that Douglas ruled out of bounds as essentially "religious." Everywhere, Lincoln said, even in the South, people knew that slaves were human beings. If southerners really believed that slaves were not human, why did they join in banning the international slave trade, making it a capital offense? And if dealing in human flesh was no different from dealing in hogs or cattle, why was the slave-dealer regarded with revulsion throughout the South?

> You despise him utterly. You do not recognize him as a friend, or even as an honest man. Your children must not play with his; they may rollick freely with the little negroes, but not with the "slave-dealers" children. If you are obliged to deal with him, you try to get through the job without so much as touching him.

People's moral intuitions could not be repressed; they would surface in all kinds of unexpected ways: in winces and unguarded expressions, in labored euphemisms, in slips of the tongue. Lincoln was on the lookout for these, and he forced his opponents to acknowledge their significance: "Repeal the Missouri Compromise—repeal all compromises—repeal the declaration of independence—repeal all past history, you still can not repeal human nature. It will still be the abundance of man's heart, that slavery extension is wrong; and out of the abundance of his heart, his mouth will continue to speak."

Douglas tried to evade the force of these observations by insisting that he didn't care *what* was chosen; all he cared about was the freedom to choose. At one point Douglas even tried to put his own theological spin on this, suggesting that God placed good and evil before man in the Garden of Eden in order to give him the right to choose. Lincoln indignantly rejected this interpretation. "God did not place good and evil before man, telling him to make his choice. On the contrary, he did tell him there was one tree, of the fruit of which, he should not eat, upon pain of certain death. I should scarcely wish so strong a prohibition against slavery in Nebraska."

Lincoln's depiction of slavery as a moral cancer became the central theme of his speeches during the rest of the 1850s. It was the warning he meant to convey in his "House Divided" speech, in his seven debates with Douglas in 1858, and in the series of speeches that culminated in the 1860 presidential campaign. In all these he continually reminded his audience that the theme of choice without reference to the *object* of choice was morally empty. He would readily agree that each state ought to choose the kind of laws it wanted when it came to the protection and regulation of its commerce. Indiana might need cranberry laws; Virginia might need oyster laws. But "I ask if there is any parallel between these things and this institution of slavery." Oysters and cranberries were matters of moral indifference; slavery was not.

> The real issue in this controversy—the one pressing upon every mind—is the sentiment of the part of one class that looks upon the institution of slavery *as a wrong,* and of another class that *does not* look upon it as a wrong. The sentiment that contemplates the institution of slavery in this country as a wrong is the sentiment of the Republican party.

Lincoln has been portrayed as a moral compromiser, even an opportunist, and in some respects he was. Though he hoped that slavery would eventually be abolished within its existing borders, he had no intention of abolishing it. Although he said, in his "House Divided" speech of 1858, that "this government cannot endure, permanently half *slave* and half *free,*" Lincoln made it clear in that speech, and in subsequent speeches and writings, that his intention was not to abolish slavery but to "arrest the further spread of it, and place it where the public mind shall rest in the belief that it is in course of ultimate extinction . . . ." In his first inaugural address, desperate to keep the South in the Union, he even hinted that he might support a constitutional amendment to protect slavery in the existing slave states against abolition by the federal government—a kind of reverse Thirteenth Amendment. The following year he countermanded an order by one of his own generals that would have emancipated slaves in South Carolina, Georgia, and Florida. In that same year he wrote the much-quoted letter to Horace Greeley stating that his "paramount object" was not to free slaves but to save the Union, and that if he could save the Union without freeing a single slave, he would do it. But when it came down to the commitment he had made in the 1850s, Lincoln was as stern as a New England minister. Slavery, he insisted, was an evil that must not be allowed to expand—and he would not allow it to expand. He struggled with a variety of strategies for realizing that principle, from gradual compensated emancipation to outright abolition, but he never for a moment swerved from the principle. A month after his election Lincoln replied in this way to a correspondent who urged him to temper his opposition to slavery in the territories: "On the territorial question, I am inflexible. . . . You think slavery is right and ought to be extended; we think it is wrong and ought to be restricted."

A Lincolnian Position on Abortion

I suggested that we can find in Lincoln's anti-slavery rhetoric a coherent position that could serve as a model for pro-life politicians today. How would this rhetoric sound? Perhaps the best way to answer this is to provide a sample of what might be said by a politician devoted to a cause but no less devoted to building broad support for it. With the reader's indulgence, then, I will play that politician, making the following campaign statement:

"According to the Supreme Court, the right to choose abortion is legally protected. That does not change the fact that abortion is morally wrong. It violates the very first of the inalienable rights guaranteed in the Declaration of Independence—the right to life. Even many who would protect and extend the right to choose abortion admit that abortion is wrong, and that killing 1.5 million unborn children a year is, in the understated words of one, 'a bad thing.' Yet, illogically, they denounce all attempts to restrain it or even to speak out against it. In this campaign I *will* speak out against it. I will say what is in all our hearts: that abortion is an evil that needs to be restricted and discouraged. If elected, I will not try to abolish an institution that the Supreme Court has ruled to be constitutionally protected, but I will do everything in my power to arrest its further spread and place it where the public can rest in the belief that it is becoming increasingly rare. I take very seriously the imperative, often expressed by abortion supporters, that abortion *should* be rare. Therefore, if I am elected, I will seek to end all public subsidies for abortion, for abortion advocacy, and for experiments on aborted children. I will support all reasonable abortion restrictions that pass muster with the Supreme Court, and I will encourage those who provide alternatives to abortion. Above all, I mean to *treat it as a wrong.* I will use the forum provided by my office to speak out against abortion and related practices, such as euthanasia, that violate or undermine the most fundamental of the rights enshrined in this nation's founding charter."

The position on abortion I have sketched—permit, restrict, discourage—is unequivocally prolife even as it is effectively pro-choice. It does not say "I am personally opposed to abortion"; it says abortion is evil. Yet in its own way it is pro-choice. First, it does not demand an immediate end to abortion. To extend Lincoln's oncological trope: It concludes that all those who oppose abortion can do right now is to contain the cancer, keep it from metastasizing. It thus acknowledges the present legal status of "choice" even as it urges Americans to choose life. Second, by supporting the quest for alternatives to abortion, it widens the range of choices available to women in crisis pregnancies. Studies of women who have had abortions show that many did not really make an informed "choice" but were confused and ill-informed at the time, and regretful later. If even some of those reports are true, they make a case for re-examining the range of choices actually available to women.

Would a candidate adopting this position be obliged to support only pro-life

163

nominees to the Supreme Court? To answer this, let's consider Lincoln's reaction to *Dred Scott* v. *Sanford,* the 1857 Supreme Court ruling that Congress had no right to outlaw slavery in the territories. Lincoln condemned the decision but did not promise to reverse it by putting differently minded justices on the Court. Instead his approach was to accept the ruling as it affected the immediate parties to the suit but to deny its authority as a binding precedent for policymaking by the other branches of the federal government. If he were in Congress, he said in a speech delivered in July of 1858, shortly before his debates with Douglas, he would support legislation outlawing slavery in the territories—despite the *Dred Scott* decision. In our analogy we need not follow Lincoln that far to see the valid core of his position. Yes, he was saying, the Supreme Court has the job of deciding cases arising under the Constitution and laws of the United States. But if its decisions are to serve as durable precedents, they must be free of obvious bias, based on accurate information, and consistent with "legal public expectation" and established practice, or at least with long-standing precedent. Since *Dred Scott* failed all these tests, Lincoln believed that it should be reversed, and he intended to do what he could to get it reversed. But he would not try to fill the Court with new, "catechized" justices (a process to which he thought Douglas had been party regarding the Illinois state bench). Instead he would seek to persuade the Court of its error, hoping that it would reverse itself. Lest this seem naive, we must remember that *he intended to conduct his argument before the American people.* Lincoln knew that in the final analysis durable judicial rulings on major issues must be rooted in the soil of American opinion. "Public sentiment," he said, "is everything" in this country.

> *With* it, nothing can fail; *against* it nothing can succeed. Whoever moulds public sentiment, goes deeper than he who enacts statutes, or pronounces judicial decisions. He makes possible the inforcement of these, else impossible.

The lesson for pro-life leaders today is that instead of trying to fill the Supreme Court with "catechized" justices, a strategy almost certain to backfire, they should content themselves with modest, competent justices who are free of ideological bias, and all the while keep their eyes on the real prize: "public sentiment." *Dred Scott* was overturned within a decade by the Civil War, but *Plessy* v. *Ferguson*—the 1896 ruling validating state-imposed racial segregation—darkened the nation for fifty-eight years before it was overturned in *Brown* v. *Board of Education.* Yet during that long night civil-rights advocates were not silent. In thousands of forums, from university classrooms and law-school journals to churches and political conventions, they argued their case against American-style apartheid. In the end they not only won their legal case but also forged a new moral consensus.

It took time—time and patience. The lesson for pro-life advocates is that they need to take the time to lay out their case. They may hope for an immediate end to abortion, and they certainly have a First Amendment right to ask for it, but their emphasis, I believe, should be on making it clear to others why they have reached the conclusions that they have reached. They need to reason with skeptics and listen more carefully to critics. They need to demand less and explain more. Whatever the outcome, that would surely contribute to the process of reasonable public discourse.

The "campaign statement" I presented above is my own modest contribution to that process. It seeks common ground for a civil debate on abortion. It does not aim at a quick fix; it is based on the Lincolnian premise that nothing is possible without consensus. At the same time, it suggests that some measures can be taken here and now, and with broad public support, to contain the spread of abortion.

Would either party, today, endorse such an approach? Probably not.

It is easy to see why Democrats would run from it. Since 1972 pro-choice feminists have become increasingly important players in Democratic Party councils. In 1976 abortion lobbies got the Democratic platform committee to insert a plank in the party platform opposing a constitutional amendment banning abortion, and since then they have escalated their demands to include public funding of abortion and special federal protection of abortion clinics. No Democrat with serious national ambitions would ever risk offending them. A long list of Democrats who were once pro-life—Edward Kennedy, Jesse Jackson, even Al Gore and Bill Clinton—turned around in the seventies and eighties as the lobbies tightened their grip on the party. In 1992 Robert Casey, the pro-life governor of Pennsylvania, a liberal on every issue except abortion, was not even permitted to speak at the Democratic National Convention.

What is more puzzling—at first glance, anyway—is the tepid reception the pro-life position has received over the years from centrist Republican leaders. In the present, heated atmosphere of Republican presidential politics, most Republican candidates have been wooing pro-life voters, obviously anticipating their clout in next spring's primaries. But in the day-to-day management of party affairs few Republican leaders have shown much enthusiasm for the cause. Among the ten items in Newt Gingrich's Contract With America there is no reference to abortion (in fact, there is no reference to any of the social-cultural issues that the Republicans once showcased, beyond demands for tougher child pornography laws and "strengthening rights of parents"). The Republican national chairman, Haley Barbour, is at odds with pro-life Republicans who accuse him of trying to scuttle the party's pro-life position.

The party's leading spokespeople include vocal abortion supporters like Christine Todd Whitman, the governor of New Jersey, and William Weld, the governor of Massachusetts, and its most prominent candidates in last year's elections—Mitt Romney in Massachusetts, Michael Huffington in California, George Pataki in New York—all declared themselves pro-choice.

It would be hard to find any Republican seriously seeking national office today who would say of abortion what Lincoln said of slavery: "The Republican Party think it wrong—we think it is a moral, a social, and a political wrong." Why? Wasn't it the Republicans who first promised to support a "human-life amendment" outlawing abortion? Didn't Ronald Reagan often use his bully pulpit to speak out in behalf of the unborn? Yes—but that was then. In 1980 the Republicans set out to woo those who were later called Reagan Democrats, and one of the means was a pro-life plank, designed to counter the plank the Democrats had put in their platform four years earlier. The wooing worked all too well. Many of the conservative Catholics and evangelical Protestants who streamed into the Republican Party in 1980 were ex-New Dealers, and they retained elements of the old faith. They may have cooled toward the welfare state, but they were not opposed to the use of government to promote social goals. Their primary goal, the outlawing of abortion, would itself involve the use of government; but even beyond that, these new "social conservatives" never really shared the Republicans' distrust of an activist government. Republican leaders thus greeted them warily. These Democrats-turned-Republican were seen to be useful during elections but a nuisance afterward. During the Reagan years they were given considerable verbal support, which at times greatly helped the pro-life cause (as, for example, at the UN International Conference on Population in Mexico City in 1984, when Reagan officials helped push through a final report stating that "abortion in no way should be promoted as a method of family planning"), though it never got beyond lip service. During the Bush Administration even lip service faltered as Republican officials decided that their party's "big tent" needed to accommodate the pro-choice view. "Read my lips," Bush said, but he was talking about "no new taxes." Bush's failure to keep his tax promise was seen as a major cause of his defeat in 1992, but in the ashes of this defeat lay what Republican leaders took to be a new sign of hope: They figured they could win elections on tax-and-spend issues as long as they kept their promises; they didn't need the "social issues" people anymore.

The Republicans have thus returned to where they feel most comfortable. Back in the 1880s William Graham Sumner used to say that the purpose of government is "to protect the property of men and the honor of women." Modern Republicans would hasten to add "the property of women" to this meager agenda, but the philosophy is the same. It sees the common good as the sum of individual private satisfactions. Its touchstone is the autonomous individual celebrated by John Locke in *Of Civil Government* (1690): "Free, equal, and independent" in the state of nature, the solitary savage enters society only to protect what is his—or hers. Here is a philosophy radically at odds with pro-life premises. If a woman has an absolute, unqualified right to her property, and if her body is part of her property, it follows that she has a right to evict her tenant whenever she wants and for whatever reason she pleases. This "despotic" concept of individual ownership is Republican, not Democratic. If Democrats are pro-choice for political reasons, Republicans are pro-choice in their hearts. Talk radio's greatest Republican cheerleader, Rush Limbaugh, has also been an outspoken pro-lifer, but even Limbaugh has been softening that part of his message lately—and small wonder. Here is Limbaugh castigating the environmental movement: "You know why these environmentalist wackos want you to give up your car? I'll tell you the real reason. They don't want you to have freedom of choice." There it is. Freedom of choice: the philosophical center of modern-day Republicanism.

Well, the reader asks impatiently, if Democrats are pro-choice politically and Republicans are pro-choice philosophically, what's the point of that pro-life "campaign statement"? Who is going to adopt it? Perhaps the good folks in some little splinter party, but who else? I answer as follows: American party politics is very tricky, at times seemingly unpredictable. Who, in the early sixties, would have dared to predict that the Democrats would become the abortion party? But there was a subtle logic at work. By 1964 it was clear that the Democrats were about to become the civil rights party. The feminism of the sixties rode into the reform agenda on the back of civil rights (by the end of the decade "sexism" had entered most dictionaries as a counterpart to "racism"), and high on *its* agenda was not just the legalization but the moral legitimization of abortion. Nevertheless, it took a dozen years for the full shift to occur. I think that within the next dozen years the shift could be reversed. To explain why, I must take a long look backward, to the parties' respective positions in Lincoln's time.

Pro-Life Democrats

In the 1850s it was not the Republicans but the Democrats who were the champions of unbridled individualism. As heirs of Andrew Jackson's entrepreneurialism—and ultimately of Jefferson's distrust of "energetic government"—the Democrats were wary not only of national action but also of any concept of the common good that threatened individual or local autonomy. It was the Republicans, heirs of Whig nationalism and New England transcendentalism,

who succeeded—under Abraham Lincoln's tutelage—in constructing a coherent philosophy of national reform. In *The Lincoln Persuasion* (1993), a
brilliant, posthumously published study of Lincoln's political thought, the political scientist J. David Greenstone traced the roots of that thought to the
communitarian "covenant theology" of seventeenth-century Puritanism. Lincoln combined this theology, with its emphasis on public duty and public purpose, with the nationalism and institutionalism of Henry Clay and other leading Whigs, arriving at a position of "political humanitarianism." Lincoln's synthesis, Greenstone noted, did not deny the importance of individual development, but it did assert that "the improvement of individual and society were
almost inseparably joined." Combining moral commitment with political realism, Lincoln arrived at a concept of the public good that resonated deeply
among northerners, especially those large segments steeped in the culture of
New England. At the time of the Civil War, then, the Democratic and Republican parties were divided not only on the slavery question but also on the
larger philosophical question of national responsibility. The Democrats adopted
a position of economic and moral laissez-faire, while the Republicans insisted
that on certain questions the nation had to do more than formulate procedural
rules; it had to make moral judgments and act on them.

This philosophical alignment, persisting through the Civil War and Recon-
struction, was blurred during the Gilded Age. Then, over the course of the
next forty years, something surprising happened: The parties reversed positions. Populist Democrats in the 1890s weakened their party's attachment to
laissez-faire, and after "progressive" Republicans (whose model was Lincoln) failed to take over their party in 1912, many started moving toward the
Democrats. Woodrow Wilson welcomed them—and so, twenty years later,
did Franklin Roosevelt. By 1936 it was the Democrats who were sounding
the Lincolnian themes of national purpose and government responsibility, while
the Republicans had become the champions of the autonomous individual.

Since then both parties have veered and tacked, sometimes partly embracing each other's doctrines, but today the congressional parties stand as
far apart as they were at the height of the New Deal. President Clinton may
have muddied the waters with his "me, too, but more moderately" response
to Republican retrenchment, but in Congress the programmatic differences
between the parties are spelled out almost daily in party-line votes reminiscent of
the late 1930s. Now as then, Republicans emphasize the role of government as a
neutral rule maker that encourages private initiative and protects its fruits.
Now as then, Democrats emphasize the role of government as a moral leader
that seeks to realize public goals unrealizable in the private sphere.

If this analysis is correct, it follows that the proper philosophical home for pro-lifers right now is the liberal wing of the Democratic Party. To test this, go back to that "campaign statement" I sketched earlier and make one simple change: Substitute the word "racism" for "abortion." Without much editing the statement would be instantly recognizable as the speech of a liberal Democrat. Democrats know that racism, like abortion, cannot be abolished by governmental fiat. But they also know that it is wrong to subsidize racist teachings publicly or to tolerate racist speech in public institutions or to permit racist practices in large-scale "private" enterprises. Democrats also insist that government has a duty to take the lead in condemning racism and educating our youth about its dangers. In other words, the same formula—grudgingly tolerate, restrict, discourage—that I have applied to abortion is what liberal Democrats have been using to combat racism over the past generation. With abortion, as with racism, we are targeting a practice that is recognized as "wrong" (Hillary Clinton) and "a bad thing" (Kate Michelman). With abortion, as with racism, we are conceding the practical impossibility of outlawing the evil itself but pledging the government's best efforts to make it "rare" (Bill Clinton *et al.*). When it comes to philosophical coherence, therefore, nothing prevents Democrats from adopting my abortion position. Indeed, there is very good reason to adopt it.

It is, however, politically incorrect. Any liberal Democrat taking this stance would incur the wrath of the abortion lobbies. Protests within the party would mount, funding would dry up, connections with the party leadership would be severed, and there might be a primary challenge. Because politicians do not court martyrdom, the intimidatory power of these lobbies is formidable.

But no power lasts forever, and power grounded more in bullying than in reason is particularly vulnerable in our country. Within the liberal left, from which the Democrats draw their intellectual sustenance, there is increasing dissatisfaction with the absolutist dogma of "abortion rights." Nat Hentoff, a columnist in the left-liberal *Village Voice,* wonders why those who dwell so much on "rights" refuse to consider the bare possibility that unborn human beings may also have a few rights. Hentoff, who is a sort of libertarian liberal, sees a contradiction between abortion and individual rights, but the socialist writer Christopher Hitchens may actually be more in tune with the communitarian bent of post-New Deal liberalism in his critique of pro-choice philosophy. Hitchens caused an uproar among readers and staffers of *The Nation* in 1989 when he published an article in which he observed with approval that more and more of his colleagues were questioning whether "a fetus is 'only' a growth in, or appendage to, the female body." While supporting abortion in some cases, he insisted that society has a vital interest in restricting it. What struck him as ironic, and totally indefensible, was the tendency of many leftists suddenly to become selfish individualists whenever the topic turned to abortion.

> It is a pity that . . . the majority of feminists and their allies have stuck to the dead ground of "Me Decade" possessive individualism, an ideology that has more in common than it admits with the prehistoric right, which it claims to oppose but has in fact encouraged.

Hitchens's critique of the pro-choice position comes from his socialist premises, but even some liberal critics closer to the center have adopted a similar view. *The Good Society* (1991), by the sociologist Robert Bellah and his associates, reads like the campaign book of a decidedly liberal Democratic politician, someone who might challenge Bill Clinton from the left in 1996. The root of what is wrong in America, it says, is our "Lockean political culture," which emphasizes "the pursuit of individual affluence (the American dream) in a society with a most un-Lockean economy and government." When the authors get to the topic of abortion, they again see Lockeanism as the culprit: It has turned abortion into an "absolute right." In place of this kind of extreme individualism they suggest we consider the practices of twenty other Western democracies.

> There is respect for the value of a woman's being able to choose parenthood rather than having it forced upon her, but society also has an interest in a woman's abortion decision. It is often required that she participate in counselling; she is encouraged to consider the significance of her decision, and she must offer substantial reasons why the potential life of the fetus must be sacrificed and why bearing a child would do her real harm.

Despite its use of the strange term "potential life" (a usage favored by Justice Blackmun) for a living fetus, Bellah's formulation expresses coherently what modem liberalism points toward but usually resists at the last minute: a responsible communitarian position on abortion. It is not the same as my campaign statement, but it is within debating distance, and setting the two statements side by side might bring together in civil debate reasonable people from both sides.

Of course, neither position would pass muster with NARAL, NOW, the ACLU, and other pro-choice absolutists. But at some point, I think, sooner rather than later, the grip of these lobbies will have to loosen. One lesson of last year's congressional elections is that the Democratic Party will suffer at the polls if it is perceived by the public as the voice of entrenched minority factions. For better or worse, the Republicans articulated a philosophy in 1994, while the Democrats, by and large, believed that all they had to do was appeal to "their" people. The party needs to rediscover the idea of a common good, and the abortion issue may be as suitable a place as any to start. But the Democrats will first have to break free of the abortion lobbies. That will be a formidable challenge, though not an impossible one. As the political scientist Jeffrey Berry has observed, one of the most startling features of modern American politics is how quickly political alliances can shift. National politics, Berry writes, no longer works by means of "subgovernments"—cozy two-way relationships between particular lobbyists and politicians. To-day we live in a world of "issue networks," in which many lobbies vie for attention. Something like this, I believe, is starting to happen on women's issues. One of the fast-growing feminist groups in the country right now is Feminists for Life (FFL), which has offices nationwide and has recently moved its headquarters to Washington, D.C. Founded in the 1970s by former NOW members who had been expelled for their pro-life views, FFL supports almost the entire agenda of feminism except "abortion rights." Citing the pro-life stands of the founders of American feminism, including Susan B. Anthony and Elizabeth Cady Stanton, they view themselves as reclaiming authentic feminism. Gay-rights groups, usually allied with the abortion lobbies, now include PLAGAL, the Pro-Life Alliance of Gays and Lesbians. In issue networks, Jeffrey Berry observes, alliances can be composed "of both old friends and strange bedfellows"; there are "no permanent allies and no permanent enemies." The new pragmatic alliances of gays and straights, religious believers and secularists, feminists and traditionalists, may soon be demanding seats at the Democratic table. It would not be surprising if they were welcomed as liberators by many Democrats who have been forced to endorse a Me Decade ideology at odds with the spirit of their party.

Pro-Choice Republicans

What about the Republicans? Where are they headed? It is hard to say. As already noted, on a range of domestic issues the party seems to have embraced a philosophy of possessive individualism that has a distinctly pro-choice ring to it, and in this respect is no longer the party of Lincoln. Lincoln's Republicanism, as Greenstone pointed out in *The Lincoln Persuasion,* combined a Whiggish sense of national responsibility with a New England ethic of moral perfection. Then as now, Republicans believed in capitalist enterprise and fiscal prudence—but in those days they put them in the service of broader humanitarian goals. "Republicans," Lincoln said, "are for both the *man* and the *dollar;* but in cases of conflict, the man *before* the dollar." This was true for a long time in the Republican Party. Theodore Roosevelt's notion of "stewardship" had traces of the Lincolnian synthesis of humanitarianism and institutional responsibility; early in this century many of the Progressives came from Republican backgrounds. Even in the 1950s Eisenhower's brand of "modern Republicanism" faintly echoed the old tradition of active government and moral leadership. Someday, I think, it will be rediscovered. It is a noble tradition.

Right now, though, it is out of season. The Republicans are on a laissez-faire roll. The strategy of their leaders is to marginalize right-to-lifers, get their plank out of the platform, and avoid any more messy debates over social issues. They see a golden opportunity to win more recruits by appealing to yuppies and other libertarians who hate taxes and welfare but like "abortion rights." What can be said to these shrewd Republican leaders? In shrewdness and wiliness it would be hard to match Abraham Lincoln. Let us, then, listen to Lincoln as he warned against weakening his party's anti-slavery plank in order to win the votes of "moderates." "In my judgement," he wrote to an Illinois Republican official in 1859, "such a step would be a serious mistake—would open a gap through which more would pass *out* than pass *in*." And so today. Many Reagan Democrats came to the Republicans in the 1980s because their own party deserted them on social issues. If the Republicans do the same, many will either drift back to the Democratic Party (many of these, remember, are former New Deal Democrats, rather liberal on economic issues) or join a third party or simply drop out (many evangelicals were apolitical before Reagan came along). For every pro-choice yuppie voter the Republicans won, they might lose two from the "religious right."

In truth, however, no one can be sure about the gains and losses resulting from one position or another on abortion, and such considerations are beside my main point, which is this: It is time at last in America for the abortion issue to be addressed with candor and clarity by politicians of both major parties. There needs to be *engagement* on the topic. Right now, as the philosopher Alasdair MacIntyre puts it, the arguments pro and con on this issue are "incommensurable"—they sail past each other; the two sides are talking about different things. Part of the blame for the mindless "emotivism," as MacIntyre calls it, can be attributed to the more extreme elements in the pro-life movement, who have stifled reasoned argument with their cries of "Murder!" But much of it results from the squeamishness of pro-choicers, who simply refuse to face up to what abortion is. Nervousness, guilt, even anguish, are all hidden behind abstract, Latinate phrases. Only rarely does reality intrude. That is why Christopher Hitchens caused such a howl of pain when he published his *Nation* article on abortion. His crack about the "possessive individualism" of pro-choicers undoubtedly caused discomfort, but what must have touched a raw nerve was his description of abortion itself. After sympathizing with the emotions of rank-and-file members of the pro-life movement with their "genuine, impressive, unforced revulsion at the idea of a disposable fetus"— Hitchens added,

> But anyone who has ever seen a sonogram or has spent even an hour with a textbook on embryology knows that emotions are not the deciding factor. In order to terminate a pregnancy, you have to still a heartbeat, switch off a developing brain and, whatever the method, break some bones and rupture some organs.

Here, then, is the center of it all. If abortion had nothing to do with the stilling of heartbeats and brains, there would be no abortion controversy.

Suppose, now, I were to define the controversy in this manner: It is a fight between those who are horrified by the above-mentioned acts, considering them immoral, and those who are not horrified and do not consider them immoral. "Unfair," most pro-choicers would say. "We are also horrified. Have we not said that we abhor abortion? Have we not called it wrong? Have we not said it should be rare?" All right, then, let the debate begin: How rare should it be? How can we make it rare? In what ways, if any, can public institutions be used to discourage abortion? If abortion means stilled hearts and ruptured organs, how much of that can we decently permit?

In this debate I have made my own position clear. It is a pro-life position (though it may not please all pro-lifers), and its model is Lincoln's position on slavery from 1854 until well into the Civil War: tolerate, restrict, discourage. Like Lincoln's, its touchstone is the common good of the nation, not the sovereign self. Like Lincoln's position, it accepts the legality but not the moral legitimacy of the institution that it seeks to contain. It invites argument and negotiation; it is a gambit, not a gauntlet.

The one thing certain right now is that the abortion controversy is not going to wither away, because the anguish that fuels it keeps regenerating. Some Americans may succeed in desensitizing themselves to what is going on, as many did with slavery, but most Americans feel decidedly uncomfortable about the stilled heartbeats and brains of 1.5 million human fetuses every year. The discomfort will drive some portion of that majority to organize and protest. Some will grow old or weary, and will falter, but others will take their place. (I have seen it already: There are more and more young faces in the annual "march for life.") Pro-life protests will continue, in season and out of season, with political support or without it. Abortion, a tragedy in everyone's estimation, will continue to darken our prospect until we find practicable ways of dealing with it in order to make it rare. But before we can even hope to do that, we have to start talking with one another honestly, in honest language.

What We Can't *Not* Know

J. Budziszewski

He came out of the blue to talk with me about abortion. I usually avoid discussing the issue with graduate student activists; what they want is free debating practice. This one, I thought, might be an exception. No doubt he wanted free debating practice, too, but something in his manner suggested a troubled mind, and I suspected that he was nearing his crisis.

There is a certain pattern in these conversations. He announced that he wanted to talk about biology, not theology. When his biology got in trouble, he switched to medical history. When the same thing happened to medical history, he switched to the history of canon law. Then he escaped to philosophy of jurisprudence; then theology. When his account of Christian theology was punctured, he complained that I was speaking from faith. When I pointed out the articles of his secularist faith, he returned to biology. Then it was medical history again, and so on. At each step he became more nervous than before. For several weeks we went on, but he was only trying to evade the hounds.

Of course I tried to close in. I showed that he was repeating spent arguments. I asked why it was necessary to keep shifting ground. I returned him to the point: A baby is there, and you're killing him. Time after time he was reduced to silence. But silence made him even more nervous than speech, and he finally broke off.

Several years have passed. We run into each other sometimes; he passes me with an absent-minded greeting, then stops, turns, tells me he has thought of answers to all my points and that he will soon come to tell me about them, then disappears again.

We say people do not know the truth about abortion. I believe the problem is altogether different: They *do* know it, but they hide it from themselves. As one post-abortive woman explained to me, "I used to treat my conscience like an abusive mother treats her child. When she beats her, the child wants to cry. But her mother says, 'Don't you dare cry! Don't you act like you have any reason to cry! Don't you even think about crying!' Underneath the child still hurts, but finally she learns to keep quiet no matter what."

So we are in a paradox. The law is really known, but it can really be denied. It is really written on the heart, but our fallen race tries to suppress and overwrite what is inscribed there.

J. Budziszewski is an associate professor in the departments of government and philosophy at the University of Texas at Austin. His latest book is *The Line Through the Heart: Natural Law as Fact, Theory, and Sign of Contradiction* (ISI, 2009).

For defenders of life, the paradox is confusing. We understand the *ought* of abortion, but not the *is* of it. We know it is wrong and must be stopped, but not how it sits with the human heart. We comprehend that the natural law is law and therefore *right* for all, but not that it is nature and therefore *known* to all. We have heard that it is written even on the hearts of the nations, but we don't really believe this is true. Too often, then, what we call belief in natural law is really only moral realism: a belief in objectively true moral principles. And so, too often, we misread the times and play from weakness.

So let us distinguish between mere moral realism and belief in natural law. Let us see what difference they make in theology, in abortion politics, and in the facts of women's lives. Let us try to understand the heart better, and study how to play from strength.

If there were no law written on the heart, there could be no true converse between believers and non-believers—about abortion or about anything else that mattered. Short of complete renewal of the mind by grace, there could be no persuasion on any subject. A Christian in the public square might as well be speaking in another language.

Often enough it feels as though we are, and sometimes theologians have spoken as though this were literally true. Thinkers as diverse as Karl Barth and Stanley Hauerwas have held that because every term gains its meaning from the story or system of thought to which it belongs, the statements of believers and non-believers will have no meaning in common even when they use the same words. They might both speak of the "sanctity of life," for instance, but there is no common ground, no point of contact, no real connection between them. The story of Jesus "teaches us to be suspicious of any political slogan that does not need God to make itself credible."

These claims are completely true. But are they the whole truth? To believe so is to take the world's pretense of ignorance at face value. I believe that this is a mistake. We are right to suppose that our stories and systems of thought do not in themselves supply a point of contact with non-believers, but we are wrong to suppose that there *is* no point of contact—it is established not by us, but by God Himself in revelation.

How could this be true? Isn't revelation precisely what non-believers reject—what keeps the two parties apart? Not so: Special revelation can be rejected, but general revelation can only be suppressed.

As to special revelation, an examination of Scripture shows at least four different forms. By the works of God in history, He set apart for Himself a people of promise and delivered them from oppression. (Joshua 24: 1-18.) By the Law of Moses, He told His people what sin is. (Romans 7:7-13.) By prophecy, He foretold their deliverance not only from oppression but from sin. (Isaiah 52:13-53:12.) Finally was Messiah Himself, Jesus Christ, who took their sins upon Himself. (John 3:16, Romans 3:23-24, 5:6-8, 7:4-6.) Each of the earlier revelations paved the way for the later ones. For example, Scripture teaches explicitly that the works of God in history were a preparation for the Law of Moses, and that the Law of Moses was a preparation for the Gospel of Jesus Christ.

None of this gives us the promised point of contact with non-believers, but the Bible also maintains that God has not left Himself without a witness even among the pagans. By contrast with special revelation, provided by God to the community of faith, this revelation is general because it is provided by God to all mankind. At least five different forms of general revelation are mentioned in the Scriptures. First, the testimony of creation speaks to us of a glorious, powerful, and merciful Creator. (Psalm 19:1-6, Psalm 104, Acts 14:17, Romans 1:20.) Second, we are made in the image of God, thereby acquiring not only rational and moral capacities, but also the intuition of an unknown Holy One who is different from our idols. (Genesis 1:26-27, Acts 17:22-23.) Third are the facts of our physical and emotional design, in which a variety of God's purposes are plainly manifest. (Romans 1:26-27.) Fourth is the law of conscience, written on the heart, which, like the Law of Moses, tells us what sin is. (Romans 2: 14-15.) Fifth is the order of causality, which teaches by linking every sin with consequences. (Proverbs 1:31.) So it is that unconverted gentiles, who have neither waited at the foot of Sinai nor sat at the feet of Jesus, are still accountable to God.

What concerns us here is the *moral* part of general revelation, usually called the natural law, which is grounded by the second through fifth ways of general revelation. Because of the influence of the pre-Christian thinker Aristotle, most natural lawyers focus on the third. I am focussing on the fourth—the law of conscience, written on the heart. One reason is that Scripture is especially clear and emphatic about it. Another is that the new sort of pagan views guilt as a sort of wart or mole that has to be hidden, cut out, or scarred over. Scripture speaks of this too: The very heart on which God has written his law is estranged from itself. It needs to be not only informed, but transformed. Until this is accomplished, by the grace of God, we discern His law more through the consequences of its violation than through the witness of clear conscience, and even that instruction may be ignored when we need it most. Yet a seared and scarred heart is still a heart: tough and withered outside, but tender within. Scripture, then, comes down unequivocally for natural law, not mere moral realism. Now let us bring this to bear on abortion.

The same facts are interpreted by belief in natural law in one way, but by mere moral realism in another. What facts? Facts like these: That abortion is called wrong by some and right by others. That most of those who call it wrong call it killing. That most of those who call it killing say that what it kills is a baby. That most of those who call it killing a baby nevertheless think it should be allowed. That most of those who think it should be allowed nevertheless think it should be restricted. That proportionately, more and more people favor restrictions. Yet that proportionately, more and more people have had or been involved in abortions. The reason these facts are puzzling, the reason they need interpretation, is their contrariness. In particular, if abortion kills a baby then it ought to be banned to everyone, but if it only excises an unwanted growth then it is hard to see why it should be restricted at all; yet most people do not reason so consistently, and those who do are considered extremists.

Mere moral realism interprets such contrariness like this. The problem of human sin, it says, is mainly cognitive: It has to do with the state of our *knowledge.* There is a real right and wrong, but we don't know what it is and are trying to find out. In the meantime we hedge our bets, so logical consistency is an unreasonable expectation. One side wants unrestricted abortion, the other wants none at all; what is more natural than to split the difference? Searching for islands of clarity in a dark and trackless sea, we may get lost and sail in circles, but we are doing the best we can.

Belief in natural law views the same contrariness quite differently. Surely we do have thoughts like those above, but they are only on the surface of the mind. The problem of human sin is not mainly cognitive, but volitional: it has to do with the state of our will. By and large we do know what is right and wrong, but wish we didn't. We only make believe we are ignorant and searching—so that we can do wrong, condone it, or suppress our remorse for having done so in the past. Spurning the paved and posted road, we lounge in the marsh; throwing away the map, we groan that we haven't got one. Our great and secret fear is that to admit that abortion should be banned would be to admit the gravity of what we have already done or countenanced. Because we really know its gravity already, we do admit—but then again we don't. We feed scraps to our hearts to hush them, but only scraps, to keep them small. Abortion, yes, but not without a waiting period. Abortion, yes, but not in the last trimester. Abortion, yes, but not by procedures that withdraw the baby partly from the womb—not where his legs can be seen to kick, his hands can be seen to open and close, and we are deprived of the pretense of his nonexistence.

If the word of God is true, then the second interpretation is the right one. We know on the authority of Scripture that some things are known to nonbelievers apart from Scripture. One can disbelieve in the natural law, but one can't not know the natural law. Therefore we can be certain that every woman carries in her heart what she has cut from the dimness of her womb, and every man wears around his neck what he has refused to carry in his arms. The burden, I think, is greatest for her. She may try to hush her conscience when she kills her child, but it croons and murmurs anyway as though it were a baby itself.

The difference it makes that we *do* know the natural law is most heart-rendingly dramatized in the lives of post-abortive women. Day after day their stories play out in hundreds of crisis pregnancy centers across the United States and Canada. Asked if she has ever suffered emotional complications from an abortion, the woman usually says "No." Once again, mere moral realism would bid us take her denials at face value; she knows not what she has done. Yet there are cracks in the facade.

"Don't speak to me about fetal development," says one woman. "It makes me think about my abortion, and I'm trying to move on." Then there is the housewife who "hasn't had any problem," but admits to having nightmares and flashbacks about her abortion; the teenager whose experience was "just fine," but who doubled her weight and began suffering panic attacks in the months after aborting; the college student who says abortion "solved her problem," but who lapses into suicidal depression whenever its anniversary draws near; the girl under parental pressure who says "I didn't want a baby the way my life is now," but who later admits that she did; and the professional who declares her abortion was "what I needed," but whose eyes fill with tears when she speaks of it.

Many of these women go on to have a second, third, or even more abortions. Asked why, they give various answers. One says "I couldn't let down my parents," another, "I couldn't interrupt my education," another, "You have to understand that I'm a selfish woman and I get what I want, so I abort." Often they speak as though their previous abortions had made no difference, but there is always a hidden story. There is the outwardly religious girl leading a double life, who had her first abortion even though she knew it was wrong, and her second for fear that God would "do something to the baby" to punish her for the first. There is the Vietnamese woman who had her first out of anger because her husband had been unfaithful, and her second because "I wanted to be able to hate myself more for what I did to the first baby." She has got her wish.

Then there is the working woman who says "I couldn't be a good parent," amends her remark to "I don't deserve to have any children," and still later adds "If it hadn't been for my last abortion, I don't think I'd be pregnant now." One does not need to be Daniel to read the writing on that wall. When she says she could not be a good mother, what she means is that good mothers do not kill their children. She keeps getting pregnant to replace the children she has killed, but she keeps having abortions to punish herself for having killed them. With each abortion the cams of guilt make another revolution, setting her up to have another. She can never stop until she admits what is going on.

The stridency of the abortion movement should not deceive us. Not many women become pro-abortion activists and therefore have abortions. On the other hand, many women have abortions and therefore become pro-abortion activists. In the early days of the cult, prominent feminists used to blazon their having had abortions in full-page signature ads in a parody of general confession. Of course they denied then, as they deny now, that what they were confessing was wrong, and mere moral realism takes their protestation of ignorance seriously: If they say they are ignorant, then they must be. But if there is a law on the heart, then conscience is deeper than consciousness. Consciously the activists may deny that they have done ill; unconsciously they know they have, and seek absolution in politics. They seek to expunge the guilt of killing their children, not by repenting and throwing themselves upon the Lord of Mercy, but by getting others to join in the killing.

This facade is also cracking. In 1977, when the rift was still unseen, *The New Republic* stoutly editorialized that "There clearly is no logical or moral distinction between a fetus and a young baby; free availability of abortion cannot be reasonably distinguished from euthanasia. Nevertheless we are for it. It is too facile to say that human life always is sacred; obviously it is not." Writing in the same magazine in 1995, however, abortion proponent Naomi Wolf struck a different note, describing the practice as real sin which incurs real guilt and requires atonement.

Yet she is for it too.

But proponents of abortion give *arguments* for it: Doesn't this prove that they don't know the natural law? On the contrary, it proves that they do. Defenders of evil are not indifferent to morality; they rationalize it, like fallen men. Just as truth is employed in all lies, so natural law is employed in all rationalizations. The mutinous heart can find no other tenets on which it might base its insurrection than those that are written upon it already. Its revolt is a sham, for all it can do is pull a few ordinances from the ranks, fatten them up, and use them to beat down the others. It derives the very strength of its rebellion from the law itself. It exploits the fact that the moral precepts qualify each other to make them suppress each other.

Abortionism illustrates this perfectly: Like a slaughterhouse that lets nothing in the animal go to waste, boiling even hooves down into glue, the cause enlists every movement of life in the cause of death. Even compassion takes its turn. Unwanted children must be spared the sorrows of this world, so let us spare them the burden of being in it. Let us no longer have pity and kill not; let us have pity and therefore kill. Let us cut them in pieces with knives, pierce their skulls with scissors, and suction out their brains with tubes, all to be merciful and kind.

This is how sin and error always work; having nothing in themselves by which to convince, on what other resources but good and truth could they draw to make themselves powerful and plausible? A virus cannot reproduce except by commandeering the machinery of a cell. In the same way, sin cannot reproduce except by taking over the machinery of conscience. Not a gear, not a wheel is destroyed, but they are set turning in different directions from their wont. Evil must rationalize, and that is its weakness. But it can, and that is its strength.

The mode of sin's reproduction also explains why so many other things change when we tolerate an evil like abortion. Wise men have warned for years that tolerating abortion will make conscience weaker. The idea is that every evil we condone lowers our barriers to the next; if we cannot see what is wrong in killing our babies, then we will be less able to see what is wrong in killing our grandparents. Good so far as it goes, this warning is based on mere moral realism and gravely understates the danger. Because it traces sin only to ignorance it fails to appreciate its dynamism. The infected conscience does not necessarily become languid; it may become more active, but in a perverted way. The evil we condone does not merely lower our barriers to the next—it drives us on to it.

How is this the case? Think what is required to justify abortion. Because we *can't not know* that it is wrong to deliberately kill human beings, there are only four options. We must deny that the act is deliberate; we must deny that it kills; we must deny that its victims are human; or we must deny that wrong must not be done. The last option is literally nonsense. That something must not be done is what it *means* for it to be wrong; to deny that wrong must not be done is merely to say "wrong is not wrong," or "what must not be done may be done." The first option is hardly promising. Abortion does not just happen; it must be performed. Its proponents not only admit there is a "choice," they boast of it. As to the second option, if it was ever promising, it is no longer. Millions of women have viewed sonograms of their babies kicking, sucking their thumbs, and turning somersaults; even most feminists have given up calling the baby a "blood clot" or describing abortion as the "extraction of menses."

The only option left is number three: to deny the humanity of the victims. It is at this point that the machinery slips out of control.

For the only way to make option three work is to ignore biological nature, which tells us that from conception onward the child is as human as you or me (does anyone imagine that a dog is growing in there?)—and invent another criterion of humanity, one which makes it a matter of degree. Some of us must turn out more human, others less. This is a dicey business even for abortionists. It needs hardly to be said that no one has been able to come up with a criterion that makes babies in the womb less human but leaves everyone else as he was; the teeth of the moral gears are too finely set for that.

Consider, for instance, the criteria of "personhood" and "deliberative rationality." According to the former, one is more or less human according to whether he is more or less a person; according to the latter, he is more or less a person according to whether he is more or less able to act with mature and thoughtful purpose. Unborn babies turn out to be killable because they cannot act maturely; they are less than fully persons, and so less than fully human. In fact, they *must* be killed when the interests of those who are more fully human require it. Therefore, not only may their mothers abort, but it would be wrong to stop the mothers from doing so. But see where else this drives us. Doesn't maturity also fall short among children, teenagers, and many adults? Then aren't they also less than fully persons—and if less than fully persons, then less than fully humans? Clearly so, hence they too must yield to the interests of the more fully human; all that remains is to sort us all out.

So conscience has its revenge. We can't not know the preciousness of human life—therefore, if we tell ourselves that humanity is a matter of degree, we can't help holding those who are more human more precious than those who are less. The urge to justify abortion drives us inexorably to a system of moral castes more pitiless than anything the East has devised. Of course we can fiddle with the grading criteria: Consciousness, self-awareness, and contribution to society have been proposed; racial purity has been tried. No such tinkering avails to change the character of our deeds. If we will a caste system, then we shall have one; if we will that some shall have their way, then in time there shall be a nobility of Those Who Have Their Way. All that our fiddling with the criteria achieves is a rearrangement of the castes.

Sin ramifies. It is fertile, fissiparous, and parasitic, always in search of new kingdoms to corrupt. It breeds.

What does it mean then to play from weakness, and what would it mean to play from strength? All apologetics includes two movements, explanation and exposé: for honest confusion can be dispelled, but smokescreens can only be dispersed.* Most people know how to deal with honest confusion; smokescreens are what defeat us. Being mere moral realists, we mistake them for honest confusion and respond by explaining still more. The futility of doing so is that although one may be instructed out of error, no one is ever instructed out of denial. Playing from strength is distinguishing between the two cases, dealing with each in the way it requires—whether we encounter it in politics, polemic, or the care of the soul.

Smokescreens are more common in certain kinds of discussions than in others. For example they are more common in politics than physics, not because the data are less clear in politics but because the motive for deception is greater. In morals, smokescreens are especially common, because added to the motive to deceive others is the motive to deceive oneself. But moral smokescreens are also the easiest to discern, and for a simple reason. The mass of the electron is not found in conscience, nor is the principle of legislative checks; but the moral law is inscribed upon the heart. Therefore, if we say we know nothing of particles or parliaments, we may well be speaking truth, but if we say we know nothing of the sanctity of life, "we deceive ourselves, and the truth is not in us."

The hardest habit to break—but it must be broken—is refuting every argument. Those who will not be disciplined by conscience are hardly likely to be disciplined by reasoning; they use arguments to disguise and distract, not to sift for truth. A better habit is simply keeping things honest. First, we should challenge every euphemism. *"Oh, you're pro-choice,"* we can say; "I thought you were only pro-abortion. Then does the baby have a say about being cut to pieces?" In the second place we should concretize every abstraction. "You spoke just now of late-term abortions," we can say; "I am thinking of the procedure in which the baby's legs and torso are pulled out into the air, then his brains are sucked out and his skull is crushed so that it can be pulled out too. Is that the one you mean?" Finally our own speech should be plain. Abortion is not a "medical" matter, because no one is healed, and we do not "consider" it killing, for it plainly *is* killing. And the little one is a "baby," not a "fetus," and a "he" or a "she," not an "it."

Even simple questions can disperse smokescreens if well-timed. "Morals are all relative anyway," said one young man. "How do we even know that murder is wrong?" My friend replied, "Are you in real doubt about the wrong of murder?" The young man's first response was evasive: "Many people might say it was all right." "But I'm not asking other people," pressed my

---

* I owe this insight to the Rev. Christopher Hancock, formerly of Virginia Theological Seminary, presently Vicar of Holy Trinity Church, Cambridge, England, who bears responsibility for neither the way I express it nor the application I make of it.

friend. "Are you at this moment in any real doubt about murder being wrong for everyone?" There was a long silence. "No," the young man admitted; "no, I'm not." "Good," my friend answered, "then we needn't waste time on morals being relative. Let's talk about something you really are in doubt about."

A few moments passed as the young man's face registered comprehension; then he agreed. Another approach to dispersion of smokescreens is playback. "You've asked a lot of questions," I observed to a challenger. "Have you noticed a pattern in our conversation?" "What do you mean?" he asked. "I mean," I returned, "that you interrupt each of my answers by asking another question from a different direction." He considered. "I guess I do," he said; "Why do I do that?" "Why do you think?" I countered. "I guess because I don't want to hear your answers," he replied. "Okay, then," I told him, "let's talk about why you don't."

The man who said "philosophy is the assembling of reminders" spoke more truly than he knew. One can disbelieve in the prime moral truths, but one can't *not* know them; though theories may differ about how we know them, the great thing is to remember that we do. Nothing new can be written on the heart, but nothing needs to be; all we need is the grace of God to see what is already there. We don't want to read the letters, because they burn; but they do burn, so at last we must read them.

This is why the nation can repent. This is why the killing can be stopped. This is why the culture of death can be redeemed. "For I know my transgressions, and my sin is ever before me . . . a broken and contrite heart, O God, thou wilt not despise."

Of Life, the Law, and Roses

Sandi Merle

On New Year's Eve, as I (soberly) watched the millennium ball drop down the tower in New York's Times Square, I reflected on the difference the turn of the century was making in my life.

Actually, my life had taken a different turn five years earlier. But, I asked myself now, could I have imagined in the 1980s or even the early '90s that I would one day be routinely referred to by the press as the "organizer of Jewish opposition to partial-birth abortion," or the "female, Jewish voice of the pro-life movement?" The answer was No. Not because I was pro-choice, or as I now call it "anti-life"—I wasn't. But because back then I had considered my position a private inclination, one that need not be discussed in public.

All of that changed for me one day in 1995, when I overheard a conversation which included this comment: "Yes, dear, but abortion is a Catholic issue." I was struck by the ignorance it betrayed, as well as the pain on the face of the woman to whom it had been directed. I had no choice but to inject my personal views. (I've been known to do that. God forgive me; *mea culpa.* I'm afraid it's not even a recessive gene.)

I introduced myself to the speaker and asked if she'd mind repeating her remark about abortion and Catholics. She didn't mind at all. When she was finished I said, "Oh my, then I suppose the Shoah [Holocaust] is a Jewish issue. How foolish of me . . . I thought they were *both* issues of humanity." And, as the words escaped my mouth, I knew that my life was about to change—again. I had allowed myself to speak about abortion in public . . . I was exposed. And I was ready—for the third time in my life—to become an advocate. (I had previously dealt with patients' rights issues; and I'd also counseled parents on the psychological sequela following a child's crib death. The reader may recall that in the late '60s, Crib Death, or Sudden Infant Death Syndrome (SIDS) as it's called today, was still a tragic mystery: Parents often blamed themselves and, in some not-so-rare instances, were harshly interrogated by the authorities, which only added to their already insurmountable grief. Having had a dear friend who was trying to survive this crushing experience—I got involved.)

When we are young, if we are so inclined, we embark on excursions to save the world. As we mature, we try taking short journeys to save a little

Sandi Merle, who died in 2006, was a novelist and Broadway lyricist. She was also a member of the Lay Advisory Council of the New York Board of Rabbis and served on the Board of Jewish/Catholic Dialogue of the City of New York.

comer of it. Somehow, when I wasn't looking, I became old enough to ask: "What *is* a good life? How is it measured? How do I inhabit my space in the world productively and with grace? How do *I* make a difference?" It was then that I realized our victories are not really ours. They are God's. We are merely His tools. Victory comes in defending what we know is right. Or, as Mother Teresa so beautifully put it: "We are not called to be successful but to be faithful."

It was with that faith and a desire to fulfill a prophecy found in a tractate of Talmud—"He who saves one life saves the world"—that I set out to help save God's beautiful creation by publicly promoting the sanctity of every human life. My original idea, which I had thought simply ideal, proved not so easy to execute. I had hoped to bring together youngsters from a Catholic school in the New York Archdiocese and a Hebrew school choir, to perform a song I had specially written for such an occasion: "Think about the Children." The rabbi in charge left the decision to his liberal, female, pro-choice choir leader, who gave the idea a thumbs down. (Surprise!)

But I couldn't ignore His call. So I looked for another way to respond. The emergence, in the latter half of '95, of news reports about legislative attempts in Congress to outlaw something called "partial-birth abortion," and my subsequent investigation into the subject, galvanized me into new action. There are those who do not know that the Catholic and Jewish faith groups are natural allies in the pro-life cause. It became my dream that by coming together as one, by seeing in each other the oneness with God, in whose image and likeness we are all created, we could make a joint statement denouncing partial-birth abortion and accomplish that which had once seemed impossible: to stand together, shoulder to shoulder, Catholic and Jew, forming a bodyguard of intelligence and compassion, enabling us to save life. (You may find it interesting, at this juncture, to learn that in the Hebrew language, the root word for compassion [*rachamim*] is *rechem* . . . womb.)

In the Jewish faith, we are taught that when something of great importance needs to be addressed, we go directly to the top (i.e., lining up for hours to visit with the Rebbe). So, I did; I went to the top. Had I known then what I know now—that one does not do that in the hierarchical order of the Catholic Church—I would not have pursued the road I did and might never have had the opportunity or the inspiration to become so totally involved with and dedicated to the pro-life cause. But in this case, ignorance was bliss, and "going to the top" meant sharing my ideas with New York's John Cardinal O'Connor. In early December of '95, I had attended a private reception honoring the fiftieth anniversary of the Cardinal's ordination, and was struck by his easy manner and kind aura of approachability. So later that month, I wrote him a letter, in which I related that his openness and public eloquence were inspiring me to come out of the private closet about my own commitment to the pro-life position.

Not long after, the Cardinal wrote back to me. We corresponded for several months, then one day, I got a call from one of his aides who said the Cardinal would like to meet with me: "Are you available on June 23rd?" "Are you kidding?" I wanted to say. Instead, I just blurted out, "I'll be there!"

We met at the Cardinal's residence. "Don't disturb me for anything other than Mother Teresa's phone call," I heard him tell his aide. He motioned for me to sit in a rocking chair next to him. I did but stayed perched on the edge of my seat the whole visit—not an easy pose to hold. I wasn't prepared for the profound attention the Cardinal paid to me and my idea for a Catholic-Jewish alliance to fight partial-birth abortion. We spoke, we sipped tea; he asked, I answered; I asked, he answered; he taught and taught and taught; I listened, I learned, I cried. (I've been known to do that.) But by the time I left our meeting, I felt that my life as a budding pro-life activist had been waiting for his witness.

Walking home, I recalled the first time I had met His Eminence—shortly after his arrival in New York, at a reception hosted by the New York Board of Rabbis to welcome the new archbishop and to introduce him to a diverse cross-section of the Jewish community. A woman a few steps ahead of me in the receiving line noticed the red rose on the lapel of the Cardinal's coat and asked, "Would that be the Rose of Sharon, Your Eminence?" Without missing a beat, he replied, "No, dear lady. This is the rose which lives in my heart for all the beautiful, unborn roses not allowed to live." Well . . . I warned you . . . I cry. When it was my turn to shake his hand, I was a wreck! His Eminence's answer had so visibly affected me, he was compelled to inquire about my health. I assured him I was fine. Embarrassed? Oh, yes. I prayed for a new handkerchief or a swift demise, whichever came first.

But that had happened on another day, a long time ago. Today, back on a busy Manhattan sidewalk after our first private meeting, I faced east and said: "*Hineni.* I am here!" Just as Abraham had answered God, I answered, on behalf of all the beautiful roses not allowed to live: "I am here." And I knew exactly what needed to be done.

Defying conventional wisdom, I chose the most difficult, albeit the most provocative path. I would create an organization for Jewish women in the Arts—the most liberal of all women—to speak out against partial-birth abortion. It would be a base from which to start. I would not insist on pro-life purists: just those willing to speak out against this heinous abortion procedure. But first, I had to educate these women! Partial-birth abortion, suppressed by the media, was the best-kept secret in town.

Whenever asked how I, a Jewish female in the arts, became so radically involved in "pro-life" advocacy, I explain: Because I'm Jewish and have a mandate to help those who cannot help themselves; because I'm female and have been on the responsible end of the umbilical cord; and because, as a writer, I have an obligation to provoke thought. (In my heart, though, I know I owe it all to a remarkable Catholic cleric whose heart is a sanctuary for beautiful, unborn roses.)

As I began talking to women about joining me, I had to keep reminding myself that there are those who, while not comprehending the full and beautiful truth about the sanctity of all human life, do see some of it. It was incumbent on me to reach out to them, gently, in words and actions that would not frighten, in order to invite them into a fuller understanding of the truth. If they felt attacked or threatened, I would lose them.

"*Partial-what*?" Yes, some thought they might have heard the term, but what was it really? Surely it couldn't be anything so gruesome as the procedure I was describing, because *that* would never be acceptable in American society—I stopped crying and started instructing.

My first undertaking was to teach Jewish laws and ethics to Jewish women, including some friends of mine. That proved more traumatic than cathartic. I remember my grandmother telling me: "Mamalla, when you find two Jews in debate, you will find three opinions." Case in point: Jewish law mandates that the mother's life must be saved first if threatened during pregnancy, which is in keeping with the Jewish principle of saving existing life. If the child in the womb is considered a "pursuer" or "aggressor" (*rodeph,* in Hebrew) it *must* be aborted to save the mother.

But, in every other situation, when there is no such mortal threat, abortion is diametrically opposed to Jewish law and is prohibited. Partial-birth abortion is *always* prohibited, for it is written: "Once the head or the greater part of the body has emerged, we do not set aside one life for another." That is a direct quote from Jewish law. But, with abortion in general, what is meant by "threatening life"? Is it physical, mental, emotional, financial? Actual physical harm is the only threat I can accept, definitely *not* the "threat" of interfering with a woman's ability to climb the corporate ladder. If we don't draw the line on the side of life, then we become modern-day Pharaohs, as in the days of Moses, rather than life-saving midwives. (For those of my friends who failed to admit to the truth about partial-birth abortion, because it "chipped away at their right to rule over their bodies," yet wanted to remain my friends just the same, I had only one request. I refused to permit them to use the Hebrew toast *"L'Chaim"* [To Life] when I was present.)

In 1997, I was ready to officially launch STOP (Standing Together Opposing Partial-birth), a small but strong cadre of Jewish women in the arts, who would take the case against partial-birth abortion to synagogues, schools and theatrical organizations all over the country, as well as give interviews to secular and religious newspapers, magazines and special-interest groups. Among the women on STOP's roster are the actress Lainie Kazan; comic/impressionist Marilyn Michaels; cabaret singer Julie Budd; actress Vicki Stuart; executive director of the Independent Women's Forum Barbara Ledeen; columnist Mona Charen; author Midge Decter; publisher Susan Roth; talent agent Suzanne Schachter; and cabaret artist Judy Scott. Our mission is to inform people that the only reason for a partial-birth abortion is to produce a dead baby, and to convince them that these murders of convenience must be banned. (Only recently have we all learned about the sale of intact fetuses and fetal body parts; that *greed* is at the bottom of it all.)

After founding STOP, I became acquainted with the Institute for Religious Values and its president, Chris Gersten. Chris had put together a list of some thirty rabbis willing to have their names published in an open letter to Congress, in opposition to partial-birth abortion. Using my own rabbinical contacts (which I'd hoped would one day be put to good use), I helped him build up the list of rabbis sympathetic to our cause. Today that list is 200 strong, and represents all denominations of Judaism. Meanwhile, Chris referred me to several female journalists and authors he knew who he thought would be interested in joining STOP.

My ongoing crusade against partial-birth abortion has included an active letter-writing campaign to members of Congress. By 1998, I had become almost obsessed. In May of '97, the Senate had passed the partial-birth abortion ban for the second time (the first was in December of '95), but it was vetoed, again for the second time, by President Clinton in October. The Senate vote to override was due to come up in June (1998).

I chose to concentrate my attention on Senator Joseph Lieberman of Connecticut. Why? It is widely known that Senator Lieberman is an Orthodox Jew. To another Jew, that would suggest a conservative political orientation. I knew that this time around his would be a swing-vote. I had also recently read the book *Diamonds of the Rebbe: The Lubavitcher Rebbe, Famous Personalities and You* by Mordechai Staiman. In it, there is an account of Joseph Lieberman telling the rabbi Rebbe Menachem M. Schneerson about his desire to help protect all that God had created. Lieberman's exact words were: "Part of my involvement in politics has to do with my Jewish education and the whole tradition in Judaism of an obligation to try to do justice, to try to better the community and to try to make a difference. If you believe in God as the Creator of the world, then the natural environment is part of Creation and should be protected and sustained. The Garden of Eden story, and the concept of stewardship in Noah's protection of all the other living creatures from the flood, are important and powerful metaphors, parables and lessons." His words.

I may forget where I put my keys, or leave umbrellas in taxis, but I remember Genesis! "So God created man in His own image; in the image of God He created him; male and female, He created them, 'Be fruitful and multiply; fill the earth and subdue it . . .'"

Please trust me: No matter how much pressure I may have applied to Senator Lieberman—be it via appeals to guilt, logic or Bible—I was never anything but respectful. I reminded him of his eloquent, televised speech berating the U.S. president for behaving in such a disgraceful, immoral fashion in his personal life: The senator had complained that he could no longer watch the evening news on TV in the company of his young daughter.

But nothing worked. He didn't even extend me the courtesy of a reply. I took his nonchalance as a disgraceful rebuke of great magnitude, and pressed on. After all, this was not about a cigarette tax or redwood trees. This was about killing babies! Would it be appropriate for the senator's young daughter to see *that* on television?

Knowing, as many people do, that Joseph Lieberman would walk five miles to cast a vote on the Sabbath, and that he walked to synagogue every Saturday morning because he is a God-fearing, religious man, it was, shall I say, "arranged," that one Saturday morning he would be intercepted by a dear friend of his, a man who is the "rabbi half" of a Washington D.C. power couple. The rabbi talked his heart out, trying to change the senator's mind, heart and, most important, his vote. Lieberman's reply to the rabbi: "Stay away from this!"

As it turned out the vote to override Clinton's veto didn't come up in the Senate until September 18. By then, I had read and re-read the chapter on Lieberman in Staiman's book. Now it was 11 p.m. on the night before. I had her phone number, so I did it: I called Marcia Lieberman. No. . . not his wife, not his daughter, not his sister—the woman I called was Senator Lieberman's mother! Why not? I too am the mother of a wonderful man. We would speak the same language.

"What do you want from me?" she asked. "I'm a woman in my 80s; what can I do?" I told her what I thought she could do. I asked her what *she* thought about partial-birth abortion. She knew it was "wrong," she said, but also knew she would not be able to convince her son to change his vote. I reminded her of the senator's meeting with the Rebbe, described in Staiman's book. She had been present, and remembered it all. Did I have "*chutzpah*"? No. I was desperate! My last words to her were: "In your heart, you know if the Rebbe were alive, your son would keep his word and protect God's creation." She agreed and hung up. The vote the following morning was two short of the two/thirds majority necessary to override Clinton's veto.

Senator Joseph Lieberman's was one of those two votes.

In November 1998, I was privileged to be invited to attend the first major conference promoting a pro-life, Catholic-Jewish dialogue. Titled "Affirming the Sanctity of Human Life," it was sponsored by the Institute for Religious Values and Catholic University, and took place at CU's Columbus School of Law in Washington, D.C. Actor Ben Stein was guest speaker; I was proud to be asked to chair the panel on partial-birth abortion.

The unique group for which I was responsible consisted of eight people. There I was with a recently-broken left foot in full cast (which I tried to hide, not to be seen as going after the sympathy vote), along with two other members of STOP, three rabbis sporting beards of three different lengths, and two Sisters of Life (the religious order founded in 1991 by Cardinal O'Connor himself; the sisters are "dedicated to the protection and enhancement of the sacredness of human life"). We all made quite a picture—but, together, we became giants!

It was at this conference that I created a bit of a stir by stating publicly that, since partial-birth abortion occurs in the intra partum stage of pregnancy, it is not covered by *Roe* v. *Wade,* which addresses only ante partum . . . the stage prior to labor and delivery. (This made a great headline in the Washington *Times* the following morning.)

When my panel took a break, I was approached by a member of the audience who told me that a friend of hers, Dr. Mary Nicholas, of the Stein Research Institute (for biomedical issues), was looking for someone with whom to co-author a book on partial-birth abortion. I contacted Dr. Nicholas immediately, and after meeting, we agreed we would begin writing in December, and that the book would take the form a Jewish/Catholic dialogue.

On learning that another vote on a partial-birth abortion ban was expected to come to the Senate floor in the late spring of 1999, we wrote our hearts out, hoping to have the book ready for publication before the vote would take place. Meanwhile, I continued my letter-writing campaign, first to *all* members of Congress who supported the president, and then again, this time to the nine Jewish senators who opposed the ban. (Arlen Specter of the great commonwealth of Pennsylvania was the only Jewish senator voting to ban partial-birth abortion.)

Dr. Nicholas and I, realizing that it would be nearly impossible to get a publisher in the secular sector, contacted my friend Father John Bonnici in the Family Life/ Respect Life Office of the New York Archdiocese, and he arranged for us to meet with the editors of the *Human Life Review,* to ask their advice.

It was a providential meeting. Editors Faith and Maria McFadden and Anne Conlon gave us some suggestions; but they also had an idea. One of the other organizations in their office is a pro-life lobbying group, the Ad Hoc Committee in Defense of Life (founded by the late J.P. McFadden); though it would not be possible to publish the whole 250-page book, the Committee could publish a lengthy booklet in time for the vote, if Mary and I could edit the manuscript down.

To make a long story shorter, both the vote on a partial-birth abortion ban and the book were delayed, but the booklet—*From the Hunter's Net: Excerpts from a Jewish/Catholic Dialogue on Partial-Birth Abortion*—was published in June, 1999. Thousands of copies were distributed over the summer. We knew the importance of getting the information contained in the booklet to every member of Congress, the Supreme Court Justices, and the New York State legislators, who were also deliberating on a state ban. All one hundred members of the U.S. Senate received hand-delivered copies. And last October, they voted for the third time to ban partial-birth abortion, but again, sadly, without a veto-proof majority.

Recently, I became Director of Life Issues at the Institute for Religious Values. My role there encompasses everything from the sanctity of human life to anti-Semitism to Catholic-bashing—even the current problem in Nazareth involving a Mosque slated to be built directly in the shadow of the Basilica of the Annunciation. In 1998, I accepted a seat on the Board of Directors of a hospital in Israel with a *pro-life* agenda. This is unusual in a country with a high incidence of abortion. Incongruous, I know, for a country built on the ashes of Nazi infanticide, but, for that reason, at least the procedure of partial-birth abortion is anathema to Israelis. To quote Professor Yigal Halperin, OB-GYN and Associate Director of Assaf Harofel Medical Center: "In Israel we do not perform the heinous procedure called partial-birth abortion. It is enough that the Serbs do similar things to the Croatians."

Last year, I resigned from a well-known, national Jewish organization of which I had been a lifetime member. The organization had presented an award to Hillary Clinton for her work on behalf of children. In her acceptance speech Clinton spoke strongly of her pro-choice platform and (of course) mentioned her support for her husband's veto of the ban on partial-birth abortion, which had, by then, passed both houses of Congress. I immediately contacted the vice president of programming, asking for an opportunity to present the opposing viewpoint. After several weeks of waiting for an answer, I received one. The "powers that be," all of whom "respected my position," felt it would be a "slap in the face" to the woman they had just lauded. I saw this as a pretty good tradeoff. But alas, it was merely a cliché and I am non-violent. So I walked away from the organization, because if I hadn't, I could no longer raise my own glass to Life (*L'Chaim*).

There are days, though, when I feel I am just spinning my wheels; days when I feel unsuccessful, unnecessary, and very tired. On one such day last fall, I read two horrifying news reports regarding abandoned newborns . . . one left to die on a conveyor belt in a Brooklyn factory, the other, tossed like so much garbage into a trash receptacle in midtown Manhattan.

My mind turned to another, happier day in June, when I had been introduced to New York City District Attorney Robert Morgenthau at a spectacular event he was hosting in honor of Cardinal O'Connor. Morgenthau is also Chairman of the Board of Trustees of the Jewish Heritage Museum/A Living Memorial to the Holocaust. Believing, as I do, that every so-called coincidence is a God incidence, I sensed Mr. Morgenthau and I had "a future" together.

So, after reading of those two dreadful incidents of murder, which are becoming a weekly, sometimes daily nightmare, I wrote the District Attorney about the horror of newborns being treated like chattel. But—realizing that some of their mothers were very young and very scared—I asked him to consider a single piece of legislation, one that would offer safe haven for babies, and a guarantee that the mothers of those babies would not be arrested, providing they brought the newborns to safe-houses. Abortion, I assured him, was ugly enough, but every baby born should be a baby who lives.

In that first letter, I offered to help form an interreligious group of qualified professionals who could be of assistance. (Those people do exist—the wonderful women who are the Sisters of Life, for example.) The District Attorney replied quickly: The "proposal is an important and interesting one," he wrote. He also told me that he was putting it in the hands of the Chief of the Domestic Violence Unit and his own Executive Assistant. Robert Morgenthau is a good man. I believe he will help us. We are still in the correspondence stage, but we are *not* just spinning our wheels: we are moving.

Whenever I have felt that I had done all I could do without accomplishing much, another baby cries out for help and another idea awaits to be hatched and nurtured. We cannot afford to rest. "Silent Scream," Dr. Bernard Nathanson's film depicting the harrowing progress of an actual abortion, keeps me awake some nights. We must stop the infanticide. We must prepare for the next vote in Congress—there will be a next, and a *next,* if necessary. We must refuse to cast our own votes for any candidate who does not support the sanctity of human life. And we must help others to realize that, sometimes, even God's battles have to be fought in the political arena.

So what started as a song, "Think About the Children," and a dream of standing together, Catholic and Jew, have become the apogee of my life's work. It defines me. It is who I am. Whether it is Pope John Paul II, Mother Teresa, the Lubavitcher Rebbe, or His Eminence Cardinal O'Connor . . . Whether Rabbis David Novak, Moses Birnbaum, Joseph Ehrenkranz, Marc Gellman, David Lincoln, Emanuel Rackman, or Barry Freundel; whether it is Mother Agnes Mary Donovan and the Sisters of Life or Fathers John Bonnici, Benedict Groeschel, Frank Pavone, or James Loughran . . . Msgrs. Ferdinando Berardi, Philip Reilly, John Woolsey, Gerald Walsh, and so many others, we must be inspired by all of them. They are all our teachers.

And they need us as well, to continue to proclaim the sanctity of every human life, to really believe. And to cultivate and nurture beautiful roses. Living roses. And to that end, let us all say: *"Hineni.* I am here!"

The Born-Alive Infants Protection Act of 2000

Hadley Arkes

Chairman Canady, Members of the Committee: My name is Hadley Arkes. I am currently the Edward Ney Professor of Jurisprudence and American Institutions at Amherst College. I've taught at Amherst since 1966, with the exception of several years in which I have been in Washington on leave and visiting at places like the Brookings Institution and the Woodrow Wilson Center at the Smithsonian Institution. My main interests as a writer and a teacher have been focused on political philosophy, public policy, and constitutional law. I have written, in that vein, several books, published by Princeton University Press, including *The Philosopher in the City* (1981), *First Things* (1986), *Beyond the Constitution* (1990), and *The Return of George Sutherland* (1994). I have had a strong interest in the so-called "life issues," of abortion and euthanasia, but those interests spring from the central concern in my work, which involves the moral ground on which the laws would have to find their justification.

The bill introduced by Congressman Canady, HR-4292, the "Born-Alive Infants Protection Act," offers the most modest and the gentlest step that is imaginable in dealing with the question of abortion; and at the same time it is the approach that goes most deeply to the root of things. That combination, of the gentlest measure, and the measure running deepest, offers the best chance we have seen, over the past 27 years, to draw all sides into a conversation, and achieve the kind of settlement of this issue in our politics that can only be achieved by the political branches. The political branches are more sensitive than the Supreme Court to the range of opinions in the country on this vexing issue of abortion, and yet the issue has been more explosive and troubling in our politics precisely because it has been kept under the exclusive control of the courts. It has been detached then from the political arena, the arena of ordinary discourse, among ordinary people, about the things that are right or wrong.

The refrain has been heard, at every turn, that abortion is one of the most emotional and divisive issues in our politics. That cliché happens to conceal the fact that there has been, for years, a remarkable measure of consensus in this country on abortion, a consensus that draws in Democrats as well as Republicans, pro-choicers as well as pro-lifers. But that consensus has not

Hadley Arkes, the Edward N. Ney Professor of Jurisprudence and American Institutions at Amherst College, appeared before the House Committee on the Judiciary on July 20, 2000, in support of the Born-Alive Infants Protection Act of 2000. This is his complete testimony.

been able to manifest itself in our laws, because the opinions of the public have not been allowed to shape the laws that the courts will permit. At the same time, I've made the argument over the years that our problems here would not be solved even if the elves could come in the middle of the night and remove *Roe* v. *Wade* from the records of our law. Even if that decision were overruled overnight, the distemper and rancor in our political life would not be removed. For many people would feel themselves dispossessed of something they have been encouraged to regard by now as one of their first freedoms under the Constitution, a right that anchors all of their other rights to privacy and sexual freedom.

Evidently, we would need a conversation before we could begin to legislate on this question. But what makes that conversation possible is the fact that there has been, as I say, a surprising degree of consensus that has not been allowed to manifest itself on this matter of abortion. We know, for example, that even people who call themselves "pro-choice" do not think that all abortions should be permitted. Indeed, they have expressed a willingness to restrict, through the law, a large number of abortions that are now permitted in the law. The news that took years finally to break through to the American public is that the laws on abortion in this country, fashioned by the courts, permit abortion for any reason at all, through all stages of the pregnancy and even, as we have seen, at the time of a live birth, with the partial-birth abortion. But the surveys, on all sides, have shown for years that only about 22-27 percent of the public supports this policy of abortion on demand, for any reason, at any time. Even many people who call themselves pro-choice do not think that abortions should be performed in the late stages of pregnancy, and for less than weighty reasons. People may support a right to abortion under some circumstances (most notably, when the life of the mother is endangered), but many of them still hold that a human life should not be taken for the sake of removing financial strain in the family, removing barriers to the career of a woman, or serving the convenience of the parents.[1] Most people do not think that abortions should be performed because the child is likely to be deaf or blind, and the opposition to abortion for these reasons is often quite independent of the age of the unborn child. My own surmise here is that most people think it would be wrong to take the life of *any* person because he happens to be deaf or blind or handicapped. And if they think this kind of killing would be wrong at any age of the victim, they may well conclude that the principle would be indifferent, in the same way, to the age of the child in the womb.

I could go on, but these points have been documented well by now in the public surveys. And yet, this constellation of opinion, rather stable over 25 years, has had no significant impact on the laws on abortion, shaped and sustained by the courts. Congressman Canady's bill offers the chance finally to let that opinion of the public manifest itself in our laws. It does that, also, in the gentlest and most powerful way by beginning the conversation at the place that should command the most overwhelming consensus across our political divisions: the place where we act simply to preserve the life of the child born alive, the child who *survives* an abortion. That moment marks the earliest possible time, associated with an abortion, when the interests of the pregnant woman can be separated entirely from the interests of the child. Even if *Roe* v. *Wade* articulated an unqualified right on the part of a woman to end her pregnancy, the pregnancy would now be over. No right to end the pregnancy would require at this moment the death of the child.

And of course no one, at that moment, claims to be suffering any doubt that we are dealing with a human being—as though the offspring of homo sapiens could have been anything less than human at any phase in its life. This is the first moment then, under our current law, when we should be able to declare, with unchecked conviction, that the law may extend its protections over that child. Or to put it more precisely, that is a moment in which it could be said for that child engaged in an abortion what could be said for any other child, or person, in the country: namely, that the claim of the child to the protections of the law could not possibly pivot on the question of whether anyone happens to "want" her. At this moment we are invited to consider whether we could not in fact say then of the child, as we would of any other person, that she bears an intrinsic significance as a human being; that any right on the part of that child to live cannot hinge any longer on the interests or convenience of any other person.

We would be in a condition truly miserable if we could not count on certain natural human sympathies at work to protect the child, and there seems to be a normal tendency on the part of parents and hospitals to supply that care to the child who surprises everyone by surviving the abortion. And yet, the law frequently comes into play precisely because parents do not always have this inclination to protect their children. As we have ample reason by now to know, some parents may be inclined to abuse or even kill their born children. In the case of abortion, the matter is complicated for us by the fact that the very logic of "abortion rights" seems to create a momentum in principle to let the child die. Jill Stanek, who is joining us today in this hearing, offers a report from a respectable hospital in our own time where that logic has been allowed to play itself out in real cases. She reports on the so-called "live birth" abortions, where children are delivered and simply left unattended, to die. I take it as a blessing that we are still capable of reacting with shock, when these cases spring up, but they should have ceased long ago to have caused surprise. From the logic of abortion rights, after all, the case for letting the child die could be eminently plausible. Under the common law, for centuries, well before *Roe* v. *Wade,* it was understood that a woman did not have to keep an unwanted child. She could give that child up for adoption. Even now, we may contend, the "remedy" for an unwanted child should not be found in destroying the person who is unwanted, but putting that child into hands that would nurture her. The passion for abortion is fed in no small part by the sense, commonly felt, that it would be far easier for a woman to kill an embryo or fetus than to give up what is so evidently a child, and a child who is *hers.*

The Marxists would find here an expression of bourgeois attitudes on property—that it is easier to kill the unborn child than to give up what is "yours." No matter how we phrase it, the passion is quite evidently there, and without it, as I say, one cannot account for why women would seek their remedy in abortion rather than adoption. It was that sense of the matter, I think, that lay behind Judge Clement Haynsworth's move, in 1977, to take that passion and restate it as a doctrine of law. In a case called *Floyd* v. *Anders,*[2] in 1977, a child of about 25 weeks of gestation had survived an abortion, had undergone one surgery, and lived for 20 days before he died. The question had been posed as to whether there had been an obligation to preserve the life of that child. And the answer, tendered by Haynsworth, was no. After all, the mother had decided on an abortion, and therefore, as Haynsworth said, "the fetus in this case was not a person whose life state law could protect." To put it another way, the right exercised by the mother should not be frustrated, or negated, by the accident that the child happened to live. Or to put it more baldly, the right to an abortion must entail nothing less than the right to an "effective abortion," or a dead child.

Several years later, in *Planned Parenthood* v. *Ashcroft* (1983), Justice Powell noted, in a footnote, a doctor who had made that argument quite explicitly: that the right to an abortion meant an effective abortion or a dead child. Justice Powell pronounced that opinion "remarkable."[3] From that comment, offered in passing in a footnote, even some pro-life lawyers have drawn the inference that the Supreme Court has rejected that argument. One lawyer also recalls, in this vein, that the Supreme Court actually reversed the holding in *Floyd* v. *Anders,* or rather sent the case back for a reconsideration. But in an opinion *per curiam* the Supreme Court sent the case back on the ground that "the District Court *may* have reached [its] conclusion on the basis of an erroneous concept of 'viability,' which refers to potential, rather than actual, survival of the fetus outside the womb."[4] In all strictness, none of these comments, or moves, marks an explicit rejection of the claim that the right to abortion entails the right to an "effective abortion." As any lawyer should know, to state that this claim is "remarkable" is not exactly the same as pronouncing it "wrong," and still less is it to explain the grounds of its wrongness.

That question, simple but primary, becomes the subject of our business here, with the "Born-Alive Infants Protection Act." As any philosopher or social scientist knows, a description of an outward act hardly serves as an explanation or an account of that act. "Smith goes to the garage of his neighbor, Jones, and takes the hose hanging on the wall." From that description of the outward act, we cannot say just yet whether the sentence describes a theft, or whether Smith had permission for taking the hose. Even if he didn't have permission, he might have been borrowing it, to put out a fire in his home, and with the intention of returning the hose. In a similar way, we can draw no inferences about the understandings at work in our law when we are told say, that "the dominant practice, among parents, doctors, and hospitals, is to preserve the life of a child who survives an abortion." The fact that they do this, or do it most of the time, does not reveal anything to us about the grounds on which they are acting, or the principles that actually govern their actions. That is the question posed in this simple move by Congressman Canady: The bill gives us the chance to fix in the law the principle that actually protects the child. And if that is not in fact the principle that explains the motivations of people on all sides, then that is something quite important for all of us to learn.

For those of us who have advocated this bill, the principle would run, as I have suggested, in this way: We think that the inclination to protect the child with the law must imply that the child has a claim to the protection of the law that cannot pivot on the question of whether anyone "wants" her. The child, that is, has an *intrinsic* dignity, which must in turn be the source of rights of an intrinsic dignity, which cannot depend then on the interests or convenience of anyone else. When parents commit infanticide with a child two or three years old, we no longer ask whether the child was straining the parents, or whether the child was unwanted. If we understand that we are dealing with a human being, reasons of convenience and self-interest become radically inadequate in supplying a "justification" for the killing of the child. We would think that the same understanding must come into place for the child who survives the abortion. Now if such a principle cannot be invoked on behalf of that child—if our friends on the other side of the issue of abortion would protect the child but not share these premises of ours—then we would earnestly invite them to explain the principle they would put in its place. If we haven't stated here the reasons that we cast over the child the protections of the law, then what are those reasons?

We are in fact anxious to hear them if people contend in this case that we have it wrong. But we should lodge a proper warning: Any attempt to finesse, or fudge, the question at this point is bound to bear tell-tale signs, and what it would "tell" would be quite ominous for anyone that the law protects now with any kind of a right, including that "right to abortion." For example, let us suppose that someone says, "I would protect the child because the child elicits in me a sense of sympathy." But if that were the ground, the explanation has to do more with *ourselves,* with *our* feelings, and with *our* sense of what is pleasing or satisfying to *us,* or agreeable to our own interests. By implication, of course, there would be no obligation to protect the child when that course of action did not serve our interests or convenience.

My own sense is that people on either side of the controversy over abortion would not be satisfied with that kind of rationale, and that they would see instantly that there is something deeply wrong in it. But if that is the case, does it not become clear, by implication, as to what we must say instead? Must we not be moved to say that there is something of an intrinsic dignity in the child, or any other human being, something that compels our respect, quite apart from anything in our self-interest? If that cannot be said for the child, newborn, at these first moments, then what can be said for any of the rest of us at any other time, for any other right? If we cannot speak those words, we would seem to imply that none of us has a claim to be respected, or a claim to be the bearers of rights, unless our presence, or our rights, suit the interests of those around us. What would even a "right to abortion" mean under those circumstances? Would it not be then a "right" that depends on the sufferance of others—a right that can be abridged or removed when it no longer suits the interests of a majority, or of those who exercise power?

Frankly, I don't see how we can refuse to protect the child at this point without producing a revolution in our law and deciding that, from this day forward, we will treat as a nullity the laws on infanticide. And of course we cannot say, in an offhand way, that infanticide has ceased to be a big deal without backing into the claim that homicide itself has ceased to be a big deal. People may try to finesse the matter by saying that we should wait perhaps a few days, or a week or two, before we extend the protection of the law to the newborn. But that would simply be a thinly disguised way of saying that we will wait in protecting the child until we are clear that the child is acceptable to someone, that it is in someone's *interest* to keep or "want" that child.

If I am right, and there is no way of getting around this matter, then Rep. Canady's modest bill does the service of compelling us to face this elementary question about the human person, the question that stands at the heart of the thing. I would not conceal my own hope or expectation here: Once this first premise is planted, it must project itself back into the situation of the child even while still in the womb. After all, if we come to the understanding that the child has an *intrinsic* significance as a human being; that her claim to be protected by the law does not pivot on whether anyone wants her; then how could that intrinsic significance be affected by anything as contingent or "extrinsic" as whether she is only two days or two weeks before birth, or whether she is attached by an umbilical cord to her natural mother? How could it hinge on the question of just where she happens for the moment to be lodged or where she is receiving her nourishment? Nothing in her intrinsic significance could be affected by things of this kind when she leaves the womb; by the same logic, it cannot be affected by such things a few days or weeks earlier, when she is still in the womb.

I happen to think myself that, once that first premise is granted, the argument to justify abortion can probably be unravelled step by step. It would be my own purpose to keep taking those steps, one at a time, and keep putting the question to people on the other side, who would be reluctant to waive the right to abortion under any set of circumstances. I would indeed raise the question of the child in late term, the child of the "wrong" sex, the child afflicted with handicaps. But that is to say, I would earnestly press the question with people on the other side, and attempt to persuade them step by step. None of us can foresee just how far that process may run. It is still open to people on the other side to refuse to go along, to insist that they have not been persuaded. They may not in fact see that the willingness to protect the child at birth bears implications for the protection of the child even earlier. But if so, what can we do except keep the conversation going? Yet, with each step we would have succeeded in saving another cluster of lives, even a handful of lives. And for those lives that are saved, the whole project must be eminently worth doing.

In the meantime, our friends on the other side must be affected by this burden: Over the last few years, we have seen a controversy in Australia over the treatment of children who survive abortions, and we have seen the most chilling statement on this matter put out in South Africa by the Department of Health, the agency that oversees the practice of medicine in that country. In 1997, the Department put out new guidelines, instructing doctors and nurses that "if an infant is born who gasps for breath, it is advised that the foetus does not receive any resuscitation measures."[5] In Australia, this past April, a controversy was ignited when doctors, and certain agencies, actually registered their opposition when an agency of the government advised that babies who survive abortions should be given medical care. Mr. Gab Kovacs, the chairman of Family Planning Australia, insisted that babies born at an early gestational age had no realistic chance of survival, and they should be left to succumb. Those are civilized countries, with legal systems based on the British model. But what seems to be at work in both places is a vibrant strand of opinion, holding that the logic of abortion rights entails that right to an "effective abortion" or a dead child.

And anyone who follows the decisions of the Supreme Court in this country would know that the Court took us just a step shy of that threshold at the end of June with its decision in *Stenberg* v. *Carhart*. Justice Breyer, in his opinion for the Court, argued that the partial-birth abortion (Dilation and Extraction [D&X]), as grisly as it is, could still be estimated as safer for the pregnant woman than the more familiar method of dismembering the child in the womb. As Breyer explained:

> The use of instruments within the uterus creates a danger of accidental perforation and damage to neighboring organs. Sharp fetal bone fragments create similar dangers, and fetal tissue accidently left behind can cause infection and various other complications.[6]

Is the implication not obvious? The avoidance of the usual method of abortion now warrants killing a child with 70 per cent of the body dangling out of the birth canal. On the same premises, would it not be even safer to deliver the child whole and simply let it die? For the doctor could then wholly avoid the insertion of instruments into the uterus or the dismembering that would allow fetal parts to be left behind, where they could be the cause of infection. With these steps, the Court has brought us to the threshold of out-right infanticide, and it takes but the shortest step to cross that threshold. One must wonder then whether the majority in *Stenberg* v. *Carhart* is preparing us for a holding even more advanced and astounding. But the point is that it will have ceased to be astounding if we offer no response and permit no line to be drawn finally at infanticide.

To our friends then who say that this bill is not needed, we would have to say: Look about you, and see plainly what is there. People who share your position think there is not the slightest inconsistency in claiming that there is a right to a dead child, and that the child who survives the abortion has no claim to the protection of the law. The people who make this argument, unashamedly, think that it is not only consistent, but virtually entailed, or made necessary, by the logic of "abortion rights." As you look about you in this country, can we not see, in fact, a notable drift in the same direction, with hospitals such as Christ Hospital in Oaklawn, Illinois, or with the appointment of Prof. Peter

Singer to Princeton University? That a leading university would appoint to a prestigious chair an outright defender of infanticide is but one sign in a drift of some parts of liberal opinion, to be far more accepting of infanticide, or at least to break down our moral reservations about infanticide. This is a problem, then, for the liberal contingent in our politics. The new acceptance of infanticide is being absorbed now in the body of their doctrines and their commitments as a political party. If they think that the refusal of care to the child who survives the abortion is, as we say, "over the top," then it has become a matter of high urgency for them finally to say that—and to do something now, both modest and emphatic, to draw that line.

In making that decision, there is no way gentler than the one Congressman Canady and his colleagues have put before us. Still, I am sure that we shall encounter people who would try to steer around the question by saying, "We agree with you, but these are rare cases, and as modest as this measure is, it is the first step that allows the Congress to be legislating on abortion. It is the first step toward involving the government in these private questions of abortion."

There are several layers of fallacies involved in this argument, and I don't expect the least acknowledgement that arguments of this kind will emanate from some of the same people who were passionate, several years ago, in advocating the passage of the Freedom of Choice Act. That was an effort to codify in our statutes the holding in *Roe* v. *Wade*. The political figures and professors who championed that measure apparently did not think that there was anything in the Constitution that barred the Congress from legislating on the matter of abortion, when it came to protecting and promoting abortion. Toward that end, the full resources of the federal government could indeed reach that private matter of abortion, whether it involved the performing of abortions in the military outposts of this country, or providing counseling and support of abortion in private facilities with federal funds.

But there is a curious screening that comes along with this argument when we turn to restrictions on abortion. And what is screened out, most notably, are the powers of Congress and the very design of the Constitution in the separation of powers. When people argue that the federal government should not be involved in these decisions, I usually ask whether they mean that some effort should be made under Art. III, Section 2, to keep the federal courts from intervening in these questions. But that is not what they mean, and one nearly has the impression that the federal courts are somehow not part of the federal government. The federal courts intervened decisively in this matter of abortion in the early 1970's, and in *Roe* v. *Wade* the Supreme Court virtually swept away the laws that restricted abortion in the fifty States.

Was that not an intervention of the federal government?

The federal courts have addressed the question of abortion in all of its dimensions, from the use of prostaglandins, and the methods of abortion, to the facilities in which these surgeries may be performed. But we may earnestly ask: How could the judicial branch of the government have the authority to deal with abortion in all of its dimensions, while the legislative branch would not have the slightest authority to address it in any dimension? A contention of that kind simply wars with the most fundamental things that should be understood about the American Constitution, especially by lawyers and members of Congress. Chief Justice Marshall once remarked on this axiom of the Constitution in *Cohens* v. *Virginia,* in 1821: "[T]he judicial power of every well constituted government," he said, "must be co-extensive with the legislative, and must be capable of deciding every judicial question which grows out of the constitution and laws."[7] To put it another way, any issue that arose under the Constitution and laws of the United States had to come within the jurisdiction of the federal courts. And yet, even jurists are persistently taken by surprise by the corollary of that axiom: Any issue that comes within the competence of the judicial branch must come, presumptively at least, within the reach of the legislative and executive branches. After all, if the Court can articulate new implications of the Fourteenth Amendment—if the Court can proclaim, say, a deeper right on the part of black people not to suffer discriminations based on race—did Congress not have the power to act on the same clause in the Constitution in vindicating those rights? Congress did exactly that in 1964, and it acted with the wider range of flexibility that a legislative body can summon, when it is not confined, in the style of courts, to the task of addressing cases in controversy between two parties.

We might put the matter finally in this way: If the Court can articulate new rights under the Constitution—including a right to abortion—the legislative branch must be able to act, on the same ground in the Constitution, in filling out those rights. But in filling them out, the legislature must have the power to mark their limits or their borders. It should be as plain as anything could be that what is not tenable under the Constitution is that the Supreme Court can articulate new rights—and then assign to itself a monopoly of the legislative power in shaping those rights. The genius of the separation of powers is that no one branch can be in complete control over the laws or its own powers. The provision on bills of attainder, for example, means that Congress may not legislate guilt or direct prosecutions under the laws it passes. Congress must work by defining in impersonal terms the nature of the wrong it would forbid, and it must work with the awareness that the law it passes will be placed in other hands to be administered. That is to say, the power to prosecute under the laws may be placed in hands unfriendly to those men and women in Congress who frame the laws. But as John Locke pointed out, that state of affairs provides a wholesome caution to the legislators: "[T]hey are themselves subject to the law they have made; which is a new and near tie upon them to take care that they make them for the public good."[8] In other words, they have an inducement not to pass laws that they would not willingly see enforced even against themselves. In that respect the logic of the separation of powers draws on the logic of a moral principle: Do not legislate for other people a rule that you would not see applied universally, to yourself as well as others. That is a wholesome principle governing the government in general—which means that it is no less wholesome when applied to the judicial branch as well as the legislative.

The Congress did not inject the federal government into the matter of abortion; it was the Supreme Court that did that with crashing cymbals, and reverberations continuing to our day. Since *Roe* v. *Wade,* the Congress has not exercised its legislative authority to restrict or cabin or scale down in any way the rights that were proclaimed in that landmark case. But now we are at a point at which the Court has struck down the effort of legislatures in 30 States to protect children at the point of birth from one of the most grisly abortions. The Court has brought us to the very threshold of infanticide, and we are asked now to take a deep breath, avert our eyes, and simply get used to the notion that the right to abortion will be spilling past the child in the womb, to order the deaths of children outside the womb. It has become more critical than ever, at this moment, that a line be drawn. Any right must have its limit, including the right to abortion, and if that limit is not found in outright infanticide, we must ask: where could it possibly be? Congress is acting here in the most modest way simply to establish that limit. As a practical matter, it will affect only a handful of cases, but as I say, it will convey lessons running deep.

As we have come to understand, important principles may be vindicated even in a single case. Ollie's Barbecue in Birmingham, Alabama, was one family restaurant, but the Civil Rights Act of 1964 was tested and vindicated in the case of that one, local establishment. There may be a score of cases facing us here, with the infants who survive the abortion; and yet the principle has an import that goes well beyond the number of cases. But even so, even if we have but a handful of cases, would there not be a vast good contained in the move to save this handful of lives? From the massive volume of abortions in this country—from that 1.3 million carried out each year—why should we not take even this small gesture and rescue, from that ocean of deaths, a handful of lives? Why should we disdain that project as an undertaking too small for this Congress? Let us not confuse the modest with the insignificant.

Lincoln once remarked, in a famous line, that "in *giving* freedom to the slave, we *assure* freedom to the *free*—honorable alike in what we give, and what we preserve."[9] In this case, we might say that, in setting in place these most elementary protections for human life, we are securing the ground for all of our rights, for the born as well as the unborn. This is the gentlest step to take, and to paraphrase Lincoln from another occasion, let the vast future not lament our having failed to take it.

NOTES

1. See "Abortion and Moral Beliefs: A Survey of American Opinion," Washington, D.C., February 28, 1991, p. 38. The study was conducted in the field by the Gallup organization, and commissioned by Americans United for Life, a pro-life group. But the survey was designed by Profs. James Davison Hunter (University of Virginia), Carl Bowman (Bridgewater College), Robert Wuthnow (Princeton). And more recently, see CNN/USA Today/Gallup poll: April 30-May 2, 1999.
2. 440 F. Supp. 535, at 539 (1977).
3. 462 U.S. 476, at 485, n. 7 (1983).
4. *Anders* v. *Floyd,* 440 U.S. 445 (1979); emphasis added.
5. See "Abortion Babies 'Should be Left to Die,'" by Angella Johnson, African News Service, March 17, 1997. One female doctor declared that the directive was "inhuman and against all my principles." Other reports suggested that as many as 50 percent of the nurses and "health workers" in the country would refuse to comply.
6. Slip opinion, Section I B.
7. 6 Wheaton 264, at 384.
8. John Locke, *Second Treatise on Civil Government,* Sec. 143.
9. Lincoln, Message to Congress (December I, 1862), in *The Collected Works of Abraham Lincoln,* ed. Roy P. Basler (New Brunswick, N.J.: Rutgers University Press, 1953), Vol. V, p. 537.

[*The Born-Alive Infants Protection Act passed both the House and Senate by unanimous consent in 2002, and was signed into law by President George W. Bush on August 5 of that year—Ed.*]

Together—for Life

Richard John Neuhaus

I should imagine that everybody here, without exception, has been to many, many such meetings; at least meetings that roughly fall under the umbrella of pro-life concern. And one of the most important things, I think, for all of us to remind ourselves of—and to be reminded of again and again—is that we're going to be at a lot more meetings, God willing. That there is no end point to the great cause of life that brings us together. We are signed on for the duration and the duration is the entirety of the human drama, for the conflict between what John Paul II calls the culture of life and the culture of death is a permanent conflict. It is a conflict built into a wretchedly fallen and terribly ambiguous human condition.

And so those who have been recruited, who understand themselves by virtue of their very faith in God, their very having-been-chosen-by-God, the God of life—those who *understand* that, know that they are in this for the duration, and that everything that has been the pro-life movement of the last 30-plus years has been the prelude, has been the laying of the foundation for the pro-life movement of the 21st century and of the 22nd century, and of all the centuries, however many more there are to come.

That understanding is absolutely essential to the kind of commitment, the kind of devotion, the kind of self-surrender that has made the pro-life movement one of the most luminous illustrations of the human capacity for altruistic, genuinely other-regarding activities, indeed, not only in the American experiment, but in world history. Never before, I think it fair to say—ponder this—have so many people given so much over so long a period of time for a cause from which they have absolutely nothing to gain personally; and indeed in which they have, in many cases, *lost*—at least by any ordinary calculation of benefits: lost time, often friendships, or gained a great deal of opprobrium and misunderstanding on the part of others and, in many cases, have been jailed and arrested, and have paid deep fiscal penalties.

It is an inspiring thing to have been part of this first 30 years of this phase of what is called the pro-life movement. And we dare not be weary. We dare never give in to what sometimes seem to be the overwhelming indications that the cause is futile. We dare never give in to despair. We have not the

---

Fr. Richard John Neuhaus (1936-2009) was the founding editor of *First Things* and the author of many books, the last of which was *American Babylon* (Basic Books, 2009). This is the text of an address he gave at a conference at Fordham University, April 24, 2001, titled "Exploring How Jews and Christians Can Work Together to Sanctify Human Life."

right to despair. And finally, we have not the reason to despair.

It is a grand thing, it is among the grandest things in life, to know that your life has been claimed by a cause ever so much greater than yourself, ever so much greater than ourselves. In our American public life today, there's much talk about a culture war—sometimes in the plural, culture wars. It's a phrase that I've used, it's a phrase we've used in *First Things* from time to time, and people sometimes are critical of that. And they say, Oh, isn't that an alarmist kind of language, isn't that an inflammatory kind of language to use, to talk about wars?

Well, maybe. It's a contestation, if you prefer the word contestation. It's a conflict, certainly very, very deep. But it does have a warlike character to it. And if it *is* war, it's good to remember who it was that declared this war; who is waging a defensive war, and who an aggressive war. It was not our side that declared war. We were not the ones who decided on January 22, 1973, that all of a sudden everything that had been entrenched in the conscience and the habits and the mores *and the laws* of the people of this nation with respect to the dignity of human life and the rights bestowed upon that life— that all of that was now to be discarded. That in one, raw act of judicial power, which of course the *Roe* v. *Wade* decision was, every protection of the unborn, in all 50 states, would be completely wiped off the books.

Astonishing thing. It is important for us to remember that most of those who were on the side of what was then called liberalized abortion law, now called pro-choice, were as astonished as everyone else by *Roe* v. *Wade.* Nobody expected that the Court would simply abolish abortion law, would simply eliminate even the most minimal protections of unborn life.

That, of course, is not the only occasion upon which a war was declared that creates what today is called the culture war. There are many, many other points in the culture. Sometimes we simply refer, perhaps too vaguely and too generally, to *the Sixties,* but certainly under sundry revolutionary titles, all claiming to be great movements of liberation, was explicitly lodged and advanced and argued for in the name of warfare, a counterculture intended to overthrow, presumably, the oppressive, stifling, life-denying character indeed of Western Civilization itself and all its works and all its ways. It was to be an exorcism, if you will, of what was perceived to be a maliciously oppressive cultural order of which we are a part, with respect to sexuality— always weaving in and out and coming back to the question of sexuality: marriage and divorce and education policy and a host of things.

And so war was declared and war followed. And it will continue to look very much like a war. It is our responsibility not only for strategic or tactical reasons, but very importantly for moral reasons, to make sure that it doesn't become warfare in the sense of violence and bloodshed. It is our responsibility to advance our arguments in this great contestation with civility and with persuasiveness, knowing that sound reason and the deepest convictions engendered by Judeo-Christian moral tradition both strongly support the cause of life, which will ultimately prevail.

Professor Bernard Dobranski, dean of Ave Maria Law School, noted the motto of Ave Maria, *Fides et Ratio,* faith and reason. And these two are seldom so powerfully conjoined as in the pro-life cause. We are constantly in the process of saying to those who claim that we would impose our values, and even worse impose our religion, upon others: No. Our response is: Let us reason, let us come reason together about what is the foundation of human life.

Let us come reason together about what are—as everybody should understand—moral questions about how we order our life together. The dean said that all of law is moral, all of politics is moral, ultimately.

What is politics? I think the best shorthand definition of politics that anybody's ever proposed is Aristotle's. And Aristotle said politics is free persons deliberating the question how ought we to order our life together. *Free persons deliberating the question how ought we to order our life together.* And the "ought" of that definition is clearly a moral term.

Every political question of consequence is a moral question. What is fair? What is just? What serves the common good? Fairness, justice, good: These are all moral terms. We are the ones who are prepared to enter into the dialogue, if you will: the ongoing conversation, within the bounds of civility, as to how we ought to order our life together, including the question who belongs to the *we*—the most elementary of all political questions.

Who belongs to the *we*? Who is entitled to our respect? Who is entitled to protection?

This conversation, this argument, in unwarlike ways, in civil ways, in persuasive ways, will prevail incrementally, piece by piece, sometimes moving, it seems, more backward than forward. But we're accustomed to that; we should be. We know that we've signed on for the duration, we know that the conflict between the culture of life and the culture of death is nothing less than the story of humankind. Humankind trying to find a better way, a more just way, a more humane way of ordering our life together, and of protecting all those who belong to the *we*.

Our goal. I think in the last few years it's been a very encouraging thing that across the spectrum of those concerned in various ways with the cause of life, there is an agreement on how we formulate our goal. What is it, that goal? The goal is every unborn child protected in law and welcomed in life.

I'm glad to say that, during the 2000 presidential campaign and since, President Bush has consistently reiterated that as the goal. When asked, "What do you mean when you say you're pro-life?" I mean that we must work as a society for a time in which every unborn child is protected in law and welcomed in life.

Now we all know that we will never get to that time. There will always be abortions just as there will always be other forms of homicide, and there will always be robberies, and there will always be child abuse. We know that, because we are unblinkingly realistic about the nature of the human condition and of our lives within it. But we also know what is that realistic goal that, step by step, with wisdom, with courage, with unfailing commitment, we are working toward.

It is a great question of what it is that keeps you going. Each of us, I think—Jews and Christians, those of us who by the grace of God have been called to the community of the God of Israel, whether as Christians or Jews—it is for us to know that finally this is His cause before it's our cause. That He is the Maker of heaven and earth and the Author of life. And that every human life is inestimable, invaluable (that is to say no price can be put upon it), a meeting between the finite and the infinite. That every human life is destined from eternity and called to eternity, with God, from God. And if one believes that, it is not whistling in the dark, or simply trying to keep up spirits or wearing a bright yellow smiley button to say that the cause of life will prevail. John Paul II, as you know, frequently speaks about the beginning of the third millennium as a springtime—a springtime of Christian unity, a springtime of Jewish/Christian understanding; a springtime of world evangelization, a springtime of the renewal of human culture.

And people sometimes ask, well, how can someone like Karol Wojtyla, who became John Paul II, say that? Someone who has lived through the 20th century, the bloodiest and most horrendous of all centuries in human history, lived through everything that would seem to contradict such a disposition, such an anticipation of a springtime? I mean he lived *through* Nazism, he lived *through* Communism, he saw the slaughter and the horror. And people ask, how can he be so optimistic about the human project, about the future? And the answer, of course, is that he's not optimistic at all. Nor does he call us to be optimistic. Optimism is not a virtue—it's simply a matter of seeing what you want to see, and not seeing what you don't want to see.

Hope is a very, very different thing. Hope is looking into the heart of darkness and seeing at the heart of darkness that there is reason for hope. Because for Christians looking at the Cross, as we've just done during the Easter period, at the heart of darkness and Christian understanding is God

Himself in Jesus Christ. And the last word belongs not to darkness, but to love, to the resurrected life, to the vindication of hope.

So we know what the goal is: every unborn child, every old person considered expendable, all the radically disabled (physically, mentally)—everyone protected in law, welcomed in life. We work for that, relentlessly, the culture of life versus the culture of death. It is one of the greatest encouragements of recent years, for which the organizers of this conference can accept the due thanks of all of us, that there has been a growing convergence between significant sectors of the Jewish community and of the dominantly Christian pro-life cause of the last 30, 40 years; important for many, many different reasons. Not so much because it adds numbers or adds clout, but because it bears more powerful, more credible witness to what we mean when we speak together about the God of life, and renew, by such speech and by such witness and by such work, what society once meant by human beings created and endowed with inalienable rights.

It is among the contributions of this great cause to renew the constituting convictions of the American democratic experiment, which are very, very much under assault on many different fronts.

I remember years ago where my own personal involvement in the pro-life cause really began, long before *Roe* v. *Wade,* when it was then called the movement for the liberalization of abortion law here in New York and California and Hawaii. In the Williamsburg/Bedford-Stuyvesant section of Brooklyn, in St. John the Evangelist Church of which I was pastor, I read an article in *Harper's* magazine by Ashley Montagu, an anthropologist at Princeton (where does Princeton get these kinds of leaders?). And this article was about what makes a life worth living. And he ran through, as you might imagine, a number of criteria of what constituted a life worth living. Obviously physical health, being in a solid, secure family situation, having economic security and prospects of an educational and career future. I think there were ten or eleven criteria, measures of a life worth living. And I recall it was an Advent Sunday in 1964—I realize I don't look that old—and I was standing at the altar at St. John the Evangelist looking out at the three or four hundred people there attending the liturgy. And I realized, looking over all these black faces of people—almost all very poor—that in Ashley Montagu's judgment not one of them had a life worth living. Not one. Not one could meet more than two or three of the criteria, in his view, necessary to a life worth living.

And this—I have to say it—hit me: Kaboom! A great evil is afoot here. What is this man saying? And people who say these things and think this way—what are they saying? They're saying, of course, what anybody should recall if they're at all literate about the history of which we are a part; they're saying that there are very, very large numbers of people living lives that are not worthy of life. And anybody who has any literacy with regard to the times in which we live will recognize that phrase, and where it was used before: *lebensunwertes Leben.* Life that is not worthy of life. Which, of course, was the centerpiece of the genocidal, unspeakable practice of the Nazi regime: that we presume to decide which lives, indeed, are worthy of life and have any claim upon our attention. In short, we decide who belongs to the *we.* And we exclude those with whom we do not want to deliberate how we ought to order our lives together.

It's an astonishing thing: I know that it's very controversial and precisely because it is controversial it is necessary to touch on the ways in which there are parallels and non-parallels between that unspeakable horror of the Holocaust and today's culture of death. When my dear, dear friend John Cardinal O'Connor first came to New York, he spoke very straightforwardly about the parallels of the Holocaust. And it caused a great deal of controversy, and many in the Jewish community (but not only in the Jewish community) said, well, you have to be very careful in making that analogy. And they were right. And Cardinal O'Connor took that very much to heart and was from there on very, very careful indeed.

But at one point, all of us—Christians and Jews and whoever understands what's at stake here—have to understand that there is this crucial commonality. There is this lethal point of logic shared by these two dreadful phenomena: that we put ourselves in the position of deciding that certain peoples, by virtue of their race, their religion, their culture, their size, their disability, their language, name it—are *lebensunwertes Leben.* And that is the lethal logic that motors the madness of killing, whether it be partial-birth abortion, whether it be euthanasia, whether it be the willingness to destroy life in order to create the perfect baby, or to clone those who are considered the superior types of our species. Whatever mechanism and whatever cause and technological manipulation is being advanced in the tide of the culture of death has always at its center the lethal logic of *lebensunwertes Leben.* We're up against something very ominous, where evil is indeed afoot. The things that I've mentioned—partial-birth abortion has already been mentioned, other developments, eugenics, cloning, genetic engineering. And it is an ominous thing that in the last three years it has become respectable again to use the word eugenics.

Eugenics basically means good births, of course, but much more than that, it means the programmatic effort to redesign the *humanum,* create a superior, better kind of human being and, of course, the flip side of that is to reduce or eliminate inferior types of human beings. Eugenics was an elite cause, and a liberal cause and a progressive cause beginning in the late 19th century and the early part of the 20th century. And then, of course, with the Second World War and with Hitler and the Holocaust, the idea of eugenics was totally discredited. The word was *verboten,* taboo. Nobody used the word "eugenics."

But now in the last two or three years—keep your eyes open, look at the books that are being published, read the leading opinion journals—it's becoming respectable again to talk about eugenics. And the people who talk about it say, well, of course there was that unfortunate episode, that unpleasantness back there around the middle of the century in Germany. But that really was an *aberration* and now we have to get back on track with the great cause of designing a better humanity. Dealing with human beings essentially as things, as products which are to please our consumer tastes. And if they don't, like any other consumer product, they simply can be rejected or eliminated or tossed out. That's a very, very ominous thing.

But I did not come here to discourage or to depress. It's very important, crucially important for us to remember, in this great contest between the culture of life and the culture of death and the form that it takes in what are called the culture wars of our society, how much we have to be thankful for.

You recall, back in the late sixties and then in 1973, when the *Roe* v. *Wade* decision came down, the New York *Times* said—and all of the rest of the media echoed the proposition—that the abortion question had at last been settled. That was the word that was used; the Supreme Court had *settled* the abortion question. And here we are, almost 30 years later, and it's the most unsettled question in American life.

And that in itself is reason for hope. It's reason for hope that all the brightest and the best and their institutions in our society, almost without exception, in 1973 said that this question is over. Don't talk about it any more; don't argue about it any more. It is settled. All of the major universities and the voices from the academy, the philanthropic world, the prestige media, go across the board: The powerful—those who control the commanding heights of culture—were unanimous that this question was settled.

There was only one major institution in American life that dissented, and that was the Catholic Church, the bishops of the Catholic Church. Not as powerfully, not as articulately, not with the determination or the skill that they ought to have had. But they said, No way, wait a minute. This can't be right. This is a very, very dangerous thing.

We are counting up reasons for hope, reasons to encourage us. Now look where we are. Today we have the Evangelical Protestants, of all varieties, solidly committed to the pro-life cause. At the time of *Roe* v. *Wade* and still five years after *Roe* v. *Wade,* the Southern Baptist Convention, the largest single Protestant association in the country, with more than 15 million members, was passing resolutions in favor of legalized abortion. It was the great work of Francis Schaeffer and a handful of others that turned around the whole of that almost one-third of the American public that is Evangelical Protestantism.

And the Jewish: how very, very important this is. For a long time now some of us have been involved in the Christian/Jewish dialogue. (Again, I'm much older than I look.) And going back, I remember at Concordia Seminary in St. Louis, Missouri, Rabbi Saul Bernard, who, thank God, is still with us. He was then the interreligious director of the Anti-Defamation League and would go around almost like an itinerant evangelist to Protestant seminary and Catholic, with this message about a strange phenomenon called the Christian/Jewish dialogue. And he first embroiled me in that. And I've never been able to get out of it, nor wanted to get out of it ever since.

Along the way it was by the grace of God my great good fortune to become a friend of someone for whom I thank God every day, Abraham Joshua Heschel, who was perhaps the most influential and admired Jewish theologian of this century, at least in America. Heschel did not live long enough, or it did not come together in quite the right way, for him ever to be entirely as clear as I thought he ought to have been on the question of abortion and the related questions of *lebensunwertes Leben.* But Heschel did understand what was involved. Heschel said that just to *be* is a blessing; just to live is holy. And he spoke and wrote magnificently about the pathos of God suffering with His wounded creation.

Heschel had another line which is never to be forgotten, I hope. With regard to Jewish/Christian dialogue he said interfaith dialogue begins with faith. And what is happening here in this meeting, and what is happening more generally in our society as all of us give ourselves to this, and we pray our efforts succeed, is a meeting in faith. Obviously there are deep differences between Jews and Christians, and the deepest of differences, as St. Paul wrote in Romans, chapters nine through eleven, probably await the end time, the *eschaton* of the final coming of the kingdom of God and the Messianic age, ever to be sorted out and resolved.

But along the way we are together pilgrims in faith, and pilgrims of faith, seeking to do the will of the God of Israel Who is the Author of Life. And that has to be much more than strategic and tactical considerations, as important as they are; that has to be the center of what brings us together in this meeting and what, from this meeting, will, by the grace of God, build and build into an ever greater cooperation. So much has already been happening that is hopeful. The issue is not settled; it's the most unsettled in our life today. A few years ago the Boston *Globe*—which has a fiercely pro-abortion, anti-life editorial posture—wrote an editorial after one of the numerous studies that have come out, that some of us have been looking at for decades now, about the public attitudes on abortion. And the Boston *Globe* ruefully, regret-fully said, we must face the fact (meaning those who support *Roe* v. *Wade* must face the fact) that 75 percent of the American people believe that abor-tion should not be legal for the reasons for which 95 percent of abortions are obtained. That's right.

It's a remarkable thing. And encouraging: The prestige media and the universities and the philanthropies and related institutions and persons who are perceived as controlling the commanding heights of culture do not have nearly the control that they think they do. Not nearly, thank God. The fact is that despite an almost unanimous and relentless campaign to have abortion accepted—not simply accepted as a purely private matter, and one that has to be entirely outside the scope of public purview or concern or control, but accepted as a positive good—they know that they have lost the argument publicly.

They hold on relentlessly with their fingertips. On partial-birth abortion, they even demand that infanticide (which surely this is) must be permitted. And why? Not because they are in love with infanticide; just out of simple human feeling, we must allow to our brothers and sisters on the other side that many of them find this as repugnant as do most feeling, thinking human beings. But they hold on to this because they dare not give an inch; because they believe that if even an inch is lost, their whole house of cards will come tumbling down.

And there is an element of truth to that. I think there is a strong element of truth to that. They know they have lost the argument.

We cannot be euphoric. We must always be terribly sober in estimating what the future holds. But I do believe that with this administration in Wash-ington, we are at long last seeing a political expression of what for a long time has been a much deeper, moral, cultural turning in American life.

I always remind myself, and tell others, of Psalm 146. Psalm 146, as you know, says, Do not put your trust in princes, even when they're your princes and you're a bit more hopeful about them than you are about others. But I *am* hopeful that this administration has, in a way that is deeper than the political calculation, understood at least in part what is at stake. You remember we shouldn't be naive about this. And we know there are going to be disappoint-ments. We know there are going to be tears. We know that. All of us are grownups. I recall President Reagan, when he would talk about negotiating arms control with the Soviet Union, would say, "Trust but verify."

And so also with respect to this administration, or anybody else in the political arena who seems to be an ally, it should not only be "Trust but verify," but also "Trust and maintain the pressure," and *that* all of us must do in the political arena. We must do it together.

It is an encouraging thing again, the heroes in the Jewish community, and among them my dear friend Rabbi Marc Gellman, whom you'll be hearing from later, who is sometimes described as being the only Reform pro-life rabbi in the country. And there is Nat Hentoff, who has just with breathtaking consistency and relentlessness acted upon the principles that made him such a hero of the Left, and in some issues still a hero of the Left, but who understood that he could not live with himself, he could not be Nat Hentoff except at the price of breaking ranks over this most elementary question of the status of the least among us.

Heschel used to say a society is measured morally not by how it treats people along the strength-lines in the society, but how it treats people along the fault-lines of the society. Nat Hentoff has understood that, and Chris Gersten and so many others.

It is more difficult for our Jewish brothers and sisters than it is for us, especially for us Catholics and for Evangelical Protestants today. It is much, much more difficult; because so many countervailing, counter-cutting forces and memories are in play, sometimes painfully. But for most American Jews, outside of the most observant, Orthodox community, the great belief, the right belief has been that the more secular the society is, the safer it will be for the Jews. A Reform rabbi friend of mine some years ago said, When I hear the phrase Christian America, I see barbed wire. That's hyperbole, of course, but one has to understand what he intends to say.

At least in the 20th century, especially following the Second World War, in the dominant Jewish communities, the dominant intellectual, cultural, organizational forces were committed to what I have described as the naked public square; public life excluding as much as possible religion and faith-based morality. The great Leo Pfeffer himself, a believing and observant Jew, won court case after court case basically arguing that democracy required the radical secularization of public life, the removal of any transcendent reference to the public belief.

What we see in our Jewish brothers and sisters represented here, and in many, many other places around the country—and I speak now to you who are Christians and Catholic first—what we see here are some courageous people, some thoughtful people who have come to recognize in various ways that the naked public square, a public life that is devoid of the transcendent, of religion and religiously based morality, is a very dangerous place. It is a very dangerous place because where there is no transcendent inhibition against evil, there is no transcendent inhibition against the evil also of, for example, anti-Semitism. And where there is no transcendent aspiration to good that is given public expression in politics and in law, there is no transcendent inhibition of evil.

We are given the task of reviving, at many, many different levels, working together, the high promise and the vitality of the American democratic experiment. We are the ones who are urging the renewal in all of this, who are urging that we come together and deliberate how we ought to order our life together, beginning with who belongs to the *we*. We are the ones who are prepared, if you will, to compromise with respect to this measure or this law or that law, fully knowing that what is uncompromisable is the goal of every unborn child protected in law and welcomed in life. That can never, never be compromised. But on the way to that goal, political and legal compromise is not morally compromising; indeed it is morally imperative. We are the ones who want to reason together. We are the ones who have that confidence in the mutually reinforcing power of *fides et ratio*. Of faith and reason.

Well, I have gone on too long. Jews and Christians are the future not only of the pro-life movement in this country, but of reviving an understanding that the God of Israel, whom we all worship, is indeed at work and alive, providentially directing not only life in this century but of His entire creation.

Last year there was a mark of new maturity, very encouraging, positive, and of historic importance in the Jewish/Christian dialogue, with the issuing of a statement called *Dabru Emet* (*Speak the Truth*), on Jewish understandings of Christians and Christianity, published in the November issue of *First Things* and signed by over 170—now, I understand, well over 200—Jewish scholars. And among the things that this underscores is that we have an ultimate obligation for a moment that has never before happened in the history between Jews and Christians, and that in fact can only happen here in the United States.

Because it is only here that there are enough Jews, and enough Christians, mutually confident, mutually secure in their relationship to one another, to enter honestly into continuing conversation, and to continue an exploration of what the God of Israel intends for us and for the nation and the world of which we're a part. This is a new thing, this dialogue. What this meeting is about is one critically important facet of this new thing that God is doing, and that is moving the conversation from the theological and philosophical and historical and the sorting out of all the grievances and anxieties of a long, tortured history, to the question: What shall we do now? What is it that we are obliged to do now?

And what we are obliged to do now is to bear witness together; and more than bearing witness, to effectively collaborate together in advancing the arguments along with many others, until finally they find effective political and legal expression, and, most important, find expression in the everyday habits and mores of the American people. To secure the conviction that there is no such thing as *lebensunwertes Leben.* To persuade our fellow citizens that every life is a juncture between the finite and infinite purpose, destined from eternity and called to eternity.

Whether we will prevail or how we will prevail, this cause will prevail, this truth will prevail, because it is the truth of the God of Life.

Singer and the Song

Jo McGowan

My thirteen-year-old daughter eats very little. Moy Moy is nearly five feet tall and weighs only fifty-six pounds. For the last eight years, Moy has been regressing. Her developmental age is now that of a four-month infant. Part of her condition (a neurological degenerative disorder) is a slow dis-coordination of the muscles needed to chew and swallow, so that, although she wants to eat, the effort is simply too much for her.

It is one of life's little ironies that I read the article about Princeton Professor Peter Singer's encounter with Harriet McBryde Johnson this week, while my husband and I are trying to decide whether the time has come for Moy to undergo a gastrostomy—a surgical procedure to insert a tube directly into her stomach so that we can continue to feed her now that she can no longer feed herself. Professor Singer would have no trouble making the decision.

Or so he thinks. Professor Singer doesn't know Moy Moy.

Based on the facts—she cannot walk or speak or do anything whatever for herself and she seems to have no self-awareness—she would probably qualify for his definition of a waste of space. Our taking care of her is, in his words, "a little weird."

But, as I say, he doesn't know her. He couldn't guess that her presence in our lives has transformed us, that she has brought us close to people we would never have known and now cannot think of life without. He couldn't imagine her magnetic charm, her delightful, adorable nature. He couldn't know that because of her, a school has been created in India which takes care of the needs of hundreds of children with special needs, employs nearly forty people, generates millions of rupees in donations and creates awareness and a sense of community in a way that no ordinary school ever could. She is a mini-Empire all on her own.

He also didn't know Shivani, one of Moy Moy's classmates. Shivani died last month, of starvation brought on by depression. Shivani had a severe mental and emotional disability. Her behaviour was erratic and often violent and she created chaos in her family. They were very poor and a year earlier, her father, an unemployed tailor, also suffering from depression, had committed suicide. Shivani was deeply attached to him and had been unable to adjust to life without him. She stopped eating gradually and slowly wasted away.

I tell both stories to make the point that, as Ms. Johnson insists, "disabled

Jo McGowan is a columnist for *Commonweal* magazine. She and her family live in Dehra Doon, India, where she has founded Karuna Vihar, a school for children with special needs.

lives are not subject to debate." Moy Moy is beautiful, easy and appealing (and well-off) while Shivani was beautiful, intensely difficult and poor; neither of them, however, need to justify their right to exist to Professor Singer, any more than he needs to justify his to me. His views offend me, but I don't plan to suggest he be killed because he holds them.

In spite of his intelligence, Professor Singer has a limited understanding of the world and, it seems, little imagination. He has no idea of what the world would be like without Moy Moy and Shivani. None of us does, really, but those of us who, like me, once had only a peripheral understanding of disability and now have it as the centre of their existence, can testify to the before and after phenomenon with some authority.

My own "quality of life" has improved dramatically since Moy Moy's birth, and not only because of the difference she herself has made to me, but also because of the many other people with disabilities I have met through her. I live differently now. I think I am a better person.

I agree with Ms. Johnson that people with disabilities are not here to provide awareness training to the rest of us. They are not here to inspire anything either: not love, not a sense of gratitude. Like the rest of us, they are just here. But, also like the rest of us, sometimes their presence *does* inspire: love, gratitude, generosity, kindness. I do not think I am being sentimental when I say that people with disabilities inspire, on average, more than people without. I have worked in the field of special needs now for nearly a decade. It used to amaze me that in every institution I visited, without exception, I would find a collection of truly wonderful people. Now I take it for granted.

While I admit that the profession attracts a certain type of person in the first place, it is also true that many character traits develop only through practice. People who make a habit of accepting others as they are, of valuing their efforts and championing their smallest achievements *become* people of depth and understanding. The world would be a poorer place without them.

In a recent column, Professor Singer says that he is not surprised by Catholic opposition to voluntary euthanasia and assisted suicide because Roman Catholicism is authoritarian, discouraging critical thinking in its followers. "Starting from the position that God has put us here on earth for a purpose, they see suicide as something like desertion from the military, except that the suicide is disobeying orders from the Supreme Commander. Voluntary euthanasia they regard as even worse than suicide, since it involves the intentional killing of an innocent human being."[1] Whether I agree with his analysis of Catholic opposition or not, his criticism is a valid one. Many of us do accept the teachings of the Church uncritically and it does no one any service. As a Catholic, I accept Singer's observation as a challenge to examine the assumptions I make, without even knowing I am making them. We all need to be called to account, to give reasons for things we profess.

In the same spirit, I challenge Professor Singer to look at his own assumptions. The moral validity of choosing abortion is a case in point. Abortion in some circles is such a sacred cow that it is difficult to honestly consider any proposal that questions its legitimacy. And if we accept abortion, as Professor Singer rightly points out, there is no reason not to accept infanticide. It's what we have been saying from the very beginning. The problem here is in Professor Singer's *assumption* that the argument for abortion is so perfect as to admit of no further debate. This is far from being the case.

As it happens, however, I don't actually worry too much about Professor Singer's views. Whatever his reasons for propounding them—making his name in the world, a taste for controversy, a desire for excitement—when it came to the test, he couldn't practice them himself. His own mother, who was, by all accounts, a brilliantly intellectual woman and a physician with an active practice, has Alzheimer's. In spite of her expressed wish not to be allowed to live in such a state, should it ever come to that, Singer has not had her done away with. Instead he spends large sums of money providing her with round-the-clock nursing care, unassisted by Kevorkian or any of his colleagues.

However he justifies it in his own mind (he says "I think this had made me see how the issues of someone with these kinds of problems are really very difficult. Perhaps it's more difficult than I thought before, because it's different when it's your mother")[2], Singer cannot deny his generosity, his love, or his humanity.

Professor Singer is obviously a man of great sensitivity—he cares about his mother, about animals and about the environment. It seems inconceivable that he would not consider the possible consequences of his proposal to do away with handicapped infants, born or unborn. I would like to invite him to forget the fact that the lives we are discussing are human and simply think of them as mammals. As he well knows, ecosystems are nothing if not interdependent. The slightest disruption can have far-reaching and often disastrous effects. Usually these effects are things we would never have guessed.

In the Redwood forests of California, for example, large scale logging operations created havoc with the natural habitat of the spotted owl. The spotted owl is what is known as a "keystone species"—an organism which plays a crucial role in its environment and whose removal results in massive ecological damage. As logging in the Redwoods continued and the spotted owl population declined, rodents increased, upsetting the delicate balance of the forest ecosystem and causing a ripple effect of destruction to other creatures and plant life. An interesting sidelight to this particular conservationist vs. big business battle is that the spotted owl's habitat is also the home of the

"Pacific yew," a tree whose bark may hold the cure for ovarian, breast and lung cancer. Had conservationists not won the day for the owls, this potentially life-saving discovery for humans might never have been made.[3]

A more elegant example (if disabled babies are spotted owls, that makes Peter Singer a rodent) are the lichens, colonizing organisms which so enrich the soil that given their presence, even areas devastated by volcanic ash can eventually support life. Lichens are astonishing: They do not require nitrogen in the soil because they can get it from the atmosphere! Their fungus rots what biological matter there is, manufacturing the phosphorous that plants need to grow; they also hasten the disintegration of rock, yielding valuable nutrients in the process. Lichens are enormously important in arctic ecosystems and their destruction could have immense and catastrophic ecological impact.[4]

One of the interesting things about "keystone species" is their seeming insignificance to the unknowing eye. Spotted owls and lichens, forsooth! But it should come as no surprise. The stone which the builders rejected became the cornerstone.

Children with disabilities enrich our lives in ways we cannot begin to fathom. Those of us lucky enough to be ecologists in this particular ecosystem can make grateful lists of rocks they have disintegrated and nitrogen they have created from thin air; the rest—including Professor Singer—will have to take our word for it. These spotted owls are too important to do without. We don't even know half of what we would be missing if they were not with us.

Life is wonderful and unpredictable and full of surprising twists and turns. Intellectual capacity and self-awareness are very well in their way, but they are not the beginning and the end. Brine shrimp, an endangered species whose habitat happened to be in the proposed path of a major railways project in California, were considered important enough that the railway was re-routed. No one was quite sure what might happen if they were eliminated and that doubt was what saved them.

Hooray for the conservative caution that errs on the side of life and possibility. Three cheers for the brine shrimp who just might be another "keystone species." And let's hear it for babies like Moy Moy, about whom there is no doubt whatsoever. Damn everything but the circus![5]

NOTES

1. *Free Enquiry*, 22 (2) 2002.
2. Interview by Michael Specter, Sept. 1999.
3. "The Green Fuse: An Ecological Odyssey" by John Harte, University of California Press, Berkeley, 1993, pp. 93-94.
4. *Ibid*, p. 23.
5. e.e. cummings.

Scheidler's Supreme Victory

Stephen Vincent

"Pro-life action news: Mark Wednesday, Feb. 26 [2003] in red letters because it is one big red letter day for the pro-life movement. We were having a slice of cherry pie for breakfast when we got word that the U.S. Supreme Court had ruled 8 to 1 that we are not racketeers."

With these words, Joseph M. Scheidler announced victory over the National Organization for Women and other pro-abortion forces in a case that had lasted 17 years and come to symbolize the struggle between the culture of life and the culture of death. Hanging in the balance was nothing less than the good name of the pro-life movement. Scheidler and his Pro-Life Action League are now using the victory to infuse new energy into the movement against abortion.

The decision, written by Chief Justice William H. Rehnquist, not only vindicates the peaceful protests of pro-lifers who pray, counsel, or picket outside clinics. It also protects social protestors and civil-rights activists of all stripes from crippling lawsuits brought under the Racketeer Influenced and Corrupt Organizations (RICO) act. Recognizing the threat the case posed to practitioners of all sorts of civil disobedience, a number of organizations that are far from being pro-life filed amicus briefs on Scheidler's side. The day after the decision, a Chicago *Tribune* editorial described it as a victory for free speech.

Conscious of its image as a champion of free speech and civil rights, NOW long ago posted a Q & A about the case on its website to appease liberal supporters. The lead (leading) question says it all: "Are Scheidler's protests like those of the Civil Rights movement . . . or the Ku Klux Klan?"

With such rhetoric hurled at him, Scheidler was proud to state after the Court's decision: "It's nice to know the First Amendment is still in force, even for pro-lifers in this country."

A Man for Many Seasons

Colorful, quotable, and irrepressible, Joe is known among his supporters as the grandfather of the pro-life movement. Yet to NOW and other pro-abortion forces he is not a grandfather but a godfather mobster in the mold of

Stephen Vincent writes from Wallingford, Connecticut.

fellow Chicagoan Al Capone. NOW brought civil charges of extortion under RICO—and used images of Scheidler sporting his signature black hat and bullhorn to back up the portrayal of him as an anti-choice gangster. NOW also presented spurious testimony to associate Scheidler with every act of violence ever committed against an abortion clinic or an abortionist. (This journal has covered the case extensively, with a forum on the use of RICO in Summer 1998 and a study of the questionable testimony in Fall 2000.)

Scheidler never let his opponents stop him, although every aspect of his personal and professional life was placed under a microscope and he was threatened with bankruptcy. His suburban Chicago house was placed in escrow to enable him to post a $440,000 bond while appealing a lower-court judgment. Throughout the legal ordeal that began in 1986 he was active at the clinics, counseling, praying, and persuading women to turn away from abortion. He even played with the mobster image, continuing to wear his black hat and introducing himself at rallies as a "racketeer for life." In November 2002—with oral arguments before the Supreme Court scheduled for December, a time when most appellants would shy away from controversial actions—Scheidler was making waves in the media and abortion capital of New York, helping to launch a campaign in which pro-lifers hold up posters of aborted babies in high-traffic areas. It was more than simply (and literally) an in-your-face tactic. Scheidler wanted to dramatize his belief that the charges against him amounted to a phantom case that could not be taken seriously.

"The case didn't slow us down," he reflected a few days after his Supreme victory. "I would say that it pepped us up. We didn't know how much time we had before we would be shut down by the courts. We always knew, though, whether it's by us or someone else, the battle goes on because it's right."

"The biggest problem," he continued, "was hiring people for our [Pro-Life Action League] operations because we couldn't guarantee that we'd still be in business the following year. They tried to make me out as the man running all these pro-life operations nationwide. It was very flattering, but it just wasn't true."

In a victory letter to friends and supporters addressed to "Dear Fellow Former-Racketeers," he stated, "As much as I have enjoyed being known as a 'racketeer,' I am now happy to have been vindicated."

One of his regular action news updates (phone hot-line messages that he's been composing since 1974) put the Court's decision in perspective: "Abortion will end one day just as surely as the day came when slavery was outlawed . . . Pro-life attorneys think this Supreme Court victory will open new action against other unconstitutional restrictions on pro-life activities. The court must recognize that it is unconstitutional to have special laws against people who disagree with abortion." He cited as examples the federal Freedom of Access to Clinic Entrances (FACE) Act passed during the Clinton years, and the "bubble zones" imposed by local governments that keep even people who are only praying away from clinic doors.

The Hand of God

A former Benedictine, who left religious life before final vows because "I wasn't cut out for obedience," Scheidler attributes victory ultimately to God. "I saw and experienced directly the power of concerted and persistent prayer," he said. "I knew without a doubt that God has His hand in this victory."

Thomas Brejcha, lead counsel for Scheidler's side, also assessed the outcome in very unlawyerlike terms. "We got not a single vote in the [Chicago] Court of Appeals, and we get an 8-1 decision from the Supreme Court," he marveled. "It's a remarkable, a miraculous turnaround."

The case was full of ironic twists. Anyone familiar with the pro-life movement knows that far from having centralized control and powerful bosses, pro-life groups are often hampered by their inability to unite. Yet NOW, in a sense, produced what it condemned. It raised Scheidler to the status of head man in legal proceedings and persuaded other pro-lifers to rally around him. As Joe goes, so goes the movement, many began to think.

Not all, to be sure. In 1999 federal appeals judge David Coar slapped Scheidler and the other defendants, Andrew Scholberg and Timothy Murphy, with a nationwide injunction. With the loose wording of this injunction, anyone working with Scheidler or adopting the methods outlined in his book *Closed: 99 Ways to Stop Abortion* could have been touched by it. Many pro-lifers shied away for fear of later being collared as cooperators in Scheidler's "network."

But enough others came to Scheidler's side, including brave donors who helped him pay his mounting legal fees. Pro-life leaders who had stood by him from the start were quick to applaud his victory. "This litigation was clearly an attempt by NOW to eliminate pro-life voices from the public square," said Dennis M. Burke, staff counsel for Americans United for Life, also based in Chicago. Judie Brown of American Life League called Scheidler a good friend "who has fought valiantly for years."

"This decision is a tremendous victory for those who engage in social protests," said Jay Sekulow, chief counsel of the American Center for Law and Justice, which filed a brief for Operation Rescue. (A related case, *Operation Rescue* v. *NOW*, was included in the decision although Operation Rescue has effectively been out of business for years.) "The ruling clearly shuts the door on using RICO against the pro-life movement."

"Abortion is not just a legal procedure. To groups like NOW it is a sacred ritual," said Father Frank Pavone of Priests for Life. "Their efforts have hit the brick wall of our nation's sacred right of protest. Long live that right!"

Francis Cardinal George of Chicago, who led a prayer vigil with Scheidler's group outside a Planned Parenthood facility shortly after the decision, stated, "If the courts had been used to stop organized sit-ins at lunch counters in the Sixties, there would have been no civil rights movement."

Columnist John Leo pointed out that the American Civil Liberties Union had opposed the passage of RICO from the start, but "they didn't fight it when it was used against pro-lifers."

Editorials in conservative and liberal papers alike applauded the decision. The *Wall Street Journal* said it upholds "the right of all Americans, left or right, to protest under the First Amendment." The Chicago *Tribune* stated: "No matter where they stand individually on the divisive issue of abortion, all Americans should applaud."

There were 74 amicus briefs filed by groups ranging from labor organizations to "tree-hugging" environmentalists to nuclear weapons protestors to the Seamless Garment Network. Also joining were high-profile Catholics more commonly associated with other issues: Maryknoll Father Roy Bourgeois, founder of the School of the Americas Watch; death penalty activist Sister Helen Prejean; Jesuit Father Daniel Berrigan; and Martin Sheen, known to millions as the President on *The West Wing*.

Craig M. Bradley, who wrote the brief for PETA, summed the issue up nicely: Scheidler & Company "wanted to shut the abortion clinics down. They didn't want to take them over. Just like PETA protestors might want to shut down an animal-rendering plant, not take it over."

The High Court agreed.

"Obtaining" a Decision

In the end, the 17-year case that made two trips to the Supreme Court was shockingly simple. To violate RICO one must commit a series of specified acts or conspire to commit these acts. Scheidler and his colleagues admitted that they had broken the law—though only laws against trespassing and related minor offenses, which don't qualify under RICO—and that they did so in concert with others with the express intent of shutting down abortion clinics. NOW claimed that by depriving or attempting to deprive clinics of their right to do business, Scheidler et al. were engaged in extortion, one of the criminal acts specified by RICO.

The Court stated, "But even when their acts of interference and disruption achieved their ultimate goal of 'shutting down' a clinic that performed abortions, such acts did not constitute extortion because petitioners did not 'obtain' respondents' property. [They] may have deprived or sought to deprive respondents of their alleged property right of exclusive control of their business assets, but they did not acquire any such property. Petitioners neither pursued nor received 'something of value from' respondents that they could exercise, transfer or sell."

The Court concluded that Scheidler's tactics more nearly constituted *coercion*, a lesser crime not covered by RICO. "If the distinction between extortion and coercion, which we find controls these cases, is to be abandoned, such a significant expansion of the law's coverage must come from Congress, and not from the courts."

The implications of the case, of course, go beyond semantic distinctions. Although Scheidler was barred from raising a First Amendment defense and NOW tried to narrow the case to anti-abortion activism alone, Scheidler's legal team succeeded in portraying pro-life protestors as being in the mainstream of civil disobedience. During oral arguments, some justices raised the First Amendment themselves, wondering aloud whether the right to free expression would not be violated by a wide application of RICO. "When we heard these statements in defense of our position, we were thinking that maybe we could win this thing," Scheidler recalls.

Justices Ruth Bader Ginsburg and Steven Breyer joined the majority with their own concurring opinion. They noted the chilling effect that NOW's application of RICO could have on all social protest, while at the same time keeping their pro-abortion credentials in order. "In the Freedom of Access to Clinic Entrances Act of 1994 . . . Congress crafted a statutory response that homes in on the problem of criminal activity at health care facilities. . . . Thus the principal effect of a decision against petitioners here would have been on other cases pursued under RICO." In other words, since we can get pro-lifers on FACE, why risk weakening PETA?

NOW attacked this position in its rants after the decision. "We will work to ensure that the [FACE act] is enforced. But that is not enough," read a press release. "FACE is too limited and doesn't reach the organizers of the violence . . . We are looking at every avenue available to us to protect women, doctors and clinic staff from these ideological terrorists."

Mood Swing

In 1994 the Supreme Court allowed the proceedings against Scheidler to continue by ruling 9-0 that he did not need to have an economic motive to be accused under RICO. Why did the Court now rule 8-1 in his favor? The technical explanation is that a slightly different legal point was under consideration; the larger implication is that the mood of the Court and the nation has shifted slightly toward life. "America, I believe, is on the brink of a new appreciation for the value of human life, especially unborn human life," Scheidler said. "We are on the cutting edge of a subtle but very clear shift in our attitudes."

Characteristically, Scheidler's victory celebration in June was not only for pro-life advocates but for all Americans. Joe is a patriot who loves his country and the freedoms proclaimed and protected by the Constitution. There were U.S. flags as well as prayers at his rally to "Bring America Back to Life."

Alongside Scheidler's populism, NOW and its sister organizations come off as angry and anti-American. The National Abortion and Reproductive Rights League showed a certain Brave New World arrogance in changing its name to NARAL Pro-Choice America. With polls showing increasing numbers of citizens opposing abortion on demand, and more young people coming out against killing unborn babies at any stage, NARAL thinks that by proclaiming America to be "pro-choice" it can make it so.

Yet the liberal tower of "choice" constructed in the Seventies is beginning to totter, as the support base ages and thins. Try as they may to refashion themselves according to the findings of Madison Avenue focus groups, the fact is that the pro-abortion forces are increasingly outsiders whose language and tactics do not resonate with most Americans. A NOW leader's argument against bringing double murder charges to include Laci Peterson's unborn baby is a perfect example of how NOW-style rhetoric has confounded common sense and left pro-abortion forces talking mostly among themselves.

It is far too soon to sound the death knell of the abortion mindset. Yet it may be time to define a new category of American malcontent that has yet to be recognized by the mainstream media. To go with the angry white male, we now have the angry white female. The poster girl, hands down, would be Fay Clayton, NOW's lead lawyer. She demonstrated her graciousness on "The O'Reilly Factor" after the decision. She attacked Scheidler and repeatedly cut off Bill O'Reilly, saying in a dozen different ways that the decision was really not a defeat, that NOW is really not finished, and that FACE gives abortion forces all the power they need to keep anti-choicers at bay. Huff and puff as she may, the Supreme Court decision speaks for itself. The name of the case itself symbolically marks a change in momentum. Though usually called by its original name, *NOW* v. *Scheidler*, the case heard by the Supreme Court was in fact the appellate version, *Scheidler* v. *NOW*. The tables have been turned on the pro-abortion movement. They've gone from bringing suit to defending.

Generating Life

The future looks bright. Against *Roe* and its progeny come Scheidler and his: seven children and (so far) 10 grandchildren. Two of his children, Eric, 36, and Annie, 26, work full-time for the Pro-Life Action League. And they are NOW's worst nightmare: educated, energetic, erudite and fully as determined as their dad. Eric, whose wife recently delivered their sixth child, handles communications and the web. Annie heads Generations for Life, which educates and mobilizes young people on abortion and a range of other issues, including chastity.

"Such a complete victory in answer to so many prayers is a tremendous encouragement to our peaceful pro-life activism," Eric Scheidler writes. "NOW's long effort to thwart our pro-life work has never stopped us from saving babies and helping women, but now we are prepared to redouble those efforts."

Partial-Birth Abortion on Trial

Cathy Cleaver Ruse

In the spring of 2004, tens of thousands of people came to Washington, D.C., for a so-called "March for Women's Lives." Organizers explained that their purpose was to protest the new threats to "choice," chief among them, the ban on partial-birth abortion.

Hollywood celebrities like Whoopi Goldberg were on the roster, as were a long list of "Honorary Congressional Co-Sponsors" such as Barney Frank and Barbara Boxer. Senator John Kerry aired a special campaign commercial that week promising to defend "the right to choose" and even hosted a "pro-choice" rally before the march.

As the preparations to defend "choice" reached a crescendo in Washington, court reporters in federal courtrooms across the country were quietly recording testimony about what that bloodless word really entails.

The Partial-Birth-Abortion Ban

In November 2003, President George W. Bush signed the Partial-Birth Abortion Ban Act, which outlaws partial-birth abortion except where "necessary to save the life of a mother."[1] This law defines partial-birth abortion as "an abortion in which the person performing the abortion—(A) deliberately and intentionally vaginally delivers a living fetus until, in the case of a head-first presentation, the entire fetal head is outside the body of the mother, or, in the case of breech presentation, any part of the fetal trunk past the navel is outside the body of the mother, for the purpose of performing an overt act that the person knows will kill the partially delivered living fetus; and (B) performs the overt act, other than completion of delivery, that kills the partially delivered living fetus." Violation of the law subjects an abortion doctor to fines and possible imprisonment up to two years, or both.

This is a most modest limitation on the otherwise unlimited right to abortion. But no prosecutions have been launched under it, because—immediately upon its enactment into law—the giants of the abortion lobby filed suit. This article will focus on the trials that ensued.

Never in the years since *Roe* v. *Wade* has such extensive evidence about the practice of abortion been placed in a public record—and it has been placed there by abortion doctors themselves.

Cathy Cleaver Ruse, Esq., the former chief spokesperson on human life issues for the U.S. Conference of Catholic Bishops, speaks and writes frequently on family and life issues.

When partial-birth abortion was first discussed in public, many people refused to believe it existed. Some in the "pro-choice" movement even accused the pro-life movement of fabricating it. Yet it was no fabrication: Dr. Martin Haskell discussed the procedure in detail at a 1992 conference of abortion providers in Dallas, Texas, titled, "Second Trimester Abortion: From Every Angle."[2] His paper stated that he "routinely performs this procedure on all patients 20 through 24 weeks LMP"[3] and uses the procedure through 26 weeks "on selected patients."[4]

As Dr. Haskell's description of the procedure became more widely known, and the existence of partial-birth abortion could no longer be denied credibly, proponents of the method made new claims. They claimed it was extremely rare, or used only in emergencies, or that the baby is already dead when it is performed. But these claims, too, collapsed in the face of investigative reports by the *American Medical News,*[5] the *Record* (Bergen, NJ),[6] and others.[7] In fact, in 1997 the Executive Director of the National Coalition of Abortion Providers admitted publicly that the method was actually common, not rare, and that the vast majority of these abortions are done on a healthy mother with a healthy fetus that is 20 weeks or more along.[8]

Despite these admissions and revelations, abortion activists continued their public-relations campaign to cast partial-birth abortion as a rare, emergency procedure, and a necessary part of the virtue of "choice"—a virtue to be protected against politicians who would intrude between a woman and her doctor (and, where politically expedient, "her god").

When the Partial-Birth Abortion Ban Act was signed into law, Planned Parenthood, the National Abortion Federation, and a number of abortion doctors aided by the American Civil Liberties Union challenged its constitutionality in federal lawsuits filed in New York, Nebraska, and California. Each suit, naming U.S. Attorney General John Ashcroft as the defendant, claimed the ban violated the fundamental constitutional right to abortion and sought a permanent injunction against its enforcement. Temporary injunctions were granted and, pursuant to a negotiated expedited trial schedule, all trials commenced in March 2004. At the conclusion of the trials, each district court ruled against the Partial-Birth Abortion Ban Act. At the time of publication, each ruling is under appeal by the Department of Justice.

While much can be said about the legal claims at issue in the trials, the purpose of this article is to provide the abortion doctors' testimony—in effect, to let the testimony speak for itself. Each trial presented similar claims and similar testimony amounting to many thousands of pages of transcripts.[9] This article will focus on the trial in the Southern District of New York brought by the National Abortion Federation and several abortion doctors.[10]

The New York trial was presided over by Judge Richard Conway Casey. Judge Casey, appointed to the federal bench by President Clinton, was not a judge from the pro-abortion-activist mold. He pressed the abortion doctors on the stand to use plain language when discussing their acts, he probed them about fetal pain, and he refused to let the plaintiffs' lawyers dictate the terms of trial. Because of Judge Casey, the New York trial testimony is the richest and most extensive of the three.

The plaintiffs' witnesses have long careers in abortion, and their association with seemingly reputable medical schools and hospitals came as a surprise to the author. Their testimony was brutal.[11] Much of the testimony includes technical medical terms or, in some cases, what seem to be hyper-technical descriptions of otherwise common acts, such as "disarticulate the calvarium" rather than "cut off the head."

Some terms bear explaining. When referring to partial-birth abortion, plaintiffs' witnesses use the terms Dilation and Extraction (D&X), Intact Dilation and Extraction (Intact D&X), or Intact Dilation and Evacuation (Intact D&E). Each of these terms refers generally to the delivery of a substantial portion of the unborn child before the child is killed. This is in contrast to the dismemberment method known as Dilation and Evacuation (D&E) where the child is dismembered inside the womb and taken out piece by piece.

For the abortion industry and their activist allies, an ultimate win in these legal challenges might prove to be a Pyrrhic victory. While the cases involve legal claims about statutory defects and the like, the admissions made in pursuit of these claims, and their astonishingly graphic nature, put partial-birth abortion—and even the abortion industry itself—on trial.

One claim against the law was that its definition of partial-birth abortion was too broad and therefore encompassed more than one particular procedure. In order to show that many procedures fall within each element of the definition of partial-birth abortion—including "performing an overt act that the person knows will kill [the baby]"—plaintiffs presented abortion doctors who described the various purposeful steps they take that they know will kill a baby.

Another claim by the plaintiffs was that the issue of fetal pain is irrelevant. In order to diminish the powerful expert testimony that partial-birth abortion causes "prolonged and excruciating pain" to the unborn child, plaintiffs used their cross-examination to make the point that other methods of abortion at this stage would be quite painful too, and perhaps even more so.

Plaintiffs' central claim at trial was that banning partial-birth abortion except in life-threatening circumstances would limit doctors' ability to use the safest and most beneficial method of second-trimester abortion. While plaintiffs'

231

experts acknowledged that the dismemberment method is used in 95 percent of second-trimester abortions,[12] they nevertheless claimed that partial-birth abortion is actually safer than dismemberment abortion. There was, therefore, substantial testimony about the comparative health risks and benefits of partial-birth abortion and dismemberment abortion. For example, plaintiffs' experts testified that uterine perforation is one of the most dangerous abortion complications, and that the dismemberment method requires more forceps passes into the uterus and therefore presents a greater chance of uterine perforation than partial-birth abortion.[13] They also testified that the dismemberment method exposes the cervix to fetal bone and skull fragments, and that this, too, presents a greater risk of uterine perforation and infection than partial-birth abortion.[14] Plaintiffs' experts testified that the retention of fetal parts in the uterus is a complication more likely in dismemberment abortions, and that such retention threatens infection, hemorrhage, and infertility.[15] They testified that dismemberment abortions require a longer time to perform than partial-birth abortions and thus increase the risks associated with exposure to anesthesia, infection, and bleeding.[16] Plaintiffs' experts also claimed that partial-birth abortion may be safer for women with certain medical conditions such as bleeding disorders and compromised immune-system conditions.[17]

The Government, however, was not able to test any of these claims made by plaintiffs' experts against the hard evidence of their medical records, as is customary in federal cases involving medical claims, because each time medical records were subpoenaed they were refused. Plaintiffs' witnesses testified that their records were under the control of the hospitals where they worked, and the hospitals refused to produce the records based upon a wholly fabricated federal "abortion records" privilege. The hospitals even filed suit in federal court to avoid having to comply with the subpoenas. Ultimately a federal appellate court ruled that the right to "privacy" protected the hospitals from having to produce the abortion records, despite the fact that patient names and other identifying information would have been redacted.

Government experts nevertheless disputed each of the plaintiffs' claims about the medical benefits of partial-birth abortion. Some of the claims were disputed on the grounds that the claimed benefit was purely hypothetical or theoretical; others, on the basis that partial-birth abortion would actually present a greater risk of harm.[18] Regarding maternal medical conditions, Dr. Steven Clark, a professor of obstetrics and gynecology at the University of Utah School of Medicine and director of obstetric education and research at the LDS Hospital in Salt Lake City,[19] testified that "there simply . . . remains no . . . maternal medical condition for which D&X would be necessary to preserve the life or health of the mother. There are always equally if not more safe alternatives that do not involve D&X."[20]

The importance of the testimony as a whole cannot be overstated, for it is nothing less than a collection of admissions by the abortion industry, under oath, about the reality of abortion.

Performing a Partial-Birth Abortion

Each of the plaintiffs' witnesses was well-versed in the grisly art of abortion. Dr. Timothy Johnson, a plaintiff in the case, is chair of the department of obstetrics and gynecology at the University of Michigan Medical School. He has performed second-trimester dismemberment abortions and observed partial-birth abortions, and was offered as an expert witness for the plaintiffs.[21]

Dr. Johnson testified from his own experience about performing dismemberment abortions, and gave his opinion about the partial-birth abortions he had observed. Dr. Johnson described observing how doctors who did partial-birth abortions "used a crushing instrument to deliver the head."[22] This provoked further questions from Judge Casey:

THE COURT: Can you explain to me what that means?

THE WITNESS: What they did was they delivered the fetus intact until the head was still trapped behind the cervix, and then they reached up and crushed the head in order to deliver it through the cervix.

THE COURT: What did they utilize to crush the head?

THE WITNESS: An instrument, a large pair of forceps that have a round, serrated edge at the end of it, so that they were able to bring them together and crush the head between the ends of the instrument.

THE COURT: Like the cracker they use to crack a lobster shell, serrated edge?

THE WITNESS: No.

THE COURT: Describe it for me.

THE WITNESS: It would be like the end of tongs that are combined that you use to pick up salad. So they would be articulated in the center and you could move one end, and there would be a branch at the center. The instruments are thick enough and heavy enough that you can actually grasp and crush with those instruments as if you were picking up salad or picking up anything with—

THE COURT: Except here you are crushing the head of a baby.

THE WITNESS: Correct.[23]

Another of plaintiffs' expert witnesses was Dr. Marilynn Fredriksen, an associate professor in clinical obstetrics and gynecology at Northwestern University Medical School. In establishing her expertise on the issue of abortion, plaintiffs' attorney asked her how many dismemberment abortions she has done in her career. She answered, "I really don't know, but probably thousands." "Thousands, plural?" Judge Casey queried. "Thousands, plural," she answered.[24] Dr. Fredriksen has also done partial-birth abortions, and in her testimony about performing a partial-birth abortion she described how she does not always need to pierce the baby's skull before completing delivery; sometimes "grasping forceps" will do the trick. Judge Casey inquired further:

> THE COURT: Excuse me. Grasping forceps, does that mean you crush the skull?
> THE WITNESS: You compress the skull, yes.
> THE COURT: You crush it, right?
> THE WITNESS: Yes.
> THE COURT: Yesterday you mentioned sometimes you use your finger, right, rather than using scissors?
> THE WITNESS: No, that is not my testimony.
> THE COURT: That's not what you said?
> THE WITNESS: No, that is not. I said the scissors would be important to make an incision at the base of the skull, but I don't use suction. I use my finger to disrupt the contents of the cranial cavity, to thereby collapse the skull and allow delivery of the fetus.
> THE COURT: So you use your finger to get the contents of the skull out rather than sucking the contents of the skull out, is that correct?
> THE WITNESS: Yes.[25]

Dr. Cassing Hammond, another plaintiff in the case who has performed "thousands" of abortions,[26] is an assistant professor in obstetrics and gynecology at the Northwestern University School of Medicine. According to his own testimony, Dr. Hammond *does* use his finger—or scissors, or anything else on his table that will get the job done—to puncture the baby's head:

> Q. Dr. Hammond, do you always use scissors or other instruments to breech the fetal head or the fetal neck in the course of doing an intact D&E of this kind?
> A. Not always. It depends on the fetus. If you've got a fetus that is earlier in gestation, the skull, or calvarium, it is soft. It isn't as firmly formed. So in those cases you can often do this just with your finger, you do this digitally. In some cases the scissors probably after 20 weeks I am more likely to use them. We actually have a number of instruments on the table that I can use, whatever seems like it is going to be most effective.[27]

Dr. Stephen Chasen, another plaintiff, is associate professor of obstetrics and gynecology at the Weill Medical College of Cornell University. He has done 500 abortions in his career, including 200 dismemberment and 75 partial-birth abortions.[28] In his expert testimony he described the way he finds the place on the baby's head to puncture: "I place a clamp on the front part of the cervix and, applying mild traction to this, it exposes the skin at the back of the fetal neck at the site through which I place the scissors. So I can in almost all cases actually visualize the spot through which I place the scissors.[29]

On cross-examination, counsel for the Government walked him through the steps he takes in a partial-birth abortion:

Q. You wrap a small sterile towel around the fetus, because it is slippery, and after the legs are out you pull on the sacrum, or the lower portion of the spine, to continue to remove the fetus, right?

A. Right.

Q. When the fetus is out to the level of the breech, you place another, larger towel around the first small towel, right?

A. Right.

Q. You gently pull downward on the sacrum until the shoulder blades appear, right?

A. Right.

Q. Then, with your hand on the fetus's back, holding it with the towel, you twist in a clockwise or counterclockwise motion to rotate the shoulder, right?

A. Right.

Q. The shoulder in front or the arm in front is swept out with your fingers, and then you rotate the other side of the fetus to sweep out the other arm, right?

A. Right.

Q. Then the fetus is at a point where only the head remains in the cervix, correct?

A. That's correct.

Q. That is when you make the decision based on the gestational age and the amount of cervical dilation, whether the head will fit out intact, whether you can tuck the head of the fetus to its chest, or whether you have to decompress the skull to remove the fetus's head, right?

A. It is based on the size of the fetal head and the cervical dilation. I don't directly consider the gestational age.

Q. If you are able to deliver the head by flexing the chin against the fetal chest— and you have been able to do this several times . . . Doctor?

A. There have been a few occasions, yes.

Q. Then you remove the fetus with the towel, you put it on the table, and you turn back to the woman to deal with the placenta, right?

A. That's right.

Q. If you can't do that, you know you are going to have to crush the head, and so you take a clamp and you grasp the cervix to elevate it, and then your assistant there in the operating room will pull down on the fetus's legs or back, gently lowering the fetus's head toward the opening of the vagina, right?

A. Right.

Q. That is when you put two fingers at the back of the fetus's neck at the base of the skull where you can feel the base of the skull, and then you puncture the skull with the scissors, right?

A. I usually can see it as well as feel it. But yes.

Q. At that point you see some brain tissue come out, and you are 100 percent certain that you are in the brain, so you open the scissors to expand the hole, remove the scissors, and put the suction device in the skull, right?

A. Correct.

Q. You turn on the suction, and typically the fetus comes right out with the suction device still in its skull, right?

A. Right.[30]

Dr. Gerson Weiss, a plaintiff and expert witness at trial, is chair of the department of obstetrics and gynecology and women's health at the UMDNJ-New Jersey Medical School. He claims to have done approximately 1,500 to 2,000 abortions, including 300 to 500 dismemberment and partial-birth abortions.[31] Dr. Weiss testified that, not only is the baby's neck visible in a partial-birth abortion, but also a portion of the baby's head: "Visualize in your mind this. The cervix has to be dilated enough to allow the entire trunk of the fetus to pass through it. The neck of the fetus is much smaller than the shoulders and the trunk but a larger thing, the shoulders and the trunk have passed through. So, not only is the neck through but a portion of the skull which is vividly, you know, exactly where it is and you see it, it's above the neck."[32]

Judge Casey questioned Dr. Weiss about finding the place on the baby's head to puncture:

THE COURT: You do it by feel, don't you?

THE WITNESS: You always feel it. It's right there where your finger is.

THE COURT: If you feel it you can't see it.

THE WITNESS: Usually you see it. So, when it's right there you can usually, under direct vision, insert a sharp instrument into the skull or, at worst, by feel, not blindly, because you know exactly where it is and you feel it with your finger.[33]

The fact that the baby is alive during the partial-birth procedure—a fact formerly contested by abortion activists—was confirmed by a number of plaintiffs' witnesses.

Dr. Carolyn Westoff, a plaintiff and expert in the case, is a professor of epidemiology and population and family health in the School of Public Health at Columbia University. She has performed hundreds of abortions including dismemberment and partial-birth abortions, fifty of which she performed or supervised in 2003.[34] Dr. Westoff testified that there is "usually a heartbeat" when she commences delivery in a partial-birth abortion, and that when she collapses the skull, the fetus is living.[35]

The fact that the baby is still living at this point in the abortion was also confirmed vividly here by Dr. Johnson in a series of questions from Judge Casey:

THE COURT: An affidavit I saw earlier said sometimes, I take it, the fetus is alive when they crush the skull?

THE WITNESS: That's correct, yes, sir.

THE COURT: In one affidavit I saw attached earlier in this proceeding, were the fingers of the baby opening and closing?

THE WITNESS: It would depend where the hands were and whether or not you could see them.

THE COURT: Were they in some instances?

THE WITNESS: Not that I remember. I don't think I have ever looked at the hands.

THE COURT: Were the feet moving?

THE WITNESS: Feet could be moving, yes.[36]

What Do Abortion Doctors Tell Their Patients?

Judge Casey displayed a keen interest in learning whether, and to what extent, abortion doctors inform their patients about the details of the abortion procedures they will perform. The following is an exchange between Judge Casey and Dr. Johnson:

THE COURT: When you describe the possibilities available to a woman do you describe in detail what the intact D&E or the partial birth abortion involves?

THE WITNESS: Since I don't do that procedure I wouldn't have described it.

THE COURT: Did you ever participate with another doctor describing it to a woman considering such an abortion?

THE WITNESS: Yes. And the description would be, I would think, descriptive of what was going to be, what was going to happen; the description.

THE COURT: Including sucking the brain out of the skull?

THE WITNESS: I don't think we would use those terms. I think we would probably use a term like decompression of the skull or reducing the contents of the skull.

THE COURT: Make it nice and palatable so that they wouldn't understand what it's all about?

THE WITNESS: No. I think we want them to understand what it's all about but it's—I think it's—I guess I would say that whenever we describe medical procedures we try to do it in a way that's not offensive or gruesome or overly graphic for patients.

THE COURT: Can they fully comprehend unless you do? Not all of these mothers are Rhodes scholars or highly educated, are they?

THE WITNESS: No, that's true. But I'm also not exactly sure what using terminology like sucking the brains out would—

THE COURT: That's what happens, doesn't it?

THE WITNESS: Well, in some situations that might happen. There are different ways that an after-coming head could be dealt with but that is one way of describing it.

THE COURT: Isn't that what actually happens? You do use a suction device, right?

THE WITNESS: Well, there are physicians who do that procedure who use a suction device to evacuate the intracranial contents; yes.[37]

Judge Casey pursued this line of questioning with Dr. Westhoff as well:

THE COURT: I want to know whether that woman knows that you are going to take a pair of scissors and insert them into the base of the skull of her baby, or her fetus. Do you tell her?

THE WITNESS: I do not usually tell patients specific details of the operative approach. I'm completely—

THE COURT: Do you tell her that you are going to then, ultimately, suck the brain out of the skull?

THE WITNESS: In all of our D&Es the head is collapsed or crushed and the brains are definitely out of the skull but those are—

THE COURT: Do you tell them that?

THE WITNESS: Those are details that would be distressing to my patients and would not—information about that is not directly relevant to their safety.

THE COURT: Don't—whether it's relative to their safety or not—don't you think it's since they're giving authorization to you to do this act that they should know precisely what you're going to do?

THE WITNESS: That's actually not the practice I have of discussing surgical cases with patients.

THE COURT: I didn't ask you that. I said don't you think they ought to know?

THE WITNESS: No, sir, I don't.[38]

Judge Casey questioned Dr. Chasen about the information he gives his patients before a dismemberment abortion:

THE COURT: Do you tell them straight out what you are doing? No sugar coating, just you tear it off and remove it in pieces?

THE WITNESS: There is nothing I can do to make this procedure palatable for the patients. There is no sugar coating.

THE COURT: I didn't ask you that, Doctor. I know it is not pleasant. I want to know whether or not these people know, have a fully-educated discussion with you what you are going to do.

THE WITNESS: We have a full and complete discussion about the fact that in most cases the fetus will not pass intact through the cervix and in many cases—

THE COURT: No, let's go back. I asked you a simple question. Do you tell them you are going to tear limbs off?

THE WITNESS: I don't have simple discussions with my patients. I have involved discussions. I can share with you what I tell my patients.

THE COURT: Go ahead. I am asking you, do you tell them you tear it off?

THE WITNESS: I initiate the discussion in general terms, and they always include the possibility that destructive procedures will be done to facilitate removal of the fetus.

THE COURT: Do you do it in nice sugar-coated words like that?

THE WITNESS: My patients are under no illusions and they don't regard that as sugar-coating and they are usually devastated—

THE COURT: How do you know, Doctor, do you see into their minds?

THE WITNESS: These are patients most of whom I have cultivated a relationship [with], and I can tell.[39]

The Issue of Fetal Pain

The only pain expert at trial was Government witness Dr. Kanwaljeet Anand.[40] Dr. Anand testified that "[f]etuses that are beyond 20 weeks of gestation can feel pain." He explained that, by this age a baby can respond to sound, light, and taste, indicating that the central nervous system is functioning and that the baby is conscious; all of the skin surfaces and mucus membranes have sensory receptors; and all of the anatomical structures needed to perceive and process pain are present and functional.[41] He testified that evidence demonstrates that "between 20 and 30 weeks of gestation there is the greatest sensitivity to pain."[42]

Dr. Anand explained why the partial-birth abortion procedure will cause "prolonged and excruciating pain to the fetus" beyond 20 weeks of gestation: "Given the increased sensitivity to pain at that period of gestation, the parts of the procedure associated with grasping the lower extremity of the fetus, of manipulation and rotating the fetus within the confines of the uterus, of delivering the fetus through an incompletely dilated cervix as well as the surgical incision made at the back of the head, the puncturing of the intracranial cavity through . . . the membranes that covered the brain, all of those parts of the procedure would be associated with prolonged and excruciating pain to the fetus."[43]

Moreover, anesthesia administered intravenously to a pregnant woman would not have an impact on the baby "because the concentrations that are generated in the fetal blood would not be effective."[44] In fact, to ensure that there was a state of fetal anesthesia, Dr. Anand testified, "we would need to give anywhere from five to 50 times the dose of regular anesthetic that is used for the mother,"[45] which would produce "a very high likelihood of toxic side effects in the mother."[46]

Plaintiffs offered no expert witness to counter this testimony. Rather, in order to diminish the powerful evidence that partial-birth abortion causes "prolonged and excruciating pain," plaintiffs used their cross-examination of Dr. Anand to make the point that *other* methods of abortion at this stage would be quite painful, too. For example, plaintiffs' counsel asked Dr. Anand to compare the pain inflicted by a partial-birth abortion to the pain inflicted by a dismemberment abortion:

Q. Are you familiar with the dismemberment D&E?

A. I am familiar with it to the extent that I have read about the procedure. I have not performed any of those procedures.

Q. In a dismemberment D&E, it is your opinion, isn't it, that at 20 weeks of gestation a fetus undergoing that procedure would experience severe pain?

A. That is correct.

Q. Isn't it true, Doctor, that assuming the same gestational age, a D&E procedure involving dismemberment would be more painful to a fetus than a D&X procedure?

A. That is possible, yes.[47]

When plaintiffs' counsel inquired about pain caused by an induction abortion procedure, Dr. Anand testified that "as a result of the induction procedure there would be pain associated to the fetus."[48] Finally, when plaintiffs' counsel pursued the possibility of pain caused by injecting a needle into the baby's heart, Dr. Anand testified that the baby would feel pain "from the point of entry of the needle into the fetal body to the point when fetal demise occurs as a result of cardiac arrest."[49]

Questions to plaintiffs' abortion experts about fetal pain produced some of the most fascinating testimony in the trial. In questions to Dr. Hammond about what he tells his patients, Judge Casey pursued the issue of fetal pain:

THE COURT: Do you tell them whether or not it hurts the baby?

THE WITNESS: We have that conversation quite a bit with patients, your Honor.

THE COURT: And what's your answer?

THE WITNESS: We say several things to the patient, your Honor. First of all, we tell the patient that it's controversial what exactly—what the fetus experiences of pain at various gestational ages. We share with them the fact that even for normally developed fetuses people debate the beginning of sensation of the fetus. They debate at what gestational age the fetus is able to interpret pain as we think about it. We share with the patients that even though there are speculations about these things among normal fetuses, when you start dealing with the kind of circumstances that we confront where a baby may not have its forebrain or may not have its brain . . . which is in essence a completely disrupted and in some cases spinal cord, that there is no data that lead us to know what the baby feels.

THE COURT: How about when there is no anomaly instead of all these exceptions, how about when there is no anomaly?

THE WITNESS: We say that there is a possibility and one of the things that we are doing with most of these patients after 16 to 18 weeks is they're all under IV anesthesia . . . which may confer some pain control to the fetus. We also share with them their alternatives and we share with them the fact that we really don't know what the fetus feels and some of the other things that they can do for pain. For example, frankly, your Honor, I think we sugar coat some of the other options and we share this with patients . . . But the honest truth is, how do we know that taking this huge instrument and poking it into the baby's heart and injecting a poison hurts any less than my rapidly cutting the umbilical cord or transecting the spinal cord with my scissors? Or how do we know that poisoning the environment that the baby is in with digoxin is any more painful or less painful than my doing a very rapid D&E . . . So what we are really asking the patients that I see is, which do you think is going to hurt worse for your fetus?[50]

Judge Casey pursued the issue of fetal pain with Dr. Westhoff as well:

THE COURT: Do any of [the patients] ask you whether or not the fetus experiences pain when that limb is torn off [referring to a dismemberment abortion]?

THE WITNESS: I do have patients who ask about fetal pain during the procedure, yes.

THE COURT: And what do you tell them?

THE WITNESS: I, first of all, assess their feelings about this, but they of course, even notwithstanding the abortion decision, would generally tell me they would like to avoid the fetus feeling pain. I explain to them that in conjunction with our anesthesiologists that the medication that we give to our patients during the procedure will cross the placenta so the fetus will have some of the same medications that the mother has.

THE COURT: Some.

THE WITNESS: Yes, that's right.

THE COURT: What do you tell them, does the fetus feel pain or not when they ask?

THE WITNESS: What I tell them is that the subject of the fetal pain and whether a fetus can appreciate pain is a subject of some research and controversy and that I don't know to what extent the fetus can feel pain but that its—

THE COURT: Do you tell them it feels some pain?

THE WITNESS: I do know that when we do, for instance an amniocentesis and put a needle through the abdomen into the amniotic cavity that the fetus withdraws so I certainly know based on my experience that the fetus [will] withdraw in response [to] a painful stimulus.[51]

Judge Casey also discussed the issue of fetal pain with Dr. Johnson:

THE COURT: I heard you talk a lot today about dismemberment D&E procedure, second trimester; does the fetus feel pain?

THE WITNESS: I guess I—

241

THE COURT: There are studies, I'm told, that say they do. Is that correct?

THE WITNESS: I don't know. I don't know of any—I can't answer your question. I don't know of any scientific evidence one way or the other.

THE COURT: Have you heard that there are studies saying so?

THE WITNESS: I'm not aware of any.

THE COURT: You never heard of any?

THE WITNESS: I'm aware of fetal behavioral studies that have looked at fetal responses to noxious stimuli.

THE COURT: Does it ever cross your mind when you are doing a dismemberment?

THE WITNESS: I guess whenever I—

THE COURT: Simple question, Doctor. Does it cross your mind?

THE WITNESS: No.

THE COURT: Never crossed your mind.

THE WITNESS: No.[52]

Judge Casey also questioned Dr. Frederiksen about partial-birth abortion and fetal pain:

THE COURT: Do you tell them whether or not that hurts the fetus?

THE WITNESS: I have never talked to a fetus about whether or not they experience pain.[53]

THE COURT: I didn't say that, Doctor. Do you tell the mother whether or not it hurts the fetus?

THE WITNESS: In a discussion of pain for the fetus it usually comes up in the context of how the fetus will die. I make an analogy between what we as human beings fear the most—a long protracted painful death.

THE COURT: Doctor, I didn't ask you—

THE WITNESS: Excuse me, that's what I tell my patients.

THE COURT: But I'm asking you the question.

THE WITNESS: I'm sorry.

THE COURT: And I'm asking you whether or not you tell them that.

THE WITNESS: I feel that [the] fetus dies quickly and it's over quickly. And I think from a standpoint of a human being our desire is that we have a quick death rather than a long, protracted death—

THE COURT: That's very interesting, Doctor, but it's not what I asked you. I asked you whether or not you tell them the fetus feels pain.

THE WITNESS: I don't believe the fetus does feel pain at the gestational ages that we do, but I have no evidence to say one way or the other so I can't answer the question.[54]

Judge Casey also questioned Dr. Chasen about partial-birth abortion and fetal pain:

THE COURT: Does it hurt the baby?

THE WITNESS: I don't know.

THE COURT: But you go ahead and do it anyway, is that right?

THE WITNESS: I am taking care of my patients, and in that process, yes, I go ahead and do it.

THE COURT: Does that mean you take care of your patient and the baby be damned, is that the approach you have?

THE WITNESS: These women who are having [abortions] at gestational ages they are legally entitled to it—

THE COURT: I didn't ask you that, Doctor. I asked you if you had any care or concern for the fetus whose head you were crushing.

THE WITNESS: No.[55]

Conclusion

Like the "collective amnesia" that is said to occur when a culture forgets a common experience, abortion requires a kind of collective blindness. *Roe v. Wade* made the Constitution blind to the personhood of children not yet born, and this blindness was exhibited in all its pitiless brutality in the trials on the partial-birth-abortion ban. The testimony was a bracing, if brief, reprieve from the layers of euphemism that cloak the truth about abortion.

For abortion doctors on the witness stand, removing those layers was not always an easy process. Perhaps the best example of this was Dr. Westhoff's tortured explanation for why she does not like the new law against partial-birth abortion: "I mean, I know what my purpose is . . . to empty the uterus in the safest way possible. Yet, this language implies that I have this other purpose, which is to kill the fetus. So, to me, it's like—kind of like there is an elephant in the room besides me and my patient . . . there is somebody judging what my purpose is in bringing the fetus out a certain way."[56]

On this point she was quite right: There is someone else in the room. Seven justices in *Roe v. Wade* closed the eyes of the law to the unborn child upon uttering the infamous words, "We need not resolve the difficult question of when life begins."[57] But in the case of a partially born child, even the Supreme Court cannot continue the charade forever. The law simply cannot say that there is no person there.

Congress and dozens of states, with overwhelming public support, have worked to ban partial-birth abortion precisely because of what happens to that someone else in the room. And no matter the outcome of the current trials on the federal ban, the effort will continue until this inhumane practice is eradicated from American public life.

NOTES

(Full transcripts are available from:http://www.priestsforlife.org/pba/index.htm. The follow-ing transcript legend may be of help in finding testimony. Plaintiffs'experts: Dr. Johnson, day 3; Dr. Hammond, days 3-4; Dr. Westhoff, days 4-6; Dr. Fredriksen, day 7; Dr. Weiss, day 8; Dr. Chasen, day 9. DOJ's experts: Dr. Lockwood, day 10; Dr. Anand, day 11, Dr. Sprang, day 12, Dr. Clark, day 13; Dr. Cook, day 14.)

1. Partial Birth Abortion Ban Act of 2003: 108th Congress, 1st Session, Section 1531.
2. He described the procedure this way: "With a lower [fetal] extremity in the vagina, the surgeon uses his fingers to deliver the opposite lower extremity, then the torso, the shoulders and the upper extremities. The skull lodges at the internal cervical os [the opening to the uterus] . . . At this point, the right-handed surgeon slides the fingers of the left hand along the back of the fetus and "hooks" the shoulders of the fetus with the index and ring fingers (palm down) . . . and takes a pair of blunt curved Metzenbaum scissors in the right hand. He carefully advances the tip, curved down along the spine and under his middle finger until he feels it contact the base of the skull under the tip of his middle finger . . .. [T]he surgeon then forces the scissors into the base of the skull or into the foramen magnum. Having safely entered the skull, he spreads the scissors to enlarge the opening. The surgeon removes the scissors and introduces a suction catheter into this hole and evacuates the skull contents." National Abortion Federa-tion, Second Trimester Abortion: From Every Angle, Fall Risk Management Seminar, September 13/14, 1992, Dallas, Texas; Presentation, Bibliography & Related Materi-als, Martin Haskell, M.D., *Dilation and Extraction for Late Second Trimester Abor-tion,* pages 30-31.
3. "LMP" refers to measuring the length of pregnancy from the mother's last menstrual period, rather than from conception.
4. *Id.* at 28.
5. "Medicine adds to debate on late-term abortion," *American Medical News,* American Medical Association, Vol. 40, No.9 (March 3,1997).
6. "Abortion: Activists Lied," *The Bergen Record,* February 27, 1997.
7. Barbara Vobejda and David Brown, "Discomforting Details of Late-Term Abortions Intensify Dispute," *Washington Post,* September 17, 1996; *Media Matters, PBS* tele-vision series, January 1997. Hosted by Alex Jones and reported by Terry Eastland.
8. "An Abortion Rights Advocate Says He Lied About Procedure," *New York Times,* All (February 26, 1997).
9. The transcripts in their entirety can be found online at http://www.priestsforlife.org/pba/index.htm.
10. Individual plaintiffs were Mark Evans, Carolyn Westoff, Cassing Hammond, Marc Heller, Timothy Johnson, Stephen Chasen, and Gerson Weiss.
11. There was the occasional light moment. When an expert for the plaintiffs said abortion is safer than childbirth, for example, Judge Casey inquired, "safer than childbirth?" "Yes, your Honor," she replied. "Would you recommend abortions rather than child-birth then?" he asked. "If a woman wants to have a baby, she should definitely go the full nine months," she answered.
12. Tr. New York: Day 5, Page 3: 12-13 (Westhoff).
13. See Grunebaum, Hammond, Westhoff, Johnson, and Fredriksen testimony.
14. See Hammond, Johnson, Chasen, and Westhoff testimony.
15. See Grunebaum, Hammond, Fredriksen, Westhoff, and Chasen testimony.
16. See Grunebaum, Hammond, Weiss, and Chasen testimony.
17. See Hammond, Johnson, Weiss, Grunebaum, Chasen, Westhoff testimony.

18. See testimony of Dr. Charles Lockwood, Dr. M. Leroy Sprang, Dr. Curtis R. Cook, and Dr. Steven Leigh Clark.
19. Dr. Clark has authored over 170 peer-reviewed scientific articles, is an editorial consultant for peer-reviewed medical journals, and has been named by his peers to the list of "Best Doctors in America" every year for over a decade.
20. Tr. New York: Day 13,2377: 22-2378-2 (Clark).
21. Tr. New York: Day 3: 388:4-390:19 (Johnson).
22. Tr. 466: 9-15 (Johnson).
23. Tr. 467: 6-15 (Johnson).
24. Tr. New York: Day 6, page 93: 2-10 (Fredriksen).
25. Tr. 1141: 6-9 (Fredriksen).
26. Tr. 517: 5-19 (Hammond).
27. Tr. New York: Day 4, page 32: 1-9 (Hammond).
28. Tr. New York: Day 9, page 60: 13-19 (Chasen).
29. Tr. New York: Day 9, page 102: 20-25.
30. Tr. New York: Day 9, page 182: 5-7 (Chasen).
31. Tr. New York: Day 8: 1312: 18-25; 1314: 25-1315: 3 (Weiss).
32. Tr. 1351: 5-11 (Weiss).
33. Tr. 1351: 21-25 (Weiss).
34. Tr. New York: Day 4, page 170: 16-page 171:2 (Westhoff).
35. Tr. New York: Day 5, page 72: 1 (Westhoff).
36. Tr. 468: 12-25 (Johnson).
37. Tr. 515: 24-516: 1 (Johnson).
38. Tr. New York: Day 5, page 21: 8-10 (Westhoff).
39. Tr. New York: Day 9, page 69: 3-page 70: 9 (Chasen).
40. Dr. Anand, a Rhodes scholar with an Oxford doctorate in the hormonal and metabolic responses of premature infants, is a professor of Pediatrics, Anesthesiology, Pharmacology and Neurobiology at the University of Arkansas for Medical Sciences and Director of the Pain Neurobiology Laboratory at the Arkansas Childrens' Hospital Research Institute.
41. Tr. New York: Day 11, page 35-page 36: 24 (Anand).
42. That is because "the early development of the receptors and the density of these receptors is much greater in the fetal skin as compared to an older child or adult" (Tr. New York: Day 11 page 46: 22-25, page 47:1(Anan)) and because "inhibitory mechanisms or mechanisms that may modulate" are not yet developed (Tr. New York: Day 11 page 105: 1-11 (Anand).Tr. New York: Day 11 page 61: 1-3 (Anand).
43. Tr. New York: Day 11, page 54: 14-23 (Anand).
44. Tr. New York: Day 11, page 60: 13-17 (Anand). The circulation of the mother and the circulation of the baby are separated by the placental membrane, and "drugs that are circulating in the mother's blood have to get across this placental membrane and reach sufficient enough concentrations in the fetus' blood in order to then cross the blood brain barrier and have an impact on brain cells in the fetus." Nor did Dr. Anand assert that general anesthesia administered to the mother would produce an adequate amount of pain control in the baby. Tr. New York: Day 11 page 60: 23-25, page 61: 1-3 (Anand).
45. Tr. New York: Day 11, page 66: 5-12.
46. Id. On cross-examination Dr. Anand stated that general anesthesia in various gaseous forms would equilibrate fairly quickly across the placental barrier and would produce some levels of anesthesia in the fetus.
47. Tr. New York: Day 11, page 100: 3-14 (Anand).
48. Tr. New York: Day 11, page 104: 7-12 (Anand).
49. Tr. New York: Day 11, page 107: 12-17 (Anand).

50. Tr. New York: Day 4, page 87: 5-page 88: 13 (Hammond).

51. Tr. New York: Day 5, page 8: 3-8 (Westhoff).

52. Tr. New York: Day 3, 513: 1-8 (Johnson).

53. Dr. Anand explained in his testimony that the International Association for the Study of Pain's official definition of pain states that the inability to communicate verbally does not negate possibility of experiencing pain.

54. Tr. New York: Day 6, page 121: 4-page 122: 1 (Fredriksen).

55. Tr. New York: Day 9, page 101:14-page 102: 1-2 (Chasen).

56. Tr. California: Day 1 (*Planned Parenthood* v. *Ashcroft*, C03-4872 PJH), page 80: 10-16 (Paul).

57. *Roe* v. *Wade*, 410 U.S. 113 (1973) at 159.

Postscript

On April 18, 2007, the Supreme Court upheld the Partial-Birth Abortion Ban Act by a vote of 5 to 4. Justice Anthony Kennedy wrote the opinion for the majority, in which Chief Justice John Roberts and Justices Scalia, Thomas, and Alito joined. Justice Ginsburg wrote a dissent in which Justices Stevens, Souter, and Breyer joined.

Leroy Carhart and the other abortion doctors and organizations claimed the law on its face was unconstitutionally vague and an undue burden on a woman's right to choose abortion. The Court disagreed, concluding that the law was sufficiently clear about the conduct it prohibited, that the anatomical landmark ("any part of the fetal trunk past the navel is outside the body of the mother") ensured that partial-birth abortion was the only procedure within the law's reach, and that disagreement in the medical community about the procedure's necessity did not make a health exception obligatory.

The question before the Court had been whether the law was unconstitutional on its face, leaving open the possibility that the law could be found to be unconstitutional as applied in a particular case with particular facts. As of this writing, no such challenge has been filed, which tends to support the argument that there are, in fact, no circumstances where this procedure is neccessary.—CCR, August, 2010

Roe Hovers Like a Malign Shadow

Michael M. Uhlmann

Concerning yesterday's decision in *Gonzales* v. *Carhart* [April 18, 2007], a few preliminary observations based on a very quick reading:

The Supreme Court's abortion jurisprudence remains a singular embarrassment. That fact is well known by, and infuriating to, *Roe*'s sophisticated supporters and foes alike. Despite what NARAL, Planned Parenthood, as well as their sisters, their cousins, and their aunts say for public consumption, they are well aware that the right to abortion is not now, and never has been, etched into constitutional stone. It rests, and always has rested, on the flimsiest of legal rationales, and on studied avoidance of the facts of life before birth. No matter how hard it has tried—and God knows, it has tried—the Supreme Court has been unable to escape the inevitable consequences of these failures.

The short history of abortion litigation from 1973 until the present hour is the history of an increasingly embattled pro-choice majority struggling to explain and justify its prior rulings. Yesterday, the majority lost one of its members and slipped into the minority; for how long we cannot tell. But consider this: Thirty-four years after the Court enacted *Roe* (I use the verb intentionally), the justices could do no better than 5-4 in deciding what they had previously decided. And this: The Court's own syllabus of yesterday's decision required six and a half pages of closely printed 10-point type to explain what happened. These are not what one would call measures of a coherent or confident body of law.

Here, a brief *tour d'histoire* may be helpful. The central problem with *Roe* (indeed, with all the cases that have followed in its wake) is that it never addressed what, or more precisely who, is killed during abortion. The Court, per Justice Harry Blackmun's majority opinion, thought it sufficient to describe the unborn child as a "potential" human being, implying that it was something different from (and less valuable than) an actual human being. In neither instance did the opinion offer the slightest factual evidence or philosophical reasoning to explain the difference, nor has any subsequent decision of the Court bothered to do so. The entirety of abortion litigation has proceeded on the premise that the only cognizable set of rights in question belongs to the pregnant woman. There is, of course, the little problem of the pesky fetus; his or her presence must be nominally acknowledged in some sense, to be sure,

Michael M. Uhlmann, a founding editor of the *Human Life Review,* teaches American law and politics at Claremont Graduate University. The following essay was first published on the website of *First Things* (*www.firstthings.com*) and is reprinted with permission.

but no more than is necessary to get on with the essential business at hand—justifying the woman's right to do pretty much as she wishes.

As for the woman's right itself, Blackmun stated—to say "argued" would give him too much credit—that the Constitution protected her decision to abort her unborn child. This right was said to derive from a right of privacy, the putative existence of which had been discovered by the Court only eight years before and was said to reside in "penumbras formed by emanations" from various constitutional provisions. The strength of the woman's right, Blackmun went on to imply, varied inversely with the child's age *in utero*: It was essentially incontestable during the first trimester, somewhat less so during the second, and theoretically extinguishable during the third. He further implied that once the child reached "viability," by which he meant the capacity to survive outside the womb, it became a rights-bearing creature.

Roe's reference to trimesters and viability, however, were deceptive shadow play, for at all stages of fetal gestation, concern for the woman's life or health could trump any claims that might be made on behalf of the child. The Court underscored the latter point in a companion case, *Doe* v. *Bolton*, by ruling that health included mental health and that mental health incorporated a subjective sense of complete well-being.

The 1973 abortion cases accomplished two goals at once, but only the first was intentional—to make abortion on request the constitutional law of the land. The second was an inadvertent by-product of the justices' naïve arrogance, demonstrating that they had little understanding of the subject they had so cavalierly removed from legislative control: The initial opinions, by raising more questions than they answered, guaranteed that the Court would become a permanent council of statutory revision on all matters touching abortion. As the states pressed the Court for answers on what they were or were not permitted to do, the justices wandered deeper and deeper into a legislative morass without benefit of map or compass.

Might a legislature require a married woman to first seek her husband's consent before obtaining an abortion? Require a doctor to preserve the life or health of the fetus after a pregnancy has been terminated? Ban saline abortions? Mandate waiting periods? Compel the creation of detailed medical reports? Require parental notification or consent before minors could undergo abortion? Forbid public funding of abortion? Declare that life begins at conception? Ban the use of public facilities for performing abortions? Require testing to determine extra-uterine viability?

As these and a host of other questions of legislative policy presented themselves in subsequent litigation, it became painfully apparent to all close observers, including the justices themselves, that *Roe* offered precious little guidance. Having misread common law and statutory history, and having cashiered constitutional precedent as irrelevant, the justices had no choice but to fabricate new law more or less *ex nihilo*. Gloss after gloss was layered upon the 1973 rulings until very little remained of *Roe*'s original rationale, other than the ritual invocation of a constitutional right to abortion, whose provenance and justification became harder and harder to explain or sustain. By 1989, Blackmun's argument, including his deceptive trimester schema, resembled nothing so much as a child's blanket that had been washed until it had more holes than fabric. *Roe*'s reasoning, strictly speaking, is not much honored today by anyone—least of all by the justices, who have abandoned essentially everything but its conclusion.

Roe nevertheless survives as symbol, and a very powerful symbol it is. A confused and confusing pro-choice majority on the Court clings to it like a drowning man clutching at a life preserver. Aging feminists rally 'round it as the *sine qua non* of their liberation from antediluvian religious authority and male bondage. Postmodernists of various stripes, who look to the Court as the font of endlessly evolving constitutional aspiration, continue to hail it as the moral equivalent of *Brown* v. *Board of Education*. *Roe* also hovers like a malign shadow, omnipresent even if not always explicitly acknowledged, over increasingly nasty judicial confirmations; and in the larger political realm, the case remains the supreme iconic representation of the differences that divide "red" and "blue" America. No Democrat can hope to be nominated without performing obsequies before *Roe*'s altar, and the current boomlet for Rudy Giuliani notwithstanding, it seems unlikely that a Republican can be nominated who fails to distance himself from the decision's moral and legal implications.

Thirty-four years after *Roe* fecklessly sought to settle the question by removing it from legislative control, abortion agitates the body politic as few other issues, and the justices are more perplexed and divided than when they began. In recent years, a slim pro-choice majority of the Court has sought to salvage what it could from *Roe*'s shards by re-potting the right to abortion in the Due Process Clause of the Fourteenth Amendment. The prevailing test now holds that a regulation of abortion will not survive judicial scrutiny if it imposes an "undue burden" on the pregnant woman's decision.

The new approach, however, has proven no more availing than *Roe*'s original theory, which the Court had regularly invoked to strike down even modest restrictions on abortion. Law professors and their students, who have infinite faith in the power of words to compel results they favor, insist that "undue burden" establishes a reasonable bright-line rule that only fools would contest. In application, however, the rule is but a rhetorical mask that disguises the radical subjectivity of the judgment being rendered. In *Planned Parenthood* v. *Casey* (1992), a sharply splintered majority employed the test for the first time to sustain diverse restrictions on abortion, including an informed consent requirement, a mandatory twenty-four-hour waiting period, a parental consent requirement for minors, as well as various recordkeeping and reporting regulations. In prior cases, however, the Court had decreed similar provisions to be unconstitutional. Did this mean that the justices had now abandoned *Roe* in all but name? Even as the Court upheld the regulations, the plurality opinion in *Casey* went beyond anything Blackmun said in *Roe* by endorsing the right to abortion as but one expression of a high-fallutin' theory of individual autonomy that, it said, lay at the heart of the Constitution. *Casey*, in short, appeared to point in two directions at once.

Casey did one thing more: It muted the talk about privacy and shifted the constitutional ground for abortion into the more comfortable territory (for the majority at least) of the Due Process Clause. This enabled the Court to *assume*, without actually having to argue, the existence of a substantive right to abortion, thus empowering the justices to decide whether a particular abortion regulation was or was not unduly burdensome. Having thus altered its own rationale for abortion, the Court then had the brass to say that it would be unseemly to overrule *Roe*. Sticking with precedent, after all, is the very essence of the rule of law, and for the justices to be seen shifting now this way and now that would undermine faith in the Court as our ultimate guide to constitutional meaning. This is constitutional *chutzpah* of the first order.

If you find all this bewildering and infuriating, you are hardly alone. Whatever else *Casey* sought to accomplish, it demonstrated for all the world to see that the justices themselves were hopelessly adrift. Witness the Court's syllabus of the decision:

O'Connor, Kennedy, and Souter, JJ., announced the judgment of the Court and delivered the opinion of the Court with respect to Parts I, II, III,V-A, and VI, in which Blackmun and Stevens, JJ., joined, an opinion with respect to Part V-E, in which Stevens, J., joined, and an opinion with respect to Parts IV, V-B, and V-D. Stevens, J., filed an opinion concurring in part and dissenting in part. Blackmun, J., filed an opinion concurring in part, concurring in the judgment in part, and dissenting in part. Rehnquist, C.J., filed an opinion concurring in the judgment in part and dissenting in part, in which White, Scalia, and Thomas, JJ. joined. Scalia, J., filed an opinion concurring in the judgment in part and dissenting in part, in which Rehnquist, C.J., and White and Thomas, JJ., joined.

Given this disarray, it was hardly surprising, in the Court's next major outing on the subject, *Stenberg* v. *Carhart* (2000), that Justice Stephen Breyer practically twisted himself into a pretzel to overturn Nebraska's prohibition against a barely disguised form of infanticide. Along the way, however, he lost Justice Anthony Kennedy, who had co-authored the rhapsody to autonomy in *Casey*'s plurality opinion. Kennedy's *Stenberg* dissent was welcome news indeed, but his collective musings on abortion gave us no confidence that he would remain on the side of the angels. All one could tell for sure was that the constitutional case for abortion now rested on little more than increasingly desperate assertions of judicial fiat. The "undue burden" test was only the latest rhetorical cover for what five or more justices on any given day "feel" about abortion and its limits.

Congress replied to *Stenberg* by enacting the Partial Birth Abortion Ban Act of 2003, the statute in issue in yesterday's litigation. Congress paid its respects at the house of *Roe* while refusing to concede that *Roe* protected all forms of late-term abortion. Based on reliable (although not undisputed) medical testimony, it found that partial-birth abortion was never medically necessary, and it took care to describe with precision (which *Stenberg* said the Nebraska law had not) the prohibited procedure. It also refused to include a specific health exception. Various plaintiffs argued that the Act was unconstitutional on its face because it contravened standards set forth in *Roe*, *Casey*, and *Stenberg*. Specifically, they alleged that the Act unduly burdened a woman's right to choose a second-term abortion, that its terms were impossibly vague, and that it lacked a specific maternal health exception.

First the good news. A 5-4 majority, with Kennedy writing, sustained the statute against these facial challenges. Kennedy distinguished *Stenberg* by saying that Congress (unlike the Nebraska legislature) had taken sufficient care to define the prohibited procedure with reasonable specificity. He further noted that the absence of a maternal health exception was not *per se* fatal, because Congress had found that partial-birth abortion was never medically necessary. Accordingly, the Act did not run afoul of *Casey*'s undue burden standard.

Kennedy's opinion is a step in the right direction, albeit a modest one. The decision, along with last year's ruling in *Ayotte* v. *Planned Parenthood* (rejecting a facial challenge to New Hampshire's parental notification statute) will increase the burden on those who wish to strike down even modest restrictions on abortion. The majority (at least for the time being) is not going to roll over every time the spirit of *Roe* or *Casey* is invoked as a reason to strike down abortion regulations. Plaintiffs, who have had rather an easy time of it over the years when launching facial challenges, will have to work harder to overturn statutes they don't like. As a practical matter, that is all one can say for sure about yesterday's ruling.

Proponents of abortion will, of course, scream to the heavens that *Roe* has been effectively eviscerated. Don't believe it for a minute. It is very much alive and well, as is *Casey*. The Court, and the Court alone, remains the final judge of what may or may not constitute an undue burden. All the Court decided yesterday was (a) that there might be a valid legislative role in a very narrow category of late-term abortions; and (b) what constitutes an undue burden will have to await the specific application of the Act's provisions to particular facts.

If you're inclined to be optimistic, you might place some modest hope in the prospect that Kennedy's opinion opens the door ever so slightly to an examination of what fetal viability means. But I wouldn't count on it. Once the Court starts down that road, it will have to examine and discuss the characteristics of unborn children—an undertaking it hitherto studiously avoided, and for good reason. Still, *Carhart* is the first occasion in which a majority has even nodded in the direction that late-term abortions might be legally problematic. *Roe* disingenuously implied as much, only to ensure that the implication was swallowed by the maternal health exception at all stages of fetal gestation.

Now for the not-so-good news. Justice Kennedy made it clear that maternal health remains a viable constitutional standard. Indeed, he all but invited litigation that would present that issue in specific circumstances. What may be slightly less clear today than two days ago is that the maternal health exception may not be an absolute trump. Only time will tell.

Justice Ruth Bader Ginsburg wrote a stinging dissent, which was joined by Justices Stevens, Breyer, and Souter. Kennedy's altogether modest hint that *Roe* may not have mandated abortion on demand under any and all circumstances was treated by Ginsburg as a total rejection of the Court's abortion jurisprudence. This is either rhetorical posturing or a measure of her capacity for legal fantasy.

In the first place, Kennedy's opinion does nothing of the sort. It sustains the main thrust of *Roe* and *Casey* without substantial qualification. Secondly, what does Ginsburg make of the fact that *Casey* upheld a variety of procedural regulations? Her opinion reads *Casey* as if its paean to autonomy was the be-all and end-all of the abortion controversy; that is, she reads it as if its muting of *Roe*'s privacy rationale was mere rhetorical sleight-of-hand. Privacy and due process, it would seem, are for Justice Ginsburg just different labels for the same thing, which is to say, an absolute right to abortion. She seems genuinely puzzled that Kennedy fails to get it. Her position, of course, gives the lie to Blackmun's trimester schema and to the dicta about viability, which for Ginsburg and her allies seem to be so much wink, wink, nod, nod rhetoric that no one ought to take seriously.

The justice's angry opinion will, of course, be cited chapter and verse by the usual suspects. When the next vacancy opens on the Court, you can count on its becoming a centerpiece of the next nasty confirmation hearing, which will surpass all hitherto existing nasty hearings in vituperation. It will do so because the law of abortion, now more than ever, rests on nothing more than arbitrary judicial will. That being the case, it's the number of votes, not constitutional reasoning, that matters. Liberals have known this from the minute *Roe* was handed down. *Carhart* reminds them that the rationale for abortion can no longer be sustained by mere pretense; only a stronger assertion of judicial fiat will do; and that now requires, more than ever, a secure fifth vote. Put on your body armor.

The Victory of the Abstract Over the Real

Harold O.J. Brown

According to the third-century Christian theologian Origen of Alexandria, freedom consists in the ability of the mind to know the good and the ability of the will to choose it. The late French philosopher Paul Ricoeur defined sin as the guilty abuse of freedom. In the modern West, we pride ourselves on our freedom, but freedom is easily abused where true knowledge is lacking. Wrong knowledge leads to wrong choices, nowhere more dangerously than when the choices concern human life. In Milton's *Paradise Lost*, the first humans are offered the chance for forgiveness because they were deceived. Satan, self-deceived, was not. Today we humans are acting like Milton's Satan. Modern man has set new records of self-deception; and his best tool is language.

In *La tête coupée. Le secret du pouvoir* (*The Severed Head*: *The Secret of Power*), the French mathematician Aaron-Arnaud Upinsky explains how our language blinds us to truth. He describes an age-long war between what he calls "strong language" and "true language," between nominalism and realism. True language tells the truth; it describes reality. Strong language manipulates. True language is the language of wisdom and knowledge. It is, or should be, the language of the friends of truth: the scholar, the scientist, the philosopher, the theologian. Strong language is the language of power. Those who abuse it rule; those who accept it obey. Upinsky has moved the nominalist controversy out of the medieval framework and sees it as a far more universal problem. Today it deprives us of freedom by destroying our ability to know the good.[1]

On a radio talk show in Chicago, a caller demanding federal financing of abortion revealed that she herself had had four abortions. When the host asked what she thought abortion was, she replied: "It's kinda like killin' the baby." That's kinda like true language. Can we imagine former President Bill Clinton claiming, "Killing babies should be safe, legal, and rare"? The victory of nominalism over realism, the replacement of true language with strong language, leaves us with *la tête coupée*, unable to think. The mere mention of words such as "judgmental," "racist," and "homophobic," among others, blocks all intelligent discussion of the merits of a case.

There is no better example of manipulation by strong language than the victory of "choice" over "life." Wishing to avoid the negative implication of

---

Harold O.J. Brown (1933-2007) was an ordained Congregationalist pastor and prominent evangelical author. He was also a co-founder of the Christian Action Council (now Care Net).

always being "against," opponents of abortion began to call themselves "pro-life." We should—in the words of a popular song of the World War II era "accentuate the positive, eliminate the negative." All too few anti-abortionists realized that their cause is not the defense of "life" as an abstract principle, but the defense of babies, each one an individual human life.

One anti-abortion billboard asks, "What does an abortion cost? One human life." That is true language. A bumper sticker reads, "Life is a choice. Choose life." That reveals a good intention, but it is a bit misleading. The woman who decides to carry her pregnancy to term is not choosing "life," but a baby, one particular human baby, who will soon make very specific individual demands on her. The difference between being pro-life in general and choosing to give birth to a particular baby is like the difference between approving of love in general and loving one person in particular. Calling themselves "pro-life" entangled the anti-abortionist movement in questions of capital punishment and war. It would have been better to stay "anti-."[2]

After a slight setback in *Webster* (1988), the pro-abortionists began to sense popular opinion moving against them and their enthusiasm for the bloody procedure of abortion. Suddenly they hit on a better word: choice. Abortion is messy, choice is clean. Let's say choice.

"Choice" is a wonderful term. It is something that everyone wants. It stands for freedom. Life is absolute; one either lives or does not. It cannot be lost and regained like choice. Choice is a function, a process. It can be used or left unused. It can be given up and taken back. What is at stake in each abortion is not a general principle but a particular substantial reality. It is not life as a principle but an individual life. Each life is not an abstraction, it is a *personal* reality, one that exists only for one particular unborn human who will no longer be if abortion is chosen.[3]

Choice and Freedom

Choosing to abort empowers the woman doing the choosing, leaving her standing in autonomy and freedom. Choosing to have the baby limits her freedom. According to many in the crisis-pregnancy ministries, the thought of losing freedom seems far more important to many women than concern for the baby to be aborted. They are very conscious of their own individuality and of their rights and see the unborn child, "the fetus," as a threat to their personal autonomy, not as another person. We used to think it sufficient to show the woman that she is carrying a real human being. Sometimes that helps—for example, when she sees the baby in a sonogram—but all too often this individual human reality is less powerful than the thought that that little being, whatever we call it, is depriving her of her autonomy.

As far as she and others are concerned, being "pro-choice" brings with it no necessary obligations, financial or otherwise. Before becoming pregnant, she was a free woman, just like a man. Pregnant, she has become someone else, an expectant mother. If she keeps the baby, she becomes a single parent with all the burdens that that entails. If she gives it up for adoption, she is no longer a mother either. The unwanted pregnancy first made her an expectant mother, which she did not want to be, and threatens to make her a single parent. Giving it up for adoption deprives her of that too, making her twice a loser. Abortion is so much neater. In the current vernacular, it offers closure.

To decide for life brings duties and burdens. The social, physical, emotional, and other problems that caused a woman or girl to want an abortion will usually remain, aggravated by the demanding presence of the baby. Abortion opponents are often accused of being indifferent to her problems after delivery. Supposedly all that they want is to impose their own morality on her. Abortion providers generally think that they have done all that is required when the abortion is done, leaving her to enjoy her regained freedom.

Contrary to "pro-choice" propaganda, for most abortion opponents, concern does not end with the birth of the child. They recognize that helping a troubled woman to give life brings a duty to help her master the problems that come with the birth of a new baby, whether he or she is to be put up for adoption or raised by the mother. A large network of crisis-pregnancy care centers offers help and care before, during, and after birth. Many will even help a woman who has chosen to abort, for instead of providing closure, the abortion choice seldom leaves her unwounded. The group with which I am most familiar, Care-Net/Christian Action Council, has over 700 centers with 10,000 volunteer workers. Given the huge number of abortions performed every year in the United States, this is far from enough, but at least it shows that there is more to opposing abortion than just passing laws against it.

Individualism in the Extreme

In *The Social Contract,* Jean-Jacques Rousseau says that freedom requires the abolition of every particular dependency. This is the freedom that abortion advocates offer. For women with unwanted pregnancies, it affirms their freedom, their autonomous authority as individuals, not their duties as wives and/or family members. Although in principle it respects the woman's rights, sometimes it is not her own choice that she is exercising, but the demand of a husband, a lover, or her family. In this context, the crisis-pregnancy center's ministry often helps a woman really to choose freely, for herself, to resist the pressure of others to abort.

To abort appears to liberate the woman seeking abortion. It also liberates the rest of society from the burdensome duties that might arise with the birth of an unwanted child. Thus it is not only the choice to abort that expresses individualistic autonomy; the choice to support the right to choose abortion also frees supporters from any responsibility for unwanted children. Thinking themselves benevolent towards the woman seeking an abortion, the pro-choicers rid themselves of all subsequent obligations to her or to the child who might have been.

The one who tells the pregnant woman that abortion is wrong, that she has no right to abort, is asking her to assume responsibilities of all kinds, for care, love, food, clothes, and schooling up to and perhaps beyond college. Of course, a child can also bring blessings and benefits, but these are not as easily quantified in advance, especially when a woman is in distress. An aborted child brings no further expenses and burdens, or so it is assumed.

Contrary to popular opinion, no abortion, even one that is medically recommended, leaves the would-have-been mother totally unscarred. To point this out is true language, not strong. It will be condemned as a pretext to interfere with the right to choose.

Ancient Precedents

Abortion, being dangerous to the woman, was infrequent in ancient times. It was punishable by law in the Code of Hammurabi (18th century B.C.) and other ancient law codes and is forbidden in the original Oath of Hippocrates. Rome and some other ancient societies did give the father the right to "expose" a newborn child, i.e., to abandon it in a wilderness, but even in Rome itself abortion was illegal. Today such "exposure" would be seen as infanticide, child murder, yet in the United States and much of the rest of the modern world the pregnant woman has the right to "expose" the unborn child to termination in abortion.

A child, once born, brings immediate and ongoing duties to his or her parents; someone has to take responsibility. The child who is aborted, "safely and legally," as President Clinton liked to say, brings no evident additional costs and duties to its would-have-been mother. Despite any emotional or psychological damage she may have suffered, having exercised her "right to choose" the woman goes on, again free to choose—including, if that be her wish, having conceived again, to abort again. The baby, deprived of its right to live, cannot choose. It is gone; indeed, in the eyes of the pro-abortionist, it never was. There are few among the advocates of choice who are willing to say what the German *Bundesverfassunggericht* (high court) said in its 1975 decision: "The usual language, termination of pregnancy, cannot conceal the fact that abortion is a homicidal act."

Abstraction over Reality

To prefer the right to choose over any right of the unborn child to live is to prefer an abstract principle, choice, above that which is tangible and real, a developing human. The right to abort exalts the right of the existing, mature individual to order a homicidal act, whether we call the victim embryo, fetus, or as the old common law did, *enfant en ventre de sa mère,* infant in its mother's belly. Whether or not one recognizes the being in the womb as a person to be protected by law, whatever one calls it in strong language, in truth it is a unique, individual being: It cannot be subdivided into other entities, and it cannot be restored or duplicated if it is destroyed. As it is not yet capable of demanding individual rights, when pro-lifers speak for it, they appear as a "they," as interfering Others, working against the "I" of the woman choosing abortion.

The Father and the Family

The right to abort exalts the woman against the father and the family, regardless of her civil or social status, i.e., of whether or not she is married or is a minor. Although in nature many pregnancies are spontaneously aborted, deliberately terminating a developing life is clearly *contra naturam.* It negates the reality of paternity and the rights of the father. Abortion law as it now stands gives the woman the absolute right to abort, whether or not the child is conceived within marriage, or she is still a minor under parental authority.

The father has no right to terminate the child before it is born but he has the obligation to support it once born, whether he wanted it or not.[4] The right of the father to have a child and of the family to perpetuate itself through children is subordinated, at least during the period of pregnancy, to the absolute power of the woman. In a strange way, for nine months the abortion community awards the pregnant woman a right no other person or agency ever has enjoyed, the right to deny life to one to whom she is in the process of giving it.

In nature the right to have a child always belongs to more than one person, at least to a couple, implicitly to a larger family. A commonsense understanding of human reproduction requires the cooperation of both sexes for more than the biologically necessary moment of begetting. Unlike the kid of the mountain goat, which can stand up the day it is born, the human child needs years of care and teaching. The new mother needs protection and support. Christian liturgies speak of marriage "as long as ye both shall live"; common sense as well as natural law teaches that those who bring a child into the world should stay together for many years at least. Similarly, because parents, as they grow old, may themselves need support, most human societies have taught that their grown children have a duty to help them. What duty to support aged parents will be felt by a child whose brothers and sisters those parents have aborted?

The right to abort is viewed by some feminists as the cornerstone of woman's dignity, her right to be free from artificial constraints. It implies that freedom praised by Rousseau, "the abolition of all particular dependencies." In a society where the right to abort is dominant, there is no room for fathers, sisters and brothers, aunts, uncles, cousins, grandparents, for family at all. The woman—but not the man—enjoys a temporary autonomy, the right of the individual as such over the family and over society.

This special autonomy undermines the basic building unit of society. The family disintegrates with the disabling of the marriage covenant. The plaintive voices opposing "homosexual marriage" on the ground that having a father and a mother is better for children go unheard when children have no value: Marriage is no longer "an honourable estate, established by God" (as in the old *Book of Common Prayer*) but only an association of fully autonomous, interchangeable individuals.

Total Victory

The license to abort any unwanted child represents the complete victory of strong language—"choice"—over true language, "baby." It represents the victory of the abstraction over reality. This is a victory of symbols and slogans over human beings. To the extent that we value ourselves as humans made in the image of the Creator who endowed us with rights, we must make individualistic autonomy second to the survival of the individual baby and of the family. We must value the true language of actual life above the strong language of abstract choice. Then, perhaps, when we sing "God bless America," we will not need to fear a voice from heaven, "Why should I bother?"

NOTES

1. Nominalism is by no means only a medieval phenomenon. It is represented today by concepts such as logical positivism and postmodernism.
2. The late James McFadden, founding editor of the *Human Life Review*, preferred the true language of "anti-abortion" to the strong variant, "pro-life."
3. Freedom to choose is a positive thing only if at least one of the possible choices is a good. Having to choose between being hanged and being shot is not.
4. Currently the National Center for Men is filing suit, claiming that the obligation of fathers to support a child they did not desire is a violation of the equal-protection clause of the U.S. Constitution. During pregnancy, the woman's right is absolute; the father's right does not exist. [*The lawsuit was dismissed in 2006 by a U.S. District Court in Michigan; that decision was upheld by the U.S. Court of Appeals (6th circuit) in 2007—Ed.*]

My Controversial Choice to Become Pro-life

Nat Hentoff

It took me a long time, when I was much younger, to understand a conversation like the one a nine-year-old boy was having recently at the dinner table with his mother, a physician who performs abortions. I heard the story from her husband when he found out I'm a pro-lifer. "What *is* abortion?" The 9-year-old asked. His mother, the physician, tried to explain the procedure simply. "But that's killing the baby!" the boy exclaimed. She went on to tell him of the different time periods in the fetus's evolution when there were limits on abortion. "What difference," her son asked, "is how many months you can do it? That's *still* killing the baby!"

I didn't see that an actual baby, a human being, was being killed by abortion for years because just about everyone I knew—my wife, members of the family, the reporters I worked with at the *Village Voice* and other places—were pro-choice. But then—covering cases of failed late-term abortions with a live baby bursting into the room to be hidden away until it died—I began to start examining abortion seriously.

I came across medical textbooks for doctors who cared for pregnant women, and one of them—*The Unborn Patient: Prenatal Diagnosis and Treatment* by Drs. Harrison, Golbus and Filly—turned me all the way around: "The concept that the fetus is a patient, an individual (with a DNA distinct from everyone else's), whose maladies are a proper subject for medical treatment . . . is alarmingly modern . . . Only now are we beginning to consider the fetus seriously—medically, legally, and ethically."

I also began to be moved by a nationally known pro-life black preacher who said: "There are those who argue that the [woman's] right to privacy is of a higher order than the right of life. That was the premise of slavery. You could not protest the existence of slaves on the plantation because that was private (property) and therefore outside of your right to be concerned." (His name was Jesse Jackson, but that was before he decided to run for president, and changed his position.)

So, in the 1980s, in my weekly column in the V*illage Voice*, I openly and clearly declared myself to be pro-life. That was—and still is—the most controversial position I've taken. I was already well known around the country as a syndicated columnist (appearing then in the Washington *Post*) reporting on assaults on free speech and civil liberties as well as focusing on education,

Nat Hentoff, a long-time syndicated columnist, has authored many books, including *The War on the Bill of Rights and the Gathering Resistance* (Seven Stories Press, 2004).

police abuse, and human rights violations around the world.

Much of that writing was controversial, but nothing as incendiary as being targeted as a pro-lifer. Some of the women editors at the *Voice* stopped speaking to me; and while I had been a frequent lecturer on free speech at colleges and universities, those engagements stopped. The students electing speakers were predominantly liberals and pro-choicers. They didn't want this pro-life infidel on their campuses.

I was still winning some journalism awards, the most prestigious of which was one by the National Press Foundation in Washington "for lifetime distinguished contributions to journalism." I'd been told by the head of the foundation that the selection committee's decision had been unanimous. But as I came into the building to accept the award, a committee member told me there had been a serious and sometimes angry debate about my being chosen.

"Some on the committee didn't think that my reporting was that good?" I asked. She hesitated. "No, it wasn't that." "Oh," I got the message. "They didn't think a *pro-lifer* should be honored." "Yes," she nodded, "that was it."

A very pro-choice law professor I knew did invite me to debate him at his college, Harvard. When I started, the audience was largely hostile, but soon I sensed that I was making some headway, and my debating partner became irritated. "If you're so pro-life," he shouted, "why don't you go out and kill abortionists?" I looked at him, and said gently, "because I'm pro-life." That response seemed to register on some of the students.

During other public debates in various settings, I challenge pro-abortionists to look at photographs in multi-dimensional ultrasound sonograms of infants waiting to be born: their eyes, the moving, outstretched fingers and hands. I have read of women who, on being shown a sonogram of their child, decided not to have an abortion. And I greatly welcomed the news that on May 29, 2009, Nebraska's unicameral legislature unanimously voted for a bill that its supporters called "The Mother's Right to See her Unborn Child Ultrasound Bill." It is now the law in that state that before an abortion, the mother has to begin to get to know—through a sonogram—the child she is thinking of killing.

And, even more likely to prevent abortions is this breaking development reported on June 30, 2009, on lifesitenews.com: "A London art student— Jorge Lopez, a Brazilian student at the Royal College of Art in London—has developed a revolutionary new step in prenatal imagery that allows parents to hold a life-size model of their unborn baby." Using four-dimensional ultrasound images and MRI scans, plaster models can be built "that can delineate the unique form of each child." Says inventor Lopez: "It's amazing to see the faces of the mothers. They can see the full scale of their baby, really understand the size of it."

And really understand that it *is* a unique human being!

On this basic issue, there was an interesting conversation on the June 18 episode of Jon Stewart's popular TV "Daily Show." Stewart is pro-choice, and his guest, former Arkansas Governor and presidential candidate Mike Huckabee, is pro-life. Said Huckabee: "To me the issue is so much more than about abortion. It's about the fundamental issue of whether or not every human life has intrinsic worth and value." Stewart asked him whether he thought that pro-choicers "don't believe that every human life has value?" Answered Huckabee: "I don't truly believe that even people who would consider themselves 'pro-choice' actually like abortion [but] they haven't thought through the implications . . . of their conclusions." Huckabee then made the crucial point that 93% of abortions in America are elective—they are not based on the health of the mother. Therefore, he went on, this trains future generations to believe that "it's OK to take a human life because that life represents an interference to our lives—either economically or socially."

Stewart became defensive, saying he had affection for his own children before they were born. "I think," he said, "it's very difficult when you look at an ultrasound of your child and you see a heartbeat—you are filled with that wonder and love and all those things." But Stewart was still not against abortion, explaining: "I just don't feel personally that it's a decision I can make for another person." And that brings us back to what the nine-year-old boy told his mother, who performs abortions: "That's *still* killing the baby"—whoever decided to abort that human being. To say it's a decision you can't make for someone else allows a life to be taken.

Years ago, as a reporter, I came to know Dr. Bernard Nathanson, who, at the time, was a wholesale abortionist, having performed more than 75,000 abortions. Then one day, he looked at the lives he was taking, and stopped. Why did he change his mind? In an interview with the Washington *Times* (reported on lifenews.com on June 12), Dr. Nathanson said: "Once we had ultrasound [sonograms] in place, we could study the fetus and see it was a member of our community. If you don't do that, you're just a creature of political ideology. In 1970," Nathanson continued, "there were approximately 1,100 articles on the functioning of the [human] fetus. By 1990, there were 22,000. The data piled up swiftly and *opened a window into the womb*." (Emphasis added). And there was a baby—certainly a member of our community!

Eventually, Dr. Nathanson converted to Catholicism, and the late Cardinal John O'Connor of New York presided at the event. I had come to know the Cardinal—first as a reporter, writing what eventually became a book about him, and then as a friend. From our first meeting, I had told him I was an atheist and a pro-lifer. He never tried to convert me; and the day after former abortionist Dr. Bernard Nathanson became a Catholic, the Cardinal called me: "I hope we don't lose you because you're the only Jewish atheist civil-libertarian pro-lifer we have." I assured him he would not lose me, as I realized that for this high-level member of the Catholic hierarchy, my becoming a pro-lifer was decidedly not controversial.

However, I continued to be banished elsewhere. When the dean of the graduate school of Antioch College said he would like to establish there a Nat Hentoff Gaduate School of Journalism, I was stunned. No institution has ever been named after me. I accepted, but the day before I was to leave to meet the faculty, the dean—clearly embarrassed—called me to tell me that because many in the faculty were strongly opposed to having a dean opposed to abortion, they would resist the appointment. So, even now, no institution has ever been named after me, and that's just as well. I much prefer to speak for—and be responsible for—only myself.

In debates with pro-abortionists, I frequently quote a writer I greatly admire, Mary Meehan, who often writes for the *Human Life Review*. Mary was active in the anti-Vietnam-War and civil-rights movements, and wrote an article for *The Progressive* magazine, many of whose readers have similar backgrounds. For years, I was a columnist for *The Progressive* and, as far as I know, I was the only pro-lifer on the staff—and probably among the readers. Mary Meehan shook up both the staff and the readers when she wrote:

> Some of us who went through the antiwar struggles of the 1960s and 1970s are now active in the right-to-life movement. We do not enjoy opposing our old friends on the abortion issue, but we feel that we have no choice . . . It is out of character for the left to neglect the weak and helpless. The traditional mark of the left has been its protection of the underdog, the weak, and the poor. The unborn child is the most helpless form of humanity, even in more need of protection than the poor tenant farmer or the mental patient. The basic instinct of the left is to aid those who cannot aid themselves. And that instinct is absolutely sound. It's what keeps the human proposition going.

Whether you're on the left or the right—or an independent, as I am—it's also vital to keep in mind what Barbara Newman has written in *The American Feminist*, the national magazine of Feminists for Life: "If it is wrong to kill with guns, bombs, or poison, with the electric chair or the noose, it is most tragically wrong to kill with the physician's tools."

Way back, a German physician and humanist, Dr. Christoph Hufeland, wrote: "If the physician presumes to take into consideration in his work whether a life has value or not, the consequences are boundless, and the physician becomes the most dangerous man in the state." Once human life is devalued unto death, many of us born people who are sick and in need of costly care—especially as we grow older—can be left to die because our "quality of life" isn't worth keeping us alive.

Having been out of step all these years, I have learned the most fundamental human right is the right to life—for the born, the unborn, the elderly who refuse to give up on life. My daughter, Jessica, recently sent me a button to wear to proclaim the essence of what she and I believe to be Constitutional Americanism: "No, you can't have my rights—I'm still using them."

The Child Came to Us

Mary Kenny

It was J.P. McFadden who said the inspirational words to me, back in the 1990s. "We didn't choose to take on this subject," he wrote. "The unborn child came to us. And we had to defend its cause." I have often reflected on this when the cause has proved trying, or difficult, or painful. And it has always sustained me.

The pro-life cause—particularly opposing abortion—is not, I would say, a particularly beneficial career move. In Britain, where I mostly live with my English husband (though I have retained a foot in my native Ireland), being pro-life is, somehow, shall we say, *bad form.* The English have a horror of "extremism" of any kind, and they imagine you are about to berate them with your "extremist" values. People seem to feel, too, that you are setting out to judge and chide them, or that you are unnecessarily bringing a private issue into the public domain.

The late Auberon Waugh—writer and son of the very great Evelyn Waugh—who was a vague sort of Catholic remarked to me: "Oh, why make a fuss about all that. An abortion is something anyone sensible wants to forget about." There is a truth in that affirmation, and it cuts several ways: It implies that anyone who takes up the pro-life cause is a standing reproach but it admits of the fact that an abortion is at best something horrible—that it is not, as the pro-abortion advocates would have it, a neutral choice that doesn't matter very much one way or the other. Yet one doesn't wish to be cast in the stern mould of John Calvin: It seems to me that the purpose of the pro-life cause is not to be a living reproach to anyone for past sins, but to endorse the value of human life from its inception, and to signal that this principle should be as much of a moral norm as any of the other human-rights ethics which are so widely agreed upon.

In the world of the media, in which I have lived for most of my professional life, pro-life values are widely regarded with hostility, and it can become difficult, even for those of us who normally have access to the press, to publish anything about the subject in the mainstream media. After I wrote a book on the abortion theme, I was told by a leader-writer on one London newspaper (there are at least 12 national newspapers in Britain, all of them published in London, and read nationwide): "Leave it out. You're a busted

Mary Kenny is a well-known British journalist and writer. Her latest book is *Crown and Shamrock: Love and Hate Between Ireland and the British Monarchy* (New Island, 2009).

flush on this question." (Meaning, "Quit this issue"; "busted flush" is a gambling term for a broken or worn-out strategy.) On a BBC (the national British Broadcasting Corporation) radio programme I was informed that I was "obsessive" about abortion, although I had only mentioned it in passing, and it was relevant to the discussion. British *Cosmopolitan* magazine nominated me as "Misogynist of the month" after I published a piece on a pro-life issue. My response to some of these reactions has been to draw back from too much directly polemical engagement: You are no good to any cause if you are regarded as a scold or an obsessive. And it hurt being called a misogynist.

Actually, I had been a fiery young feminist from my early twenties, and was involved in founding a feminist movement in Ireland in 1970, the *Irish Women's Liberation Movement*. Another of my co-founders was Mrs. Mary Robinson, who subsequently went on to become President of Ireland, and latterly, an important personage at the UN. The IWLM was a worthy cause in its time: It was, I now see, a modernising movement which necessarily brought antiquated Irish laws into the latter part of the 20th century. There were Victorian laws enacted by British administrations which had never been taken off the statute book: restrictions which barred women from taking out a checking account without the counter-signature of a man, or from applying for a mortgage (odd in that in Irish society women were often considered more responsible than men when it came to money—certainly less likely to spend it at the local bar); regulations which very seldom admitted women to jury service (enacted by the Irish Free State in the 1920s); laws which banned married women from working for the State (commonly applied in European countries in the 1920s and 30s, during catastrophic male unemployment); fiscal arrangements which in effect neglected widows and failed to support deserted wives, and, perhaps most controversially of all, a 1935 law which forbade the importation of contraceptive devices.

Similar anti-contraception laws had existed in France (from 1920 to 1967) and in the State of Minnesota. The "suppression of fertility," as the French called it, was culturally regarded as dangerous and unnatural, and particularly so after the horrendous loss of French population after the First World War. Nevertheless, by 1970, the Irish law was archaic, and an unwarranted intrusion by the State, to forbid the importation of condoms or the diaphragm once known as the "Dutch cap." And in our feminist movement, we had some fun with demonstrations and stunts against the outdated law.

Interestingly, our feminist movement did not, at that time, confront the issue of abortion. In our consciousness-raising sessions, we simply never spoke about it. Although a British law enabled abortion to be performed—with certain token restrictions—in 1967, termination of pregnancy did not really become a worldwide public issue until 1973, with the *Roe* v. *Wade* debates in America. I think there were a number of reasons why we, in the Irish feminist movement, did not discuss abortion. There was a natural, if unspoken, element of distaste. Irishwomen would be aware that there would be deep divisions among women, even among feminists, in what was still a profoundly Catholic country—and what was also relevant, an agricultural one. When abortion did enter the public realm of discourse in Ireland in the 1980s, a correspondent wrote to *The Irish Times* to say that the only time the word "abortion" had ever been heard among farming folk (which until recently constituted the majority of Irish people) was "when the cow had failed to calf." To agriculturalists, "abortion" simply meant "failure": and indeed material loss.

Among Irish feminists at that time, there was an instinctive feeling, then, that the market wouldn't bear a pro-abortion stance—besides the ambivalent feelings of the women themselves. (It surprised me to note, more recently, that Mary Robinson now accepts the routine "right to choose" of feminist orthodoxy over the abortion question: She never showed any engagement with the subject during our shared Irish feminist movement.)

But moreover, legal contraception seemed a more focused and significant issue.

Although I have more complex feelings about contraception today—I think it is a profoundly complicated subject, and I have developed an enhanced esteem for the ideals expressed in Pope Paul VI's *On Human Life*—I would still stand by our campaign to remove the archaic law from the Irish statute book prohibiting contraception. I do not think it is the business of the state either to forbid or promulgate the use of vulcanised rubber in the matter of human sexual relations. On a pragmatic basis, too, I think it more difficult to maintain a stand against abortion when also opposing contraception. As a wise woman once said to me: "You can't be against everything."

I think it was about 1977 when I first became aware of abortion as a political issue: It was ten years after the 1967 British abortion act, which was universally marked in the United Kingdom as a liberating piece of legislation which had saved women's lives. I had returned to live in London, was married and had one child, with another expected. It was at that moment, I remember, that I thought: Wait a minute—*is* this legislation so liberating? Can it be right for the state to extinguish human life in the womb? Can't women's lives be safeguarded in ways other than by this?

Some of the arguments being advanced by pro-abortionists struck me as not only diminishing of human life, but as laughably unscientific—even backward. There were claims that the conceptus was "part of a woman's body" and "just an undifferentiated lump of jelly." I became involved with the British organisation *Life* and met groups of people who not only felt that human life must be defended, but who also cared immensely for the young women faced with problem pregnancies.

Jack and Nuala Scarisbrick, the founders of *Life*, had actually started out by inviting distressed young pregnant women into their own home, in the Shakespearean county of Warwickshire in England. Later, the network grew so remarkably that a range of sheltered houses was established throughout the country to support pregnant women. *Life*'s counselling services brought its volunteers into daily contact with women who needed to talk through a crisis pregnancy, and I came to admire not only the *caritas* involved, but also the experience, knowledge, compassion and understanding that the counsellors developed. They *never* judged the women who came to them, or sought to coerce them in any way; but tried, instead, to emphasize the positive and support them through what was often a worrying time.

From the 1970s to this day, *Life* has done admirable work in helping not only pregnant women, but mothers with young families, disabled babies (founding a hospital for handicapped babies in Liverpool, "Zoe's Place"), and extending support to men and fathers. They have also provided post-abortion counselling and encouraged studies on psychological assistance. All this has been supported by voluntary contributions, and, incidentally, I might add, in a spirit of admirable ecumenism which embraced Catholic, Protestant, Jewish and agnostic members. (In Northern Ireland, at the height of the sectarian Troubles of the late 1970s and early 1980s, I witnessed Catholics and Protestants working harmoniously and wholeheartedly together in *Life*'s cause: I saw the Rev. Ian Paisley's daughter, Rhonda, stand shoulder to shoulder with Roman Catholics—perhaps for the first time in her experience—on a *Life* platform.)

All this has passed without a single note of public recognition. Britain is a society replete with a complex honours system: The powers that be can, and do, award a rich variety of honours in the name of the Queen, and the Prime Minister has, within his gift, a large deposit of grace and favour patronage in due recognition of public service. Despite the help and support they have extended to generations of young mothers, despite the care they have initiated for disabled babies, and despite the social and welfare services they have brought into being—not to mention the human lives they have saved—the founders and personnel of *Life* have never received any honour in Great Britain. Quite the contrary—the work has been officially ignored and marginalized. It has consistently and persistently been omitted from standard reference books which provide helping services for pregnant women, and the charity has never been permitted to make a charitable appeal over the BBC (which regularly broadcasts a "week's good cause.") And indeed, I might add, neither have any of the other pro-life campaigners in Britain, all of whom do fine work which in effect supports the fabric of society.

But that is what I mean by pro-life causes not always being a beneficial career move, at least in the United Kingdom. It is simply not Politically Correct, and was not Politically Correct even before the notion was established. I realized this when Christopher Hitchens—an old friend of my husband's, who worked in London for a decade before migrating to America—confessed to me that, privately, he was anti-abortion. Really? "Yes," he said reflectively. "I reported a story in California which involved an aborted baby gasping for breath on a hospital slab—and I thought, shit, this is *revolting.*" But he declined to go public with it. Why upset the feminists? Unnecessary. I thought then of Jean-Paul Sartre's refusal to condemn Stalinism in the 1950s and 60s, for fear of distressing the Parisian working-class, who were solid Communist voters. And yet, Christopher Hitchens is a courageous man, and one day, I believe, he will make his privately held commitment on abortion public.

Throughout the 1980s and 1990s, I engaged in numerous public debates in Britain and Ireland on the abortion issue. It was often a disagreeable experience: I find it difficult to be the object of hostility and hatred. And yet, I learned a great deal and met some wonderful people. I also discovered, as the Jesuit teachers have always said, that sometimes you learn as much from your opponents as from your cohorts. Some of the people I debated against, often at Oxford or Cambridge, were chillingly cold-hearted. One woman said, when referring to a distressing case in the North of England where an aborted infant fought for breath in the hospital sluice room and even tried to cry: "Oh, aborted foetuses only cry to draw attention to themselves." Even she knew that she had gone too far with such a statement. But I also met opponents who were thoughtful and sincere and who at least had the honesty and courage to engage in open debate. Far more evasive were the pro-abortionists who would not, or perhaps could not, engage in debate at all.

I did feel gratified, though, when an opponent said to me after a debate: "I don't agree with what you say, obviously. But in some part of me, I'm glad you're out there saying it."

Debate is important; and yet now I think it is best done by younger people, or those in an active middle age who are in the full flow of oratory. As I moved torward my 60s, the historical perspective was becoming increasingly interesting, in a whole range of subjects—in culture, politics, and what I would call "values." The purpose of the senior years is to analyse the past, and to reflect upon the narrative that it opens up to us.

I am also beginning to think that there are other ways of exploring the pro-life narrative, in terms of story and drama. I wrote a book of short stories, *A Mood for Love*, in the 1980s, mostly based on abortion case histories I had encountered in research. It was not particularly successful, and may not have been well realised; and yet, the material around the theme is full of real human issues and reflections, and has tremendous creative potential. In general, fiction writers have tended to avoid the abortion issue; or to treat it in the predictably Politically Correct mode as being something associated with fanatics (see Douglas Kennedy's *State of the Union*). The field is wide open to be explored more imaginatively, and I hope that the pro-life narrative will develop in this way, as well as maintaining its platform in politics, culture and ethics.

I have come to see that it is the imagination which can be the most powerful tool of all in communication. I said I had first been alerted to the abortion issue as a political subject in 1977, but now, looking back, I think a 1966 movie first stirred a dim awareness. That film was *Alfie*, with Michael Caine. There is an abortion in that film, and we see Caine looking down at the aborted child. I remember sitting in the cinema and thinking "please don't show us the reality. Please don't." The direct Lewis Gilbert very wisely didn't: It was enough to imagine the horror.

*   *   *   *   *

My own journey through the pro-life issue has been a very small and humble part of the pattern; a pattern, though, which I believe in times to come will be regarded as being akin to the anti-slavery movement or the campaigns to rescue starving and abandoned infants. For at its core is the affirmation of life itself, and there is no higher value.

Identity, Abortion and Walker Percy

Edward Short

When a number of books about the American Civil War appeared in the late 1950s, including Bruce Catton's *This Hallowed Ground* and Shelby Foote's *Shiloh*, the novelist Walker Percy (1916-1990) accounted for the resurgent interest in the long-ago war by surmising that "the whole country, the South included, is just beginning to see the Civil War whole and entire for the first time. The thing was too big and too bloody, too full of suffering and hatred, too closely knit into the fabric of our meaning as a people, to be held off and looked at—until now."[1] Percy wrote that four years before the publication of his first novel, *The Moviegoer* (1961), which won the National Book Award. Nevertheless, it broached a theme that he would tackle again and again in his six novels: how we understand our identity, claim the inheritance of our fallen nature. In his last novel, *The Thanatos Syndrome* (1987), he returned to this theme by considering what he called "the widespread and ongoing devaluation of human life . . . under various sentimental disguises: 'quality of life,' 'pointless suffering,' 'termination of life without meaning,' etc."[2] The form of devaluation with which Percy became most concerned was abortion, though he also decried the related rise of eugenics, euthanasia, and pharmacology.

Since Western society is still waging its war against unborn children, it is not possible to step back and grasp the full import of this war. Still, Percy recognized that the grounds of this development are, in their way, as inscrutable as the grounds for the Civil War. "Not being a historian, I don't know what the cause of that war was," he admitted in one article, "whether it was fought purely and simply over slavery, or over states' rights, or, as Allen Tate once said, because the South didn't want to be put in Arrow collars."[3] What he did know was that the war against unborn children could not be understood simply as a political or even a moral debate between the pro-life and the pro-choice—if anything, it was the consequence of an even bigger and bloodier division than the one that pitted Yankees against Confederates. Beginning with Descartes in the 17th century, this division tore body and soul completely asunder and saddled the Western mind with misconceptions about the nature of human identity that have almost entirely derailed philosophy. Percy described the circumstances in which these misconceptions arose in terms that are fairly indisputable:

Edward Short is the author of a study of John Henry Cardinal Newman, titled *Newman and His Contemporaries,* to be published by Encounter Books, Spring 2011.

The old modern age has ended. We live in a post-modern as well as a post-Christian age. . . . It is post-Christian in the sense that people no longer understand themselves, as they understood themselves for some fifteen hundred years, as ensouled creatures under God, born to trouble, and whose salvation depends upon the entrance of God into history as Jesus Christ. It is post-modern because the Age of Enlightenment with its vision of man as a rational creature, naturally good and part of the cosmos, which itself is understandable by natural science—this also has ended. It ended with the catastrophes of the twentieth century. The present age is demented. It is possessed by a sense of dislocation, a loss of personal identity, an alternating sentimentality and rage, which, in an individual patient, could be characterized as dementia. As the century draws to a close [Percy wrote this in 1990], it does not have a name, but it can be described. It is the most scientifically advanced, savage, democratic, inhuman, sentimental, murderous century in human history.[4]

Here is the philosophical context in which Percy placed the emergence of abortion on demand. Before looking at how he treated the subject in his writings, I should say something about his life.

No one can read of Percy's life without seeing that his solicitude for unborn children had deep roots in his personal history. He was descended from English Protestant planters and lawyers who arrived in the South in the 18th century and settled in Birmingham, Alabama. What distinguished them most, besides their commitment to their families and their neighbors, white and black, was their constitutional melancholy. In 1917, Percy's grandfather shot himself in the heart with a twelve-gauge shotgun. Some of his depression might have been attributed to the loss of two of his children in infancy but what the root cause was no one could ascertain. Then, in 1929, family history grimly repeated itself when Percy's father shot himself with a twenty-gauge shotgun, the coroner later finding that the bullet had gone clear through the top of his head. Walker Percy was 12 at the time. Two years later, Percy's mother died when she drove her car off a bridge, which Percy always suspected had been intentional. In any case, at 14, Percy, together with his two younger brothers, was an orphan. No series of events could have better acquainted him with the vulnerability of children.

When his own vulnerability was at its acutest, his father's brother, William Alexander Percy, took Percy and his brothers into his home and adopted them. Their lives were transformed. Uncle Will was a well-respected lawyer, poet, and autobiographer who introduced Percy not only to a number of living Southern writers but to Shakespeare, Keats, Brahms, and Beethoven—not to mention Richard Wagner, whom Percy always found insufferable, "though I was dragged every year," as he recalled, "to hear Flagstad sing Isolde."[5]

But more than classical culture, Uncle Will gave Percy the gift of himself. "To have lived in Uncle Will's house," Percy later wrote, "was nothing less than to be informed in the deepest sense of the word. What was to be listened to, dwelled on, pondered over for the next thirty years was of course the man himself, the unique human being, and when I say unique I mean it in the most literal sense: he was one of a kind: I never met anyone remotely like him."[6]

This sense of the precious uniqueness of the individual would profoundly inform Percy's understanding of the abortion issue. The rigorous sense of honor that he learned in his uncle's home would also equip him to see through the tawdry sophistry that prepared the way for legalized abortion. Writing in 1973, the year of *Roe* v. *Wade*, Percy remarked of his beloved uncle, "Certainly, nothing would surprise him about the collapse of the old moralities; for example, the so-called sexual revolution, which he would more likely define in less polite language as alley-cat morality. I can hear him now: 'Fornicating like white trash is one thing, but leave it to this age to call it the new morality.'"[7] Just as important, William Percy impressed upon his nephew how vital it was for the individual to understand his true identity. In his brilliant biography of Percy, *Pilgrim in the Ruins*—published in 1992, two years after Percy's death—Jay Tolson quoted a passage from William Percy's autobiography, *Lanterns on the Levee* (1941), which goes to the heart of this issue of identity:

> Here among the graves in the twilight I see one thing only, but I see that thing clear. I see the long wall of a rampart somber with sunset, a dusty road at its base. On the tower of the rampart stand the glorious high gods, Death and the rest, insolent and watching. Below on the road stream the tribes of men, tired, bent, hurt, and stumbling, and each man alone. As one comes beneath the tower, the High God descends and faces the wayfarer. He speaks three slow words: "Who are you?" The pilgrim I know should be able to straighten his shoulders, to stand his tallest, and to answer defiantly: "I am your son."[8]

In a moving piece about his Uncle Will's three-story Greek revival house in Greenville, Miss., which included an elevator, a huge automatic phonograph known as the Capehart, a rambling garden, and a voluminous library, Percy fondly recalled the literary guests who came to visit his uncle, including Carl Sandburg and Langston Hughes, and the unforgettable vitality of the place. Yet he concluded his reminiscence by observing, "It's all gone now, house, garden, Capehart, Beethoven quartets in Victor 78s. . . . In its place, I think are neat condo-villas of stained board-and-batten siding. Only the garden wall remains. I am not complaining. I have what he left me, and I don't mean things."[9]

Here was proof that the most important lesson that Uncle Will had to impart—the lesson of the inestimable value of the individual before and beyond the graveyard—was not lost on his brilliant nephew.

Percy attended the University of North Carolina at Chapel Hill with his best friend Shelby Foote, the celebrated historian, to whom he was introduced by William Percy in 1930. The correspondence between Percy and Foote records the support they gave each other as they mined their respective quarries. When Percy was unsure about whether he was on the right track with regard to *The Thanatos Syndrome,* which caused him more artistic trouble than all his books put together, Shelby was ready with good steadying counsel. "I say you should write what you want to write about anyone anywhere," he wrote his anxious friend. "That dreadful things can come from do-gooding . . . who's going to argue with that?"[10]

After graduating from college, Percy trained as a medical doctor at Columbia, where he received his medical degree in 1941. After conducting an autopsy as an intern at Bellevue, he contracted TB. While convalescing at the Trudeau Sanatorium in the Adirondacks, he read Søren Kierkegaard and Fyodor Dostoevsky, both of whom led him to question whether science could usefully pronounce on the basal mysteries of life. In 1947, Percy converted to Catholicism and decided to pursue writing rather than medicine.

A year earlier, he had married Mary Bernice Townsend, a medical technician, with whom he raised two daughters in Covington, La., which he once described as lying "in the green heart of green Louisiana, a green jungle of pines, azaleas, camellias, dogwood, grapevines, and billions of blades of grass."[11] So many, in fact, that he once told his wife that if she would allow it, he would prefer finishing his days "in a French cottage on Rue Dauphine [in New Orleans] with a small paved patio and not a single blade of grass." Just short of his 74th birthday, in 1990, Percy died of prostate cancer. He is buried on the grounds of St. Joseph's Abbey in St. Benedict, La.

Although stylistically highly differentiated, all of his novels—*The Moviegoer, The Last Gentleman* (1966), *Love in the Ruins* (1971), *Lancelot* (1977), *The Second Coming* (1980), and *The Thanatos Syndrome* pivot on what for Percy was the all-important question of human identity.

When it came to his own identity, Percy recognized it as nurtured and sustained by his Catholic faith. He was particularly grateful for the dividends his faith paid his art. One hears so much nonsense of how faith constrains the artist: It is refreshing to hear Percy affirm how it liberated him. "I have the strongest feeling that, whatever else the benefits of the Catholic faith, it is of a particularly felicitous use to the novelist. Indeed, if one had to design a religion for novelists, I can think of no better. What distinguishes Judeo-Christianity in general from other world religions is its emphasis on the value of the individual person, its view of man as a creature in trouble, seeking to get out of it, and accordingly on the move. Add to this . . . the sacraments, especially the Eucharist, which, whatever else they do, confer the highest significance upon the ordinary things of this world, bread, wine, water, touch, breath, words, talking, listening—and what do you have? You have a man in a predicament and on the move in a real world of real things, a world which is a sacrament and a mystery: a pilgrim whose life is a searching and finding."[12] One of the reasons why Percy is such a good novelist is that he fully recognizes how well fitted the novel is to explore man's moral pilgrimage.

Percy's faith also reinforced something of the patrician steel that was a good part of his make-up. In a witty piece called "Why Are You a Catholic?" (1990), he recalled how outré his conversion was in a region not known for its fondness for the Roman Church. When the subject of religion came up in the South, he pointed out, it did so usually as "a challenge or a provocation or even an insult":

> It happens once in a while, for example, that one finds oneself in a group of educated persons, one of whom, an educated person of a certain sort, may venture such an offhand remark as: *Of course, the Roman Catholic Church is not only a foreign power but a fascist power.* Or when in a group of less educated persons, perhaps in a small town barbershop, one of whom, let us say an ex-member of the Ku Klux Klan—who are not bad fellows actually, at least hereabouts, except when it comes to blacks, Jews, and Catholics—when one of them comes out with something like *The Catholic Church is a piece of s**** then one feels entitled to a polite rebuttal in both cases, in the one with something like, "Well, hold on, let us examine the terms power, foreign, fascist—" and so on, and in the case of the other, responding in the same tone of casual barbershop bonhomie with, say, "Truthfully, Lester, you're something of a s*** yourself, even for white trash—" without in either case disrupting, necessarily, the general amiability.[13]

Such unflappable independence of mind would stand Percy in good stead when he went up against the equally bigoted pro-abortion Establishment. But even before the abortion issue arose, he knew that he was not in sync with the consensus of most of his contemporaries, especially those in the medical and academic fields. In a 1987 interview he described what he called the "Holy Office of the Secular Inquisition":

> It is not to be confused with "secular humanism," because . . . it is anti-human. Although it drapes itself in the mantle of the scientific method and free scientific inquiry, it is neither free nor scientific. Indeed it relies on certain hidden dogma where dogma has no place. I can think of two holy commandments

which the Secular Inquisition lays down for all scientists and believers. The first: In your investigations and theories, thou shalt not find anything unique about the human animal even if the evidence points to such uniqueness. Example: Despite heroic attempts to teach sign language to other animals, the evidence is that even the cleverest chimpanzee has never spontaneously named a single object or uttered a single sentence. Yet dogma requires that, despite traditional belief in the soul or the mind, and the work of more recent workers like Peirce and Langer in man's unique symbolizing capacity, Homo sapiens be declared to be not qualitatively different from other animals. Another dogma: Thou shalt not suggest that there is a unique and fatal flaw in Homo sapiens or indeed any perverse trait that cannot be laid to the influence of Western civilization. Example: An entire generation came under the influence of Margaret Mead's *Coming of Age in Samoa* and its message: that the Samoans were an innocent, happy, and Edenic people until they were corrupted by missionaries and technology. That this turned out not to be true, that indeed the Samoans appear to have been at least as neurotic as New Yorkers has not changed the myth or the mindset.[14]

Here, Percy delineated the baleful outlines of political correctness, which became liberal orthodoxy in the last years of the 20th century. Denying civilized man's unique symbolizing capacity, while at the same time inflating the capabilities of savages and chimpanzees, constituted more than bad anthropology. These dogmas were an assault on the identity of the uniquely human, an assault that opened the door to the inhumanity of abortion and euthanasia, eugenics and embryo experimentation. According to this rogue science, the living were free to flout the divine source of life by determining whether the unborn should live or die, because there was no divine source of human life and therefore no concomitant uniqueness or sanctity inherent in human life. The moral Percy drew from this absence of any true sense of human identity was not candy-coated. "It is easy to criticize the absurdities of fundamentalist beliefs like 'scientific creationism,'" he wrote, "but it is also necessary to criticize other dogmas parading as science and the bad faith of some scientists who have their own dogmatic agendas to promote under the guise of 'free scientific inquiry.' Scientific inquiry should, in fact, be free. . . . If it is not, if it is subject to this or that ideology, then do not be surprised if the history of the Weimar doctors is repeated. [It was the leading doctors of Germany's Weimar Republic before the rise of Hitler and the Nazis who pioneered modern methods of euthanasia.] Weimar leads to Auschwitz. The nihilism of some scientists in the name of ideology or sentimentality and the consequent devaluation of individual human life lead straight to the gas chamber."[15]

Although he did not acknowledge as much in print, Percy was indebted to Flannery O'Connor for at least some of this point. In an essay about a young girl, a splendid candidate for abortion, who had been born with a tumor on the side of her face and one eye, the other having been surgically removed, O'Connor observed how

> one of the tendencies of our age is to use the sufferings of children to discredit the goodness of God . . . Ivan Karamazov cannot believe as long as one child is in torment; Camus' hero cannot accept the divinity of Christ, because of the massacre of the innocents. In this popular pity, we mark our gain in sensibility and our loss in vision. If other ages felt less, they saw more, even though they saw with the blind, prophetical, unsentimental eye of acceptance, which is the eye of faith. In the absence of this faith now, we govern by tenderness. It is a tenderness, which, long since cut off from the person of Christ, is wrapped in theory. When tenderness is detached from the source of tenderness, its logical outcome is terror. It ends in forced-labour camps and in the fumes of the gas chamber.[16]

In a letter to a friend in 1973, Percy also deplored this factitious pity when he related how he "heard Dr. Christiaan Barnard say that what mattered was quality of life and that therefore euthanasia could be defended. Dick Cavett asked him who made the decision about the quality of life. Said Doc Barnard: 'Why the doctors.' Now the time may come when this society does dispose of human life according to pragmatic principles, and come to look upon the 'sacredness of life' as either an empty slogan or an outgrown religious dogma. But if that happens—as in fact it already has—we're in deep trouble. . . . I think we're much more like the Nazis and Dachau than we imagine."[17]

To some, this might seem needlessly provocative. In making the pro-life case against abortion, they might argue, we should employ more measured arguments. But my own exception to Percy's statement is not that it goes too far but that it does not go far enough. Weimar did lead to Auschwitz and the gas chambers. But the sentimental nihilism that Percy accurately sees as the legacy of Weimar has led in our own time not to the gas chamber but to the abortion clinic, to destruction and degradation of human life on a scale that the Nazis would have thought scarcely possible. Comparing our own abortion industry, which has killed over 40 million unborn children, to the Nazi murder of 6 million Jews is a misleading comparison. We have been infinitely more successful in doing away with our own "life not worth living" than the Nazis were with theirs.

However, Percy was right to see a link between our ideologically perverted science and our readiness to connive at the killing of unborn children. In an op-ed piece that appeared in the New York *Times* in 1981, Percy noted an irony that the liberal enemies of the Roman Church and of unborn children continue to miss:

The con . . . perpetrated by some jurists, some editorial writers, and some doctors is that since there is no agreement about the beginning of human life, it is therefore a private religious or philosophical decision and therefore the state and the courts can do nothing about it. . . . There is a wonderful irony here. It is this: the onset of individual life is not a dogma of the Church but a fact of science. . . . Please indulge the novelist if he thinks in novelistic terms. Picture the scene. A Galileo trial in reverse. The Supreme Court is cross-examining a high-school biology teacher and admonishing him that of course it is only his personal opinion that the fertilized human ovum is an individual human life. He is enjoined not to teach his private beliefs at a public school. Like Galileo he caves in, submits, but in turning away is heard to murmur, *"But, it's still alive!"*[18]

After this unanswerable sally, it is perhaps no wonder that the editors of the staunchly pro-abortion *Times* refused even to acknowledge a Letter to the Editor that Percy sent off in 1988 at the behest of J. P. McFadden and the *Human Life Review*:

Perhaps the most influential book published in German in the first quarter century was entitled *The Justification of the Destruction of Life Devoid of Value*. Its co-authors were the distinguished jurist Karl Binding and the prominent psychiatrist Alfred Hoche. Neither Binding nor Hoche had ever heard of Hitler or the Nazis. Nor, in all likelihood, did Hitler ever read the book. He didn't have to. The point is that the ideas expressed in the book and the policies advocated were not the product of Nazi ideology but rather of the best minds of the pre-Nazi Weimar Republic—physicians, social scientists, jurists and the like who with the best secular intentions wished to improve the lot, socially and genetically of the German people—by getting rid of the unfit and the unwanted. It is hardly necessary to say what use the Nazis made of these ideas. I would not wish to be understood as implying that the respected American institutions I have named are similar to corresponding pre-Nazi institutions. But I do suggest that once the line is crossed, once the principle gains acceptance—juridically, medically, socially—that innocent human life can be destroyed for whatever reason, for the most admirable socio-economic, medical or social reasons—then it does not take a prophet to predict what will happen next, or if not next then sooner or later. At any rate a warning is in order. Depending on the disposition of the majority and the opinion polls—now in favor of allowing women to get rid of unborn and unwanted babies—it is not difficult to imagine an electorate or a court ten years, fifty years from now, who would favor getting rid of useless old people, retarded children, anti-social blacks, illegal Hispanics, gypsies, Jews . . . Why not?—if that is what is wanted by the majority, the polled opinion, the polity of the time.[19]

This can be read as something of an abstract of *The Thanatos Syndrome*, in which Dr. Tom More, a lapsed-Catholic psychiatrist, uncovers a scheme by colleagues and local Louisiana businessmen to introduce behavior-altering chemicals into the water supply. "What would you say, Tom," one of the book's smarmier characters asks, while listening to a waltz by Strauss, "if I gave you a magic wand you could wave . . . and overnight you could reduce crime in the streets by eighty percent?"[20] Dr. More recognizes that the sexual behavior of his psychiatric patients has become arrestingly pongid; their ability to remember facts has increased exponentially; and their overall deportment has become suspiciously sedate where once it was characterized by violent mood swings.

The novel's narrative is given over to Dr. More's discovery of the precise nature of the scheme, including its effects, which are revealed to be at once uproariously funny and revoltingly sinister. In his crisis of conscience, Dr. More clearly recalls another More, though Percy spares his hero the grisly consequences that befell Henry VIII's Lord Chancellor. In this superbly satirical novel, which merits a place beside the most unsettling salvos of Swift and George Orwell, Percy takes devastating aim at our arrogant contempt for the laws of God and nature, and in the process skewers pharmacology, euthanasia, eugenics, and abortion. In one representative passage, Dr. More describes the forces of change that have made poor Freud passé:

> I am the only poor physician in town, the only one who doesn't drive a Mercedes or a BMW. I still drive the Chevrolet Caprice I owned before I went away. It is a bad time for psychiatrists. Old-fashioned shrinks are out of style and generally out of work. We, who like our mentor Dr. Freud believe there is a psyche, that it is born to trouble as the sparks fly up, that one gets at it, the root of trouble, the soul's own secret, by venturing into the heart of darkness, which is to say, by talking and listening, mostly listening, to another troubled human for months, years—we have been mostly superseded by brain engineers, neuropharmacologists, chemists of the synapses. And why not? If one can prescribe a chemical and overnight turn a haunted soul into a bustling little body, why take on such a quixotic quest as pursuing the secret of one's very soul?[21]

The most effective character in the book is the one about whom Percy was most dubious.[22] Father Smith, a Catholic whiskey priest, has secluded himself atop a fire tower to protest his society's instruments of death. In modeling Smith after St. Simon Stylites, Percy was calling attention to a form of holy protest that might not be favored by monks today but which is perfectly suitable for what Percy calls our "time of apocalypse."

For some sense of what Percy might have had in mind in creating Father Smith, we can revisit what the historian Edward Gibbon had to say about the original St. Simon. When Gibbon considered the rise of monasticism in the fifth century in his *Decline and Fall of the Roman Empire*, he made a distinction between vulgar and ascetic Christians. The former were easy-going latitudinarians who "reconciled their fervent zeal and implicit faith with the exercise of their profession, the pursuit of their interest, and the indulgence of their passions." But the ascetics were different. "Inspired," as Gibbon says, "by the savage enthusiasm which represents man as criminal . . . they seriously renounced the business and pleasures of the age; abjured the use of wine, of flesh, and of marriage; chastised their body, mortified their affections, and embraced a life of misery, as the price of eternal happiness."

For Gibbon, the most patently absurd and indeed pernicious of these "wretched votaries" was Simon Stylites, a Syrian shepherd, born about 390, whose "aerial penance" required his residing 60 feet above ground on a pillar six feet in diameter, where he fasted and prayed for over 30 years. "A prince, who should capriciously inflict such tortures would be deemed a tyrant," Gibbon contended. For him, "This voluntary martyrdom... gradually destroyed the sensibility both of the mind and body; nor can it be presumed that the fanatics who torment themselves are susceptible of any lively affection for the rest of mankind. A cruel, unfeeling temper has distinguished the monks of every age and country: their stern indifference, which is seldom mollified by personal friendship, is inflamed by religious hatred; and their merciless zeal has strenuously administered the holy office of the Inquisition."[23]

We have already seen what Percy thought of the "Holy Office of the Secular Inquisition." But what is interesting about Gibbon's attack on St. Simon is that he depicted him as "cruel," "unfeeling," and "inflamed by religious hatred"—all the attributes that accurately describe the proponents of abortion, despite their attempts to appear paragons of niceness. What makes Father Smith such an enjoyable character is that he is the antithesis of nice. And yet while he is by no means a model ascetic, he is anything but cruel or unfeeling. Here Percy draws an important distinction between sentimental and true goodness. Father Smith may be a whiskey priest, he may even have wavered in his faith, but, unlike the advocates of human engineering, he is a compassionate sinner. He cares for the unfortunate; he does not spurn the misbegotten.

In one bravura section of the novel, titled "Father Smith's Confession," which has a kind of Dostoevskyian irrepressibility, Father Smith abjures the do-gooding sanctimony assumed by so many in the pro-abortion camp, without ever compromising his claim to authentic virtue. In one memorable passage, recalling his rocky stint as a parish priest, he admits: "Frankly, I found my fellow men, with few exceptions, either victims or ***holes. I did not exclude myself. The only people I got along with were bums, outcasts, pariahs, family skeletons, and the dying." Here is a St. Simon that wonderfully confounds Gibbon's caricature of sanctity, as well as his Enlightenment contempt for the mysterious, the flawed, the uniquely human. At the end of the novel, when Father Smith makes another impromptu speech, another confession, the sympathetic reader can be excused for listening to him as to a prophet, even though his creator was highly skeptical of novelists making any claim to prophecy:

> Listen to me, dear physicians, dear brothers, dear Qualitarians, abortionists, euthanasists! Do you know why you are going to listen to me? Because every last one of you is a better man than I and you know it! And yet you like me. Every last one of you knows me and what I am, a failed priest, an old drunk, who is only fit to do one thing and to tell one thing. You are good, kind, hardworking doctors, but you like me nevertheless and I know that you will allow me to tell you one thing—no, ask one thing—no, beg, one thing of you. Please do this one favor for me, dear doctors. If you have a patient, young or old, suffering, dying, afflicted, useless, born or unborn, who you for the best of reasons wish to put out of his misery—I beg only one thing of you, dear doctors! Please send him to us. Don't kill them! We'll take them—all of them! Please send them to us! I swear to you, you won't be sorry. We will all be happy about it! I promise you, and I know that you believe me, that we will take care of him, her—we will even call on you to help us take care of them!—and you will not have to make such a decision. God will bless you for it and you will offend no one except the Great Prince Satan, who rules the world. That is all.[24]

In a letter to one of his early mentors, the Catholic Southern novelist Caroline Gordon, Percy made an extraordinary admission. "Your letter has the effect of encouraging me to expectorate a chronic bone-in-the-throat. It has to do with my main problem as a fiction writer. Actually, I do not consider myself a novelist but a moralist. . . . My spiritual father is Pascal (and/or Kierkegaard). And if I also kneel before the altar of Lawrence and Joyce and Flaubert, it is not because I wish to do what they did, even if I could. What I really want to do is to tell people *what they must do and what they must believe if they want to live.*"[25]

Some have seen this as proof that Percy confused art with didacticism and was simply too honest to try to conceal the fact. But this is an unwarranted criticism. It is true that his fiction is profoundly moral. It is also true that he wrote to confront what he regarded as the spiritual desolation of post-modern man, man after Auschwitz. But the idea that these moral and spiritual objects somehow vitiated his art is false. For Percy, fiction, if undertaken honestly, was a kind of science in its own right, a way of knowing. Of course, he could be witheringly critical of the presumed reach of this form of knowing. "The novelist, I have come to believe," he declared in one essay, "is only good for one or two things—and they do not include being prophetic or making broad pronouncements about the decline of the West, the nature of evil, loneliness, God, and so forth. The embarrassment of the novelist is that after he masters his one or two tricks, does his little turn, some readers tend to ascribe this success to a deeper wisdom—whereas it is probably the very condition of his peculiar activity that he doesn't know anything else—which is to say that a person who asks a novelist anything about life and such, how to live, is in a bad way indeed."[26] Yet in the same essay he balanced this grudging assessment with a more generous measure of the practical good that the novelist can accomplish:

> If the novelist's business is, like that of all artists, to tell the truth, even when he is making up a story, he had better tell the truth no matter how odd it is, even if the truth is a kind of upside-downness. And if it is the novelist's business to look and see what is there for everyone to see but is nonetheless not seen, and if the novelist is by his very nature a hopeful man—he has to be hopeful or he would not bother to write at all—then sooner or later he must confront the great paradox of the twentieth century: that no other time has been more life-affirming in its pronouncements, self-fulfilling, creative, autonomous, and so on— and more death-dealing in its actions. It is the century of the love of death.[27]

The Thanatos Syndrome is not flawless. Its satire, at times, is too scattershot and it is structurally jerry-built. Nonetheless, what makes it a book that will continue to be read long after its critics have handed in their dinner-pails is that it provides a kind of epidemiology of abortion, an inquest into the roots of sentimental inhumanity, which one finds nowhere else. Percy does "look and see what is there for everyone to see but is nonetheless not seen." And he locates the cause for this failure of vision in our ignorance of our true identity. In 1974, in an unpublished paper given to a group interested in mental health at Louisiana State University, Percy wondered "whether or not we have settled for a view of man which is grossly incoherent by any scientific canon. That is to say, I wonder if through a kind of despair or through sheer weariness we have not given up the attempt to put man back together again, if indeed he was ever whole, or whether man isn't like Humpty Dumpty, who fell off the wall three hundred years ago, or rather was pushed by Descartes, who split man into body and mind . . ."[28]

Percy was making these speculations a year after *Roe* v. *Wade*. Of course, long before, Nazi Germany had already set up the death camps. But nearly forty years after *Roe* v. *Wade*, in America, it is clear that Humpty Dumpty's fall has had more than philosophical consequences. An incoherent view of man has resulted in a contempt for man, which, in turn, has resulted in the murder of 40 million unborn children. The Nazis justified their destruction of what they called "life not worth living" by appeals to racial purity; we justify ours by appeals to "reproductive rights," "quality of life," "family planning," "compasssion." Father Smith, the messenger of God,[29] helps Dr. More understand the meaning of these appeals: "You are a member of the first generation of doctors in the history of medicine to turn their backs on the oath of Hippocrates and kill millions of old useless people, unborn children, born malformed children, for the good of mankind—and to do so without a single murmur from one of you. Not a single letter of protest in the august *New England Journal of Medicine* . . ."[30]

Scientists could scarcely diagnose a problem to which they so blindly contributed. Percy, a scientist who was also a novelist, saw that the problem was in us: not only in our fallen nature but in our Pelagian refusal to acknowledge that fallen nature. Yet, he never counseled despair. As he has Father Smith assure Dr. More: "if you keep hope and have a loving heart and do not secretly wish for the death of others, the Great Prince Satan will not succeed in destroying the world . . . Perhaps the world will end in fire and the Lord will come—it is not for us to say. But it is for us to say . . . whether hope and faith will come back into the world."[31]

NOTES

1. "The American War" in *Signposts in a Strange Land*, edited by Patrick Samway, S.J. (New York, 1991), 72.
2. "An Interview with Zolan Abadi-Nagy," in ibid., 394.
3. "The American War," in ibid., 79-80.
4. "Why Are You A Catholic?" in ibid., 309.
5. "Uncle Will" in ibid., 55.
6. Ibid.
7. Ibid., 58.
8. Quoted in Tolson, Jay, *Pilgrim in the Ruins: A Life of Walker Percy* (New York, 1992), 17.
9. "Uncle Will's House" in *Signposts in a Strange Land*, 66.
10. *The Correspondence of Shelby Foote and Walker Percy*, edited by Jay Tolson (New York, 1997), 294.
11. "Why I Live Where I Live" in ibid., 9.
12. "The Holiness of the Ordinary," in *Signposts in a Strange Land*, 66.
13. "Why Are You a Catholic?" 305-06.
14. "An Interview with Zolan Abadi-Nagy," 395-96.
15. Ibid.
16. O'Connor, Flannery, "A Memoir of Mary Ann," in *Mystery and Manners: Occasional Prose*, selected and edited by Sally and Robert Fitzgerald (New York, 1969), 226-27.
17. Tolson, *Pilgrim in the Ruins: A Life of Walker Percy*, 439.
18. "Why Are You A Catholic?" 342.

19. "An Unpublished Letter to the Editor," in *Signposts in a Strange Land*, 350-1.
20. *The Thanatos Syndrome* (New York, 1987), 91.
21. Ibid., 13.
22. See *The Correspondence of Shelby Foote and Walker Percy*, edited by Jay Tolson (New York, 1997), 297. Percy wrote to his good friend, Shelby Foote, apropos this crucial character, "I deeply appreciate your taking time with that peculiar novel—and pinpointing what's wrong. Well, you're right. Every time Fr. Smith opens his mouth he, I, is in trouble. What I do is cut, cut, cut. Thanks to you, I'll probably cut him again. You can't get away with a Fr. Zossima these days and probably shouldn't." But, as it happened, Percy retained a good portion of the section featuring Father Smith and although many thick-witted reviewers, including Terrence Rafferty of *The New Yorker*, had no idea what Percy was up to in creating the Smith character, the decision to retain a good portion of him was artistically sound. See Tolson, Jay, *Pilgrim in the Ruins*, 469-70, for a précis of Rafferty's objections to the novel.
23. Edward Gibbon. *The Decline and Fall of the Roman Empire* (Folio Society, 1986), v. 4, 302.
24. Ibid., 361.
25. Tolson, *Pilgrim in the Ruins*, 300.
26. "Novel Writing in an Apocalyptic Time," in *Signposts in a Strange Land*, 155.
27. Ibid., 162.
28. "Is a Theory of Man Possible?" in *Signposts in a Strange Land*, 115.
29. Since the hagiographer John Coulson refers to St. Simon of Stylites as "God's messenger," the same epithet might be fairly accorded his fictional protégé Father Smith. Coulson's portrait of St. Simon is more reliable than Gibbon's. According to Coulson, "Far from being an uncouth fanatic," Simon "showed unruffled patience, gentleness and kindness to all . . . He preached daily to crowds. The Bedouin from the surrounding deserts flocked to hear him. Persians, Armenians, and Georgians thronged around him . . . Emperors consulted him and asked his prayers. The Emperor Marcian visited him incognito. He persuaded the Empress Eudoxia to abandon the Monophysites. To St. Geneviéve, remote in the far west, he sent greetings and a request for prayers. The Stylite thus proved himself God's messenger . . ." See The Saints: A Concise Biographical Dictionary, edited by John Coulson. (New York, 1958), 417.
30. *The Thanatos Syndrome*, 127.
31. Ibid., 365.

A Notre Dame Witness for Life

William McGurn

Good evening.

It is an honor to be with you on this campus. It is a joy to be here under the auspices of Notre Dame's Center for Ethics and Culture—and the Notre Dame Fund for the Protection of Human Life. This date has a special resonance for me: 13 years ago today, in a hotel room in a far part of the world, Chinese officials put a beautiful baby girl in my wife's arms—and I became a father.

The precipitate cause of our gathering tonight is the honor and platform our university has extended to a President whose policies reflect clear convictions about unborn life, and about the value the law ought to place on protecting that life. These convictions are not in doubt. In July 2007, the candidate spelled them out in a forceful address to a Planned Parenthood convention in our nation's capital.

Before that audience, he declared that a woman's "fundamental right" to an abortion was at stake in the coming election. He spoke about how he had "put *Roe* at the center" of his "lesson plan on reproductive freedom" when he was a professor— and how he would put it at the center of his agenda as president. He invoked his record in the Illinois state senate, where he fought restrictions on abortion, famously including one on partial-birth abortion. He said that the "first thing" he wanted to do as President was to "sign a Freedom of Choice Act." And he ended by assuring his audience that "on this fundamental issue," he, like they, would never yield.

These were his promises as a candidate. His actions as President—his key appointments, his judicial nominees, his lifting of restrictions on federal funding for abortion providers overseas, the green light given to the destruction of human embryos for research, his targeting of "conscience clause" protections for healthcare workers—all these actions are fully consistent with his promises. It is precisely this terrible consistency that makes it so dispiriting to see our university extend to this man her most public platform and an honorary doctorate of laws. There are good men and women working for an America where every child is welcomed in life and protected by law—and when they lift their eyes to Notre Dame, they ought to find inspiration.

So tonight our hearts carry a great sadness. But we do not come here this evening to rally against a speaker. We come to affirm the sacredness of life.

William McGurn is a columnist at the *Wall Street Journal* and an alumnus of Notre Dame University. This is the text of an address he gave at Notre Dame on April 23, 2009.

And we come with a great hope: that a university founded under the patronage of Our Lady might be as consistent in the defense of her principles as the President of the United States has been for advancing his. In a nation wounded by *Roe* . . . in a society that sets mothers against the children they carry in their wombs . . . we come here tonight because however much our hearts ache, they tell us this: Our church, our country, and our culture long for the life witness of Notre Dame.

What does it mean to be a witness? To be a witness, an institution must order itself so that all who look upon it see a consonance between its most profound truths and its most public actions. For a Catholic university in the 21st century, this requires that those placed in her most critical leadership positions—on the faculty, in the administration, on the board of trustees—share that mission. We must concede there is no guarantee that the young men and women who come here to learn will assent to her witness—but we must never forget that the university will have *failed* them if they leave here without at least understanding it. That is what it means to be a witness.

This witness is the only real reason for a University of Notre Dame. We believe that there *are* self-evident truths about the dignity of each human life, and that this dignity derives from our having been fashioned in our Creator's likeness. In this new century, these beliefs make *us* the counterculture. One does not need to be a Catholic to appreciate that abortion involves the brutal taking of innocent human life. To argue that this is a Catholic truth, or even a religious truth, is to overlook what science and sonograms tell us—and to insult the Protestants, Jews, Hindus, Buddhists, Muslims and, yes, even some atheists, who appreciate that a civilization which sanctions abortion as a human right is in some essential way writing its death warrant.

Over the years, the whole idea of truth—much less our ability to know it—has been rendered doubtful by the slow advance of a soft agnosticism that has itself become orthodoxy at so many universities. Not so at Notre Dame. All across this wondrous campus, we pass imagery that sings to us about the hope born of a Jewish woman in a Bethlehem stable. Yet we kid ourselves if we believe these images are self-sustaining. Without a witness that keeps these signposts alive, our crosses, statues, and stained-glass windows will ultimately fade into historical curiosities like the "Christo et ecclesiae" that survives to this day on buildings around Harvard Yard and the seal that still validates every Harvard degree.

For most of her life, Notre Dame has served as a symbol of a Catholic community struggling to find acceptance in America—and yearning to make our own contributions to this great experiment in ordered liberty. We identify with those who are poor and downtrodden and on the margins of acceptance because that is where the Gospel points—and because we remember whence came our own parents, grandparents, and great-grandparents.

If we are honest, however, we must admit that in many ways we—and the university that nurtured us—are now the rich and powerful and privileged ourselves. This is a form of success, and we need not be embarrassed by it. But we must be mindful of the greater responsibilities that come with this success.

For years this university has trumpeted her lay governance. So what does it say about the Notre Dame brand of leadership, that in the midst of a national debate over a decision that speaks to our Catholic identity, a debate in which thousands of people across the country are standing up to declare themselves "yea" or "nay," our trustees and fellows—the men and women who bear ultimate responsibility for this decision—remain as silent as Trappist monks? At a time when we are told to "engage" and hold "dialogue," their timidity thunders across this campus. And what will history say of our billions in endowment if the richest Catholic university America has ever known cannot find it within herself to mount a public and spirited defense of the most defenseless among us?

In the past few weeks, we have read more than once the suggestion that to oppose this year's speaker and honorary degree is to elevate politics over the proper work of a university. In many ways, we might say that such reasoning lies at the core of the confusion. As has become clear with America's debates over the destruction of embryos for scientific research, over human cloning, over assisted suicide, and over other end-of-life issues, abortion as a legal right is less a single issue than an entire ethic that serves as the foundation stone for the culture of death.

With the idea that one human being has the right to take the life of another merely because the other's life is inconvenient, our culture elevates into law the primacy of the strong over the weak. The discord that this year's commencement has unleashed—between Notre Dame and the bishops, between members of the Notre Dame community, between Notre Dame and thousands of discouraged Catholic faithful—all this derives from an approach that for decades has treated abortion as one issue on a political scorecard. This is not the road to engagement. This is the route to incoherence, and we see its fruit everywhere in our public life.

Twenty-five years ago, on a similar stage on this campus, the then-governor of New York used his Notre Dame platform to advance the personally-opposed-but defense that countless numbers of Catholic politicians have used to paper over their surrender to legalized abortion. Eight years after that, the school bestowed the Laetare Medal on a United States Senator who had likewise long since cut his conscience to fit the abortion fashion.

Today we have evolved. Let us note that the present controversy comes at a moment where the incoherence of the Catholic witness in American public life is on view at the highest levels of our government. Today we have a Catholic vice president, a Catholic Speaker of the House, a Catholic nominee for Secretary of Health and Human Services, and so on. These are America's most prominent Catholics. And they have one thing in common: the assertion that the legal right to terminate a pregnancy—in the chilling euphemism of the day—must remain inviolable.

For those who think this a partisan point, let us stipulate for the record one of the curiosities of the Republican Party. Notwithstanding the party's prolife credentials, at the level of possible Presidential contenders, the most prominent pro-choice voices in the GOP arguably belong to *Catholics*: from the former Republican mayor and governor of New York, to the Republican governor of California, the Republican former governor of Pennsylvania, and so on. Notre Dame must recognize these realities—and the role she has played in bringing us to this day by treating abortion as a political difference rather than the intrinsic evil it is. In his writings, Pope John Paul II noted the awful contradiction of our times, when more and more legal codes speak of human rights while making the freedom to deprive the innocent of their lives one of those rights. Several times he uses the word "sinister" to characterize the enshrinement of abortion as a legal right. And he states that all pleas for other important human rights are "false and illusory" if we do not defend with "maximum determination" the fundamental right to life upon which all other rights rest.

Maximum determination. Ladies and gentlemen, the unborn child's right to life represents the defining civil-rights issue of our day—and it ought to be a defining civil-rights issue on this campus.

This is not a popular witness. In our country, those who take it must expect ridicule and derision and a deliberate distortion of our views. In our culture, so many of our most powerful and influential institutions are hostile to any hint that abortion might be an unsettled question. And in our public life, one of the most pernicious effects of the imposition of abortion via the Supreme Court is that it has deprived a free people of a fair and open debate. Notre Dame remains one of the few institutions capable of providing a witness for life in the fullness of its beauty and intellectual integrity—and America is • waiting to hear her voice.

Those who say that as Notre Dame engages the world, she cannot expect her guests to share all her beliefs are right. But that is not the issue. The issue is *that* we engage them. Think of how we would have treated an elected

Senator or President or Governor whose principles and actions were given over to seeing that segregation enjoyed the full and unqualified protection of American law. We would have been cordial . . . we would have been gracious . . . we would have been more than willing to debate—but we would have betrayed our witness if ever we brought them here on the idea that all that divided us was one political issue.

My friends, the good news is that the witness for life is alive at Notre Dame. We see this witness in the good work of teachers here in this room. We see this witness in the new Notre Dame Fund to Protect Human Life. I have seen this witness in a very personal way, on the cold gym floor of a suburban parochial school on the outskirts of Washington—where 200-plus students spent a freezing January night just so they could raise the Notre Dame banner at the annual March for Life. These are but a handful of the wonderful things going on at this campus. And we know that this witness exists too in the other, unheralded acts of love designed to ensure that the unwed sophomore who kneels before the Grotto with an unexpected pregnancy weighing on her mind has a better choice than the cold front door of a Planned Parenthood clinic.

Unfortunately, people across this nation—and perhaps even here at this university—know little of these things. And they do not know because the university keeps this lamp under a basket. In her most public witness, Notre Dame appears afraid to extend to the cause of the unborn the same enthusiasm she shows for so many other good works here.

If, for example, you click onto www.nd.edu, you will often find a link for the Office of Sustainability, which happily informs you about all the things Notre Dame is doing to be green-friendly. You will find another link that defines the university with a series of videos that ask, "What would you fight for?" Each home game during the football season, NBC broadcasts one of these videos. There are more than a dozen of them—each highlighting members of the Notre Dame community who are fighting for justice, fighting for advances in medicine, fighting for new immigrants, and so forth.

Imagine the witness that Notre Dame might provide on a fall afternoon, if millions of Americans who had sat down to watch a football game suddenly found themselves face to face with a Notre Dame professor or student standing up to say, "I fight for the unborn."

Even more important, imagine the larger witness for life that would come from putting first things first. So often we find support for abortion rights measured against decisions involving war, capital punishment, and so on. All these issues deserve more serious treatment. But the debate over these prudential judgments loses coherence if on the intrinsic evil of abortion we do not stand on the same ground. What a challenge Notre Dame would pose to our culture if she stood united on this proposition: The unborn belong to no political party . . . no human right is safe when their right to life is denied . . . and we will accept no calculus of justice that seeks to trade that right to life for any other.

Now, there are different paths to this witness—and many who say they share it maintain their only problem is with the prolife movement itself: It's too Republican, it's not effective, it's too militant, and so forth. We who are prolife must admit that some of these criticisms have an element of truth. Yet those who advance them must also acknowledge that in practice such criticisms often serve not to strike out a bold new path for a more informed witness, but to rationalize a preference for remaining on the sidelines.

Tonight I ask our prolifers to open up the dialogue to your professors and classmates. Invite them in. Say to them: "Brothers! Sisters! We are not perfect, and we will be much improved by your participation. We are holding a place for you on the front lines. Come join us—and let us walk together in our witness for life."

I appreciate that for some people, the idea of Notre Dame as an unequivocal witness for the unborn would be a limit on her work as a Catholic university. The truth is just the opposite. The more frank and forthright Notre Dame's witness for life, the more she would be given the benefit of the doubt on the many judgment calls that the life of a great university entails. At this hour in our nation's life, America thirsts for an alternative to the relativism that leaves so many of our young people feeling empty and alone. This alternative is the Catholic witness that Notre Dame was *created* to provide . . . that Notre Dame is *called* to provide . . . and that in many ways, only Notre Dame *can* provide.

Let me end with a story about one of our family. His name is John Raphael; he belongs to the Class of '89; and he's an African-American who runs a high school in New Orleans. He's also a Josephite priest. In his ministry, Father Raphael knows what it is like to answer the knock on his office door and find a woman consumed by the understandable fears that attend an unplanned pregnancy. He says that one of the greatest lessons he learned about how to respond to these women came from a friend of his, who had come to him in the same circumstances. The woman was an unmarried college student, and she told him what had surprised and hurt her most was how many friends greeted her news by saying, "Oh, that's terrible."

"That young lady taught me something," says Father Raphael. "She taught me that what these women need first and foremost is to have their motherhood affirmed. For too many women, this affirmation never comes. We need to let these mothers know what their hearts are already telling them: You may have made a mistake, but the life growing within you is no mistake. That life is your baby, waiting to love and be loved."

My young friends, this night I ask you: Make yours the voice that affirms life and motherhood. Be to those in need as the words of our alma mater: tender . . . strong . . . and true. And in your every word and deed, let the world see a reflection of the hope that led a French-born priest in the north woods of Indiana to raise Our Lady atop a dome of gold.

I thank you for your invitation. I applaud your courage. And as we go forth this evening, let us pray that our beloved university becomes the Notre Dame our world so desperately needs: a witness for life that will truly shake down the thunder. God bless you all.

One Man's Evil

William Murchison

Here I go again—apologies for that self-referential start—peeking at a news story whose immediate end is a few weeks over the horizon. I did this last with respect to the 2008 election. The habit, I fear, of peeking around corners belongs to those of us who have spent too much time in the newspaper trade. We can't help it. We want to talk, which, when you are writing for a quarterly, can complicate matters.

I write, in other words, before the sentencing, in Wichita, Kans., of one Scott Roeder for the murder of Dr. George R. Tiller, on May 31, 2009. For which crime a jury convicted Roeder Jan. 29, 2010, after 37 minutes of deliberation. Roeder had, so to speak, testified against himself: "I did what I thought needed to be done to protect the children. I shot him." Little more needed saying? Hardly that. Much, much more, in my own view, needs saying, irrespective of copy deadlines.

I write—here is a considerably larger complication—knowing that whatever I say will displease particular readers, however I couch the matter. That is in fact the reason I write. We need to think about the issue raised by Tiller's murder at the hands of the self-deputized Roeder. The matter is a solemn and nasty one, and yet crucial to talk about due to the state of affairs the *Roe* v. *Wade* decision, in 1973, created for us to live amidst—a situation of sharply contrasting moral and emotional perceptions, clipped carelessly, often as not, to individual appraisals of right and wrong.

For our souls' health, we need to talk of these matters, in as level a tone as possible. Lamely, following the habits of a lifetime, I stick my hand in the air to volunteer as . . . what? Moderator? I don't know. Let's see where this goes.

Only so much detail wants recounting at this point. The facts of the case are reasonably well known. Scott Roeder, a white, middle-aged, divorced airport-shuttle driver with a history of mental problems, went to Reformation Lutheran Church on the last Sunday in May 2009. He encountered there, in the role of church usher, Dr. George R. Tiller, described by the *New York Times* as "one of the few doctors in the country to perform late-term abortions." There, in the church, Roeder shot Tiller dead. Roeder was arrested a few hours later. He showed no remorse, or sympathy either for the dead

William Murchison is a syndicated columnist and senior editor of the *Human Life Review.* His latest book is *Mortal Follies: Episcopalians and the Crisis of Mainline Christianity* (Encounter Books, 2009).

doctor's family. He had done, he explained, what had to be done to save the lives Dr. Tiller would have extinguished had he lived.

Tiller's prominence as a target was nothing new. He performed a lot of abortions—"as late as in the third semester of pregnancy," the *Times* reported. His abortion mill, as I think it not unfair to call the operation, was called Women's Health Care. He had founded it two years after *Roe* v. *Wade*. Tiller was himself the son of a Wichita doctor said to have performed abortions—"illegal operations" people called them back then, in the days before *Roe* v. *Wade*. He was a bespectacled man of 67, with the bland face of a bank teller; born the same week of August 1941 as two or three of my high-school classmates. To think—had I myself grown up in Wichita, Kans., as Tiller did, rather than in North Texas, we would have gone to the same high school; possibly golfed together or tried out the new steps on *American Bandstand*; sported crew cuts and dodged polio; attended the same 50th reunion last year amid hugs and how-ya-been's. Or, in the last case, maybe not; around reunion time, at the end of May, Tiller was dead.

Roeder may have seemed equally ordinary, early in life at least and on the surface. I do not know. It is Tiller who pulls me into the story, partly on account of our synchronicity, a thing that makes me wonder . . . how? Why? A third-trimester baby is, for God's sake—and I mean that literally, not "in vain"—a baby, all but ready to debut in the affairs of his parental and, of course, medical, patrons. Somehow my contemporary, Dr. George Tiller, raised on Lucy and Desi like the rest of us, accustomed to Rock Hudson and William Holden at the picture show, and to summer fireflies in jars, failed to take in that crucial datum. Nor was that all. Having seized the flaming torch of abortion rights, he refused to lay it down, unassailable in his conviction that what he did was exactly what needed doing.

For public purposes, the crime—the murder of George Tiller—is the central event of the narrative; that, and how we react to it. When I first thought of writing about the murder, it was the division of opinion between Roeder defenders and Roeder critics that interested me. It was certainly one thing on which the media focused: people who said, approvingly, so much for one abortionist, over against far larger numbers of people, from the small to the great, who said, whatever the killer's motives, no one should take the law into his own hands. As our mothers used to assure us back in the Lucy-Desi days, "Two wrongs don't make a right." They surely don't. One has to make very certain that roving wildmen don't get it into their heads to decide who deserves to live and who needs to die. They do, of course; it's just that we can't encourage it, because life is a more serious thing than George Tiller or Scott Roeder, either one, supposed it to be. More serious than other free agents—the Branch Davidians, for instance, or Joe Stack, who crashed his plane into an Austin office building in February—can ever have supposed.

What is it that uncouples ordinary-seeming people from the suppositions and restraints by which most of us try at least to live? Despair, anger, hatred—these sorts of emotions, of course. But something more appeared to drive the parallel, in some sense, careers of George R. Tiller, physician, and Scott Roeder, triggerman. That something was the sense of loss.

I say that. I can't prove it. Tiller's dead, and Scott Roeder, I suspect, is too far around the bend for cogent questioning. Let us talk about loss and see where we get.

Loss of what? A moral center. Better said, perhaps, *the* moral center—the one that, for all its holes and gaps and deficiencies, exercised some purchase on the minds of Americans prior to the era of *Roe* v. *Wade*. I said holes and such like. I meant it. No moral order of which I have ever heard, from Babylon and Greece to the present day, was or is without cruelty, cowardice, stubbornness, indifference, hypocrisy—enduring traits of the human race, we have to acknowledge. I mean no more than that the moral order amid which George Tiller and I grew up was demonstrably different from that which succeeded it.

For one thing, abortion was a crime back during the Lucy-Desi days. Its being a crime meant, first, of course, you shouldn't do it; but there was more to the matter. It was that the obligation of parent to unborn child—of power to weakness and vulnerability—of maturity to futurity—had a profound character that organized society had engaged to uphold. The abortion laws evidenced that insight, that determination, that public sense of a moral center on questions pertaining to human life. The First Amendment to the Constitution naturally allowed objections, angry or piteous, to that state of affairs. Louder and louder, harsher and harsher the objections grew. There followed, at last, *Roe* v. *Wade*.

On human-life questions the moral center cracked and crashed. Fragments of witness still existed—sermons and speeches; websites; the action programs of churches; journals such as the *Human Life Review*; all of it loose, informal, uncoordinated. In the official absence of a center, options multiplied, with the blessing of the U.S. Supreme Court. It was up to individuals henceforth to sort out the rights and the wrongs, the shoulds and the shouldn'ts of abortion—as indeed these individuals did. No state legislature, no state court was to stand in the way of individual discernment. The high court had made that plain.

Well, individual discernment can and does take interesting forms. It seems to have worked so in George Tiller's case. Into the cause of abortion virtually on demand he plunged with what might well be called recklessness. In 1986, his clinic was firebombed. In 1993, an anti-abortion activist named Shelley Shannon shot him five times. What was it about abortion that kept him on the case? One couldn't call his determination heroic, but there was a quality to it that stuck out a mile. He had decided somehow that the brand-new right to conceive but not deliver a live baby was of transcendent worth in . . . in what? The liberation of modern folk from the rules of dead people? No moral center—no tapestry of belief, supported by statute and exhortation—was there to make him question or actually doubt his premises. The new moral center, after *Roe* v. *Wade*, was, we don't need moral centers any more.

Neither, for that matter, did Scott Roeder, though he thought perhaps he had one. In the moral vacuum produced by *Roe* v. *Wade*, Roeder felt free to decide for himself which lives were good and which deserved elimination. The Supreme Court, without intending in the least to do so, had empowered Scott Roeder by assigning to individuals the right to make up their own minds in certain specified cases as to the worth of human life. The problem that raised was, what about other human lives? If one class of life had suddenly become vulnerable to human whim, did not that at a minimum raise the question, what about other classes of life—say, the George Tiller class? How could Dr. George Tiller's right to life outrank that of the entirely human, certainly not animal, lives he extracted in gruesome fashion from women's wombs? What was the qualitative difference? The Supreme Court, which, in the matter of unborn life, had subcontracted moral understanding to individuals, cannot have thought someone like Scott Roeder would embrace the invitation in such cold-blooded fashion. But he did.

None of this, I emphasize, is to adduce some backdoor justification for the murder to which Scott Roeder calmly confessed. It is to show how certain things lead to certain other things: how, when the lid to Pandora's box gets lifted, out fly things previously unimaginable—never intended for introduction into the world.

The moral center collapses—and life, if it goes on, flows differently and between reconfigured banks. I have not seen much made, journalistically, of the scene of the crime: the narthex of a Lutheran church, where Dr. George Tiller was handing out programs to fellow church-goers. These, one can only assume, found it un-startling to receive a church program from a practitioner of partial-birth abortion. Why would this be?

One can visit the website of Reformation Lutheran Church, 7601 E. 13th St. N., in Wichita, Kans. (www.reformation-lutheran.org) and discover a normal-seeming American Protestant church, "Christ-centered," with ministries to youth and adults (including Cub Scouts and Golfers for God) and a commitment to "Scripture, liturgy, and inspiring music." "[W]e respond with love to the needs of others," the website affirms. Further, "We respect varying points of view and consider diversity to be one of our attributes." That would seem to have cleared a space for the late Dr. George Tiller, whose commitment to abortion cannot in any case be read as offending deeply, if at all, the policy of the Evangelical Lutheran Church in America under a teaching statement dating from 1991 (www.elca.org/What-We-Believe/Social-Issues/Social-Statements/Abortion). "Induced abortion," as the teaching puts it, "is one of the issues about which members of the Evangelical Lutheran Church in America have serious differences." The church wishes members to talk about those differences "in ways that do justice to our"—that word again—"diversity." ELCA, as you will have deduced by now, is neither passionately opposed to abortion nor passionately for it. It all seems to depend on circumstances. Abortion to save the mother's life, and in cases of rape, incest, or "fetal abnormalities"—that's all right, according to the teaching. Also all right would be legislation outlawing "abortions that are performed after the fetus is determined to be viable, except when the mother's life is threatened or when lethal abnormalities indicate the prospective newborn will die very soon." Plenty of wiggle room there if you're a certain local clinic owner with a commitment to Lutheran worship. Plenty of space for personal interpretation.

George Tiller's commitment to abortion, in the face of bullets and bombs, has about it, I say, a notable quality, whatever else could and should be said about it. No less observable is the lack of evidence that the generality of fellow worshipers at Reformation Lutheran Church found the doctor's presence in Lutheran worship in any way offensive. Possibly the congregation's commitment to diversity barred the wary sideways glance when the local abortion doctor passed down the aisle.

If moral centers have given way formally in our time to diversity—and they have, for the most part—it behooves us to reckon with the likely consequences. We will not like all of them. Some are jarring in the extreme—the sound, for instance, of a revolver going off point blank on a quiet Sunday morning in a quiet Midwestern city.

The Supreme Court, in *Roe*, thought to liberate. In striking down old laws that prohibited abortion, it wiped away, supposedly, the convictions behind those laws. Though, as we see, the seven justices in the *Roe* majority were as naive as first graders if they believed a piece of official paper—an opinion by our highest court— could erase a moral/cultural instinct traceable to earliest times, the instinct to care for and protect unborn life. All the Court did was enfranchise, I suppose one could say, local-option views on a matter formerly reserved for much larger oversight—that of states responding to moral prompting of an urgent sort. With the fall of the abortion laws, it became less urgent than in quite a long time to examine or even notice the premises that underlay the old laws. One such premise was the sacredness of life—life as proceeding from the mind and the work of God. Another was the welfare of women, who were seen by various reformers as the victims of abortion quacks and butchers.

The moral center, as to abortion, consisted in the duty to protect unborn life for a complex of reasons that heavily outweighed the pleas that grew in the 1960s for the right "to control one's own body." The moral center, as to unborn life, was concerned with protection—a historic aim of government and of organized society. To the culture that began to show its face around the time George Tiller and I were leaving undergraduate life, protection savored, oddly, of oppression. It was time to free humanity from old shackles, time to empower individual appreciation of individual wants and needs (as if the United States, pre-1965, had been some factory for the obliteration of human differences!).

The old moral center had outlived its usefulness, as many saw the matter. It had to go. Rules went out; choice came in. Normlessness was the new norm—the one that did in, eventually, both Dr. George Tiller and his murderer and, in no small degree, further unsettled the normless society around them. What Tiller could do—kill—was also what Roeder could do. It required only an act of the will to see as much. One man's evil was another's good—an unstable and highly undesirable condition, even in a culture verbally committed to "diversity."

Where from here? It is hard to say. No path in life leads backwards, only forwards. The construction of a new moral center is the most urgent task of 300 million diverse Americans, relatively few of whom, one surmises, hope to see their own principles of self-determination and choice unlimited turned against them. So it fell out with Dr. George Tiller. The culture that had made him, killed him.

The Greeks gave us the definition of tragedy—the mighty laid low by personal flaws or moral mistakes. For staging directions, visit Wichita, Kans.

The Facelessness of the Unborn

Donald DeMarco

Emmanuel Lévinas, a Lithuanian Jew, is distinguished for having formulated a "philosophy of the face." Lévinas is an existentialist in the most concrete sense inasmuch as he establishes the basis for his morality not in an abstraction or in a code, but in what is written in the human face. The starting point for his philosophy is plain enough for anyone to see, if he would only make the effort and take the time to look into the face of another.

Lévinas develops his "philosophy of the face" in a most remarkable book titled *Totality and Infinity* (1961). He states that the first word of the face is "Thou shalt not kill." It is an *order*, a commandment that is registered in the very structure of the face, one that is more compelling than words, more decisive than any dogma.

According to Lévinas, in the access to the face, there is also an access to the idea of God: "To my mind," he writes, "the Infinite comes in the signifyingness of the face. The face *signifies* the Infinite . . . When in the presence of the Other, I say, 'Here I am!', this "Here I am!' is the place through which the Infinite enters into language. . . . The subject who says 'Here I am!' *testifies* to the Infinite." In this regard, the thought of Lévinas bears an interesting correlation with that of St. Thérèse of Lisieux: "*Ta face est ma seule patrie*," "Thy face is my only home"—the face which restores our own.

For Lévinas, the face-to-face encounter with the other discloses the other's weakness and mortality. The face is, as it were, naked, destitute, and without defense. Its command is: "Do not leave me in my solitude." In looking at another's face, one senses the supreme inappropriateness of violence and, at the same time, the profound obligation to love. The command to treat the other with justice is registered in the human face. But it takes a godly person to read it properly.

In a world of widespread depersonalization, in which people move about side-by-side rather than face-to-face, a reflection on the profound significance of the human face is critically needed. In pornography, for example, as psychiatrist Leslie Farber and others have pointed out, the fig leaf is transferred to cover the face. In this transference, the impersonal gains ascendancy over the personal. It also signifies a suppression of the spiritual. Where

---

Donald DeMarco is professor emeritus at St. Jerome's University, and adjunct professor at Holy Apostles College & Seminary, Mater Ecclesiae College (Canada). He is co-author (with Benjamin D. Wiker) of *Architects of the Culture of Death* (Ignatius, 2004).

the impersonal rules, morality disappears. The face, witness to the personal, is needed in order to keep morality alive.

The great Russian Orthodox philosopher Nikolai Berdyaev, like Lévinas, understood how the spiritual order can manifest itself in the human face. In *Slavery and Freedom*, he wrote: "The face of man is the summit of the cosmic process, the greatest of its offspring, but it cannot be the offspring of cosmic forces only, it presupposes the action of a spiritual force, which raises it above the sphere of the forces of nature. The face of man is the most amazing thing in the life of the world; another world shines through it. It is the entrance of personality into the world process, with its uniqueness, its singleness, its unrepeatability."

Darwinian evolution cannot begin to explain the emergence in the cosmos of the face as a bearer of the spiritual, let alone as a testimony of the Infinite. For Darwin and his disciples, the spiritual realm exists wholly outside of their limited sphere of discussion concerning physical variations and chance mutations. As the noted geneticist Theodosius Dobzhansky has pointed out, human beings properly belong to an "ethical," not a "gladiatorial" mode of existence. The "ethical" is not something that evolves from matter.

Max Picard, a Swiss psychiatrist whose book *The Human Face* Lévinas greatly admired, is recognized as "the poet of the human face." According to Picard, God enters man's face as a friend enters the house of a friend, without a stir, hardly knocking on the door. The face, for Picard, is a tempered image; it is the mildness of God that appears in the face of man. Since God is in every face, He sees His own image whenever He looks out from one face into another. In this way, for Picard, God unites faces as He fills the spaces between them. And he fills these spaces with love. The great crisis in the modern world, then, is the expulsion of God and the resulting gap between humans. Bitter loneliness ensues as the individual becomes closed in on himself.

Before Picard, physiognomy was a doubtful intellectual discipline. But when *The Human Face* appeared in 1929, it imbued physiognomy with philosophical as well as theological dignity. One writer aptly appraised Picard's work when he wrote: "The little field of human countenance becomes for him the arena of a divine comedy."

Like Lévinas, Picard finds implications of the Infinite in the finite human face: "Two human faces look upon each other. A silence ensues. A silence that does not arise from the earth, but from eternity. Two faces look upon each other, and for a moment time ceases and stands still. And all the hours that are hidden away in time begin to strike together, and as they strike, a marvelous tone dwells in the air, and, in this loud silence of the hours, eternity enters. Thus does time call up eternity." Picard goes on to say that, "The human face is the proof for the existence of God."

The face *speaks*. It speaks of love and is the beginning of all subsequent discourse. The mother's face is like the face of God for her baby. Looking into her face, the infant comes to believe that the world outside the womb is safe and trustworthy. The child picks up these messages intuitively and immediately as it studies the face of his loving mother.

The call to justice is written in the face of the human person, though it takes a godly person to see this. Those who argue that religion has been history's leading cause of violence and warfare fail to recognize this primordial fact. The Judeo-Christian tradition clearly, repeatedly, and consistently reminds its disciples that a refutation of war is written in the human face. War is unjust, and peace is not possible without justice. Consequently, peace begins when one sees the inscription in the face of the other not to kill and, by honoring that inscription, renders him justice.

The face of the unborn, however, apart from cloudy ultrasound imaging, is unseen. And even with ultrasound, the face lacks distinctiveness. Therefore, it does not incarnate the moral maxim "Thou Shalt Not Kill" in a visible way. Abortion takes place without witnessing the face of the unborn. Can we say, then, that Lévinas's philosophy of the face does not apply to the unborn? We may reason that it does apply, though by extension (and anticipation), through the faces of the conceiving parents.

Dr. Jérôme Lejeune has drawn attention to the fact that the "pupil" of the eye derives its name from the Latin word *pupilla* or "little baby girl." It is significant that all languages employ the same metaphor. In Greek, the word *chorea* means "little girl." The Spanish are more precise: *Niña del ocho* refers to "the little girl inside the eye." In Italian it is *pupilla*, while in both French and German it is *pupille*. The comparable word in Arabic is *Insan el ein*, referring to "a little being inside the eye." Iranians would speak of *mardomak* or "the little one."

At a conference in Moscow in 1992, Dr. Lejeune told his audience the following: "When the lover looks closely into the eye of the beloved, he sees his own image reflected on the spherical surface of the cornea. This tiny figure is so much more brilliant than the dark field of the pupil that it stands out. My guess is that women were the first to discover this interesting property of the spherical mirrors. That explains why most languages say 'the little girl of the eye,' and not 'the little boy.' Love sees a child in the eye of the beloved; this is a true fact."

Till We Have Faces (1956) is C.S. Lewis's last work of fiction. It is also the one he considered his best. He had been thinking about it over a period of 35 years, ever since his undergraduate days. The use of the word "face" in the title is a reference to the myth he is retelling, concerning the relationship between Psyche and Cupid. Cupid did not allow Psyche to see his face. Her intimate encounters with him were always veiled in darkness. The face also relates to a statement that Orual, Psyche's ugly sister, enunciates: "How can the gods meet us face to face till we have faces." In a letter to Dorothea Conybeare, Lewis amplifies what he means by the "face," explaining that a human being must become real before a person can expect to receive any message from divine beings, "speaking with its own voice (not one of its borrowed voices), expressing its actual desires (not what it imagines that it desires), being for good or ill itself, not any mask, veil, or persona." One's true face is a sign of personal authenticity and the locus where the finite and the Infinite intersect.

The face-to-face look between lovers anticipates not only a loving embrace, but the possibility of a child who will be formed as a result of that embrace. This may also explain why a person tends to avert his eyes when he begins to look too long or too deeply into the eyes of the other. The eyes open to a sanctuary, one that is profoundly personal. Not just anyone may be admitted. It is an area where the finite and the Infinite are conjoined.

There is a natural continuity between loving looks, intimacy, and the loving acceptance of offspring. The faces of the lovers are a prelude to accepting the "faceless" child that is the outcome of their loving intimacy. Once born, however, the child's face is the center of constant attention and amazement for the parents. The eyes of the infant will never grow larger, although every other part of his body will.

When a woman looks into the eyes of the man she loves, she finds an image and a suggestion of her subsequent maternity. *Matrimony* is rightly named for marriage since it represents the "office or duty of the mother" and not that of the man. The man has his own role to play. Marriage anticipates maternity. The child in the eye anticipates the child in the arms. The face of the child will soon be clear enough. Before that, it will be predicted in the face-to-face gaze of the lovers.

Love is creative. It possesses a momentum that brings about more love. Plato spoke about how happiness expresses itself by the desire to reproduce the beautiful. Happy people, which is tantamount to saying "loving people," want to extend their love by adding something lovable to the world. This sentiment is in accord with Lord Byron's remark: "He who would win joy must share it for happiness was born a twin." Love sets in motion a natural sequence each of whose links are alien to violence. Love is a refutation of the violence that results in death. It is a sign that killing is foreign to human relationships. Love craves continuity. It is, as some poets and philosophers have proclaimed, "the breath of eternity."

The face of the unborn is anticipated in the faces of the lovers, especially in the face of the woman, for she, like Eve her precursor, is the mother and guardian of all human life. From the viewpoint of lovers, the unborn are not faceless.

Abortion occurs because there is a disruption in the transmission of love. It is the broken link that love failed to solder. Human love is intimately and profoundly bound up with the human face. The face is the entrance of the spiritual into the cosmos, but also the point of entrance of one soul into the life of the other. The face is an entreaty to love and to honor what love produces.

Abortion is inevitable in a broken world. But brokenness is neither man's destiny nor his natural condition. We deplore brokenness and instinctively look for the healing that only love provides. We were made for continuity, not discontinuity (the latter being a dominant feature of the Media and the modern world).

Abortion also occurs as a result of discordance between the procreating man and woman where the love relationship does not have a firm root. Abortion emerges from a void. The human face is a powerful invitation to extend the being-to-being relationship. Two people, face-to-face (overcoming isolation), fall in love and want to extend that love to another being. The continuation of life has its genesis in the face-to-face relationship between a man and a woman. Through the face, one's unique personality shines, at once physical and spiritual. The physical alone cannot carry forth the legacy of love, its bearing on the future, its natural propensity to repeat itself.

Alienation enters life wherever there is a refusal to love, when self-centeredness replaces the face-to-face relationship. Abortion is a consequence of alienation. Love excludes alienation. It is accepting and integrating. It prevents the kind of voids from forming that can draw people into black holes of despair.

The face-to-face relationship is a more incarnate image of the "I-Thou" relationship that has been extensively elaborated upon by Martin Buber, Gabriel Marcel, Nikolai Berdyaev, Paul Tillich, Karol Wojtyla, and many personalist thinkers. It gives philosophy a visible and unmistakable origin. It settles the question, "When does ethics begin?"

The face-to-face relationship should not be construed as merely an antidote to loneliness, but as an opportunity for mutual giving. The impulse for generous giving is an essential feature of the human person. It is deeper and more characteristic of man in his authenticity than the more superficial desire to possess. The essential purpose of "self-mastery," writes the personalist Jacques Maritain, is for "self-giving."

Our technological world, insofar as it is technological, is a man-made mechanical construct. As a result, the realm of the spiritual tends to be excluded. Man sees himself as an individual in the mirror of his technology. The world of nature remains silent with regard to morality. The language of the day is mathematics, and meaning is associated with technological utility. It is a world pervaded and dominated by "I-It" relationships. It is not a world that encourages face-to-face relationships. In such a world it is not surprising that author Sabine Rachel can believe that "the relationship between men and women is dark, irrational and turbulent, defined by ambivalence and laced with underlying hatred. Unexpressed violence is a part of this archaic and basically primitive relationship." Jean-Paul Sartre's deathless phrase, "Hell is other people" captures the pathology of a world in which the individual is *numero uno* and others are viewed essentially as threats. It is a world in which God is expelled from the space between persons.

Nearly one hundred years ago American sociologists were complaining about how technology and materialism were fostering a diminishing number of "face-to-face" relationships. Charles Horton Cooley, for example, observed that as the metropolitan web grew tighter, human relations became increasingly depersonalized. People became less dependent on other particular people, and whatever dependence they did have on others, according to Cooley, was "confined to a highly fractionalized aspect of the other's round of activity." The sense of community began to vanish as individuals proceeded to operate mechanically from a defensive shell within which lay, unexercised, their true personalities (*Human Nature and the Social Order*, 1922).

It is superficial in the extreme to regard abortion as merely a "choice." American sociologists of the early 20th century were correct in lamenting the diminishment of face-to-face relationships. They probably did not anticipate, however, the extent to which this diminishment would advance. Lévinas, Berdyaev, Picard, Lejeune, C.S. Lewis, and other stalwart thinkers were trying to stem the tide of diminishing face-to-face relationships by arguing that love and God—the conjunction of the finite and the Infinite—are needed in order for human beings to establish authentic relationships with one another.

The chief obstacle to reversing abortion is the "facelessness" of the unborn. People do not witness the facial inscription that pleads, "Do not kill." By contrast, animal-protection groups used the Media to their advantage most effectively by showing the clubbing of seal pups in northern Canada. The televised images of young seals helplessly facing the mortal blows of hunters moved people to protest vehemently against the practice and, in many instances, to boycott all seafood exported from that country. It was as if they could see inscribed in the faces of these animals the prohibition against killing. The well-circulated phrase "Club sandwiches not seals" also proved very effective. Many celebrities spoke out against the seal hunt. The long list includes Brigitte Bardot, Pamela Anderson, Pierce Brosnan, Kevin Bacon, Adrien Brody, Christina Applegate, Martin Sheen, Juliette Binoche, David Schwimmer, and Neve Campbell. Sir Paul McCartney and his wife Heather were given an influential forum to voice their disapproval on *Larry King Live.*

The heart of the abortion problem, therefore, is not merely whether or not to choose abortion, but whether or not to establish loving, godly, face-to-face relationships with other persons. Abortion is the delayed consequence of human faces having hardened into façades (courtesy of Helena Rubenstein, Max Factor, Calvin Klein, *GQ*, or the *Wall Street Journal*). The effort to reverse abortion through political persuasions is, of course, both needed and urgent. But this effort must be accompanied by advising, inspiring, and teaching others about the irreplaceable origin of morality in the loving look on the countenance of the other. A special effort to achieve this, natural though it is, will be needed given our situation in an impersonal, technological world. We should take heart, however, in the words of personalist philosopher Jacques Maritain: "As individuals, we are subject to the stars. As persons, we rule them." We need not be victims of our environment. The primary responsibility, then, of every human being is being human. In that act of being human one finds his authentic personhood as a dynamic integration of individual uniqueness and social responsibility, and as a creative fusion of love and generosity.